SITUATING OPERA

Setting opera within a variety of contexts – social, aesthetic, historical –
Lindenberger illuminates a form that has persisted in recognizable shape for over
four centuries. The study examines the social entanglements of opera, for example
the relation of Mozart's *Die Entführung aus dem Serail* and Verdi's *Il trovatore* to
their initial and later audiences. It shows how modernist opera rethought the
nature of theatricality and often challenged its viewers by means of both musical
and theatrical shock effects. Using recent experiments in neuroscience, the book
demonstrates how different operatic forms developed at different periods to create
new ways of exciting a public. Lindenberger considers selected moments of
operatic history, from Monteverdi's *Orfeo* to the present, to study how the
form has communicated with its diverse audiences. Of interest to scholars and
opera-goers alike, this book advocates and exemplifies opera studies as an active,
emerging area of interdisciplinary study.

HERBERT LINDENBERGER is Avalon Professor of Humanities Emeritus at
Stanford University. He is the author of *Opera in History: From Monteverdi to Cage*
(1998), *The Literature in History: On Genre, Values, Institutions* (1990), *Opera: The
Extravagant Art* (1984), and *Saul's Fall: A Critical Fiction* (1979).

CAMBRIDGE STUDIES IN OPERA

Series editor: Arthur Groos, *Cornell University*

Volumes for *Cambridge Studies in Opera* explore the cultural, political, and social influences of the genre. As a cultural art form, opera is not produced in a vacuum. Rather, it is influenced, whether directly or in more subtle ways, by its social and political environment. In turn, opera leaves its mark on society and contributes to shaping the cultural climate. Studies to be included in the series will look at these various relationships, including the politics and economics of opera, the operatic representation of women or the singers who portrayed them, the history of opera as theatre, and the evolution of the opera house.

Published titles

Opera Buffa in Mozart's Vienna
Edited by Mary Hunter and James Webster

Johann Strauss and Vienna: Operetta and the Politics of Popular Culture
Camille Crittenden

German Opera: From the Beginnings to Wagner
John Warrack

Opera and Drama in Eighteenth-Century London: The King's Theatre, Garrick and the Business of Performance
Ian Woodfield

Opera Liberalism, and Antisemitism in Nineteenth-Century France: The Politics of Halévy's *La Juive*
Diana R. Hallman

Aesthetics of Opera in the Ancien Régime, 1647–1785
Downing A. Thomas

Three Modes of Perception in Mozart: The Philosophical, Pastoral, and Comic in *Così fan tutte*
Edmund J. Goehring

Landscape and Gender in Italian Opera: The Alpine Virgin from Bellini to Puccini
Emanuele Senici

The Prima Donna and Opera, 1815–1930
Susan Rutherford

Opera and Society in Italy and France from Monteverdi to Bourdieu
Edited by Victoria Johnson, Jane F. Fulcher, and Thomas Ertman

The Puccini Problem: Opera, Nationalism, and Modernity
Alexandra Wilson

Rossini in Restoration Paris: The Sound of Modern Life
Benjamin Walton

When Opera Meets Film
Marcia J. Citron

Situating Opera: Period, Genre, Reception
Herbert Lindenberger

Situating Opera
Period, Genre, Reception

Herbert Lindenberger

CAMBRIDGE
UNIVERSITY PRESS

CAMBRIDGE UNIVERSITY PRESS
Cambridge, New York, Melbourne, Madrid, Cape Town, Singapore,
São Paulo, Delhi, Dubai, Tokyo, Mexico City

Cambridge University Press
The Edinburgh Building, Cambridge CB2 8RU, UK

Published in the United States of America by Cambridge University Press, New York

www.cambridge.org
Information on this title: www.cambridge.org/9780521199896

First published 2010

Printed in the United Kingdom at the University Press, Cambridge

A catalogue record for this publication is available from the British Library

Library of Congress Cataloging-in-Publication Data

Lindenberger, Herbert, 1929–
    Situating opera : period, genre, reception / Herbert Lindenberger.
        p.   cm. –   (Cambridge studies in opera)
    Includes bibliographical references.
    ISBN 978-0-521-19989-6 (Hardback)
        1. Opera.   2. Opera–Social aspects.   3. Operas–Literary themes, motives.
    I. Title.   II. Series.
    ML1700.L564 2010
    782.1–dc22

                                                                        2010017813

ISBN 978-0-521-19989-6 Hardback

FOR CLAIRE, ONCE AGAIN

CONTENTS

Acknowledgements | viii

Prologue: Why opera? Why (How, Where) situate? | 1

1 Anatomy of a warhorse: *Il trovatore* from A to Z | 8

2 On opera and society (assuming a relationship) | 44

3 Opera and the novel: antithetical or complementary? | 62

4 Opera by other means | 84

5 Opera and/as lyric | 115

6 From separatism to union: aesthetic theorizing
from Reynolds to Wagner | 139

7 Toward a characterization of modernist opera | 174

8 Anti-theatricality in twentieth-century opera | 196

9 A brief consumers' history of opera | 219

Epilogue: Why (What, How, If) opera studies? | 263

Works cited | 280
Index | 298

ACKNOWLEDGEMENTS

Over the decade during which I worked on these essays, so many colleagues, friends, and editors have listened to my ideas, helped me with bibliographical advice, and invited me to publish versions of them or to present them as lectures, that I may, inadvertently, have omitted the names of some whose contributions should be acknowledged. Of those who come to mind most readily, I thank the following: Alan Ackerman, Frederick Aldama, Richard Begam, Karol Berger, Jane and Marshall Brown, Bliss Carnochan, Petra Dierkes-Thrun, Sidney Drell, Thomas Ertman, Joseph Frank, Jane F. Fulcher, Albert Gelpi, Philip Gossett, Thomas S. Grey, Arthur Groos, Heather Hadlock, Stephen Hinton, Blair Hoxby, Edward D. Huey, Linda and Michael Hutcheon, Victoria Johnson, David Levin, Roberta Montemorra Marvin, Roger Parker, Marjorie Perloff, David Posner, Martin Puchner, Paul Robinson, Stephen Rumph, Downing A. Thomas, Heather Wiebe, and Anne Williams. I take full responsibility for all errors and misunderstandings.

Earlier versions of some essays have been presented as lectures at the University of California, Berkeley, the University of Iowa, and the University of Washington. I thank the following for permission to include revised versions of several essays: Ashgate, for use of the Epilogue, which appeared in *Operatic Migrations: Transforming Works and Crossing Boundaries*, ed. Roberta Montemorra Marvin and Downing A. Thomas, 2006, pp. 253–63; Cambridge University Press, for use of Essays 2 and 6, which appeared, respectively, in *Opera and Society in Italy and France from Monteverdi to Bourdieu*, ed. Victoria Johnson, Jane F. Fulcher, and Thomas Ertman, 2007, pp. 294–311, and *The Cambridge History of Literary Criticism*, vol. v, ed. Marshall Brown, 2000, pp. 362–86; the web journal *Modernist Cultures*, for use of Essay 7, which appeared in a special issue, "Modernist Opera," ed. Richard

Begam, Winter, 2007; Oxford University Press Journals, for use of Essay 1, which appeared in *The Opera Quarterly* 25 (2009), pp. 97–123; and Palgrave Macmillan, for use of Essay 8, which appeared in *Against Theatre: Creative Destructions on the Modernist Stage*, ed. Alan Ackerman and Martin Puchner, 2006, pp. 58–75.

All translations, unless otherwise indicated, are my own.

PROLOGUE

WHY OPERA? WHY (HOW, WHERE) SITUATE?

INTERLOCUTOR: Still another book on opera?

AUTHOR: You mean by me or in general?

INTERLOCUTOR: Both.

AUTHOR: I still have a thing or two to say about opera.

INTERLOCUTOR: Does the world need another book on this topic?

AUTHOR: It's a much bigger topic than it seemed thirty years ago when I first wrote on it. Opera's been exploding all over the place: new audiences, new companies (and in towns where you could never have imagined opera before), new approaches to how one stages the thing, and, to top it off, as I'll show in the epilogue, a whole new area of inquiry that people are calling opera studies.

INTERLOCUTOR: How can you even speak of an explosion when we know that for most people these days classical music is giving way to popular forms?

AUTHOR: That may be true of some classical genres, but opera is flourishing more than ever. When I was growing up in Seattle during the 1930s you got only a single week of opera a year – and this from a touring group called the San Carlo Opera, which did only the most tired of warhorses, and with the flimsiest of sets, and singers who could charitably be described as of bush-league quality. Today, though I no longer live there, the city boasts its own company with a respectably sized season plus a summer *Ring* that draws international audiences.

INTERLOCUTOR: Still, why would you devote so large a chunk of your career – fully a third of the books you've done – to a form as marginal as opera? I don't mean trivial, as some people take it to be, or an "exotick and irrational entertainment," in Johnson's notorious definition.[1] I just mean that it doesn't carry the cultural weight of categories such as tragedy, epic poetry, or, to cite a subject that you've treated, historical drama. And how must it feel to you to know that most of the people in your field, literary study, really don't care about opera? In fact many of them are positively embarrassed at the thought of having to watch some huge singer, all puffed up, projecting her ridiculous words toward an adoring house. Can't you appreciate how they must feel?

AUTHOR: Probably no different from the way a vegetarian feels sharing a table with somebody audibly sucking marrow from a large bone. That's *their* problem. But please remember, the anti-operatic prejudice is a phenomenon that goes far back in time. I dealt with it earlier in writing on opera. It's not unrelated to the anti-theatrical element in twentieth-century opera that I take up here in Essay 8.

INTERLOCUTOR: You are avoiding the question by intellectualizing it. Let me put it another way: Are you perhaps trying to exploit your own particular taste for opera by concocting a project for yourself?

AUTHOR: Obviously I'm an opera fan. But as musical preferences go, I'm equally a fan of other forms of music (or should I say "classical music?" – for when I was young music meant classical music and pop forms needed adjectives to indicate you didn't mean classical). Yes, I'm as avid about the chamber, the *Lieder*, and the piano repertory as I am about opera. And about ballet and dance as well.

INTERLOCUTOR: So why pick opera among all these forms to write about?

AUTHOR: Because it transcends the usual intellectual categories. Opera extends its tentacles into all manner of territory. The various ways one can relate opera to society – the topic of this book's second essay – are as manifold as that of any aesthetic form. Its particular relations with its audiences over time – the topic of

---

[1] Johnson, "Hughes," p. 39. Johnson mentions that Hughes wrote the texts for six cantatas that, as he put it, "seem intended to oppose or exclude the Italian opera." This negative attitude toward foreign ("exotick") opera was frequent among eighteenth-century British thinkers from Addison (see Essay 9) onward.

Essays 1 and 9 – show it to be at once responsive to and also assertively manipulative of its consuming public. And by looking at recent experiments on music by neuroscientists, as I do in Essay 5, we can better understand both why opera seeks to maintain a high degree of emotional tension and also the ways that different operatic styles have found their own ways of doing this.

INTERLOCUTOR: Aren't you asking a lot of your prospective audience if you expect them to follow experiments from the sciences, including social science, as you do in Essay 2, where you insist on the relevance of a social scientist, Pierre Bourdieu, to the study of opera?

AUTHOR: I know there are people in the humanities who think that anything coming from all those distant areas has nothing to do with their concerns. They see themselves as the last bastion upholding the traditional cultural values that they assume science and social science spurn. I could easily warn them at this point to skip the neuroscience essay. But actually I want them to read this piece: even if it does not undo their anti-science bias, it may ring a bell for them about how their reactions to music, and to opera in particular, are not all that different from the other, more animal satisfactions in their lives.

INTERLOCUTOR: What makes opera so special among these satisfactions?

AUTHOR: Where but in opera, except maybe in Shakespeare, do you find the most melodramatic, silly, banal material transformed into something sublime? Where else can you find a form that keeps you in a state of intense rapture without let-up for three, and, in a few cases, even five hours? And where else, once you're sober enough to analyze what it's all about, can you find a medium situated within so many heterogeneous contexts as opera?

INTERLOCUTOR: Is that what you mean by the word *situating* in your title? What precisely *do* you mean?

AUTHOR: Opera is situated in places like the eighteenth-century theater boxes in which the local nobles play cards during the recitative while waiting for the castrato to begin his aria (Essays 2 and 5); or in the contemporary opera house where the society matrons enter on opening night to display their latest designer gowns and their latest cosmetic surgery (Essay 1); or, to move to more serious territory, opera is situated in an aesthetic theory such as Wagner's idea of the *Gesamtkunstwerk*, which sought to overturn the longstanding classical system insisting on the separation of the arts (Essay 6); or in such pleasure centers of the brain as the thalamus, the ventral striatum, and the insula (Essay 5); or in the cryptic allusions within modernist writing to the full-blown passion of nineteenth-century arias (Essay 1); or in the lovemaking of opera queens while a screechy Callas *roulade* blasts from their speakers (not further developed in this book); or in the double shock within some modernist works to scandalize both by means of musical sound and of the actions transpiring onstage (Essay 7); or in the contemporary offshoots that use and distort the operatic past to pioneer new theatrical forms (Essays 3 and 4); or in the imperial cultural policy and international power games that instigated the commissioning of what turned out to be a classic opera (Essay 2); or in the parody of what might seem too highfalutin an operatic tradition (Essays 1 and 8).

INTERLOCUTOR: You are clearly seeking to move in a multitude of directions at once. It's only honest at this point to warn you that your readers will likely feel disturbed by your shifting, and I might add, quite unconventional, modes of presentation as they move from essay to essay, like the lexicon that shapes your piece on *Il trovatore* (Essay 1), or the vignettes about specific operatic occasions in your so-called consumers' history of opera (Essay 9), and your survey of recent operatic – or rather quasi-operatic – experiments (Essay 4). And then there's that very formal essay full of theories about the various arts (Essay 6), a piece in which you abandon any attempt at wit and assume the mantle of a theorist, or at least a historian of theory. How can you claim any sort of unity, any argument even, in a book that flaunts so many incongruous styles and topics at its reader?

AUTHOR: For one thing, the three words of my subtitle – period, genre, reception – help shape nearly every essay. But I confess I prefer to pursue variety rather than unity. And I find raising questions more interesting than finding answers. In fact, readers will discover a number of paragraphs among these essays in which interrogative sentences outnumber declarative ones.

INTERLOCUTOR: So where are the answers?

AUTHOR: Readers can mull the questions over and enter into dialogue with me.

INTERLOCUTOR: And whoever heard of a prologue like this one in which the author is openly in dialogue with himself?

AUTHOR: And an epilogue too, which continues in this mode.

INTERLOCUTOR: Maybe you think you can soften your reader's resistance by advertising your own skepticism to this project. I'd like to hear you justify yourself.

AUTHOR: This book is only doing in a more overt way what I've been doing all along.

INTERLOCUTOR: How so?

AUTHOR: My way of conceiving a project is to hook a bunch of diverse essays around a single subject. My first book, for example, was unified only by the fact that all the essays – each of them in fact using a critical method different from the rest – engaged with a single work, namely, Wordsworth's long poem *The Prelude*, which I sought to place within a whole range of contexts: within the tradition of epic, of long poems in general, within modern poetry, within a long line of writings obsessed with time, within the political conflicts of the poet's time.[2] I made it clear in my introduction to this book that readers should not expect a single, overriding argument the way they could do with other people's books.

INTERLOCUTOR: That sounds plausible enough if all those heterogeneous pieces concentrate on a single work, but how do you justify writing on so amorphous a genre as opera?

AUTHOR: I did it earlier with something perhaps even more amorphous: historical drama.[3] Every one of the five sections of that book – centered around a large bundle of plays about history from totally

---

[2] Lindenberger, *On Wordsworth's* Prelude.   [3] Lindenberger, *Historical Drama*.

different periods and cultures – drew upon a theoretical construct quite different from the others. When, soon after, I decided to do my first book on opera,[4] I had a model based on my earlier work: so I could draw on social theory in one chapter, while in another I did an iconographical study showing how the act of attending an opera created some of the crucial scenes in a number of classic novels.

INTERLOCUTOR: Sounds as though you've not done what other people in most fields do, that is, commit yourself to a particular method or point of view. You surely know that readers expect this sort of thing.

AUTHOR: Committing oneself is tough when you don't really believe strongly in a single way of doing things. The harder I look at any particular method, the more holes I see in it. After my Wordsworth book came out, a well-known theorist labeled me a "perspectivist."

INTERLOCUTOR: So you think that using multiple perspectives will get you closer to the truth?

AUTHOR: Not if you aren't searching for a particular truth, or even truths. People who go for some grand theory that'll hold everything together are a bit too earnest for my tastes. I much prefer being playful with the particular perspectives I employ.

INTERLOCUTOR: Does that account for those abrupt stylistic changes that I find in what you're presenting to us now?

AUTHOR: I began to experiment with those in my second book on opera.[5] In one chapter I juxtaposed two seemingly antithetical modernist composers, Arnold Schoenberg and Kurt Weill, and then I further juxtaposed these two with the political events of the year 1930 in Germany, and I added a further complication by organizing the chapter into some seventeen brief items, much like the consumers' history of opera in this book or the essay on *Il trovatore*. And like the latter, these items in the Schoenberg-Weill chapter display their arbitrariness by organizing themselves simply in alphabetical order.

INTERLOCUTOR: Why the alphabetical organization for the piece on *Il trovatore*? Isn't this just a gimmick?

---

[4] Lindenberger, *Opera: The Extravagant Art*.   [5] Lindenberger, *Opera in History*.

AUTHOR: The essay (if you allow me to call it that) seeks to explore as many facets of audience reception as it can: *Il trovatore* as it made its way into popular movies, into Montale's hermetic poetry, into the ears of listeners greedy for their high *c*'s (even when Verdi had left them out). The only way to cover this heterogeneous material – though it's all centered on how we've devoured this warhorse of an opera over the years – is to find what you call a gimmick that will hold it all together in a rational way. The order of the alphabet provides this rational cover.

INTERLOCUTOR: So I assume you aren't expecting your reader to look for or discover an argument in this book.

AUTHOR: If readers find any argument, it's that opera, like most aesthetic phenomena, lends itself to a variety of critical voices.

INTERLOCUTOR: But with all your stylistic tricks, it's hard even to find an argument in any of your individual essays.

AUTHOR: Some offer arguments: for example, Essay 8 contends that some of the most significant operas of the twentieth century, like *Pelléas et Mélisande* and *Moses und Aron*, are deeply anti-theatrical in nature.

INTERLOCUTOR: But why do you need a whole long essay to say that? Isn't it a bit obvious?

AUTHOR: Probably so, I suspect, but the purpose of that argument is to hold a bunch of otherwise diverse operas together in order to show the quite different ways that each of them reveals its anti-theatrical stance. The argument, one might say, serves as an excuse to say something that I hope will seem interesting about these works. What a difference, for example, between the under-statedness that Debussy uses to challenge Wagnerian theatricality and the parodying of earlier operatic styles in *The Rake's Progress*!

INTERLOCUTOR: We seem to be going in circles. You speak with pride of your unconventionality and now you tell me you're also amen-able to conventional writing. How do you reconcile all these things?

AUTHOR: Why not simply let the curtain go up – and on *Il trovatore* to boot?

ABOUT

What is *Il trovatore* "about?"

a. the standard *dramatis personae* of Italian Romantic opera: heroic tenor, yearning soprano, unpleasant and unsuccessful baritone, wronged and vengeful mezzo-soprano, loyal bass, plus these people's various attendants.
b. the Romantic Middle Ages.
c. the Middle Ages as romanticized in the later novels of Sir Walter Scott.
d. the Middle Ages as further romanticized by Scott's followers, above all, in the dramas of Victor Hugo and *his* followers – most notably for *Il trovatore*, in the play *El Trovador* by Antonio García Gutiérrez.
e. the characteristic structure of arias and duets of its time: recitative leading into the cantabile, then the *tempo di mezzo*, and, finally, the cabaletta.
f. the dangers posed by gypsies (though gypsies did not yet reside in Aragon at the time the play was set).[1]
g. the gypsy's revenge, revenge becoming an emotion the audience can identify with since it is mediated by a romantically distant setting and by music that seeks to overwhelm any moral compunctions we may have (see VIOLENCE).
h. very little in the present and a lot in the past (see NARRATING).
i. two brothers separated in infancy after a gypsy bewitches one of them and, in punishment, is sent to the stake, after which her daughter steals this child and, in revenge for her mother's death,

---

[1] See the introduction to García Gutiérrez, *El Trovador*, p. 20.

seeks to throw him into a fire but mistakenly tosses her own child in, after which she raises the noble son, who, when grown up, attracts a young woman who also happens to be loved by the other brother, with whom he fights a duel, after which, having spared his rival in this duel, he in turn abducts the woman they both love from the convent she was about to enter and then, just before his impending marriage to her, goes into battle to save his supposed mother, who had been captured by his real brother, who in turn captures and jails the brother who had outwitted him in abducting the mutually beloved and who thinks he has finally won the latter, after she agrees to sleep with him if he releases the man she loves but actually poisons herself before he can enjoy her body, with the result that the brother who holds the power in turn executes his rival but is then informed by the original gypsy's daughter of his kinship to his victim.

j. the characteristic disposition of musical numbers of its time: arias, duets, trios, choruses, and a concertato at the end of a middle act.

k. the war between the Carlists and the Liberals in the Spain of the 1830s, this war being the contemporary subtext of García Gutiér-rez's play,[2] though Verdi and his librettist Cammarano would likely have been unaware of this, or, even if aware, would scarcely have cared.

l. whatever a contemporary director chooses to make it about (see X-RATED).

BRAINWORM

What can be more banal than Manrico's refrain from inside his tower cell during the Miserere? Outside the context of *Il trovatore* these notes come back to me obsessively at the most inopportune times and without giving me the opportunity to turn them off, as I can a CD player or an iPod. They belong to a musical genre that Oliver Sacks, looking at this phenomenon as a neurologist, has

---

[2] *Ibid.*, pp. 24–26.

labeled "brainworms."[3] Maddening as these notes may be, when I hear them within their appropriate context – interspersed with the male chorus solemnly intoning the Miserere and Leonora frantically assuring her lover that she will never forget him (see QUOTING and THRUST) – what can be more sublime?

c''

Any aspiring tenor looking through David Lawton's critical edition of *Il trovatore* will notice that Manrico is never granted a high *c* in Verdi's score. Not even a *b*, though at one point, inconspicuously in the first act trio, he gets a *b* flat, with the option of even lowering it to *d* flat.[4] And in what has become his showpiece, the cabaletta "Di quella pira," the critical edition reproduces nothing higher than an *a*. By contrast, Leonora is amply rewarded with high *c*'s and even a *d* flat in her two arias, while Azucena gets to show off a high *c* on top of the deep chest tones that define her personality. The Count, moreover, is expected to display an uncommonly high tessitura.

So what can a self-respecting tenor do? He simply inserts his own resounding *c*'s into "Di quella pira." Indeed, it's been that way since within a few years of the premiere of *Il trovatore*, when Enrico Tamberlick, asking the composer's permission to violate the original score after he had tried out the *c*'s in some provincial theaters, supposedly received this reply: "Far be it from me to deny the public what it wants. Put in the high *c* if you like provided it is a good one."[5]

Is Verdi's statement sufficient evidence to warrant – or even to demand – the high *c*? At one extreme one finds Riccardo Muti's insistence on playing Verdi's scores as the composer originally composed them and, as a result, brazenly challenging the audience's desires, as was evident at a performance of *Il trovatore* that he conducted in 2000 on a La Scala opening night and that invited the

---

[3] See the chapter entitled "Brainworms, Sticky Music, and Catchy Tunes," in Sacks, *Musicophilia*, pp. 41–48.

[4] Verdi, *Il trovatore*, ed. Lawton, p. 84 (m. 261).

[5] Budden, *The Operas of Verdi*, vol. II (1978), pp. 98–99.

predictable fury from the upper balconies when Salvatore Licitra omitted the expected high *c*.[6]

The question remains how one makes choices. Does Verdi's original score have more authority than later performance practices that the composer is even thought to have sanctioned? Do not these practices have the authority that attaches to long-standing precedent? Does one want to allow an audience accustomed to the high *c* to feel let down as Act III comes to its dramatic conclusion? After all, Verdi wrote the part for a particular singer, Carlo Baucardé, who had begun his career as a baritone and may well not have been able to do any better than an *a*. But then there is also a story that Baucardé himself inserted the *c* in a performance in Florence a few months after the premiere.[7]

Moreover, to what extent should later interpreters of a role be guided by the vocal peculiarities of the singer for whom the role was originally composed? By that criterion, of course, coloratura sopranos struggling for the Queen of the Night's high *f*'s should be allowed to settle for some lower note, for Mozart was able to make his demands only because the role was designed for the unusually agile voice of his sister-in-law, Josepha Hofer.

And who is to make these choices – the singer, the conductor, or the impresario responsible for hiring both of them? Does the intent of some composers, above all those of German vintage, have more authority than that of others, especially those, like Verdi, writing in a supposedly more populist mode? And does the warhorse status that a work such as *Il trovatore* is perceived to possess allow its interpreters greater or lesser freedom?

DREAM

In *El Trovador*, just before Ruiz rushes in to tell Manrique to come to his supposed mother's rescue, the hero recites the following dream to Leonor:

[6] For a detailed discussion of the issue, see Gossett, *Divas and Scholars*, pp. 124–27.
[7] *Ibid.*, p. 546 (note 49).

I dreamt that I was with you in the silent night
Near the lake that kisses the feet
Of high Castellar.
Everything lay calm; only a
Melancholy and sad moan
Lugubriously approached my ear.
Tremulous like the wind along the lake
The sinister brilliance of the yellowing moon
Sparkled sadly.
Seated there on the shore and at your side,
I strummed my lute, and sweetly it sang
Your beauty and my tender love,
And with a sad melody
The wind that murmured over the waters
Repeated my song and your sighs.
Suddenly, ominously, through the murky mist
A brilliant flash of lightning crossed,
Wounding your face with melancholic splendor.
I witnessed a specter that on the opposite shore
Wandered like a ghostly illusion
With mysterious steps;
And a doleful moan was let loose
Interrupting the nocturnal silence,
Now looking sadly at us,
Now smiling with an infernal face.
Suddenly the hurricane shakes and quivers
With hundreds of thunder-bolts,
And a thousand rays crossed,
And the ground and the mountains trembled
At its terrifying imprint.
And, enveloped in smoke, the fierce phantasma
Fled, extending its arms to me.
"Avenge me!" it said, and it threw itself to the clouds;
"Avenge me!" repeating through the air.
Cold with fright, I extended my arms
To where you were . . . You were no longer there;
And at my side I found

Only a skeleton; and when I touched it, it boldly
Turned into dust, which the violent, thunderous wind
Suddenly carried away.
I woke up startled; my head had become
A volcano, my eyes clouded;
But finally I succeed in seeing you, tender, gentle,
And your smile calms my anger.[8]

According to the scenario that Verdi sent to his librettist Cammarano, he had intended to include this dream in the opera.[9] Manrique's
violent dream (Verdi was still using the Spanish version of his hero's
name at this point) was to be recited at that spot in Act Three which
eventually housed the lyrical aria "Ah! sì, ben mio." But Cammarano
replied he had decided to eliminate the dream, which he found
"superfluous."[10] In a missing letter Verdi apparently insisted on
retaining this dream, but the librettist had the last word, reminding
the composer that the libretto already contained two long narratives,
those of Ferrando and Azucena (or of Leonora, for that matter).[11]

What if Verdi had prevailed in retaining this dream narrative?
Surely it would have resulted in a dramatic aria, one that revealed a
more troubled, introspective hero than the Manrico who emerged
in the aria that replaced the dream. With its vision of the hero's
supposed grandmother calling for vengeance, together with its
graphic description of the heroine turning into a skeleton that then
turns into dust, we have a thoroughly Gothic passage that calls
more for the sort of music that Wagner designed for his Flying
Dutchman, or even that Verdi had already given to Azucena, than
for anything we have come to associate with Manrico. Indeed, what
plans might Verdi have had for accommodating this dream to the
formal conventions of an aria, to which he was still committed at
this stage of his career? The horrors that Manrico recounts would
surely have made for a strange cantabile section – granted that "Di
quella pira" was at this point already intended to serve as the

---

[8] García Gutiérrez, *El Trovador*, pp. 151–53.
[9] Mossa, *Carteggio Verdi-Cammarano*, p. 191.   [10] *Ibid.*, p. 196.   [11] *Ibid.*, p. 215.

cabaletta. Or might Verdi have opted for a dramatic recitative like "Pari siamo" in *Rigoletto*?

Had Verdi won, as he did in most conflicts with his various librettists, we should not only have known a more rounded hero, but, as a result, our judgment of the opera as a backward-looking work might have been somewhat different, especially if the composer had given the dream the complex musical form it called for. The shape that nineteenth-century operas ultimately take lies less in the composer's initial desires than in the negotiations and ensuing compromises between him and his librettist.

ENDINGS

The ending of an opera often defines the spectator's experience more than any other single passage. *Il trovatore* has two endings: the powerful, quick, abrupt ending that we ordinarily hear and one that is lengthier by some thirty bars and that is used in the opera's Paris version, *Le Trouvère*.[12] In addition, Cammarano's original libretto was longer by several lines that help explain the actions going on in the final moments, but Verdi, after his librettist's death, shortened this text on his own in order to achieve the concise ending that we know.[13]

I once attended a performance that pasted the longer, Paris ending onto the Italian version.[14] It was impressive enough in its own way, with the male chorus in the background repeating its Miserere chant. And one could follow the action of the final moments far better than in the usual *Il trovatore*, in which the count's final line, "E vivo ancor!" virtually collides with Azucena's announcement of her revenge, with neither of them being very

[12] For descriptions of how *Le Trouvère* diverges from *Il trovatore*, see Budden, *Operas of Verdi*, vol. ii, pp. 107–11, and Lawton, "'*Le Trouvère*'," pp. 79–119.

[13] For Cammarano's text, see Budden, *Operas of Verdi*, vol. ii, pp. 64–65.

[14] The words to the Paris ending are reprinted in Verdi, *Le Trouvère, L'Avant Scène Opéra*, No. 60 (February, 1984), p. 83. A critical edition of *Le Trouvère* is being prepared by David Lawton, who edited the critical edition of *Il trovatore*.

intelligible. But with this more expansive ending, the opera had become a different thing altogether. The driving force (see THRUST) that moves the work with such intensity from its earliest bars had become a bit lax. The next time I attended the opera I was relieved to find at the end that Romantic Fate, however unintelligible the words, had once again manifested itself in all its horrifying glory.

FOURSOME

Caruso supposedly said that *Il trovatore* demanded the greatest singers in the world for each of its four major voice ranges.[15] Over the years, except for Maria Callas, I've heard everybody who, at any particular time, counted among this select company but never, alas, in the same opera and certainly not in *Il trovatore*.

GESAMTKUNSTWERK

Verdi recognized the obsolescence of *Il trovatore* even before he began composition. From a letter to Cammarano of April 4, 1851, it is clear that what he really wanted to do was something on the order of *Falstaff*, for which, given the expectations of librettists, impresarios, and audiences, he had to wait another forty years. "If operas," he writes, "had no more cavatinas, no more duets, no more trios, no more choruses, no more finales, etc., and if the whole opera were, so to speak, one single piece, I should find that more reasonable and right."[16]

Like his exact contemporary Richard Wagner, Verdi, as this remark suggests, was nurturing dreams of some artwork of the future. Is it wholly coincidental, moreover, that Verdi uttered his desire (voiced, to be sure, at various times during his career) in the same year that Wagner published *Oper und Drama* (1851), the treatise that proposed the new direction toward which he intended to steer opera?

[15] Budden, *Operas of Verdi*, vol. ii, p. 112.
[16] Mossa, *Carteggio Verdi-Cammarano*, p. 188.

Indeed, the period 1851–53, the very years of Verdi's great trilogy of which *Il trovatore* is a part, is also the period in which Wagner theorized and first set into practice a method that was to revolutionize the way that operas were composed. Whereas 1851 marked the treatise, 1853 was the year in which he published the libretto of *Der Ring des Nibelungen* and, in his celebrated vision at La Spezia on September 5, inwardly heard the *e*-flat chord that generated *Das Rheingold*.[17]

Yet to invoke Wagner in this context is also to remind us how retrograde *Il trovatore* looks within the history of opera (see JUDGMENTS) – and this despite Verdi's stated desire for seamless continuity.[18] His librettist, not to speak of singers and impresarios, would have been wholly unprepared for so violent an assault on operatic form. By contrast, Wagner, living in exile, and without any hope of getting his operas performed, enjoyed the luxury of putting his dreams into action, at least on the written page.

Verdi was of course tied to the institutional system of opera as it was practiced in Italy in his time. When he introduced innovations – for example, the creation of new voice configurations for the baritone and the mezzo-soprano[19] – he did so one thing at a time. If he was cantankerous and overly demanding with his librettists, singers, and impresarios, this stance was doubtless necessary for him to institute what changes he needed to give his works the artistic integrity that he coveted. By the time of his final two operas, the only ones that sometimes receive praise from Wagnerians, he was enough of a cultural icon to force the system to bow to his demands.

---

[17] Wagner described his vision in *Mein Leben*, ed. Middell, vol. II, p. 60.

[18] Even if Verdi's middle-period operas seem retrograde from a Wagnerian point of view, an essay on the criticism of his contemporary Alberto Mazzucato shows that during the early 1850s a shift occurred between "two diverse conceptions of opera": an earlier one in which the desires of the singer were primary, and a later one, represented by Verdi, in which the individual opera emerges as "*opus perfectum*, as monument, set in every detail by the author's will." See Della Seta, "Gli esordi della critica verdiana," p. 69.

[19] See Robinson, *Opera and Ideas*, pp. 171–79.

HEROICS

Being heroic also means being a little dumb, and Manrico is no exception. His chief functions, besides singing, are to love (both his mother and his girlfriend) and to fight. He is anything but introspective, though if Cammarano had allowed Verdi to set his dream (see DREAM), Manrico might have displayed a bit of psychological complexity. But Verdi was concerned above all with maintaining his heroism, and when Cammarano sought to change the Spanish original by letting him be wounded in a duel rather than in battle, the composer insisted on a battle wound instead: "This poor troubadour," Verdi wrote, "has so little going for him that if you take away his valor, what does he have left?"[20]

When Manrico sings well, especially if he can negotiate the unwritten c''s in "Di quella pira" (see c''), he is irresistible. But even without these superfluous notes he is like few other tenors in the repertory: lyrical and at once grandly heroic.

I have experienced three celebrated Manricos, each a singer-generation apart. But only one of these was at his best. Giovanni Martinelli, whom I heard in Seattle in 1941 with a pick-up touring company, was already over the hill. Still, despite the shards that were all that was left of his voice, one knew – from his gestures and the presence with which he commanded the stage – that here was the quintessential hero.

Luciano Pavarotti, for whom the role had not yet jelled when I heard him do it in San Francisco in 1975 (it was in fact his first Manrico), produced his usual beautiful tones but, quite in contrast to Martinelli, failed to project the necessary heroism. Not so with Franco Corelli, whose offstage serenade to Leonora, when I heard it in Rome in 1963, told me even before his appearance that I should never hear a Manrico like it again, and of course I never have. From beginning to end, from the passionate serenade to the fierce reproaches he leveled at Leonora when, in the final scene, he

[20] See Mossa, *Carteggio Verdi-Cammarano*, pp. 188–89, 190, 195. The quotation is on p. 190.

accused her of betrayal, I still hear that heroic voice in my mind when I attend performances of other, invariably lesser, Manricos.

Yet there was another great Manrico (at least to judge by his recording of the role) whom I could and should have heard. In 1956 a friend called in sick to offer me his ticket to hear Jussi Bjoerling in Los Angeles that night do the part alongside Eileen Farrell. How I wanted to go! Yet I felt obligated to prepare for my next morning's classes. In retrospect I know that my students of more than half a century ago would not remember my having to wing it as much as I might now be remembering (and boasting to have heard!) Bjoerling's Manrico. This was one of those missed opportunities that haunt you for life – like not buying Microsoft in 1986 or Google in 2004.

INTERTEXTUAL

When hearing those Verdi operas composed after *Il trovatore*, as well as *Rigoletto*, which preceded it, the listener is more aware of what is new than what is similar to earlier Italian opera. Not so with *Il trovatore*, which has long been labeled old-fashioned, with such condescending terms as "hackneyed" and "vulgar" attached to it (see JUDGMENTS).

And we surely remain conscious of the operatic past when attending this opera. In one sense it is a reworking of *Ernani*: both are built around four voices, though *Ernani* has a star bass instead of a mezzo-soprano, and in both operas we perceive these four characters more as voices than as individualized people. Both works are unremittingly heroic, and both lack the subtleties that have endeared, say, *La traviata* and *Un ballo in maschera* to sophisticated moderns. It seems no accident that both *Ernani* and *Il trovatore* were Verdi's two most resounding successes with the public when they were first performed.

Verdi's first audience might also have heard the two opening scenes as a reworking of the first scenes of *Lucia di Lammermoor*. Each work begins with a family retainer recounting mysterious problems around the estate, then gives way to the soprano's entrance aria – in both cases a celebration of her love for a stranger – though the remainder of the act goes in a distinctly different direction in each work: an ecstatic duet between the lovers in *Lucia*, while in *Il trovatore* any possible duet of this sort is thwarted by the appearance of a rival suitor. It seems no accident that both Donizetti and Verdi used the same librettist for these works.

Once serious scholarly inquiry into Verdi began – long after Wagner had been established within the musicological canon – many details within the score of *Il trovatore* could be traced to various antecedents. Ferrando's opening aria emerges as a ballade echoing innumerable such passages in French opera, most notably Raimbaud's ballade in the first act of *Robert le Diable*.[21] Leonora's entrance aria, in turn, reworks the conventions of the romance, in which a character often narrates the first glimpse of his or her beloved.[22] Specific musical echoes have been suggested, notably the funeral march of Beethoven's Opus 26 sonata in the harmonies of the Miserere.[23] The idea for the ending, in which a character unwittingly sends a close relation to execution, may well have come from an earlier opera, though not by way of the composer or librettist, but rather through the source text, for García Gutiérrez evidently adapted the brutal catastrophe of Halévy's *La Juive*, in which the Cardinal learns that the woman he has executed is his long-lost daughter.[24]

But *Il trovatore* has also been shown seeping into the other work that Verdi was working on at the time, namely, *La traviata*. Different though these operas may be in other respects, at several points thematic shapes and certain brief orchestral accompaniments, as Roger Parker has suggested, made their way from one opera into the next.[25] It does not seem wholly accidental, for instance, that the

---

[21] See Hepokoski, "*Ottocento* Opera as Cultural Drama," pp. 166–75.

[22] *Ibid.*, pp. 175–85.

[23] Osthoff, "'Pianissimo, benché a piena orchestra'," pp. 222–23.

[24] Chusid, "A New Source for *El Trovador*," pp. 208–10.

[25] See "Of Andalusian Maidens and Recognition Scenes: Crossed Wires in *La traviata* and *Il trovatore*," in Parker, *Remaking the Song*, pp. 22–41. See also Rosen, "Meter, Character, and *Tinta* in Verdi's Operas," pp. 380–82.

opening theme of Ferrando's "Abbietta zingara" is echoed in the chorus of mock-gypsies in the later opera. Whether in the repetition of musical or plot elements, experienced operagoers are always aware that somewhere – whether or not they can identify precisely where – they have heard this before.

JUDGMENTS

1853

> Last night 'Il Trovatore' was produced in a theatre overflowing with people . . . the music transported us to heaven; and, of a truth, it could not be otherwise, because this is, without exaggeration, heavenly music.[26] *Gazzetta Musicale*, Milano

1877

> *Trovatore*, – Italian of the trashiest, most hackneyed, barrel-organ type! . . . When lovers of the best in music neglect the best, the appeal has to be made to the popular crowd.[27] *Dwight's Journal of Music*

1890

> I know my Trovatore thoroughly, from the first drum-roll to the final chord of E flat minor, and can assert that it is a heroic work, capable of producing a tremendous effect if heroically performed. But anything short of this means vulgarity, triviality, tediousness, and failure; for there is nothing unheroic to fall back on – no comedy, no spectacle, no symphonic instrumental commentary, no relief to the painful flood of feeling surging up repeatedly to the most furious intensity of passion; nothing but love – elemental love of cub for dam and male for female – with hate, jealousy, terror, and the shadow of death throughout.[28] George Bernard Shaw

---

[26] Quoted in Toye, *Verdi*, p. 79.
[27] Quoted in Phillips-Matz, *Verdi*, pp. 639–40. To be sure, *Dwight's Journal* was an apologist for the new German music.
[28] Laurence (ed.), *Shaw's Music*, vol. II, p. 78.

1931

> "Il Trovatore" has been reproached with vulgarity and the reproach is not unfounded. But this vulgarity is the vulgarity of greatness, a by-product of the vitality and passion without which there can be no great art. Is Shakespeare never vulgar? Or Beethoven?[29]   Francis Toye

1956

> Its [*Rigoletto's*] success did not stop Verdi from glorifying the bad old style two years later in *Il Trovatore*, a magnificent demonstration of unprincipled melodrama.[30]   Joseph Kerman

1978

> *Il Trovatore* is unlikely to depreciate with the years. If it is not the composer's supreme masterpiece it is none the less without parallel in the whole operatic literature – a late flowering of the Italian romantic tradition possible only to one who had seen beyond it.[31]
>   Julian Budden

2010

> *Il trovatore, Simon Boccanegra*, and *Don Carlos* – my favorite Verdi operas.
>   Herbert Lindenberger

KULTUR

Does *Il trovatore* belong to high or to low culture? When I lived in Italy during the early 1960s it clearly belonged to the latter category, at least among the educated people whom I came to know there. They much preferred chamber music to opera, and if they were to be seen at the opera, it was for Wagner or Strauss, though they might compromise for *Otello* and *Falstaff*, but certainly for nothing earlier by Verdi (see GESAMTKUNSTWERK).

The attitude shown by many postwar Italian intellectuals derived from a perception that Verdi, and nineteenth-century Italian opera in

---

[29] Toye, *Verdi*, p. 320.   [30] Kerman, *Opera as Drama*, p. 164.
[31] Budden, *The Operas of Verdi*, vol. II, p. 112.

general, represented an earlier, cruder form of culture that, frankly, they found embarrassing. But this attitude actually goes further back in time, not only in Italy but throughout Europe. With the ascent of Wagnerism during the late nineteenth century, Italian opera came to seem backward, at best some form of folk art better suited to the masses than to people who saw themselves as cultivated (see JUDG-MENTS). To be sure, serious attempts were made, especially in Weimar Germany, to bring Verdi into fashion, yet it was largely those less popular operas – such as *Simon Boccanegra, La forza del destino*, and *Don Carlos* – that attracted the attention of new Verdians like the writer Franz Werfel, who prepared his own performing versions of several operas in an attempt to make the composer palatable to sophisticated tastes.[32]

Yet the present-day distinction between high and low culture had little meaning at the time that *Il trovatore* was composed, when the opera house was still an entertainment site for people from diverse classes. Opera counted as a popular form, not quite as light as, say, *opéra comique* or vaudeville, but something that could communicate with everybody. In his book *Highbrow Lowbrow*, Lawrence W. Levine has shown how pervasive opera was in mid-nineteenth-century America, from regular performances to offshoots such as the Boston Peace Jubilee of 1869 that advertised the Anvil Chorus played with sledge-hammers by a hundred firemen.[33] But Levine also describes the process by which opera was "sacralized" in the course of the century as new, more rigid canons of taste took hold.

If opera during the twentieth century was relegated to a ghetto comprising the affluent and the educated, there are signs today that the wall separating high and low culture can perhaps be broken down – or at least breached in a few spots. In view of the current fear that opera, especially in those countries with little or no state

---

[32] See Wiesmann, "'Eine verlachte Liebe.'" For a comprehensive history of the Verdi revival of the 1920s and early 1930s, together with Werfel's pivotal role, see Kreuzer, "*Zurück zu Verdi.*"

[33] Levine, *Highbrow Lowbrow*, pp. 85–168. For the sledge-hammer performance, see p. 105.

subsidy, will not have the resources to continue in its present form, impresarios are concocting new ways of enticing people to the opera. Stage directors with no previous experience in (and sometimes even no knowledge of) opera are mounting glamorous new productions utilizing the most advanced stage techniques. Major companies are presenting matinees of shortened versions of operas in English for children. Just as I finished work on this essay, the San Francisco Opera broadcast *Il trovatore* live in high definition at the local baseball stadium on a weekend when the Giants were on the road. And the Metropolitan is doing a good bit of its current repertory live in movie theaters throughout the world – and with unexpectedly high attendance. Might this mean that ordinary folk will once again be humming the Anvil Chorus?

LADIES

Culture in America, at least regarding opera, has long been entrusted to certain so-called beautiful people, ladies whose husbands are expected to accompany them to performances (though often with considerable reluctance). These female sponsors, immaculately blond, face-lifted, de-la-Renta-gowned, Bulgari-choked, see to it not only that the repertory remain conservative but that productions retain the period costumes and scenery they remember from their distant youth. An innovative recent impresario in San Francisco was excoriated after she chose the dowdy *Mother of Us All* (an opera whose plot, the old subscribers complained, goes nowhere) for an opening night – the very occasion that these ladies count on to show off their all. If only this doomed impresario had chosen the company's tired and easily available production of *Il trovatore* (whose plot, the subscribers would have found, manages to go everywhere)!

MOVIES

Il trovatore has made two significant forays into the movies: the Marx Brothers' *A Night at the Opera* (1935) and Luchino Visconti's

Senso (1954). No two films could be more different: the first, a zany Hollywood farce, the second, a sumptuously outfitted postwar Italian meditation on Italian-German relations.

The uses to which Verdi's opera is put in each film are as different as the films themselves. *A Night at the Opera* pokes merciless fun at the opera, not so much perhaps at *Il trovatore* itself but rather at opera as an institution. The film opens with a snippet of *I pagliacci* and culminates in a long sequence from *Il trovatore*. It is hardly an accident that the Marxes chose these two operas to represent the institution as a whole, for both are among the few operatic works whose titles (and even a few of whose tunes) would have been quite familiar to the middle-class movie-going public of the 1930s. (One can of course no longer count on this familiarity with the film public.) If opera as a form is known for representing emotional situations in an extravagant form, both these operas serve as extreme examples.

Within the Marxes' world (also, perhaps, within the whole American world), opera represents at once high culture and high society (see KULTUR and LADIES). In the *Il trovatore* sequence, shots of the opera alternate regularly with shots of formally clad opera patrons who, in the course of the performance, display their horror at the antics with which the Marx brothers disrupt the musical proceedings on stage. The key representative of society in this film is the benefactress Mrs. Claypool, played by Margaret Dumont, who, in various Marx films, customarily enacted the ladies whose pretensions the brothers deflated.

The upshot of all this is that social and musical pretensions need to be cut down to size. The unrestrained, corrosive wit exercised above all by Groucho suggests an anarchic social vision that leaves no room for the formalities demanded by either high society or high art. Low-brow culture emerges as the only viable alternative to the artifice represented by both the benefactress and the opera that she finances.

The antics commence immediately. When the orchestra gets to page two of the prelude, it starts playing "Take Me Out to the Ball

Game," whose sheet music one of the brothers has inserted in the score. The next thing we see is Harpo Marx swinging his violin as his brother Chico pitches to him, while Groucho moves through the audience pretending to peddle peanuts. Baseball becomes an alternative institution to opera – and a more authentic one to boot. The antics continue throughout the film with one comic trick following another, for example, a backdrop suddenly emerging to advertise the American Taxicab Company.

The capers that define *A Night at the Opera* stand at an opposite extreme from the earnest use to which Visconti puts *Il trovatore* in *Senso*. The opera performance, supposedly taking place in Venice's La Fenice in 1866, when northern Italy was liberating itself from Austria, serves as an allegorical cover for the film's plot. The glamorous heroine, Countess Livia Serpieri, is measured throughout against Verdi's Leonora, whose idealism in sacrificing herself for Manrico contrasts with Livia's betrayal at once of her Austrian lover Franz Mahler (who, like Manrico, is executed at the end) and of the cause of Italian freedom.

Indeed, the whole first section of the film is dominated by the *Il trovatore* performance. The film opens with the brief (and only) duet between the lovers, followed by Manrico's rousing "Di quella pira," which suffices to set off a demonstration in the audience.[34] This cabaletta, as Visconti must have known, was long associated with Italian patriotism during the Risorgimento: Cavour, for instance, burst into song with Manrico's music when, in 1859, he received a dispatch assuring him that France would ultimately join Piedmont in war against Austria.[35]

Although on one level the tenor's heroic stance in the filmed opera sequence contrasts with Mahler's deception of Livia, at another level it accords with the genuinely heroic action of Livia's cousin, the Italian patriot Ussino. Yet about one third of the way through the film Verdi is left behind as the background

---

[34] See Visconti, *Two Screenplays*, trans. Green, pp. 107–09.

[35] See Conati, "Higher than the Highest," p. 14.

music shifts to Bruckner's Seventh Symphony, as though to signal the turn to the Austrian enemy.[36]

Visconti's film is actually a double allegory, as its audiences showed in the controversies generated at its early showings. Just as the hero and heroine of *Il trovatore* enact an idealism that could not be emulated in the film's historical plot, so the latter represents a world that Visconti saw paralleling the betrayal of the ideals of Italian leftist partisans at the end of World War II. And in the positive use to which he put Verdi's opera, Visconti took a markedly different stance from his generation of Italian intellectuals, who tended to reject not only Verdi but also Italian opera as a whole (see KULTUR). But then Visconti was, in fact, a distinguished opera director, having staged several of Maria Callas's most famous productions – and also, a decade after *Senso*, his own version of *Il trovatore*.

NARRATING

Il trovatore may well be the only opera in which Verdi emulates Wagner in the high proportion of text devoted to retelling the past. And when it is not concerned with the past, the opera repeatedly projects a happy future – of course never to be achieved. The present, by contrast, gets short shrift throughout this opera.

The whole first scene is devoted to narrating events from the far past: the bewitching by Azucena's mother, the theft and burning of a child, and all the familiar rest. And when the second scene opens with Leonora's entrance aria, we hear the heroine's memory of meeting her unknown knight at a tournament and her later dream of his pursuing her. Her cabaletta moves to the future with her hopes – note, for example, the future tense in the words *vivrò* and *morirò* in which it culminates. Even the troubador's brief serenade that follows is future-oriented in the hope that it expresses. Only the trio that ends the act is rooted in the present.

---

[36] For studies of *Senso*'s relationship to *Il trovatore*, see Crisp and Hillman, "Verdi in Postwar Italian Cinema," and Steinberg and Stewart-Steinberg, "Fascism and the Operatic Unconscious," pp. 278–82.

And so it goes all through the opera. Azucena's "Stride la vampa," though in the present tense, recounts the burning of her mother. In her long duet with Manrico she tells her own version of the tale we had already heard from Ferrando. And the Count's aria in the following scene is built around his future hope of attaining Leonora, who, when she appears with the nuns, voices her own hopes for her future in the convent. Only with her abduction at the end of the scene do we return briefly, as at the end of Act I, to the present.

The scene in the Count's camp that opens Act III is again concerned with the past, as Azucena reshapes her story in the hope of saving herself, but once she is recognized, the ensuing ensemble allows each character to project a future for her. Manrico's aria in the second scene is built around his hopes for his impending union with Leonora, but the cabaletta, like the endings of the preceding acts, brings us back to the real present as he prepares to save Azucena.

Leonora's aria that opens the final act is future-oriented both in the cantabile and the cabaletta, though the Miserere that provides the thoroughly unconventional *tempo di mezzo* returns us briefly to the painful present. Her duet with the count that follows is built around their divergent accounts of the future, as the verb *vivrà* that generates their cabaletta conspicuously shows. In the opera's final scene the dialogue and duet between Manrico and Azucena mixes together memories of a bloody past with idyllic hopes for their future – an illusion that Azucena maintains in the ensemble that follows. But once Leonora enters, she and Manrico face up to the present, which, suppressed as it was throughout much of the opera, returns with a vengeance (literally!) as the execution and its accompanying revelation take place.

Does all this mean that what we experience in *Il trovatore* is distanced from us in time? As Carolyn Abbate has argued in *Unsung Voices*, musical narrative, to the extent that it achieves a presentness, indeed, a presence in the context of performance, works differently from literary narrative.[37] By a strange paradox, *Il trovatore*, however

---

[37] Abbate, *Unsung Voices*, pp. 3–29.

obsessed its libretto may be with past and future, actually affects its audiences with the powerful presence of an ongoing present.

ORNAMENTING

I have always wondered why I did not feel thrilled on hearing the Leonora performed in San Francisco by Joan Sutherland, whom I had revered in all her other parts. At the time – 1975 – she was still in top form. Groupies around the opera house attributed the problem to her bad back: the production was so abominably dark, they said, that her fear of falling as she groped around the set must have inhibited her singing, which, as always, was never less than competent. But I did not buy that excuse. She was not a great Leonora simply because she was ornamenting too much.

Each of her two arias, but especially the first one, was paced (as her husband-conductor-mentor Richard Bonynge made sure it was) to give her the maximum opportunity to display her vocal prowess. To find space for all the notes she (and he) wanted, she proceeded at the leisurely pace one associates with Bellini, a composer at whose works she excelled. As a result she missed the fierce momentum that should characterize *Il trovatore* from start to finish (see THRUST).

Would Verdi have approved of Sutherland's ornamentation? The great trilogy of which *Il trovatore* is the central member stands at a watershed between the still relatively florid style that marked Verdi's and other composers' operas of the 1840s and the leaner style toward which he was moving. Although the score of *Il trovatore* contains some strikingly florid passages, especially in Leonora's music, they are always contained, as it were, within the rapidly moving drama that was central to his intent. For example, as a study of the manuscript materials shows, some embellishments Verdi composed for Leonora's entrance aria and for the Count's cabaletta in Act II were simplified in the final version.[38]

---

[38] Verdi, *Il trovatore*, ed. Lawton, p. xxxii. See also Lawton's detailed discussion of Verdi's inconsistent attitude to ornamentation in "Ornamenting Verdi's Arias."

The few recorded comments by Verdi on singers' ornamentations of his work do not give us a firm answer: sometimes he approved, and at other times he did not, though his negative reactions sometimes had to do with what he saw as a performer's poor taste.[39] As Philip Gossett, who has worked not only as general editor of the Verdi critical edition but also as an advisor to many singers, has put it, "As a practical matter, it seems to me that modest variations, an occasional diminution, a turn figure, can appropriately be applied to repeated passages in Verdi when the operas are performed complete, but ornamental variations *alla* Rossini and Bellini are to be excluded."[40]

Yet given the fashion of baroque and *bel canto* operas today, together with the fact that many younger singers are training to meet the technical rigors of these works, it scarcely seems accidental that it has become difficult to find Verdi singers who can catch the right note.

PARODY

The parodying started even before Cammarano and Verdi got to work on *Il trovatore*. In 1846, several years before Verdi had even discovered García Gutiérrez's drama, the playwright had himself subjected his own, still quite popular play to ruthless parody. After nearly a decade of writing plays in the vein of *El Trovador*, his first success, García Gutiérrez moved mainly to comedy and zarzuela, though, luckily for Verdi and the later history of opera, not before he had written *Simón Bocanegra* (1843).

The result was *Los hijos del tío Tronera*, which shifts the setting of his original play from the north of Spain to the depressed south.

---

[39] Crutchfield, "Vocal Ornamentation in Verdi," pp. 14–17. Crutchfield's article demonstrates, on the basis of late nineteenth- and early twentieth-century recordings, that famous singers, many of whom had worked with Verdi, employed a wide variety of ornamentations (see Crutchfield's notations of these ornaments, pp. 21–54).

[40] Gossett, *Divas and Scholars*, p. 324.

Moreover, the characters, all of a lowly sort, speak in Andalusian dialect. Although the author retains his plot – in sharply condensed form, to be sure – the characters and incidents are all reduced to mockeries of their original selves. Manuel (formerly Manrique) recites an absurd dream to Inesilla (formerly Leonor), in which he sees her turn into a witch on a broomstick instead of the grim skeleton he imagines in the earlier work (see DREAM). When she later announces she is dying of the poison she has consumed for his sake, she receives the simple dialect reply, "Has jecho una tontería" [You've done something foolish].[41]

Il trovatore was itself often parodied in Italy together with *Rigoletto* and other popular Verdi operas. Giovanni Tebaldini, a musicologist who befriended the composer, wrote in his memoirs of seeing Verdi, in the company of his later librettist Arrigo Boito, attending a performance of one such parody, *Minestron*, in Milan in 1884. He also reported noticing "grotesque statuettes" of the two actors mimicking the Count and Manrico on Verdi's writing desk thirteen years after this performance.[42]

Operatic parody found an especially welcome home in Victorian England, in which the genre called burlesque was a popular comic form. In her detailed study of burlesques of *Ernani*, *Il trovatore* and *La traviata*, Roberta Montemorra Marvin has shown a wide range of approaches to the genre.[43] In some the original tunes were used with new (and of course comic) lyrics, while, in other examples, parodies of the aria text were attached to melodies from various popular sources such as music halls. Above all, the absurdity of operatic plots was a central concern of these burlesques, as in the following lines assigned to Ferrando in *Il Trovatore, or Larks with a Libretto* (1880):

---

[41] García Gutiérrez, *El Trovador*, p. 314. For a brief study of the parody, see Adams, "A Spanish Romanticist Parodies Himself."

[42] See Conati, *Encounters with Verdi*, p. 359.

[43] Marvin, "Verdian Opera Burlesqued."

Look here my dear
don't you attempt to make the outline clear
or to explain the plot because the story
of the original Il Trovatore
is what Dundreary'd call without a doubt
one of those things no fellow could make out.[44]

Those art forms such as epic and opera that distance themselves from everyday realism are especially open to parody. In one of his anti-operatic moments Theodor Adorno wrote, "The closer opera gets to a parody of itself, the closer it is to its own most particular element."[45] And as operas go, *Il trovatore*, with its unrelentingly high style, is a sitting duck.

QUOTING

Nobody would dream of calling *Il trovatore* a modernist text or even a proto-modernist text, a term appropriate to *Falstaff*.[46] Yet its sheer old-fashionedness makes it the ideal foil for modernist appropriation, as in the poetry of Eugenio Montale. Note, for example, the following short lyric, "Lungomare" [Seaside Walk]:

Il soffio cresce, il buio è rotto a squarci,
e l'ombra che tu mandi sulla fragile
palizzata s'arriccia. Troppo tardi
se vuoi esser te stessa! Dalla palma
tonfa il sorcio, *il baleno* è sulla miccia,
sui lunghissimi cigli *del tuo sguardo*.[47]

[The wind rises, the dark is ripped to shreds,
and the shadow you cast upon the fragile
paling shrivels. It's too late

---

[44] *Ibid.*, p. 56.   [45] Adorno, "Bourgeois Opera," p. 26.

[46] For discussions of *Falstaff* as proto-modernist, see L. Hutcheon and M. Hutcheon, "'Tutto nel mondo è burla',," pp. 926–27; Parker, "In Search of Verdi," pp. 924–35; Senici, "'Se potessimo tornare da capo'," pp. 942–43; see also my own remarks on the modernity of *Falstaff* in Essay 8.

[47] Montale, *L'opera in versi*, p. 190. Here and in subsequent quotations I have italicized the words that Montale borrows from *Il trovatore*.

to be yourself! The rat thuds down
from the palm tree, *lightning* plays about the fuse
and in the longest lashes *of your gaze.*][48]

In this love poem addressed to Clizia (his poetic name for his American friend, Irma Brandeis), Montale alludes to the count's description of Leonora from his aria in *Il trovatore*: "*Il balen* del suo sorriso . . . Sperda il sole d'un *suo sguardo.*" As Gilberto Lonardi has demonstrated in his book on Montale's operatic allusions, this is only one of several poems that play upon the same aria.[49] An Italian reader familiar with *Il trovatore* would likely recognize the allusion, but even more important, this reader would be aware of the gap that separates Verdi's world from that of the poet. Whereas the Count speaks his love in an uncomplicated manner (though he is never of course to see it fulfilled!), the poet suggests a tortured, complex relationship: in the darkening day it has become "too late" for the woman to "be herself"; her shadow "shrivels" on the "fragile paling"; and the lightning that seemed so positive in the aria is now associated with a potentially exploding fuse.

Another lyric to Clizia, "Il fiore che ripete," echoes one of the most memorable phrases spoken by Manrico in the Miserere – "non ti scordar di me" [don't forget me] – soon answered repeatedly by Leonora – "di te?.. di te?.. scordarmi di te?" [I should forget you?]:

Il fiore che ripete
dall'orlo del burrato
non scordati di me,
non ha tinte più liete né più chiare
dello spazio gettato tra me e te.

Un cigolìo si sferra, ci discosta,
l'azzurro pervicace non ricompare.
nell'afa quasi visibile mi reporta all'opposta
tappa, già buia, la funicolare.[50]

---

[48] Montale, *Selected Poems*, p. 64.

[49] For a detailed description of how Montale uses words from this aria, see Lonardi, *Il fiore dell'addio*, pp. 206–08. I am greatly indebted to Lonardi's book for the many operatic borrowings in Montale's poetry that he has discovered.

[50] Montale, *L'opera in versi*, p. 148.

[The flower on the mountainside,
which keeps repeating its
forget-me-nots from cliff
to cliff, has no colors brighter
or happier than the space
set between us.

A screech of metal is pulling us apart.
The obstinate blue is fading. In a sky
so sultry you can barely
see through it, the funicular
carries me back to the other station
where it's already dark.][51]

The two stanzas of this poem, which appears in the cycle "Motets," offer a dramatic contrast: from closeness between the lovers to their parting as the poet leaves in the funicular, from the "obstinate blue" and total clarity to the darkness that takes over. Yet in the word "forget-me-nots" the happy first stanza already anticipates the negativity of the second. As Lonardi has suggested, Montale's allusion refers at once to Manrico and Leonora's cries, to the forget-me-not flower, and to a popular song, "Non ti scordar di me," performed in a 1935 film of the same title by Beniamino Gigli.[52] This network of allusions gives this lyric about leave-taking an ironic edge that defines the pathos surrounding a farewell with a scrupulous avoidance of sentimentality.

Although, as Lonardi shows, a number of famous operas – notably *Manon, Tosca,* and *Madama Butterfly* – inhabit Montale's poetry, none is as pervasive as *Il trovatore.*[53] And quite appropriately so, for the emotional and cultural distance standing between this opera and Montale's body of poetry is nothing short of immense. Whereas the characters of *Il trovatore* sing out loud and clear, a hermetic, introspective poet such as Montale can utter only by indirection. From the point of view of the modernist poet, *Il trovatore*

---

[51] Montale, *Mottetti*, p. 55.   [52] Lonardi, *Il fiore dell'addio*, p. 202.
[53] *Ibid.*, pp. 205–06.

evokes an unselfconscious state of mind that, though it can never be restored, can at least leave its fragmentary remains in his writing. Isaiah Berlin, building on Schiller's famous distinction between the "naïve" and "sentimental" poet, once described Verdi as the epitome of the naïve artist.[54] If we translate these two terms into their contemporary equivalents, say, unselfconscious as against selfconscious, Montale's appropriation of Verdi becomes a prime example of the modernist artist's attempt to recover that lost earlier state.

REALISTIC

Opera of course is never realistic even when it calls itself *verismo*. Still, certain members of the audience wish to think they are witnessing something resembling the real world as they know it. Operatic singers, they insist, should act instead of just standing there to sing. And the characters they impersonate should have the complexity of the people they meet in real life – or at least in the movies. Scenery and costumes, moreover, should be faithful to the time and place in which the opera is set. You should, in short, forget you're hearing music and think you're experiencing some well-made Ibsen play. (Real life, to be sure, is never well made and sometimes is not very realistic.)

For people with these particular needs, *Il trovatore* doesn't quite do the trick, at least not in comparison with the two Verdi operas that came directly before and after it. The title characters of *Rigoletto* and *La traviata* suggest hidden depths that no character in *Il trovatore* possesses – not even Azucena, who simply gravitates back and forth between the two passions, filial and maternal love, that Verdi defined for her (see ZINGARA). When Violetta and the elder Germont engage with one another in their long duet, the change in their relationship that develops with each new segment displays a psychological realism totally missing in the duets in *Il trovatore*.

<hr>

[54] Berlin, "The Naiveté of Verdi." For a commentary on Berlin's essay, see Williams, "Naïve and Sentimental Opera Lovers."

The plot of *La traviata* might really have happened (it's even based on a real-life story!); that of *Rigoletto* could conceivably have happened (though that may be a stretch); but the story of *Il trovatore*, even if one can follow its labyrinthine paths (see ABOUT, SECTION 'i'), could never have happened. Yet *Il trovatore* remains the perfect opera for those who relish make-believe within an earnestly heroic mode.

SOUL

Up to then it had been a rather routine performance (like most performances, to be sure) – and this despite the presence of Leontyne Price, one of the great Leonoras of the last century. She had been singing somewhat sleepily that night, and so had the others.

But then Act IV began, and from Leonora's opening "Vanne . . . lasciami," we all knew that something had happened. Every phrase she uttered led powerfully into the next, and every segment of the remaining score, including the often omitted cabaletta to Leonora's aria, glowed with a fervor one encounters only at rare intervals in the opera house.

When it was over, I bumped into a colleague in physics who, I could tell, had felt the same vibrations that I had. "How do you account for that transformation?" I asked.

"Soul," he replied.

THRUST

Verdi is the pre-eminent composer of thrust, and no opera displays thrust more powerfully than *Il trovatore*. By thrust I mean the composer's penchant for moving the music forward constantly even with slow tempi. Rossini, to be sure, established the principle of thrust in Italian opera, but, especially in his *opere serie*, he allowed delays in his forward movement to give his singers the luxury of showing off their technical prowess. Bellini often – and also thrillingly – froze his forward movement to allow us to languish in his languid melodies. And Donizetti was only sporadically a composer of thrust.

Consider the unwavering movement pervading the next-to-last scene of *Il trovatore*, which consists of only two numbers, Leonora's aria and her duet with the Count. The orchestral opening, with its staccato triplets in the woodwinds, already suggests the urgent business ahead. Leonora's cantabile, though marked adagio, thrusts forward as her voice rises; as this section closes, her precipitous downward movement rushes us to a tentative closure, at which point the bell sounds, and the Miserere – that most elaborate of *tempi di mezzo* – takes off. For a moment, as we hear the male choir intoning its liturgical phrases, everything turns static. But Leonora's impassioned pleas to Manrico, and his equally impassioned pleas to her – all of this punctuated frighteningly by the bell – work against the static chorus to create an even more powerful forward movement than we might have experienced with only their two voices alone. Her cabaletta, with its frequent upward leaps, confirms this movement; indeed, to omit this cabaletta, as was frequently done until recent years, is to impede rather than confirm the thrust central to the scene.[55]

The duet between Leonora and the Count consists of some jaunty tunes that one could scarcely have imagined if one knew only the grim words of the libretto as these two figures negotiate with one another; yet these tunes work to propel the action forward to the brief but event-laden *tempo di mezzo* in which, in quick succession, the two swear their oaths to one another, Leonora swallows her poison, and the Count speaks out his "Vivrà," a word which, when Leonora jubilantly repeats it, sets off the allegro-brillante cabaletta, after which the duet rolls mercilessly to its fast and brilliant conclusion.[56]

---

[55] For an argument supporting the inclusion of the cabaletta, see Baldini, *The Story of Giuseppe Verdi*, pp. 217–18. Abramo Basevi, the great Verdi critic who was also the composer's contemporary, found the cabaletta a letdown; see Basevi, *Studio sulle opere di Giuseppe Verdi*, p. 285. For a measured view of the issue, see Gossett, "Verdi's Ideas on Interpreting His Operas," p. 401, and Gossett, *Divas and Scholars*, p. 264. Verdi himself omitted the cabaletta from the Paris version of the opera.

[56] For an analysis of some techniques that Verdi employs to create what I call forward thrust, see the section entitled "Tension" in De Van, *Verdi's Theater*, pp. 120–27.

What we hear in this scene is not so much music that sets a text as something more like program music: in short, music that has let itself be inspired by a text so that it may proceed in its own, purely musical way. Indeed, Verdi may well have set Leonora's aria even before he had received any text.[57] As we listen to this scene, we hear the music thrust forward with an inexorable force analogous to what Aristotle meant when he demanded that the events of a tragedy be linked to one another in a way that seems probable. The sheer momentum that drives the opera forward from beginning to end provides that illusion of probability so notoriously lacking in the libretto as well as in its antecedent play.

UPSTAGING

Common operatic wisdom has it that Azucena characteristically runs away with the show. My own wisdom – or at least my memory – tells me that the character who runs away with *Il trovatore* is the one who happens to be delivering the best performance that particular night. In my own experience, the Manrico of Franco Corelli once ran away with the show (see HEROICS), and on other occasions it was the Leonora of Leontyne Price (see SOUL) and the Azucena of Dolora Zajick. This never happened with a Conte di Luna or a Ferrando.

If Azucena is going to upstage everybody else, this can be ascribed to the fact that the soprano, the tenor, and the baritone are not the world's greatest singers in their respective voice ranges (see FOURSOME).

VIOLENCE

Violence is endemic within nineteenth-century opera, and *Il trovatore* displays perhaps more of it than any other of Verdi's major works: an

---

[57] See Parker, *Leonora's Last Act*, pp. 183–86. From a study of Verdi's sketches, Parker concludes that Verdi worked out the melody before he had received the text from Emanuele Bardare, who finished the libretto after Cammarano's death. The aria had not been included in Cammarano's initial scenario for the opera (see Mossa, *Carteggio Verdi-Cammarano*, p. 187).

abduction, a duel, a wounding on the battlefield, plus death by bonfire, poison and beheading. Yet except for the soprano's self-administration of the poison and her subsequent death, *Il trovatore*'s violence is something we know not from what we witness onstage but from its characters' still vivid memories (see NARRATING).

Violence is not the same in opera as it is in spoken drama and other non-musical forms. Although some violent films and TV shows purportedly instigate violent acts among their viewers, an opera as loaded with violence as *Il trovatore* is perfectly safe fare for the young. Once the music has taken over, it is as though the violence has been transformed into something more benign. More-over, a warhorse such as *Il trovatore*, whose audiences have usually heard much of its music over the years, works to inure its viewers against any ill effects of violence by dint of its familiarity.

A recent experiment, to be cited for other purposes in Essay 5, may shed some light on how we experience violence once it has been turned into music. Two neuroscientists, Vinod Menon and Daniel J. Levitin, imaged the brains of a group of subjects (all of them non-musicians) using functional magnetic resonance imaging (fMRI) while these subjects were listening to selected pieces from the classical repertory.[58] The researchers discovered significant acti-vation in those areas of the brain – above all the mesolimbic dopaminergic reward system – that respond to pleasurable experi-ences. Activation in, for instance, the nucleus accumbens and the ventral tegmental area showed a correlation between dopamine release and response to music.

The experiment, which used examples ranging from the high drama of Beethoven's Fifth Symphony to the soothing *Eine kleine Nachtmusik* of Mozart, did not attempt to distinguish differences in the emotional content of the works. But all of these pieces, whether tensely dramatic or gently benign, tapped essentially the same reward system within the brain. Thus, when a composer such as Verdi composes a libretto loaded with violence – and of course he

---

[58] Menon and Levitin, "The Rewards of Music Listening."

carefully sought out these subjects in the first place – he revs up his musical engine to produce the maximum of excitement in his listeners. The resulting work poses no danger to society. Like such other stimulants as food, drugs, and sex that set off the reward system in our brains, *Il trovatore* simply leaves you feeling high.

WARHORSES

An operatic warhorse is whatever can fill the house even if the cast has to be pulled off the street and the backdrops and costumes reveal their moth holes well into the orchestra section. At any particular moment in history only a few works fit this criterion. The warhorse list nowadays is topped by Puccini's biggest hits – *Bohème, Tosca, Butterfly*, and *Turandot* – plus *Carmen*, the *Barber*, and a few of Verdi's – certainly *Rigoletto* and *Traviata*, probably also *Aida*. *Il trovatore*, for long the quintessential crowd-pleaser, is barely hanging in.

X-RATED

An X-minded director in need of staged sex would find *Il trovatore* hard going. Leonora and Manrico are left alone onstage together for little more than a hundred bars – five to six minutes at best – before Ruiz rudely interrupts them to send the groom-about-to-be to rescue his mother. And how, without eliciting laughter, could one ever stage sex against that organ music or the words "di casto amor" that the two fervently (and repeatedly) sing together?

No such problem with *Rigoletto*. I remember the tremors shaking the audience in a 1973 production in San Francisco by the late Jean-Pierre Ponnelle, when he arranged for the ducal rape to be performed not offstage but in an elaborate four-poster bed – curtained, to be sure – to which the hapless Gilda was delivered just before her father arrived to plead before the courtiers. Although her father, and the audience as well, could not see behind the curtain, a director bringing this production up to current-day standards would need to open the curtain that faces the audience – and promptly send Rigoletto off to the side to keep him, unlike the audience, unaware of what is going on.

Although a graphic portrayal of the *Rigoletto* rape would expose the horror lurking beneath the opera's surface, it is hard to imagine a way of X-rating *Il trovatore* properly. To be sure, there was a 1996 Hans Neuenfels production at the Deutsche Oper, Berlin, in which, as Leonora describes her lover during her first aria, we are shown "a gigantic photograph of a scruffy Latin youth, nude except for a tattoo on each folded arm, genitalia concealed by crossed pieces of black tape."[59] Since I did not see this production, I cannot judge how convincingly it gets under *Il trovatore*'s skin. Yet it was clearly an attempt to "unsettle" this opera – to cite the term used by David J. Levin in the title of his recent book on those many productions, starting with the Patrice Chéreau *Ring des Nibelungen* of 1976, that seek to uncover the unspoken subtexts of classic operas.[60]

Suppose I were to attempt my own unsettling production of *Il trovatore*. Taking some cues from Visconti's *Senso* (see MOVIES), I'd move the setting to the turmoiled Italy of Verdi's time, with Manrico a heroic officer in Garibaldi's campaign; Leonora, an aristo-crat who has read too many Romantic novels and heard too many Romantic operas the likes of *Il trovatore*; the Count, a love-crazed landowner collaborating with the Austrians; and Azucena, just as Verdi conceived her, a primordial creature driven by passion for her mother and son. But that seems altogether tame – indeed, it would all too easily satisfy the conservative American opera public.

Since the libretto itself gives no opportunity for sexual explicit-ness, I would allow certain passages to be accompanied by filmed dreams rising above the characters as they sing. For example, the recitative of Leonora's first aria, with its dream of Manrico in battle array, could, as it turns into the aria, show her imagining her lover remove his armor to reveal himself nude – though emphatically not scruffy as in the Neuenfels production. The Count's second-act aria

[59] Paul Moor, "Horsing Around with a Classic."   [60] Levin, *Unsettling Opera*.

at the nunnery could show him strip her of the nun's habit in which she is about to appear onstage. And the duet between the two in the last act could show two films – one above each of them – the Count dreaming of raping her, while Leonora imagines him discovering that the body she has given him is nothing but a cold corpse ("fredda, esanime spoglia," as she puts it in her aside while taking her poison). Surely this would be graphic enough to earn the production its X, though it might also distract a bit from the splendid music Verdi composed for these passages.

YAWN

Nothing's so boring as a routine performance of *Il trovatore*. Even if the work's tempi are correct, the fierceness is missing; even if the Leonora sings her *fioriture* as Verdi notated them, they sound labored; even if the anvils pound down on time, you know they don't in the least mean it. Who has not witnessed a show like this at least once too often?

But why should so wondrous a work be as vulnerable as it is? There are certain warhorses that, in my experience at least, have proved pretty routine-resistant – or rather they manage to please however shabbily they may be done. I remember a wretched *Tosca* in Florence that still sent chills during its high spots. Or a third-string Met *Bohème* in Zeffirelli's plush production that still pushed one's emotional buttons at the required moments. Or a Vienna *Carmen* with a tired, superannuated cast that still charmed with its tunes.

These other warhorses, for one thing, don't demand as much from their singers as *Il trovatore*: the Toreador Song, for instance, can't compare in its rigors with the Count di Luna's "Il balen del suo sorriso," nor can "Mi chiamano Mimi" compare in trickiness with Leonora's "D'amor sull'ali rosee." At least as important, the scores of these less demanding operas seem to carry their singers and their conductors along if they more or less observe the markings, while *Il trovatore* asks for an unremitting energy from start to finish. As Shaw put it, "There is nothing unheroic to fall back on" (see JUDGMENTS).

High energy, high passion, high heroics fast dissipate in the face of routine.

ZINGARA

Azucena:

a. was *Il trovatore*'s initial reason for being. It was her role in *El Trovador* that attracted Verdi to this play, just as Victor Hugo's Triboulet had attracted him to *Le Roi s'amuse*.

b. speaks the most readable lines in García Gutiérrez's play. It is no accident that her part, like that of the other lowly characters, is in prose,[61] while the higher-born personae speak a highfalutin verse (see DREAM).

c. sings a correspondingly more earthy music in *Il trovatore* than that assigned to the other three major characters.

d. is less a character than a force of nature – these two concepts not being wholly compatible with one another.

e. represents the birth of the Verdi mezzo-soprano, who, with those chthonic tones emanating from deep within the abdominal cavity, together with her consciousness of feeling wronged, is reincarnated in Eboli and Amneris, all of whom have spawned generations of singers alternating regularly among these roles.[62] (As with most of his innovations, there are anticipations of the Verdi mezzo-soprano in French *grand opéra*, namely, Fidès in Meyerbeer's *Le Prophète*.)

f. rarely goes wrong in the hands of one of these specialists. My own most memorable ones have been Elena Obratzova, Fiorenza Cossotto, Dolora Zajick, and, most recently, Stephanie Blythe. In my mind I can still hear and see all of them cry revenge.

g. was the major single bone of contention between librettist and composer during their work on this opera. Whereas Cammarano sought to portray Azucena as demented, Verdi insisted that she

---

[61] García Gutiérrez turned the prose passages into verse for a production in 1851 at the Teatro Español. Verdi and Cammarano used the earlier, mixed version.

[62] On the development of the Verdi mezzo-soprano, see Robinson, *Opera and Ideas*, pp. 174–77.

was perfectly sane, that she was in fact motivated by "two grand passions, filial love and maternal love."[63]

h. for a while during the process of composition emerged as the prima donna. At one point Verdi was even willing to forgo an entrance area for Leonora,[64] with the result that Azucena would have had little competition.

i. was a role Verdi would love to have sung, as we can see from a comment he made after a diva asked him to recompose Leonora's entrance aria: "Why does la Barbieri undertake that part if it doesn't suit her? If she wants to do *Il trovatore* there's another part, that of the Gipsy . . . . If I were a prima donna (a fine thing that would be!) I would always rather sing the part of the Gipsy in *Il trovatore*."[65] Imagine Verdi croaking out "Giorni poveri vivea" while pleading with the Count. In my mind I can hear and see him.

---

[63] Mossa, *Carteggio Verdi-Cammarano*, p. 190.
[64] *Ibid.*   [65] Budden, *The Operas of Verdi*, vol. II, p. 68.

Why should we even speak of opera and society in the same breath? Is there, for instance, a special affinity between these two terms, and if so, is it different from or more intense than the relationships we seek to establish between other artistic forms and society – between, for instance, painting and society, comedy and society, or, to cite the title of a famous essay by Theodor Adorno, lyric and society?[1]

As we listen to these various combinations, the phrase "opera and society" seems particularly amenable to discussion. With painting, for example, one is faced with a multitude of forms, each rooted in a particular social context, from the animals depicted on the caves of Lascaux to the political messages drawn by muralists on barrio walls. Opera, by contrast, seems comfortably circumscribed. It encompasses an easily definable history extending back four hundred years in Europe and the Americas. It has flourished continuously within a discernible institution, the opera house, though also, at least in its earlier years, within aristocratic courts. And despite the substantial differences in national traditions of opera, the particular roles assigned to those who create and sustain it – impresario, singers, librettist, composer – have maintained a degree of constancy over these four centuries rarely to be found in other art forms.

The second noun in the phrase "opera and society" obviously presents a more fluid situation than the first. The term "society" encompasses a wide variety of often disparate objects: for example, the social context within which an opera is written; an idealized (or even demonized) image of a society that an opera projects; the operatic audiences for which an opera was created, as well as those that experience this opera in later revivals; and even the so-called

[1] Adorno, "Rede über Lyrik und Gesellschaft."

"on-stage societies" in Lully's operas who, in the guise of chorus and dancers, represented the different social levels during the time of Louis XIV.[2] My own concern in this essay is not to enforce a single definition of society but to note what happens – has happened, might yet happen – when we allow the terms "opera" and "society" to jostle against one another.

The most obvious questions to be raised regarding opera and society have to do with the social contexts within which individual operas, or operas constituting a particular period of operatic history, have been created. We establish a link between opera and society, for example, when we analyze Lully's mythological operas as attempts to flatter the absolute monarch who sponsored them or when we tie Schoenberg's *Moses und Aron* to a context that includes matters such as the composer's commitment to Zionism, his reaction to the dangers of Nazism around 1930, and the hermeticism that defined the role of the artist in his generation.

The questions relevant to linking opera and society are by no means limited to an opera's or a style's origins but include the whole history of interpretation and reception of this work or style. One might ask, for example, how Berlioz's rewriting of Gluck's *Orfeo*, or Wagner's of *Iphigénie en Aulide*, nearly a century after its composition, answers the needs of a new social, not to speak of musical, context. Or what the interpretive history of frequently performed pieces such as *Don Giovanni* and Gounod's *Faust* tells us about changing social biases. Indeed, what do we make of the apparent fall from grace of this latter work, now performed only sporadically but a century ago probably the most popular of all operas?

And then of course there are questions that go beyond the framework of individual works and styles. How, for instance, do we account for the rise of repertory opera somewhere in the middle of the nineteenth century? Before that, after all, audiences customarily demanded new works each season. And how might we account for the quite recent increase in demand for new works – this after it

---

[2] See Harris-Warrick, "Lully's On-Stage Societies."

had become common wisdom that audiences refused to attend operas with which they were not familiar? And what do we make of the rise of directorial opera after World War II?

And beyond these there are the larger theoretical questions. How do we speak of authorship in a form as collaborative as opera, yet also one that is dependent upon the musical distinction that only the composer can bestow? To explore this issue, we might draw analogies from other collaborative art forms: from film, for example, or perhaps from the methods of the Elizabethan theater; or even from painting during, say, the late Middle Ages or the early Renaissance, before the individual artist's authority and autonomy had become established. Perhaps we can best suggest some relevant questions at this point by looking at a particular opera. I choose Mozart's *Die Entführung aus dem Serail*, a work with which most operagoers have a passing familiarity but that is not quite the revered classic that the same composer's later operas are. To start with, let us look at the circumstances surrounding its composition.

Die Entführung was originally commissioned in 1781 for the National Singspiel, an institution founded by the enlightened Emperor Joseph II only three years before to promote a taste for German-style comic opera as an alternative to the Italian comic works that had long enjoyed favor among the Viennese public – and which, I might add, would return to imperial favor by 1783. Although the National Singspiel was dependent to some degree on French and Italian works that were, for the most part, translated into German, its mission during its brief existence was to cultivate a relatively simple, often folklike, musical style with spoken interludes between numbers.

Moreover, the production of *Die Entführung* was originally planned as part of an official visit by the Russian Grand Duke Paul. Although the opera was not finished in time for this occasion, which was intended to impress the visitors with a display of Austrian power, *Die Entführung*'s participation in a nationalist political program, both in the circumstances of its commission and in the musical style that reigned in the National Singspiel, remains part of the significance it would have had in its own time. It might be remembered that Mozart's major operatic achievement up to this point had been *Idomeneo*, a thoroughly Italian *opera seria* composed for Milan earlier during the same year that he received the Viennese commission.

But the resulting work was not quite the simple sort of *Singspiel* that reigned for the brief period during which Joseph's theater flourished. It displays in fact an uncommon mixture of styles, from, on the one hand, Pedrillo's folklike Romance as the lovers await their escape, or the so-called vaudeville near the end, in which the major characters all repeat the same simple tune, to, on the other hand, the enormously complex music characteristic of several arias assigned to Belmonte and Constanze – above all, the second-act "Martern aller Arten," which in my own opera-going experience has proved the most precarious aria within any of the composer's major works. But Mozart's mixture of musical forms, as Stephen Rumph has shown in a recent essay, can also be viewed as dramatizing what Rumph calls "the irreducible contradictions" within the thought structures of the Enlightenment.[3] One wonders what to make of this strange stylistic mixture, which some critics, notably Edward J. Dent, in his long-influential 1913 book on Mozart's operas, saw as a sign of the opera's relative failure.[4] And how do we interpret the Emperor's alleged remark to the composer that the opera contained "monstrous many notes"?[5] It is likely that this statement, which might have referred to the complex runs of "Martern aller Arten," expressed the disdain that Joseph II held for the vocal complexities of *opera seria* in favor of the Germanic simplicity characterizing other parts of *Die Entführung*. And one might ask as well what role Mozart himself played in driving the opera toward this more complex style, especially after the middle of the second act. The libretto he was using was by a well-known north-German librettist, C. F. Bretzner, and had already been set by a German

---

[3] Rumph, "Mozart's Archaic Endings," p. 195.   [4] Dent, *Mozart's Operas*, p. 138.
[5] Quoted in Bauman, *W. A. Mozart*, p. 89.

composer, Johann André, but Mozart's Viennese friend Gottlob Stephanie then made extensive revisions to this libretto – with "Martern aller Arten" being not only wholly new but also radically changing the image of the heroine that had prevailed in the original. To what extent did these revisions result from Mozart's desire to assert the autonomy of music – as he himself hinted in a letter to his father during the process of composition[6] – and to what extent from his need to satisfy the desires and needs of the Italian-style singers assigned to perform Belmonte and Constanze?

Beyond these issues our interest today is inevitably drawn to the conspicuous role played by Turkish music in this opera. To be sure, what passed for Turkish music – percussive sounds from cymbal, triangle, and loud drums, squealing sounds from the piccolo, a two-four rhythm, and a sharpened fourth degree – had long been familiar to audiences, both in street music and in opera (not to speak of such non-operatic examples as the finale of Mozart's A-major sonata, K. 331). In *Die Entführung*, we have not only the overtly Turkish Janissary choruses but Turkish moments at numerous other points, even at the opening of "Martern aller Arten," in which the Western heroine shows herself infected, as it were, by the Eastern world that she defies in this aria. Turkish music appears not only in the many operas about European maidens captured by Turks in various Mediterranean sites but even in a pre-Turkish setting like that of Gluck's *Iphigénie en Tauride*, in which it is used to characterize the primitive Scythians. (I might add that the last-named opera, in German translation, was chosen to be performed at the National Singspiel for the Russian Grand Duke when it turned out that Mozart's work could not make it in time.) As Matthew Head has shown in his full-length study of Mozart's orientalism, Turkish music, including Hungarian tunes with which it was often conflated, had a considerable history in the West for at least a generation before Mozart.[7]

[6] *Ibid.*, pp. 18–19.
[7] Head, *Orientalism, Masquerade and Mozart's Turkish Music*, pp. 67–89.

Are we to hear these sounds as a code for that newly fashionable notion of the "primitive"? Or perhaps we should hear them simply as an entertaining popular alternative to the formality of the prevailing classical style,[8] a means of aesthetic liberation analogous to the craze for chinoiserie somewhat earlier throughout Europe. And what political meanings can we read into what we hear? Since Mozart's opera was finished a year short of the century that had elapsed since the Turkish siege of Vienna, it would be difficult to argue that *Die Entführung* and other works containing Turkish music were responding to a living threat – though a few years after *Die Entführung* Austria joined Russia in a brief war against the Turks to which Mozart responded with several compositions.[9] But one recent commentator on the opera, Nicholas Till, has described European anti-Turkish policy at the time as a "cold-war stratagem of maintaining their subjects in a state of perpetual vigilance against the imagined enemy at the gates."[10] Indeed, the idea of staging this opera – or Gluck's, as it turned out – to celebrate a Russian state visit can also be seen as a means of reinforcing the central and eastern European policy of seeking to reconquer Turkish territories in the Balkans. It is significant, moreover, that the embedding of Turkish music within a Western piece goes back over a century to a time when the Turks really *were* a threat, namely, to Lully's Turkish march in *Le Bourgeois Gentilhomme*, composed in 1669 when a Turkish delegation was visiting the court of Louis XIV.

And what do we make of the ending of *Die Entführung aus dem Serail*, in which the barbaric ruler decides to let the Westerners escape in style in order to display his powers of forgiveness toward his old enemy who had banished him and who, we have just learned, was Belmonte's own father? The refrain of the vaudeville at the end keeps reminding us that anybody who is not grateful for Pasha Selim's generosity deserves contempt. The display of a monarch's magnanimity was of course an established convention for a good

---

[8] *Ibid.*, pp. 88–89.   [9] *Ibid.*, p. 56.
[10] Till, *Mozart and the Enlightenment*, p. 104.

century and a half in the endings of both dramas and operas from Corneille's *Cinna* to Mozart's own later opera, *La clemenza di Tito*. But it is also significant that in *Die Entführung* this display stems from the libretto's reviser, Stephanie, and was not present in Bretzner's original, in which Pasha Selim allows the lovers to escape only after he discovers that Belmonte is his own long-lost son. Can it be that Bretzner, writing in Leipzig for a theater in Berlin, felt no need to flatter the ruler sponsoring his work? An early reviewer of Mozart's opera, in fact, objected to the new magnanimous resolution as something that was already out of fashion everywhere except in Vienna.[11]

I have limited myself thus far to the context surrounding the origins of *Die Entführung aus dem Serail*. The social and political implications we locate in a work include not only this context but also the experience of directors, audiences, and critics in the course of its interpretive history. After being one of Mozart's most popular operas until the end of the eighteenth century, *Die Entführung* gave way in frequency of performance to the first two of the Da Ponte operas and to *Die Zauberflöte*;[12] although one could speculate that the presence of considerable spoken dialogue might have inhibited the currency of the last-named work in non-German-speaking lands, the *Singspiel* form of Mozart's final opera has not prevented its continued popular acclaim throughout the world. On the other hand, it is possible that the plot and the issues with which *Die Entführung* was concerned came to seem trivial during the earnest-minded nineteenth century. Reception theory has proposed the idea of multiple "horizons" to depict the difference between a work's effect at its inception and the experiences it offers to its readers and audiences at a later time.[13] However well we historically reconstruct the work's earlier context, the preoccupations, biases, and expectations of the later observer color the manner in which we perceive it in its later

---

[11] Bauman, *W. A. Mozart*, pp. 33–34.   [12] *Ibid.*, pp. 108–09.
[13] See Jauss, *Toward an Aesthetic of Reception*, especially the opening essay, "Literary History as Challenge," pp. 3–45.

embodiments. Take, for instance, the way that the publication in 1978 of Edward Said's *Orientalism* altered our perceptions of works in all the arts that depicted the non-Western world. Studies of *Die Entführung* since that time invariably focus on matters such as the role of the Turkish music or the difference between the musical orientalism of the eighteenth century, centered as it is on the conflict between European and Muslim values, and that of the later nineteenth century, in which the East is portrayed as at once seductive and sinister. Productions are more likely than scholarly studies to respond quickly to the possibilities offered by current events. Thus, a 1980 Munich production referred to the Iran hostage crisis at the time by offering a Pasha clad like the Ayatollah Khomeini while threatening Constanze with tortures.[14] In view of the continuing presence of Islamic terrorism in the news, an inventive director may come up with any number of scenarios linking the opera with the latest international developments.

I have lingered on a single example, Mozart's *Die Entführung*, not to provide new facts – for the observations I draw upon are well known to specialists – but to portray the interchanges between an operatic work and the external world that, though they may vary in character in different settings, can still be considered typical. My discussion has stressed the kinds of questions we ask ourselves in approaching specific operatic works: questions about the circumstances surrounding the making of a work, about the pressures upon the various agents engaged in this task, and about what happens to an opera once its original context has become remote. Above all, it should be clear that what we see as matters of aesthetics and literary or musical style cannot easily be separated from what has customarily been viewed as outside the realm of art. Thus, the stylistic choices that Mozart made in composing *Die Entführung* involved such issues as the Emperor's preference for a simple and Germanic manner, the Viennese public's preference for complex Italian vocal forms, Austrian political ambitions in eastern Europe, and Mozart's need at this

---

[14] Bauman, *W. A. Mozart*, p. 117.

still early point in his career to establish himself in the capital, in which he had recently arrived from Salzburg. Similarly, in discussing *Il trovatore* in the preceding essay, I cited such often-conflicting issues as the pressure of the Italian opera-house system, the desire of singers to be adulated by means of the high notes at their command regardless of the composer's original intentions, and Verdi's need to achieve what, among Italian opera composers of his day, was still an emerging ideal of artistic autonomy.

To what extent has the study of opera met the challenges of the questions I have raised? Certainly the last two decades have witnessed an unprecedented boom – within the anglophone world above all – in the understanding of opera as a unique phenomenon within the history of the arts. It is significant, for example, that a number of serious books have been published in recent years with the word *opera* in the title or subtitle. I say "serious" since these books are distinct in the readership for which they are designed from the popular guidebooks to opera that have flourished since at least the late nineteenth century.

I refer to such products of the boom as Paul Robinson's *Opera and Ideas*; Linda and Michael Hutcheon's *Opera: Desire, Disease, Death*; John Bokina's *Opera and Politics*; Gary Tomlinson's *Metaphysical Song*; Carolyn Abbate's *In Search of Opera*. What distinguishes books such as these is their attempt to focus not simply on a single opera, composer, or period, as most earlier serious studies of opera had done, but to attempt a definition of, an approach to, the form as a whole. Yet they are also distinguished by another fact, namely that they do not emanate from a single discipline but from a number of disciplines within the humanities and even the social sciences. Of the books mentioned here, only two, those by Tomlinson and Abbate, were written by musicologists, both of whom also use theoretical frameworks borrowed from other disciplines. Robinson is eminent as a historian of sexuality. Linda Hutcheon, based in comparative literature, has done pioneering studies of postmodernist writing. Michael Hutcheon is a medical professor specializing in pulmonology, Bokina, a political scientist.

The author of the present volume has spent his entire career within programs of comparative literature.

Although it was rare until relatively recent years for scholars to adopt the methods of disciplines outside their own, the books on opera of the last two decades are notable for their interdisciplinary borrowings. Not only do their authors come from a variety of disciplines, as I have indicated, but they have picked up their theoretical frameworks from a multitude of sources. Take, for example, Tomlinson's *Metaphysical Song*, which rethinks the whole history of opera by way of a philosophical system, namely that of Michel Foucault, and in particular the Foucault of *The Order of Things*. Thus, for Tomlinson early operas such as Peri's *L'Euridice* and Monteverdi's *Orfeo*, through their faith that music can closely match the meaning of words, fit Foucault's model of the Renaissance world of analogy and resemblance, while *opera seria*, with its highly conventionalized forms of representation in which music goes its own way whatever the words it is setting, demonstrates what Foucault called the episteme of the classical age.

Although Tomlinson's book is notable for its attempt to apply a single paradigm to opera, all the recent books on the topic display a variety of tools available in recent years within the intellectual marketplace. Robinson made use of his background as an intellectual historian in *Opera and Ideas*; Wayne Koestenbaum, of his commitment to gay and lesbian studies in *The Queen's Throat*; Abbate, of her knowledge of deconstruction and, in particular, of Lacanian theory in *Unsung Voices* and *In Search of Opera*; Michael Hutcheon, of his medical expertise in *Opera: Desire, Disease, Death*.

To what extent, one may ask, have these approaches, drawn as they are from a number of disciplines, brought us closer to an understanding of opera's relationship to society? The answer must remain mixed, for the various strands of critical theory available within humanistic study during recent decades range from the formalist to the socially-oriented. Whereas Abbate's admirable work is near the formal end of the spectrum, much recent work on opera displays a strong social focus. The boom in opera studies coincides in time, moreover, with two powerful strains within literary study – the New Historicism in the United States and Cultural Studies in Britain – that, in their varying ways, are concerned with social phenomena. To be sure, the particular phenomena one may choose to observe and to analyze are by no means the same in the various thinkers such as Foucault, Adorno, Bakhtin, and Raymond Williams whose work has helped make these moves in literary study possible.

Yet there is a way of thinking about society that has not been nearly as well represented in humanistic work as that of the thinkers I have just mentioned: I refer to the writings of the sociologist Pierre Bourdieu. If I may return once more to Mozart's *Die Entführung*, let us imagine a Bourdieu-inspired reading something on the order of his approach to Flaubert's *L'Éducation sentimentale* and its social context.[15] Such a reading would demand an understanding of the cultural landscape of Vienna during the later eighteenth century: the clash between national and foreign musical traditions, between native-oriented Emperor and cosmopolitan public, with this clash embedded within the uneasy mixture of styles that Mozart's opera displays. It would also demand an immersion into a particular social milieu, with its class biases and its institutional conflicts, that those of us who have attempted global approaches to opera have not hitherto performed. And it would also demand an understanding of the differences in the historical situation of the arts in the eighteenth-century German states and nineteenth-century France. Bourdieu's analysis of the artistic and literary fields in Flaubert's time can take for granted the conflict between a difficult, avant-garde form of art and a more easily consumable, commercially-oriented mode. Neither side of this conflict is easily applicable to *Die Entführung*, within which neither the "native German" nor the *opera seria* component could be labeled avant-garde in our normal use of this term.

---

[15] Bourdieu, *The Rules of Art*, pp. 1–140. For an application of Bourdieu to the French musical scene in the early twentieth century, see Fulcher, "Shifting the Paradigm from Adorno to Bourdieu."

But there are other aspects of Bourdieu's work relevant to understanding the social foundations of opera. One might note, for example, that the 1963 questionnaire whose results form the basic argument of *Distinction*, his study of how differing social classes in France value and consume art, includes the names of three operas, *La traviata*, *Götterdämmerung*, and *L'Enfant et les sortilèges*,[16] each of which appeals to differing class tastes. For example, *La traviata* is listed with *Rhapsody in Blue* and Buffet's paintings among the "moyen" and "déclassé" works favored by the petite bourgeoisie,[17] while *L'Enfant et les sortilèges* joins *The Firebird* and Kandinsky's paintings as pleasing to what he calls the "new petite bourgeoisie" who originated in the upper classes and who seek to hold on to their legacy through their avant-garde tastes.[18] Although these three operas constitute only a small number of art works in many genres that fill the charts and analyses of *Distinction*, Bourdieu's book suggests that a study of the use of opera by various group formations – not simply in recent years but throughout the history of the form – to ground their identity and to claim distinction would shed light from an angle that has not received the attention it deserves.

But Bourdieu can also be used to tell us something not only about opera but about the problems we encounter in the study of opera. Take, for instance, his analysis, in *Homo Academicus*, of the power relationships in the French university system. Bourdieu presents graphic descriptions of the dependency that researchers experience toward the senior professors who sponsor their careers, with the result that the system encourages them to conform to established norms in a particular field.[19]

To apply Bourdieu's conclusion to the study of opera, one might note that music departments, above all in the United States and Great Britain, subscribed to a positivistic research model long after this model had become outdated in English departments. As a result, the study of opera by musicologists, at least until the 1980s, seemed

---

[16] Bourdieu, *Distinction*, p. 516.   [17] *Ibid.*, p. 327.   [18] *Ibid.*, p. 362.
[19] Bourdieu, *Homo Academicus*, pp. 84–127.

retrograde compared to the study of literature. Although some musicologists writing about opera in recent years have, as I have shown, adopted paradigms from other fields, many of the books constituting what I have called the boom in opera study emanated from scholars who were not only outside music but who could bring to bear on opera approaches that had become prestigious in their own fields. And once the positivistic model had lost its once exclusive hold on music departments, musicologists could call on these same approaches to gain the advancement and security necessary for survival within the university system.

Let me move beyond these perspectives suggested by Bourdieu's work to suggest some areas that those engaged in the study of opera and society might profitably pursue. I pose here the question of what constitutes the social experience of opera, both in the course of the form's history and during the present day. We might ask, for example, what is unique about this experience, above all when one compares opera with other representational arts, indeed even with other audience-centered events that we do not necessarily classify within what Bourdieu calls the aesthetic field.[20]

One thing that characterizes the social experience of opera is the extreme diversity of opera audiences, both in the course of history and in the present day. To take only the latter, as I developed in detail elsewhere,[21] opera invites a wide variety of spectators ranging from the passive viewer motivated chiefly by social ambition (and who might well spend the middle act of the opera at the bar) to the avid fan with eye and ear intent upon every gesture and sound. Moving back in time, one notes sharp distinctions in the distance that audiences maintain between themselves and the action within an opera: at one extreme, the participation of the courtly audience in the age of Louis XIV, and, at the other extreme, the large gap between the audience and the heroic, larger-than-life action going

---

[20] See the section entitled "Three States of the Field," in Bourdieu, *The Rules of Art*, pp. 47–173.
[21] Lindenberger, *Opera in History*, pp. 265–82.

on behind the proscenium in the public opera houses that have flourished since the first ones in Venice in 1637. Moreover, audience behavior in the course of operatic history has varied considerably: at one extreme one can point to the noisy boxholders in eighteenth-century Italy playing cards and eating dinner while ignoring the long recitatives, yet engaging in wild demonstrations once the aria has begun,[22] and, at the other extreme, the silent spectators in the darkened theaters that have prevailed from Wagner's Bayreuth down to the present day. And as I shall show in Essay 9, which examines some representative performances since the form's beginnings, audience expectations about what they seek to experience at the opera have been colored by matters such as their political commitments, their generic biases, and the charisma of particular singers.

Comparisons among musical genres have tended to stress formal attributes rather than different audience experiences. To cite the work of a single composer, one might note the ways one customarily distinguishes between Handel's operas and oratorios: thus, we cite the fact that, whereas the former are in Italian, the latter are in English; the former on historical and literary themes, the latter on religious and occasionally mythological ones; the former staged, the latter unstaged; the former with only rare choruses, the latter with considerable choral music. On only one point of comparison does the difference in audience experience enter the picture, namely, the fact that Handel's operas were sponsored and frequented by the aristocracy, the latter by a bourgeois public. Yet this last-named point is the most important single factor that distinguishes Handel's oratorios from his operas, for the changes in language, subject matter, and musical style were all occasioned by, indeed derive from, the change of audience.

Once we make the social experience of opera central to an investigation, opera's role among the arts looks different from what

---

[22] For an anthropology-influenced study of the interaction of audience and stage action in *opera seria*, see Feldman, *Opera and Sovereignty*, especially pp. 1–96.

a more formal analysis would reveal. We ordinarily think of opera as a blend of two other forms, the spoken theater and music. But if we stress audience experience, other relationships emerge. Adorno, in his sociology of music, describes the opera audiences in the eighteenth and nineteenth centuries as similar to the cinema audience in the twentieth century.[23] For Adorno, with the exception of a few "high-art" works such as the operas produced by Schoenberg and his school, opera is essentially a popular form, one that he, in fact, treats with a certain disparagement. When he juxtaposes chapters on opera and chamber music,[24] the reader wonders if the category "music" in the title of his book can really apply to both genres.

A study of audiences would reveal certain affinities between opera, on the one hand, and film and sports events, on the other. When opera fans send pirated tapes of performances to distant fellow fans, or when they recite statistics about individual singers, they display a form of passion that, except for the adulation granted an occasional instrumental star, does not ordinarily manifest itself within other forms of classical music. The passion for opera sometimes verges on fanaticism, with fans willing to travel half way around the world to attend some much-vaunted production or to hear a favorite singer, or, for those with less ample resources, to camp out in front of the opera house the night before to assure themselves a standing-room place.

The social experience of opera throughout the form's history has been entangled in complex ways with the economic realities that make operatic performance possible. Since opera has traditionally counted as the most costly of all the performing arts, the public's role has varied according to the type and degree of subsidy offered to an opera company. These state subsidies have played a major role in making possible – as with the German companies of the late twentieth century – a high degree of innovation, both in repertory and production style, regardless of what the public has demanded; to put it another way, a high-subsidy system enables a company to view its

---

[23] Adorno, *Introduction to the Sociology of Music*, p. 80.   [24] *Ibid.*, pp. 71–103.

role as enlightening, and not simply entertaining, its audience about the possibilities of operatic art. By contrast, North American companies, subsidized as they are not by the state but by a combination of ticket sales and private donations, have been forced to a more conservative repertory and type of production in order to cater to the tastes of their audiences and donors. The history of opera financing reveals a none-too-subtle relationship between money and art: one could cite examples such as the craze for spectacle in seventeenth-century Venice that necessitated keeping instrumental accompaniment to a minimum; or the presence of a gambling casino in Naples's San Carlo that allowed both the musical and visual extravagance of Rossini's *opere serie*.

Yet there is another aspect of the social experience of opera that does not lend itself as easily to precise and concrete description as the matters I have discussed above. I refer to the peculiar hold that opera has exercised on the emotions of its audiences. Despite sharp differences in period and national styles, opera has maintained an identity and a staying power over the centuries that is rare among aesthetic forms. Indeed, the means by which particular styles take hold of their audiences can be related to the social contexts within which these styles flourished. At one extreme, one might point to the relative lack of musical continuity in *opera seria*, catering as it did to a public that allowed its social activities in the boxes to be interrupted only for momentary thrills from the seemingly superhuman voice of some star castrato. At the other extreme one notes the seamless musical web of music drama, designed as it was for an audience submitting itself to the high emotions of the Wagnerian sublime.

The emotional hold of opera upon its spectators is also related to the fact that opera offers a communal experience to diverse persons who, even if they do not overtly communicate with one another, establish a bond inside the opera house with others whom they assume are experiencing similar reactions. This bond is not unlike those formed in other representational forms such as the spoken theater, film, sports events, and rock concerts. What separates opera from spoken theater and film is the intensity of opera, by means of which the audience often comes to feel it is participating in emotions and passions distinct from those it allows itself to engage with in its everyday world. As Essay 5 will show, recent research on how the brain processes music offers insights into how we respond to differing levels of musical intensity. The forms that this intensity takes, and the audience's expectations of the way it may react, of course change from period to period, from composer to composer. The intensity of a Handel aria, especially in the *da capo* section (see Essay 5), differs from the sustained frenzy of, say, *Il trovatore* (see Essay 1), which differs from the slow hypnotic spell exercised by *Saint François d'Assise* (see Essay 8).

One might argue, to be sure, that certain films, for instance, those that cultivate advanced modes of visual and audial simulation, have come to rival opera in intensity. And one can speak as well of the communal experience in sports events, in which intensity is achieved through the suspense about a game's outcome and through the bonds created in the stadium by means of the enmity exercised toward the rival team. But the rock concert may well provide the closest analogy to the communal experience of opera. In both cases the audience senses a strong separation between the world of daily routine and the larger-than-life beings (a largeness created to a great degree by the amplifying system as well as the stage lighting) who perform before them. Both invite the traditional discourse of the sublime when spectators seek to account for their experiences. And both manage to retain something of the communal experience even when their music is simulated by electronic means by the listener alone with an iPod or with a computer accessing *YouTube*, for the implied presence of others somewhere sharing this experience (whether in a live performance or in the listener's imagination during solitary listening) remains at the edge of one's awareness. And, as Essay 4 will suggest, the lines between rock concert, rock album, and rock opera can be quite fluid.

There is still another form of representation with which opera intersects, namely the religious service. Indeed, in the present day the boundaries between rite and operatic performance have become blurred. Verdi's *Requiem* is often dubbed "operatic" in character. Such comparatively chaste religious works as the Bach Passions, composed as they were for church performance, are now sometimes mounted in the opera house. And Handel's oratorios, though not designed to be heard in church as the Bach Passions were, are also entering the operatic repertory.

Yet my concern here goes considerably beyond "crossovers" of this sort. In the course of the past century many spectators have come to treat the communal opera experience as something akin to a rite, sometimes as a supplement to, even as a substitute for, what the traditional religions have offered. One could view the Bayreuth experience, and above all the particular experience that Wagner intended his audience to undergo in *Parsifal*, as modeled after religious practice. But the religious analogy is not limited to the earnest and often somber world of Wagnerian music drama. Almost any good opera can serve the contemporary spectator as a mode of religious experience. The length of performance is comparable to that of many religious services. Like a church, the opera house works to isolate those who attend from the everyday world that they have temporarily left behind. And like a rite, opera employs both visual and auditory resources to draw its spectators into the new world it has created.

To return to an earlier example, Mozart's *Die Entführung aus dem Serail*, worldly though it may seem, is as likely as any opera to render this sort of experience. As it moves through its diverse and seemingly incompatible styles – the contemplative music of its two principals, the simple tunes of its servant characters, Osmin's intrusive eruptions, the boisterous *à-la-turque* choral passages – the audience undergoes a cycle of shifting feelings and moods whose magnitude one could never predict from a reading of the libretto alone. When realized to its fullest in the opera house, *Die Entführung*, like all the best operas, gives its spectators cause to believe that something miraculous has happened in an otherwise secular world.

3 | Opera and the novel: antithetical or complementary?

As the common wisdom goes, novel and opera would seem antithetical to one another. For one thing, they are wholly different media: the one a printed form designed for private reading, the other a dramatic representation meant to be performed. The novel is not only consumed privately, but it supposedly focuses upon the private experience of its characters and in turn encourages its readers to reconsider their individual life experiences. By contrast, opera, located as it is in large sonorous spaces, patronized by the so-called beautiful people (whoever they fashion themselves to be at any particular moment of history), and attended by hordes of avid fans relegated to the cheaper parts of the house, can count as the most public and social of art forms.

This appealing model of two media in powerful confrontation with one another served me well when, years ago, I wrote a chapter on the many opera scenes contained within novels for my first book on opera.[1] The scene at the opera, whether centered in social interactions in the lobby or boxes, or in the action onstage, has been an ongoing *topos* in the novel as a way, one might say, of distinguishing between the ordinariness of the everyday life that is its essential subject matter and the extravagance, as my book's subtitle suggests, of the world of opera. However absurdly operatic goings-on are depicted, as in the opera scenes in *La Nouvelle Heloïse* and *War and Peace*, from the novelist's point of view opera served as a medium embodying the high style, performing actions that, in earlier centuries, had been the task of forms such as epic and romance. When a novelistic character such as Emma Bovary or Natasha Rostov goes to the opera, I argued, the writer takes the opportunity to assert the

[1] Lindenberger, *Opera: The Extravagant Art*, pp. 145–96.

identity, even, in many cases, the superiority of the novel. As a genre whose prestige, until well into the twentieth century, remained below that of other literary genres, the novel could invoke the *topos* of an operatic visit as a means of validating its seemingly lowly style and the commonplace events that it so painstakingly recorded.

Yet as I reconsider my remarks in that chapter, I recognize that my observations on the relation of these two media had not been sufficiently historicized, that they were relevant above all to the novel and opera of the nineteenth century. Is it possible that these media have wider, more varied meanings for us today than they did even a few decades ago? In the course of this essay I shall attempt, first, to recapture an earlier, narrower conception of both novel and opera than we have at present and, second, to suggest some direc-tions that we may take to rethink their relationship. As the discus-sion develops, the neat antithesis with which I began, and that I took for granted in my chapter on operatic scenes in the novel, may well be open to question.

If we look back a half century and more to ask how the best and also the most persuasive minds talked about the novel and about opera, what we see would look strange and provincial to many today. Within the anglophone world the most influential model for the criticism of fiction was F. R. Leavis's book of 1948, *The Great Tradition*, which opens with these ominously prescriptive words, "The great English novelists are Jane Austen, George Eliot, Henry James and Joseph Conrad – to stop for the moment at that compara-tively safe point in history."[2] To be sure, in the course of his argument, Leavis adds D. H. Lawrence to his list (as it turns out, the only Englishman among the major English novelists), and he grudgingly finds a place for two Victorian novels, *Wuthering Heights* and *Hard Times*, by authors who otherwise do not make his favored company.

It is hard for a later generation to recognize the power that Leavis once exercised on criticism. Indeed, as late as the 1970s I encountered

[2] F. R. Leavis, *The Great Tradition*, p. 9.

graduate students from Commonwealth countries who mouthed his theories as received doctrine – often blind to the vital postcolonial literature that was developing in their homelands. Leavis's all too cogently argued notions were based on a long-traditional idea of the literary critic's role, a role that goes back to Samuel Johnson and even further back to Dryden, namely, that criticism must above all educate and elevate readers' tastes, teaching them to discriminate among authors and texts. For Leavis, what distinguishes the few authors who make it to his list of "greats" is "that they not only change the possibilities of the art [of the novel] for practitioners and readers, but that they are significant in terms of the human awareness they promote; awareness of the possibilities of life."[3] However vague this criterion for greatness may sound, what emerges from his close analyses is that his favored authors – to use some of his characteristic words and phrases – write with "complexity," "maturity," "moral intensity," "moral interest in human nature."[4]

Leavis's standards for greatness were so high that his recommended canon is very small indeed. The rest of novelistic history is of little importance except for what it tells us of the social conditions that encouraged bad reading habits. The gap between great literature and mere entertainment remains huge for Leavis and his school. Even Dickens, except for *Hard Times*, was relegated to the status of "a great entertainer,"[5] though in later years, a repentant Leavis found an honored place for Dickens in his great tradition.[6]

Leavis's canon was expanded to a degree by a book of comparable authority that appeared nearly a decade later, Ian Watt's *Rise of the Novel*, which added three eighteenth-century novelists, Defoe, Richardson, and Fielding, to the later writers whose greatness Leavis had championed. Watt approaches these authors both in sociological and philosophical terms by demonstrating the rise at once of a new

---

[3] *Ibid.*, p. 10.   [4] *Ibid.*, pp. 115, 98, 18, 154, respectively.   [5] *Ibid.*, p. 31.
[6] See the book jointly co-authored by Leavis and his wife, Q. D. Leavis, *Dickens: The Novelist*. Although Leavis characteristically did not admit to past errors, at one point in this book (pp. 213–14) he qualifies his earlier designation of Dickens as an entertainer.

middle-class reading public during the eighteenth century and of a new concept of individuality. The larger contextual range that Watt displayed was to some degree due, as he himself acknowledged, to a landmark study of the British reading public by Leavis's wife, Q. D. Leavis, but it also derived from the regular mentoring that he had received at an early stage of his writing from Theodor Adorno during the latter's exile in California.[7] As in Leavis's work, Watt's focus is on realism, indeed, on several forms of realism that he shows developing in the course of the eighteenth century: first, a realism of presentation – for example, Defoe's attempt to render authenticity of experience – and, second, what he calls the realism of assessment – for example, Fielding's dedication to evaluating the world he has rendered.[8]

A similar validation of the realistic tradition in fiction governs Erich Auerbach's classic work of 1946, *Mimesis*, significantly subtitled *The Representation of Reality in Western Literature*. Taking the whole of Western literature as its domain, *Mimesis* is not, like, Leavis's and Watt's books, devoted to the novel, yet it too, as its subtitle suggests, gives primacy to the realistic tradition in a number of genres. Indeed, what we ordinarily call novels occupies only a small segment of Auerbach's broad panorama, which consists of texts from the Old Testament to modernist novels of the 1920s. For Auerbach the high points within Western literature occur when three particular features converge within a single work: depiction of "everyday reality," "seriousness" of tone, and a "tragic" approach. This convergence occurs at only rare moments: in passages of the Bible, in the *Divine Comedy*, and in the French realist writers, in particular, in Stendhal, Balzac, and Flaubert.[9] As one reads through this rich and intellectually generous book, one recognizes that the author's enthusiasm resides above all in this last group of writers.

---

[7] Watt, *The Rise of the Novel*, pp. 7–8. Q. D. Leavis's influential early book was *Fiction and the Reading Public*.

[8] Watt, *The Rise of the Novel*, pp. 32–34 and 288, respectively.

[9] Auerbach, *Mimesis*, especially the chapter on these three French novelists, pp. 454–92.

It is noteworthy that these three major critical works of the mid twentieth century, despite the different novelists that each enshrines as canonical, privilege writers who, in one way or another, can be called realist. And it is also noteworthy that these critical writings date from a time when modernism had already produced its major texts. The only modernist whom Leavis admits to his "great tradition" is Lawrence, who, at least from a formal point of view, is the least radical of the major anglophone modernist novelists. And Leavis's chapter on Henry James expresses disdain for the author's more modernist later novels in favor of those from his middle period. For Auerbach, despite the searching and sympathetic analysis of *To the Lighthouse* in the final chapter of his book, the modernist novel is clearly a falling off from the great realist works of the preceding century.

This privileging of the realist novel can be related to the distinction between novel and romance that had been a common theme in critical discourse for well over a century. The novel, whether or not one classified individual instances as realist, was supposedly devoted to the so-called "real," and this was the domain that Leavis's "mature" reader was expected to inhabit. Romance, on the other hand, was the place to which you resorted for wish fulfillment, for escape from the responsibilities of the real world, for what was characteristically dubbed mere entertainment. And it was a *topos* of criticism that the most important ancestor of the novel was *Don Quijote*, a book devoted, among many other things, to exposing the dangers of romance as well as anticipating the techniques of self-conscious narration that many major novelists were to practice in later centuries.

If we turn to the best writings on opera of the mid twentieth century, we find biases similar to those marking discussions of the novel. Consider Joseph Kerman's *Opera as Drama*, published in 1956. The most powerful and influential study of opera of its time, this book proposed a small, limited canon of great operas as exclusive as Leavis's canon of novels. Unlike the latter, however, the operas that passed Kerman's rigorous test – some dozen or so works straddling the course of operatic history from Monteverdi's *Orfeo* through *Le nozze di Figaro, Tristan und Isolde, Pelléas et Mélisande,* and thence down to the still recent *The Rake's Progress* – could not be dubbed "realistic." After all, an extravagant form such as opera can scarcely be deemed realistic in the way that prose fiction or drama are; even that movement within opera labeled *verismo* did not produce a single opera worthy of Kerman's short list.

Kerman's criterion for the aesthetic success of an opera is the ability of the composer, as the title of the book suggests, to make the music function as drama. Although his stress remains on the music, not on the libretto, his concept of the properly dramatic is drawn from literary theory, specifically the critical tradition deriving from Aristotle. Since this tradition places a premium on a certain clean-cut, inevitably shaped dramatic form, most operas, above all those with a florid vocal style or long ceremonial scenes, do not pass muster; indeed at the time that Kerman was writing, the Handel operas had not yet entered the general repertory, and only Maria Callas had by then demonstrated the dramatic potential of the so-called *bel canto* operas.

Like Leavis and the most eminent literary critics of his era, Kerman attempts above all to train his readers to develop a discriminating taste, or, as he puts it at the start of his study, "to provide a basis for standards."[10] Just as Leavis seeks to make his readers grow beyond the *Jane Eyres,* the *Vanity Fairs,* and the *Tesses* that they all too readily embraced, so Kerman shames his audience into shunning the *Il trovatores, Toscas,* and *Rosenkavaliers* that cater to its desire for simple thrills or mere sentiment (one remembers Leavis's disparagement of Dickens as an "entertainer"). Kerman's much-cited label for *Tosca,* "that shabby little shocker," gives some indication of the huge gap separating educated from popular taste at mid century.[11]

Whereas Kerman offers his readers a small group of operatic masterpieces to offset the large number of repertory works that fail as musical drama, Adorno, in "Bourgeois Opera," an essay exactly

[10] Kerman, *Opera as Drama,* p. 6.   [11] *Ibid.,* p. 254.

contemporary with Kerman's book, condemns the medium as a whole as the product of what, in a celebrated section of *Dialectic of the Enlightenment*, he and Max Horkheimer had called the "culture industry."[12] For Adorno, opera's affinities with the culture industry begin early in the nineteenth century with Meyerbeer's historical extravaganzas, which he sees as ancestors of the Hollywood films that he had excoriated in his earlier essay with Horkheimer. Adorno finds that even those operatic scores he most reveres, like the *Wozzeck* and *Lulu* of his former composition teacher Alban Berg, make compromises by cultivating a certain showiness (as in Lulu's coloratura style) and a retreat from reality (as in Wozzeck's dream visions).

What Adorno attacks in this essay is not so much individual operas, as Kerman does, but what Nietzsche, in *The Birth of Tragedy*, had called the "culture of the opera,"[13] above all what both Nietzsche and Adorno see as this culture's inauthenticity. The culture of opera manifests itself, for instance, in the fact that, as Adorno puts it, "costume is essential to opera: in contrast to a play, an opera without costume would be a paradox."[14] (Little did Adorno know that within a couple of decades of this essay it would become *de rigueur* in the more advanced German theaters to do opera in modern dress.) The culture of opera is so tied to unchanging routines that, as he says, "Opera runs head on into the aesthetic barrier of reification,"[15] a point he exemplifies by projecting a *Lohengrin* production that outrages its audience by substituting a beam of light for the clichéd swan. (Again, little did Adorno know that within a short time after the essay the swan would be banned from any self-respecting *Lohengrin*.) The routinized nature of operatic culture is preserved, according to Adorno, by "that type of

---

[12] Adorno, "Bourgeois Opera." The essay was originally presented as a radio talk in Germany in 1955. The discussion of the culture industry is in Horkheimer and Adorno, *Dialektik der Aufklärung*, pp. 128–76.

[13] Nietzsche, *The Birth of Tragedy*, p. 114.

[14] Adorno, "Bourgeois Opera," pp. 25–26.   [15] *Ibid.*, p. 27.

operatic audience which always wants to hear the same thing and suffers the unfamiliar with hostility."[16]

Opera for Adorno is culpable as well of a failure to engage the mature intelligence. At one point he writes that "some of the most authentic operas, like *Der Freischütz*, but also *Die Zauberflöte* and *Il Trovatore*, have their true place in the children's matinee and embarrass the adult."[17] Similarly, Leavis had frequently cited "maturity," both on the part of the novelist and of the reader toward whom the novel was directed, as a prime criterion for aesthetic value.[18]

Adorno's dismissal of operatic culture does not mean that he lacked respect for certain opera scores. Thus, the three major nontonal stage works by Berg and Schoenberg, *Wozzeck, Lulu,* and *Moses und Aron,* engaged his critical attention in detailed and lovingly written essays.[19] His posthumous and fragmentary study of Beethoven mentions *Fidelio* at various points as an analogue to Hegel's philosophy, as expressing the ideology of the bourgeoisie, and as re-enacting the French Revolution.[20] And his collected writings also include a surprisingly sympathetic essay on *Carmen.*[21]

Behind these discussions of both novel and opera in mid century one notes an underlying and not fully expressed theme, namely, that neither novel nor opera quite counted among the highest forms of art. As far as the novel is concerned, this statement may seem exaggerated: after all, one can cite a century and a half of vigorous defenses of the novel, from Friedrich Schlegel's "Letter on the Novel" of 1800,[22] through the theories propagated in Flaubert's

---

[16] *Ibid.*, p. 41.   [17] *Ibid.*, p. 26.

[18] See, for instance, F. R. Leavis's approving citation of Virginia Woolf on *Middlemarch* as "one of the few English novels written for grown-up people" (quoted in *The Great Tradition*, p. 50).

[19] The Berg operas are discussed in his large-scale monograph, *Berg: Der Meister des kleinsten Übergangs*, in Adorno, *Gesammelte Schriften*, vol. XIII (1971), pp. 428–34 and pp. 471–90. Adorno devoted a lengthy essay to *Moses und Aron* in *Gesammelte Schriften*, vol. XVI (1978), pp. 454–75.

[20] Adorno, *Beethoven*, pp. 14, 29–30, and 164, respectively.

[21] Adorno, *Gesammelte Schriften*, vol. XVI (1978), pp. 298–308.

[22] F. Schlegel, "Brief über den Roman," in *Kritische Schriften*, pp. 508–18.

correspondence and James's prefaces, down to the pronouncements of Forster, Lawrence, and Woolf.

Yet these defenses also suggest a certain nervousness about the status of the novel in relation to other, more traditional forms. For many centuries epic counted as the most prestigious literary form, though by the eighteenth century, just when the novel, as defined by Watt, was entering its triumphant period, verse tragedy came to inhabit the pinnacle. It is significant that a number of Victorian novelists, most notably George Eliot and Thomas Hardy, composed ambitious verse dramas – as of course did nearly all the major British nineteenth-century poets. By the nineteenth century, moreover, lyric poetry came to share top rank – to some degree even displacing poetic drama – all of which left the novel as a genre in constant need of eloquent defense. It is symptomatic of this uneasy status of the novel that Leavis originally titled two of the essays that made their way into *The Great Tradition* "the novel as dramatic poem."[23]

Although the ranking of literary genres goes back for centuries, with the novel long assigned an inferior status, the categorization of musical forms was never as rigid, doubtless because there was no long-standing classical tradition within music as there was within literature. In the course of the nineteenth century, however, the new concept labeled "absolute music" made opera appear suspect. Opera, after all, was a popular form with a certain theatrical stink to it. Wagner, to be sure, sought to endow opera (no longer, of course, to be called opera in his hands) with the aura attached to absolute forms such as the symphony and string quartet. Wagner's move to turn opera into something more high-minded than it had been in the past is comparable to the attempts of novelists such as Flaubert and James to give their chosen form the aura of the higher literary genres. The sharply pared-down operatic canon that Kerman advocated in his book is,

---

[23] This title was attached to F. R. Leavis's essays on *Hard Times* and *The Europeans* when they were originally published in his journal *Scrutiny*: the essays appeared, respectively, in vol. 14 (1946–47), pp. 185–203 and vol. 15 (1947–48), pp. 209–21.

in turn, an attempt to look back at the whole history of the form to what he considers salvageable for a mature and serious listener in the mid twentieth century.

I might add at this point that two significant literary theorists active at mid century presented approaches to the novel distinctly at odds with those of Leavis, Watt, and Auerbach: I refer to Mikhail Bakhtin and Northrop Frye. For Bakhtin, for instance, the novel encompassed more varied forms of writing, as well as a far greater temporal spread, than it did for other critics of the time. The Bakhtinian novel starts in antiquity and moves down the ages until it culminates in the work of Dostoevsky, whose polyphonic style set the model for what, looking back in time, this critic sees as the greatest novels, which for him are also the greatest literary works. Unlike the other mid-century critics I have discussed, Bakhtin does not necessarily privilege works in a realist mode. Among Bakhtin's multivoiced novelists, for example, Rabelais, to whom he devoted his most widely read single book, occupies a special place; Auerbach in *Mimesis* had provided a pioneering analysis of the Rabelaisian style, which ultimately he found wanting because, unlike the writing of nineteenth-century French realists, it "excludes deep feeling and high tragedy."[24]

Bakhtin did not, as far as I know, write at length on opera, yet he illustrates his important concept of "re-accentuation" with an operatic example. By re-accentuation Bakhtin sought to define how works of the past – often flattened in their effect over time – are perceived and rewritten in new ways. Re-accentuation works in a particularly discernible way when we see a work that was conceived in one medium translated into another medium. Bakhtin's prime instance here is the transformation of Pushkin's novel in verse, *Evgeny Onegin*, into Tchaikovsky's opera. Whereas the novel *Onegin* was intimate and ironic, the opera, despite characters bearing the same names, has been re-accentuated into an entirely different sort of work – earnest, romantic, and distinctly non-ironic – with the

---

[24] Auerbach, *Mimesis*, p. 282.

result that those familiar with the opera have often come to perceive the novel in what Bakhtin calls a "philistine" manner.[25]

For Northrop Frye the realist novel favored by his contemporaries is only one spot on a spectrum of works in prose, which also includes the romance, the autobiography and the anatomy, a form shared by his own *Anatomy of Criticism* and many older works such as Burton's *Anatomy of Melancholy* and Rabelais's book.[26] Indeed, any particular work for Frye is likely to include elements drawn from other spots along the spectrum. Frye's task is to discover and describe not only what prose fiction encompasses but what is to be found in all realms of literature. Yet there is one literary mode that all of Frye's writing, and *Anatomy of Criticism* in particular, seeks to propagate and defend above all others: the romance. As such, Frye stood in conscious defiance of the values assumed by the major critics of the novel in mid century.

Although Frye did not write explicitly about opera, I can record a suggestive comment, made during a seminar that I took from him in 1951 as he was starting to think out that larger system which eventually became *Anatomy of Criticism*. In response to my question about where opera fits among the various genres, he answered that opera, any opera in fact, was a manifestation of romance, and he promptly, and also extemporaneously, launched into an extended analysis of *Die Zauberflöte*, demonstrating how this opera reworked a myriad of images and turns of plot endemic to the whole history of romance. At one point the Leavisite in me objected that Schikaneder's libretto was a very bad piece of writing, to which Frye replied that Mozart's music picked up the libretto's romance themes and transformed them into something higher. (Parenthetically, I might add that long after this interchange an alternate text of *Die Zauberflöte* was discovered with far superior lyrics that also happen to suit the voice better than those of the standard version.)[27]

---

[25] Bakhtin, *The Dialogic Imagination*, p. 421.
[26] Frye, *Anatomy of Criticism*, pp. 303–14.
[27] See Freyhan, *The Authentic* Magic Flute *Libretto*.

Though Bakhtin's critical writing goes back to the 1920s, his crucial work was deliberately ignored in his home country until near the end of his life, nor was it discovered in the West until the late 1960s. And Frye, though influential in the anglophone world during the 1960s and 70s, spoke for a long while as a minority voice challenging many of the assumptions of his contemporaries. Yet Bakhtin's and Frye's questioning of the limitations of the novelistic canon prevailing in their time is relevant as well to the limitations set by Adorno and Kerman.

If we fast-forward to the present from the once-influential mid-century studies of the novel and opera that I discussed above, it is amazing how much the landscape has changed. Who, for instance, feels the need to reproach listeners and readers for feeling moved by, say, *La Bohème* or *Jude the Obscure* or enjoying the shudders of *Salome* or *Dracula*? After a succession of critical paradigms that have promoted canons based on a traditional notion of good taste, or on new perspectives such as gender, ethnicity, and postcolonialism, it is no wonder that some of us have developed a certain canon fatigue in recent years. We are living at a time when many individuals take advantage of the multitude of musical and literary forms available to them. The same iPod may house "Stairway to Heaven," Miles Davis's *Kind of Blue*, Arvo Pärt's *Tabula Rasa* and Siegfried's Funeral Music. And a particular person, moreover, may be at once a crime-novel addict, a reader of Jane Austen, and a member of a study group meeting regularly to decipher *Finnegans Wake* page by page.

What most entices us today is not so much a desire to restrict ourselves but rather to learn what is and has been out there in literature, music and all the arts. Take, for example, the project on the novel that was initiated by Franco Moretti more than a decade ago and that he is pursuing with collaborators in a number of countries. For Moretti the novel encompasses not only those works produced within the last two centuries in Europe and the Americas, but also those going back to antiquity, as well as novels emanating from obscure places not regularly represented by literature faculties. And the form for him includes not only the canonical works or those we honor with terms like "high art" and "for the discerning reader" – to go back to the characteristic vocabulary of sixty years ago – but a multitude of texts usually scoffed at by literary academics.

Needless to say, no one person can speak knowingly of more than a small number of texts. To understand the novel as a worldwide phenomenon, Moretti has had to enlist the aid of many others, and he has also coined a term, "distant reading," to describe the process of surveying and placing the countless novels that do not lend themselves to fulfilling that mid-century imperative dubbed "close reading."[28] He has also explored the significance of extra-textual phenomena, such as the modes by means of which novels were published and circulated in diverse times and places, and of the ways that new subgenres of fiction break off from older forms to create new ones.[29]

The ease with which Moretti and other scholars today are able to examine the novel without worrying, as their predecessors did, about the form's value in relation to other genres, or about whether they need to elevate their readers' taste, is a sign that the novel has by now achieved a hegemony over lyric poetry and drama both in college curricula and in the proportion of scholarship devoted to it. During my undergraduate years, courses on poetry, drama, or on individual literary periods outnumbered those on the novel, examples of which one encountered mainly within the various period courses that formed the core of a major. But by the late 1980s, the demand for poetry had declined to such a degree at my own university that we felt forced to introduce a mandatory poetry course for all undergraduate English majors.

This relatively recent triumph of the novel has also provided an opportunity for scholars to expand our conception of what the form encompasses. After all, we no longer feel the need to defend the novel against other genres – as in the long struggle to separate it from romance, or in Bakhtin's desire to pit the multi-voiced novel

---

[28] Moretti, "Conjectures on World Literature," pp. 56–58.
[29] For examples of these investigations, see Moretti, *The Novel*.

(or polyphonic or heteroglossic novel, to cite the terms he used at various points in his career) against its supposed predecessor, the monologic epic.[30]

Whether we define the novel as something that effectively began in the eighteenth century, or as far back as ancient and medieval romances,[31] we can also treat it as a member of some larger genus that one may simply term "narrative." As such it need not confine itself to prose: after all, Pushkin and Elizabeth Barrett Browning produced widely read verse novels as late as the nineteenth century. If the distinction between verse and prose no longer remains central, narrative may also include within its orbit those long poems from past ages labeled epic and romance that traditionally served as antitheses to the novel, and against which the novel asserted its identity. Nor is fictionality necessary to narrative; after all, there have been times in which stories that we now deem fictions were taken to be the truth by their tellers and their readers – or at least their degree of truthfulness was not an issue.

If we look at narrative as a long *durée*, of which the novel, whatever temporal limits we impose on it, represents only a short segment, it becomes clear that there exists a large range of circumstances under which it can be produced, transmitted, and consumed. This was brought home to me during my student days when, on my first trip abroad, I found myself in Morocco, which was still under French control at the time. My fellow traveler and I arrived at night and chose to stay in the Arab rather than the French quarter. When we looked out the window the next morning we witnessed a scene on the central square that surely, I surmised, would have thrilled the young Flaubert. Directly below our window we saw a snake charmer, a fire eater, and, most exciting to a graduate student in

---

[30] See Bakhtin's essay, "Epic and Novel: Toward a Method for the Study of the Novel," in *The Dialogic Imagination*, pp. 3–40.

[31] For examples of studies that argue for a continuing tradition of the novel since antiquity, see Bakhtin's essay, "From the Prehistory of Novelistic Discourse," in *The Dialogic Imagination*, pp. 41–83; Doody, *The True History of the Novel*; and Pavel, *La Pensée du roman*.

comparative literature, a bard chanting what must have been some Arab epic. His listeners came and went at varying intervals, but as long as they remained in the group they seemed quite wrapped up in the narrative he was reciting – or was he improvising? At that point I was only vaguely familiar with the researches into oral epic by Milman Parry and Albert Lord,[32] enough so, however, that I thought of the South Slavic bards they had recorded and by implication of the supposedly improvising great Homer himself.

What this taught me most of all was that the history of narrative belongs only partly to the silent, isolated reader; that, probably for much of human history, narrative was something performed publicly before groups that, like modern theater audiences, consciously shared and collectively reacted to what they were witnessing. Nor can one classify oral narrative solely as verbal, for it has often been accompanied by one or more musical instruments. But the performative mode can sometimes include texts written for silent reading: witness Chaucer reciting his stories before the English court, or the public readings of the latest installment of a Dickens serial, or, for that matter, the audiobooks that have replaced silent reading for harried commuters.

I have been trying to suggest that what we can call "narrative" represents a much larger and messier category than that subcategory "the novel," which, in its more or less realist mode, was celebrated and demarcated by earlier critics such as Leavis and Watt. One might think of the various forms of narrative as existing along a spectrum such as the one Frye proposed for prose forms, yet a spectrum capacious enough to accommodate stories of greatly varying length, from all known human cultures, and ranging from those intended for performance – often with musical accompaniment – to those designed for the silent reader.

By contrast, opera seems a far more limited category. After all, we speak of opera as a form that was initiated in Italy just four centuries

---

[32] These researches were, much later, described in detail in Lord, *The Singer of Tales*.

ago and that is rooted in the public opera house (though for its first generation, before the founding of the first public opera houses in Venice in the late 1630s, opera was situated in noble and papal palaces). As the preceding essay stressed, few art forms have enjoyed as continuous a tradition of techniques and conventions as opera, which, despite considerable differences in style over the course of its development, has resolutely maintained a certain identity: a continuing attempt to unite words and music, scenic representation, and a combination of individual and group voices with instrumental accompaniment. The public's view of what constitutes opera was even more circumscribed a half century ago than it is today. At the time that Kerman and Adorno wrote those critiques of opera described earlier, the active repertory was relatively narrow. It crossed over just a hundred fifty years of operatic composition, from Gluck's *Orfeo ed Euridice* (1762) through *Der Rosenkavalier* (1911) – even the now-popular *Turandot* (1926) was little performed until well into the late 1950s. And this repertory was pretty much the same in most opera houses, except that a few operas remained confined to national borders, Weber's *Freischütz*, for example, in the germanophone countries, or Gounod's *Mireille* in France, or Smetana's *Libuše* in the Czech domain. Although the old warhorses of mid century have survived to the present, today's operatic repertory has been expanded to include musical and performance styles quite foreign to an older generation of operagoers: the varied forms of Baroque opera from Monteverdi through Handel; a whole panoply of *bel canto* operas; modernist works that were once guaranteed to alienate the operatic public – all are now common fare. And this public now even seems willing to attend newly commissioned pieces, as long as these are embellished with well-known singers and are accorded theatrically compelling productions.

Yet if opera is to be defined institutionally by the fact that it emanates from the opera house, it is also clear that composers and directors have seriously stretched the traditional boundaries of opera in recent decades. Steve Reich, who dislikes the operatic voice, has concocted multimedia events in *The Cave* and *Three Tales* (the latter of which is called a "video opera" and which I discuss in more detail in the next essay) that combine the recorded speech of representative political voices with his electronically enhanced musical ensemble. Or consider the last three large vocal works of John Adams. *El Niño* (2000), though seemingly organized as an oratorio with poems on the Nativity from various sources in Spanish, English, and Latin, was designed to be performed with stage movements by its singers and with Peter Sellars's filmed backgrounds creating a current-day political allegory. *Doctor Atomic* (2005), designed for performance in opera houses, remains, like his earlier *Nixon in China* and *The Death of Klinghoffer*, easily definable as a work based on political events familiar to its audience. But another operatic foray, *A Flowering Tree* (2006), is more difficult to situate. Commissioned by Peter Sellars for a festival in Vienna and afterwards performed in symphony halls rather than opera houses, it belongs to that new category dubbed "semi-staged," with three singers, one of them a narrator, plus three dancers interpreting the singers' actions, all of them utilizing those parts of the stage not occupied by the instrumentalists.[33]

Adams's two recent attempts to extend the possibilities of opera beyond the confines of the opera house – what in the next essay I call "opera by other means" – might remind us that opera is not quite as monolithic an institution as I earlier implied. Ever since comic opera developed in the early eighteenth century as distinct from *opera seria*, separate venues were created to segregate lighter from heavier fare. *Opera buffa* in Italy, *opéra comique* in France, and the *Singspiel* in the germanophone world could cater to patrons of a lower social order than the "higher," more earnest forms of musical drama.

---

[33] To be sure, Adams himself refers to *A Flowering Tree* as an opera. See his discussion of the work in his autobiography, *Hallelujah Junction*, pp. 294–310. In an earlier chapter on *El Niño* (pp. 237–67), he writes that this work was planned to "exist either in a fully staged version with the orchestra in the pit or as a simple unstaged oratorio" (p. 240). The uncertainty of how and where these two works should be performed doubtless derives from the economic hurdles of putting on full-blown operatic productions. Of the three works I mention here, only *Doctor Atomic* (discussed by Adams on pp. 268–93) was commissioned by a regular opera company.

Although the classics within these lighter forms are now well entrenched within the opera house, the distinction persists in the United States today in the gulf that separates the operatic repertory from the Broadway musical. What distinguishes the latter from opera is not simply its alternation of sung and spoken passages: after all, *Die Zauberflöte, Fidelio*, and *Carmen*, which now count as full-fledged operas, retain the spoken texts endemic to the theaters for which they were originally composed. It is sometimes said that what separates the Broadway musical from opera is the fact that the former amplifies voices electronically, while the latter demands voices able to project on their own in the theater.[34] But this distinction simply begs the question: more fundamentally, the Broadway musical offers a form of entertainment perceived by its fans (many of whom also happen to be operagoers) as more relaxing, more pop-oriented, less high-minded than what they expect in the opera house. Yet several Broadway musicals – notably Bernstein's *Candide* and Sondheim's *Sweeney Todd* – have made it into the opera house in recent years. It is as though the classical status they have achieved as musicals – like *Die Fledermaus* and *Die lustige Witwe* among operettas – has rendered them worthy of opera-house performance.

Throughout its history opera has been flanked by other forms to which it is closely related: for example, the melodrama in early nineteenth-century France, a mode of spoken drama accompanied by music that also left its imprint on subsequent operas. Or note the oratorio in early eighteenth-century Rome; for a short period during which overtly theatrical performance was banned, the oratorio allowed the essential musical forms of opera to continue in sacred guise. Or note the role that the oratorio played for Handel; when, as I indicated in the preceding essay, the demand for his operas petered out, the oratorio gave him the opportunity to transform both his style and his audience, from an operatic mode consisting mainly of

---

[34] For an account of how the advent of the microphone drove the traditional operatic voice from Broadway, see the chapter "After the Microphone" in Grant, *The Rise and Fall of the Broadway Musical*, pp. 35–49.

virtuoso arias designed for an aristocratic public, to a simpler style of aria that alternated with large choral passages and that also cultivated a new bourgeois audience to replace the earlier patrons of his operas.

I bring up these issues to suggest the variety of genres that make up that larger category we might call simply "musical drama." Opera, which, as I have noted, contains its own variety of forms under its institutional umbrella, is only a single, though also central, genre among these. Just as the novel, as I mentioned earlier, can be seen as an instance within that capacious category called narrative, so the long Western tradition of opera from Monteverdi to John Adams may appear a bit different to us when we view it as one among a number of forms developed throughout the world in which music is combined with dramatic performance.

This notion of opera as only a single form of musical drama was illustrated for me in 2006 when I attended a performance by a traveling company of *The Peony Pavilion*, the famous Chinese work that dates from the end of the sixteenth century, just before the first Western operas were performed in Florence and Mantua. Fearing that the musical and dramatic conventions of this Chinese opera (must we even attach our Western generic title to it?) would be totally foreign to me, I approached this performance with some trepidation. Imagine my surprise to find it just as moving and absorbing as any Western opera was for me the first time that I experienced it. To be sure, I was aided by the presence of that new teaching aid labeled supertitles, and also by the fact that the original had been considerably condensed, with many arias and much of the recitative omitted. But otherwise, at least from what the program notes told me, we were getting the real thing – Chinese musical instruments and Chinese vocal inflections. During the 1950s I had attended a performance of Beijing opera, a later development that communicated with a Western mind much less readily than the Kunju form of which *The Peony Pavilion* counts as the most celebrated example.

Whether or not we choose the term "opera" for non-Western musical dramas, the fact remains that much of the world's drama is cast in musical, or at least partially musical, form. Even within the Western domain, music plays a role – sometimes central, sometimes only peripheral – in many periods: for example, Greek tragedy, medieval miracle plays, and the Elizabethan and Spanish Golden-Age theater. The absence of music in French classical tragedy, or in realist plays of the last century and a half, is the exception rather than the rule. Can one, for instance, imagine a film without background music? The few that have long stretches without music, for example Ingmar Bergman's *Virgin Spring*, keep their viewers aware of the lack of background sound. Films and television dramas without music can, in fact, give an audience an uneasy feeling, as also Jerome Robbins's music-less ballet *Moves: A Ballet in Silence* is distinctly meant to do. Moreover, since many narrative forms in diverse cultures are customarily performed publicly with musical accompaniment, the line between musical drama and narrative remains far less strictly defined than most traditional genre theory would lead us to believe.

And just as some recent studies of the novel are casting a wide net in both time and place, so it is possible that we may expand our understanding of musical and dramatic forms to encompass traditions that developed independently of the West. My own experience attending *The Peony Pavilion* has led me to wonder how well, say, Javanese and Japanese puppet plays or Japanese Noh drama might communicate with foreign audiences. To be sure, novels can be translated and transmitted far more readily than musical dramas, which, to cite the examples I mention above, have remained bound to their own cultures and are otherwise known mainly to ethnomusicologists and specialists in the various Asian literatures.

During the last couple of decades, critics of both the novel and opera have proved quite adept at situating texts and their creators within their appropriate social and historical contexts. To engage successfully in this work, one needs to be immersed in a particular context, with the result that scholars remain highly specialized in individual periods and national historical traditions. Moreover, visual artifacts from non-Western cultures have proved more readily communicative to the general public in the West than literary and musical ones. Without specialized knowledge at its disposal, this public makes contact more easily, for instance, with Javanese puppets on display in museums than it could with the actual plays in which they are designed to appear.

Might we imagine a somewhat different mode of investigation, one that seeks to view texts not simply in relation to their immediate contexts, but also in relation to texts from other, often distant cultures? How, for instance, do the musical and dramatic conventions of Noh drama differ from those of other Asian or African dramatic forms? And how do any of these differ from the Western conventions with which we are familiar? In recent years writers and composers familiar with more than a single culture have sometimes sought to join elements of two cultures into a single, as it were, hybridized artifact. The British-educated African dramatist Wole Soyinka has, in *Death and the King's Horseman* (1975), brought together the drums and chants of Yoruban ritual with the chatter of the colonial administrator who seeks to suppress this ritual. And Tan Dun, educated musically both in China and the United States, has in his recent opera *The First Emperor* (2006) juxtaposed Chinese with Western instruments within the same orchestra, while his singers alternate vocal inflections that might have come from *The Peony Pavilion* with others of a distinctly Puccinian cast.[35]

I raise these questions about cross-cultural interchanges on the part of both scholars and artists in order to lead to a further question: can we perhaps locate any cultural universals that cut across artistic forms? I recognize that even to mention universals is to violate one of the central assumptions of cultural studies, a field of inquiry that insists on the uniqueness of individual cultures and their artifacts. Yet the notion of universals has re-entered the intellectual marketplace through the findings, first, of Chomskian linguistics and, more

---

[35] For a searching analysis of *The First Emperor*'s stylistic hybridity – mixing Eastern (and not simply Chinese) and Western music, moving between neo-Romantic and postmodern styles – see Sheppard, "Blurring the Boundaries."

recently, through the investigations of neuroscience, which, by means of research on how the human brain processes information, has, among other things, opened the possibility of demonstrating the varying ways that people perceive and react to different art forms.[36]

In the course of this essay I have concentrated on two large generic categories: narrative, which I treated as an extension of what we ordinarily call the novel, and musical drama, which sought to extend the concept of opera. But I have said little about that traditional third category, the lyric. Plato, one remembers, introduced the idea of a triad of modes into Western criticism by defining each of the three modes according to its method of presentation: in the lyric, for instance, the poet speaks in his own voice; in drama he speaks only through others; while in epic, a mixed form, he speaks at times for himself and at other times through his characters.[37] Although the criteria for demarcating these three modes have differed over the ages, it is remarkable how the triad of epic (or at least narrative), drama, and lyric has persisted in critical discourse since Plato. My discussion has suggested that the gap between novel and opera, or, by extension, between narrative and musical drama, was not as absolute as the critical tradition (whatever the criteria being used to distinguish the genres) has ordinarily taken it to be. If we examine the history of lyric from the point of view I have developed here, we may find its boundaries extend beyond those we commonly assign to it, and we may well discover certain continuities between lyric and the other two modes. Essay 5 will attempt a new way of locating the lyric elements in opera.

---

[36] See my essay "Arts in the Brain." Essay 5 will apply some ideas from this essay to suggest what these investigations might tell us about opera.

[37] Plato, *The Republic* (Book III), in *The Dialogues of Plato*, vol. I, pp. 655–57.

TEN RECENT INSTANCES

Two *Rodelinda*s

How do you find an appropriate means for staging an opera set in barbarous Lombardy during the supposedly darkest of ages (*c.* 700 AD)? Do you research what brutish clothes and crudely fortified buildings would have shaped these operatic characters' lives? But that would be too much the way of the nineteenth century, which wanted its theater and fiction to represent an earlier world "as it really was." Or do you imitate the way that *Rodelinda*'s parent play, Corneille's *Pertharite, Roi des Lombards* (1653), was likely staged, that is, in the elegant theatrical dress of the dramatist's own time? Or do you go to the equally elegant operatic dress, often Roman, but never medieval, prevailing at the time – 1725 – that *Rodelinda* was first performed? To be sure, the title character, sung by the famous Francesca Cuzzoni, wore what Horace Walpole described as a "brown silk gown, trimmed with silver," that he pronounced "vulgar and indecorous," though as he admitted, "the young adopted it as a fashion."[1]

Had there been a continuing performing history of *Rodelinda*, audiences would likely have settled happily for whatever setting had become customary by the end of the nineteenth century (doubtless a medievalizing one). But Handel's operas were not performed between his own lifetime and the early twentieth century – and, until a decade or so ago, only at the most sporadic intervals. To be viable today, these operas, like all *opere serie*, need a strong directorial idea imposed upon the long succession of individual arias that would otherwise hamper the audience's ability to discover any dramatic

---

[1] Quoted in Dean and Knapp, *Handel's Operas*, pp. 589–90.

action holding an individual opera together. So how can an enter-prising opera director communicate with a contemporary audience? Two recent productions have sought to mediate the temporally and psychologically distant events of *Rodelinda* by means of a common medium, namely, early film.

The production directed by Jean-Marie Villégier for Glyndebourne in 1998 evokes the world of silent films. Characters communicate by means of the exaggerated gestures that were felt to be necessary for silent actors to make themselves "heard." Yet these gestures seem wholly appropriate to the anything-but-silent singers voicing the strong and varied affects governing the arias that make up an *opera seria*. The heroine's costumes are at least as gaudy as Walpole found Cuzzoni's. To approximate the totalitarian world – usurpations, imprisonment, attempted murder – within which the plot moves, the director chose to clothe the functionaries in snappy fascist uni-forms and the usurper Grimoaldo in formal attire.

The second production, directed by David Alden for Munich and San Francisco (2004–05), is as seedy as the earlier one is sumptuous. Its cinematic point of reference is Hollywood *film noir* of the 1930s. Handel's arias are sung amid claustrophobic city streets, with a glaring neon sign reading "BAR" at the start of the second act. If the original plot's nastiness takes the form of fascist posturing in the earlier production, in the later production the story plays itself out in a world of Mafia intrigue. Guns and knives are brandished without the slightest provocation. A slick black car, presumably prepared for a quick getaway, is parked onstage. Sinister-looking, hatted men in double-breasted suits or slick jackets walk the streets.

Each of the productions meticulously reproduces Handel's score, which means that they go on for over three hours not counting intermissions. Although the Munich/San Francisco production uses a modern orchestra, the Glyndebourne version employs the period-instrument Orchestra of the Age of Enlightenment which, in its TV credits, boasts that it uses the opera's recent critical edition. Unlike the performances of the 1920s at the beginning of the Handel revival in Germany, when castrato parts were taken over by lower male voices, these use counter-tenors for the two castrato roles of Bertar-ido and Unulfo. And, with few exceptions, the *da capos* remain in place. Like many other contemporary productions that choose a setting not stipulated in the score, the two *Rodelinda*s combine theatrical outrageousness with meticulous musical authenticity.

Kentridge/Monteverdi, *Il ritorno d'Ulisse in patria*

Musically, the *Ulisse* performance I witnessed in 2009 was even more meticulously authentic than the two *Rodelinda*s. The instrumental group approximated the ensemble that Monteverdi likely employed: three plucked instruments – chitarrone, archlute, and baroque harp – and five string instruments – two baroque violins, viola da gamba, cello, and lirone. The singers were all early-music specialists. The only less-than-authentic musical element was the fact that the score was cut to about 100 minutes, some three-fifths of its length, yet since editions derive from a manuscript based on performances with which the composer had no likely connection, achieving authenticity remains at best a questionable goal.

Theatrically, this *Ulisse* was even further removed from its origins than the *Rodelinda*s were. For one thing, the actors were life-size puppets rather than singers. But the singers were also very much in view, as were the puppeteers. Indeed, the characters moved about the stage in threes – puppet, puppeteer, singer – as though they were Siamese triplets. The stage occupied two levels, with the characters moving up and down from one to the other. Between these two levels the orchestra sat in a semi-circle, their movements almost as conspicuous to the audience as those of the characters.

As though this visual component were not enough, still another action took place above these levels. A large screen upon which Kentridge's animated charcoal drawings, as well as borrowed images, are projected competes with the moving character-triplets and the instrumentalists for the audience's attention. The images on the screen tell a story that is parallel to, or, one might say, counter-pointed with, that of the opera. The Ulisse on the screen is a contemporary South African lying in a hospital bed after surgery and full of feverish dreams represented in the drawings. The doubling is also mirrored on the stage, where a second puppet-Ulisse represents his modern embodiment. What the latter Ulisse shares with his classical prototype is the idea of a wound – the famous scar by which the original Greek character is identified – and, as the director puts it, "the muscle of the human heart,"[2] which he reproduces in often ghoulish anatomical drawings to suggest the surgery that the modern character is undergoing. Indeed, the history of medicine dominates much of what we see on the screen: images of body parts from medical textbooks, pictures of anatomy lessons, and contemporary scans which are meant to comment both upon the modern patient's suffering and healing as well as those of the operatic hero. "It is through these scans," Kentridge writes, "through Ulisse himself (his anxieties) that we get to his vision of Penelope and the suitors. Rooting the opera part in his post-operative delirium gives a way of dealing with the problem of the classical theme, the early music, the late 20th-century production."[3] Kentridge, in short, has found a means to make suffering – both mental and physical – unpleasantly graphic so that modern audiences cannot help but react.

And as we listen we come to recognize that Monteverdi's "representational" style of speaking in music – the *stile rappresentativo* – has found a way to render suffering as few composers have ever been able to do. When I attended this production (in one of its later embodiments, with its original puppeteers, the Handspring Puppet Company, but with a new musical ensemble, the Seattle-based Pacific Operaworks) I at first remained conscious of the gaps between the diverse elements of the performance – between puppets and human beings, early music and a contemporary narrative, classical antiquity and the modern world, animated film and real body movements – but within a short while everything blended into a

[2] Quoted in Christov-Bakargiev, *William Kentridge*, p. 148. A description of the original Brussels production, together with Kentridge's notes and reproductions of some of his drawings, can be found on pp. 142–49.
[3] Ibid., p. 146.

single experience. In the course of preparing his production, Kentridge spoke of these gaps in the following way: "The sense has to be of Ulisse Eckstein (a 20th-century man in a hospital bed) leading us into the world of the opera. This world, though referring to the 1940s and 1950s, might also allude to the world of classical Greece and 17th-century Italy. So, for example, a doctor's 40s-style stethoscope forms the basis of the ancient Grecian bow that the suitors have to pull."[4] Kentridge's style of animation, I might add, allows him to transform the most diverse objects into one another with considerable ease.

Behind the central role that suffering plays within this work, there stands a larger allegorical project that, over the years, has guided Kentridge's activity as graphic artist, film-maker, and theater and opera director, namely, the agony experienced within his native South Africa. The *Ulisse* production dates from the first years after the African National Congress took over the country and began the healing process after the nearly half century of official apartheid that marked Kentridge's childhood and growing up. His parents in fact were both political activists defending victims of the earlier regime. The social messages within opera have rarely found an advocate as appropriate as Kentridge.

Kentridge/Mozart, *Die Zauberflöte* in the museum

Although I never attended Kentridge's 2005 production of *Die Zauberflöte*, prepared for the Brussels Théâtre de la Monnaie and later seen in several other venues, I saw some offshoots at a Kentridge retrospective at the San Francisco Museum of Modern Art in 2009. It seems significant that a figure known variously as graphic artist, filmmaker, and theater and opera director should have a multimedia presentation of his work displayed in an art museum.

The space devoted to *Die Zauberflöte* included three staging areas, with the spectators sitting on benches placed in two different directions, so that they could move from one spot to the other when the music for each segment started playing. In the first staging area was a

---

[4] *Ibid.*, p. 143.

large blackboard upon which Kentridge's key images for the *Zauber-flöte* production were projected; Kentridge had created these with charcoal and pencil on white paper, then photographed them so that his drawings came out white and grey on the black background. The images include Masonic symbols, ancient Egyptian temples, various geometric configurations inspired by Egyptian forms, and birds of various sorts, including one held by the artist himself as though he were Papageno. The music for the blackboard presentation is the overture to the opera, drawn from the celebrated recording conducted by Sir Thomas Beecham in Berlin in 1938.

Once the overture is over, the audience turns to a large box showing a proscenium and several layers of stage flats that mimic the stage production. Kentridge's animated images are projected onto an opening at the back. Programmed puppets enact key moments of the opera, which is here reduced to about twenty minutes, with the music, like the overture in the earlier blackboard performance, drawn from the Beecham performance. The recording was chosen not only because of its intrinsic quality but also for a particular political meaning that it lends to our experience of the opera. As Kentridge explains in an interview, "When we hear Sarastro singing his aria in that great Thomas Beecham recording of 1938 in Berlin, we cannot help but think of the nonsense of those words in the light of that political era in German history. There is here the notion that behind many great works of art lies some form of barbarism, some cruelty."[5] It is evident that this artist is aware of Walter Benjamin on the barbaric substratum of great art.[6] I might add that during the many years in which I have played this recording, I felt myself forced to listen, as it were, contrapuntally, conscious both of how magnificent the performance was and of how inappropriate it seemed to hear the work's ideology mouthed by Nazi-employed musicians led by a British conductor. Moreover, the

---

[5] Kentridge, *Flute*, p. 35.
[6] "There is no document of civilization which is not at the same time a document of barbarism," in Benjamin, *Illuminations*, p. 256.

whole project was put together by a British record producer, Walter Legge (who himself, many years later, married a member of that *Zauberflöte* chorus, the then still unknown young Nazi party member, Elisabeth Schwarzkopf); Beecham's and Legge's first choice for Sarastro, the Jewish bass Alexander Kipnis, was, not surprisingly, unacceptable to the Nazis.[7]

The third component of this museum installation presents an incident from German colonial history for which *Die Zauberflöte* provides an ironic commentary. This component, entitled *Black Box/Chambre Noire*, was commissioned by the Deutsche Guggenheim, Berlin, and shown in 2005, the same year as the *Zauberflöte* production; Kentridge refers to *Black Box* as a "footnote" to the production.[8] At the showing I attended, viewers of *Black Box*, whose performance lasted a half hour, turned around on their benches after watching the opera excerpts. Like the preceding segment, *Black Box* consisted of a proscenium with a series of flats and an open background upon which Kentridge's images were projected. The "characters," besides those projected on the background, consisted of flat figures moving on rails. At the front, viewers see a megaphone and a figure holding a sign reading "Trauerarbeit," Freud's term from *Mourning and Melancholy* to denote the process with which the "work" of mourning frees us from the melancholy induced by a trauma.[9]

The mourning in which viewers are invited to participate is the massacre of the Herero people in German Southwest Africa (the present Namibia) in 1904. The event counts today both as the opening genocide of the twentieth century and as Germany's first foray into this activity. After a number of German colonial farms were raided by natives, with some 150 Germans killed, Kaiser Wilhelm II sent General Johann von Trotha to the colony to help "pacify" the region. A report from Trotha speaks of the need to "annihilate" the Hereros and also calls the conflict a "racial

[7] See Jefferson, *Elisabeth Schwarzkopf*, pp. 75–76.   [8] Kentridge, *Flute*, p. 33.
[9] "When the work of mourning [*Trauerarbeit*] has been completed, the ego becomes free and uninhibited again." In Freud, "Trauer und Melancholie," p. 199.

struggle."[10] As a result of this struggle, the Germans succeeded in killing what is estimated at three quarters of the native population – a lesser percentage, to be sure, than that of the European Jews under German occupation some forty years later. The colonial administrators sent a number of native skulls to Germany for scientific investigation to help advance German investigations of racial difference.

The imagery in Kentridge's projections consists of a variety of pictures and documents relating to the massacre: skulls, people hanging from trees, newspaper clippings from the time, old maps, drawings of ancient cameras (which give *Black Box* its title, among the other meanings Kentridge sought to convey by this designation),[11] pages of account books, and names of persons involved in the incidents. The moving figures show attackers hitting their victims with weapons. The musical score for *Black Box* by Philip Miller juxtaposes themes from native music of the region with passages from *Die Zauberflöte*. Thus, Sarastro's noble "In diesen heil'gen Hallen" is linked to an image of two figures beating down a third. While the March of the Priests is played, a list of Hereros killed by the Germans is projected. My first impression was that the fine sentiments voiced by Sarastro and the priests provide a simple contrast of Enlightenment humanitarianism with the brutality of the images. But Kentridge, in remarks delivered at the Deutsche Guggenheim for the opening, made it clear that his intentions were more complex: the enlightened principles for which Sarastro, whom he labels a "well-meaning tyrant," stood were also those practiced by Robespierre two years after the opera's premiere as well as, in our own time, by Pol Pot in Cambodia.[12] Just as a remark quoted earlier alluded to Walter Benjamin, Kentridge here applies the

---

[10] Quoted in Kentridge, *Black Box*, p. 101.

[11] Besides signifying the black box of early cameras, the title refers to the British term for chamber theater and to the black box that reveals the details of an airplane crash. For Kentridge's explanation of how each of these three meanings is relevant to the work, see *ibid.*, p. 51.

[12] *Ibid.*, p. 47.

famous Horkheimer-Adorno thesis on the Enlightenment to the totalitarianism that supposedly emanated from eighteenth-century rationalism.[13]

In placing his political views overtly into *Black Box*, Kentridge is able to distinguish what is appropriate in an opera production from a performance piece wholly his own. "Do I do *The Magic Flute* as *Black Box*, simply as a colonial interpretation of the opera?" he asked himself, to which he answered, "But I couldn't see a way of doing that and being true to this particular opera. It would have been pushing the opera into the service of an idea."[14] But at one point he succumbed to this "colonial reading." Among the animals that Tamino charms in the opera production is that African beast, the rhinoceros. Near the end of *Black Box* Kentridge quotes some footage from a silent film showing Germans cruelly killing a rhino, who thus becomes a symbol of the native people we had watched being killed earlier. This footage worked so powerfully for the original museum audience that the director found a way of accommodating it to the opera production when the latter reached New York: while singing the words "In these sacred chambers / Revenge is not known," Sarastro is shown killing the animal – to which Kentridge adds that this insertion elicited "howls of protests from many people in the production."[15]

Wilson/Waits, *The Black Rider: The Casting of the Magic Bullets*

It defies easy classification. Is it opera? The subtitle, with its overt allusion to Weber's *Der Freischütz*, suggests the genre with which the Hamburg audiences (for whom it was originally created in 1990) would have associated it. Although *Der Freischütz*, as mentioned in the preceding essay, has never acclimated itself outside the germanophone world, these audiences would quickly have recognized the

---

[13] See Horkheimer and Adorno, *Dialektik der Aufklärung*, especially the opening essay, "The Concept of Enlightenment," pp. 9–49. Note, for example, the line, "For the Enlightenment is totalitarian like no other system" (p. 31). The authors were writing during World War II at the height of the Nazi regime.

[14] Kentridge, *Flute*, p. 32.   [15] *Ibid.*, p. 35.

redoing of the Wolf's Glen scene, the pact with the devil, and the shooting of the hero's beloved at the end.

But then the music and lyrics we hear in *The Black Rider* are not by Weber and his librettist, but rather by Tom Waits, who, though influenced here by Brecht and Weill, is ordinarily classified as a pop artist. Shall one call this a pop opera? Moreover, since the book was written by that hero of the Beat Generation, William Burroughs, might one think of *The Black Rider* as perhaps the prime example of Beat opera?

Hardly so, for neither of these terms would do justice to the central contribution of the director, Robert Wilson, who conceived it and put it all together and who also occupies his own, distinctly avant-garde niche within contemporary theater. Indeed, anybody attending *The Black Rider* for the first time would likely be less aware of the plot or even the music than of the contorted, typical Wilson-like stances by means of which the characters define themselves and communicate with one another. Our attention remains centered on heads that stare without moving; bodies that climb slowly over one another; stiff, stretched-out hands and arms. All else – the music, words, lighting, the often bizarre costumes and makeup – serves to confirm and supplement what we see the something-other-than-human figures doing.

To judge from Wilson's own instructions, recorded in a documentary about the Hamburg production, much of the meaning we are to find in the work derives from the stage movements, which, as in much of his work, proceed at a snail's pace. At one point Wilson, citing Martha Graham, tells the cast to move "as though you're carrying the universe." At another point he asks them to act "angular, crazy, off-balance" and at still another to move as though they were "under water." These movements mediate between and hold together a piece whose book and music Wilson saw as going in distinctly different directions: whereas he describes Waits's music as "cloudlike," he sees Burroughs's text as "down to earth."[16]

---

[16] Janssen and Quinke, *"The Black Rider" Documentary.*

In view of the dominant role of movement, one might be tempted to call *The Black Rider* a dance piece. Wilson himself classifies it as "music theater" on his website, which also maintains separate categories for his "theatrical works," for example, *Death, Destruction and Detroit*, and the operas that he has staged, for example, such standard works as *Lohengrin* and *Alceste*, as well as the quite non-standard *Einstein on the Beach*.[17] Yet Wilson's characteristic stage movements are evident within all the genres he lists there.

Beyond the primacy of movement, *The Black Rider* is notable for its obsession with guns, magic bullets, redness, and blood. Although shooting was already central to *Der Freischütz*, *The Black Rider* takes the obsession considerably further. Indeed, whereas the heroine of the former is brought back to life after the accidental shooting by her lover, the heroine of the latter actually dies. (Is it accidental that Burroughs himself, long before writing this play, had killed his own wife – accidentally or perhaps not?) A tag we hear early in the work, "You see that gun, it's not for fun," sticks in one's ears throughout the performance.

As in *Der Freischütz*, the gun craze here is closely connected to the hero's pact with the devil. Like innumerable nineteenth-century works in various genres (for example, Byron's *Manfred*, Chamisso's *Peter Schlemihls wundersame Geschichte*, many Gothic novels, Meyerbeer's *Robert le diable*, Ibsen's *Peer Gynt*, Offenbach's *Les Contes d'Hoffmann*) this opera moves like a satellite around Goethe's *Faust*. But Wilson too has often shown a penchant for the Faust situation, having staged such pieces as *Peer Gynt*, Gertrude Stein's *Dr. Faustus Lights the Lights*, and even that most popular of all operatic versions, Gounod's *Faust*. As such *The Black Rider* occupies a generic place among its creator's Fausts.

Cocteau/Glass, *La Belle et le bête*

Here is a full-length opera (1995) that cannot be produced on the stage, for it remains inexorably linked to a classic film (1946). To be

---

[17] On the difficulties of classifying *The Black Rider*, see Salzman and Desi, *The New Music Theater*, pp. 261–64. Wilson's website is www.robertwilson.com.

sure, it can be (and has been) performed in a theater and symphony hall if the soloists are willing to stand aside for the film to provide the major visual experience. There is a long tradition of operas superimposing themselves on existing plays. *Pelléas et Mélisande*, as Essay 8 will develop in detail, essentially recreates Maeterlinck's play with only minor cuts and changes; yet Debussy maintained the freedom to allow his opera to breathe at its own pace: opera, after all, moves more slowly than spoken drama. Strauss too superimposed his *Salome* on Oscar Wilde's play; yet the change of language from French to German, and the need he felt to delete large segments in order to keep up the musical frenzy, results in a work quite different in pace from its original.

The wonder of Cocteau's film is the delicacy with which the *auteur* represents a romance between a young woman and her animal suitor (the latter ultimately is transformed back to his original human state). With his silky mane and pleasing human voice, the *bête*, despite the threats that he presents, is about as appealing as any bear might conceivably be. Fairy tales were common enough in cinema at the time, but they ordinarily took the form of animated movies in color. *La Belle et le bête* demonstrated that a fairy tale could succeed by means of straight black-and-white photography, though Cocteau managed to create magic through such surrealistic special effects as the disembodied arms that move the candelabras around in the *bête*'s house.

Cocteau's film seems so satisfying, so complete in itself, that one may wonder how a superimposed operatic score could embellish it. After all, it has its own film score, by the distinguished composer Georges Auric, who introduced some memorable music at discrete moments while allowing much of the film to run without accompaniment. But like all operas based on earlier works (even on earlier operas), Glass's version creates its own world, even though what we witness visually is identical to what viewers of the film already knew.

Glass's music, unlike Auric's, is through-composed, and it always remains conspicuously in the foreground. Moreover, his repetitive minimalist style underlines the hypnotic quality that Cocteau's fairy tale already possessed. The constant but also gradual changes in harmony that mark the Glass style also work to define the mood shifts characterizing the film, above all, the differences between the everyday world of the family and the at-first frightening world associated with the *bête*.

The constraints to which Glass subjected himself in superimposing his score onto an existing film are most evident in his treatment of the characters' dialogue. Since he was coordinating sung speech with the slower pace of spoken words, his characters are forced into quicker rhythms than they would ordinarily employ in an opera. Although their timings are the same as those of the actors, it would have been impossible to lip-sync these two distinct modes of speech, and viewers thus remain conscious of a gap between film and opera. To find a method of speaking operatically that could be timed with speech, Glass created rhythms – something derived from talk yet also far more heightened than talk – reminiscent of those used by Debussy, Ravel, and Poulenc in their stage works. Indeed, the musical version of *La Belle et le bête* remains squarely within the tradition of French opera – suave, wise, thoroughly enchanting.

Mayer/Armstrong/Green Day, *American Idiot*

Rock concert, rock album, rock opera: how do we distinguish between these generic categories? The concert, with its theatrical lighting and its musicians moving about the stage in a way that the decorum guiding a classical concert does not allow, easily invites the adjective *operatic*. And, as I suggested in Essay 2, the audience experience at a rock concert has much in common with the audience experience of opera. The rock album customarily reproduces what a particular group does at its concerts, and its listeners, whether in their memories of the concert or in what they imagine it to be like in the flesh, find their own ways of visualizing the concert on their CD player or iPod. Thus, from concert and album it is only a short way to opera.[18]

American Idiot, which opened at the Berkeley Repertory Theatre in September, 2009, further theatricalizes the already quite theatrical album issued in 2004 under that name by the punk-rock group Green Day. The huge set, climbing up behind an uncommonly high proscenium, is papered over with rock-band posters and various icons of contemporary celebrity culture, all of this punctuated with innumerable television monitors of various sizes set in the walls up to the ceiling. The changing images on the screens express a typical punk-rock irreverence, as one notes when viewing the American flag upside down on all the monitors. The director and co-author, Michael Mayer, who calls the album "an opera, ready to be staged,"[19] kept the numbers in their original order, although he also asked for several extra songs from the group. And since opera characteristically needs a plot and characters, he supplemented the album hero, Jesus of Suburbia, renamed Johnny in the opera version, with two other characters to represent conventionality: Tully, who enlists in the service and goes off to some Middle East war, and Will, who gets married, has a child, and displays all the predictable frustrations of suburban life. But Johnny, to the extent that he takes off for adventures in drugs and sex, also pursues a convention of sorts, namely, the rebellion against ordinary middle-class life as it has been defined since the 1960s. The rebellion that the characters express is aimed at once against parents ("We're fucked up . . . / And Mom and Dad are to blame") and against patriotism ("Maybe I am the faggot America / I'm not a part of a redneck America"). The in-your-face attitude of

---

[18] The term *rock opera* has been used to designate a number of rock performances and albums that created plots around the songs making up the performance. Among the most notable is *Tommy* by The Who, whose album of 1969, after a change in the plot, was turned into a 1975 film, in which the titular hero, played by the group's vocalist Roger Daltrey, uses the cinematic medium to sing while swimming, riding a glider, climbing a mountain, and rushing through a blazing fire.

[19] Luppert, *"American Idiot,"* p. 14.

1960s rock has here been updated, from objections to the Viet Nam war to questioning of recent American ventures in the Middle East.

Yet the plot, as in eighteenth-century *opera seria*, is only the pretext for what is central to the opera, namely the songs and, almost as important, the visual spectacle. And, as in *opera seria, American Idiot* consists of a succession of songs, though, unlike its predecessor, without recitative. Indeed, the only interruptions to the songs come in some short spoken passages interspersed between a few songs, for example, in Johnny's letter, "Dear Mom, I shot drugs for the first time today," which he speaks instead of sings. (In nineteenth-century Italian opera it was conventional for letters to be spoken rather than sung.) Again, as in *opera seria*, musical and dramatic variation is achieved through the fact that every song represents a particular emotional stance such as sadness, defiance, or supplication. Yet the audience's experience in a rock opera like *American Idiot* is quite different from that of the eighteenth-century opera-going public, which, as I show in the next essay, expected the high intensity of the arias, each of which builds to the vocal pyrotechnics of the *da capo*, to alternate with the relative relaxation afforded by the long recitatives separating these arias. *American Idiot*, by contrast, allows no laxness. It goes on without break for ninety minutes, to the point that performers and public alike reach a visible point of exhaustion. To employ the terms I shall invoke in the next essay, a rock opera keeps blood flowing into the pleasure centers of the brain without let-up. (Within the standard operatic repertory only those intermission-less shockers like *Salome* and *Elektra* achieve a comparable intensity.)

Yet to the extent that rock is based on traditional harmonies, a work such as *American Idiot* is considerably more conservative musically than many twentieth-century operas, especially those of Schoenberg and Berg. And the rock singing voice is unrelated to any traditional operatic mode; indeed, it stands at an opposite extreme from the full-blown vocal style of the nineteenth century, and it is quite different as well from the restrained recitative style of the earliest operas. If anything, the rock voice can be seen as a version (unintentional, surely) of Schoenbergian *Sprechstimme*, though considerably faster-paced and usually a good bit more frantic. The instrumental ensemble of *American Idiot* contains only eight musicians, roughly the same number and, indeed, with similar instruments, as the ensemble of the early Venetian operas. (The original Green Day album had only a trio of musicians.) Yet the volume achieved by amplification makes the ensemble sound considerably louder even than the hundred-plus orchestra required for many Strauss operas.

Is there a future for a rock opera such as *American Idiot* in the opera house? Not that it would be unacceptable on aesthetic grounds, even if the older audience members should refuse to classify it as music. But there is a new generation of operagoers for whom rock was mother's milk. The chief barrier to rock in the opera house is institutional, for *American Idiot* demands a wholly new performing ensemble. (To be sure, when Monteverdi's *Ulisse* is done authentically, as in William Kentridge's production, all but a few members of the opera-house orchestra would need to be furloughed.) Even if *American Idiot* and other rock operas never make it into an ordinary opera-subscription series, rock is affecting opera in another way: just as jazz has been invading "serious" music for a whole century, so rock – its rhythms, its anti-operatic vocal style, its use of electronic devices – is leaving its traces on many contemporary composers. For example, Steve Reich, whose dislike of the vibrato-ridden operatic voice is legendary, cites the precedent offered by amplification in rock to justify his use of the "thin" voice customary within early music.[20] John Adams, whose early tastes were shaped to a degree by popular music of the 1960s, has written of the power exercised on him by some major rock artists.[21] And certain "serious" composers such as Reich and Glass have, in turn, influenced rock.[22] Indeed, the iron curtain that long walled the serious off from the popular is fast breaking down.

---

[20] Reich, *Writings on Music*, pp. 157, 173, 200–01. See also Sachse, *Sprechmelodien, Mischklänge, Atemzüge*, p. 212.

[21] Adams, *Hallelujah Junction*, pp. 40–41, 197, 234.

[22] On Reich's influence on rock, see Potter, *Four Musical Minimalists*, pp. 249–50. On Glass's influence on rock, see *ibid.*, pp. 339–40.

Korot/Reich, *Three Tales: Hindenburg, Bikini, Dolly*

Over the centuries, prominent composers have ordinarily been expected to find their way to opera. Even the anti-vibrato Steve Reich has pursued his own, idiosyncratic operatic path, first with *The Cave* (1993), about the Israeli-Palestinian conflict, and next, and more ambitiously, with *Three Tales* (1998–2002), which uses the latest video technology to examine the dangers of modern technology: the result is a high-tech opera, or rather a piece of music theater, as Reich and his wife and collaborator Beryl Korot prefer to call it.

Each of the three tales treats what for Reich and Korot is a defining moment in the history of modern technology: first, the burning of the dirigible Hindenburg, Nazi Germany's supposed technological marvel, in 1937; next, the American testing of the still-new atomic bomb on Bikini atoll in the late 1940s and early 50s; and, finally, the cloning of the sheep Dolly in 1997. Like that equally science-minded but much more generically traditional later opera, John Adams's *Doctor Atomic*, *Three Tales* seeks to make music theater a means for conveying social concerns.

Similarly to *The Cave*, *Three Tales* was designed in its early performances to be heard in several theaters in which the video was accompanied by a live ensemble. Before the final two tales had been composed, I attended a performance of *Hindenburg*, paired with commentary by its two creators, on a video screen in a large symphony hall. The designated musical ensemble consists of two sopranos and three tenors (vibrato-less voices!) plus keyboard, four percussionists, and string quartet.

Both the sound and visual effects possible in video are essential to the viewer's experience. Indeed, as Korot explains, technological advances after the completion of *The Cave* enabled her "to combine photography, film, video and drawing all within a single frame," with the "complexities coming from the relationships between the images and the timings of the images on five different screens."[23] *Three Tales*, in fact, creates a new musical language in which sight

---

[23] Reich and Korot, "A Theater of Ideas," p. 10.

cannot be separated from sound, text cannot be separated from its musical embodiment, and the repetitiveness and interweaving of images, texts, and music haunt and disturb the viewer to an uncommon degree. Speech rhythms, especially when we hear them repeated and varied, become part of the musical fabric. Reich and Korot have created a means of communication that sidesteps the old question as to whether words or music are primary in opera: words present themselves in multiple forms at once, as visual text that we also hear spoken, at the same time that we watch the speaker and hear the vocalists sing the text.

In *Dolly*, a long line of science and technology celebrities, including Richard Dawkins, James Watson, Stephen Jay Gould, and Ray Kurzweil, appear briefly in video extracts with short quotes, some of which are then projected as visual text and sung. It is as though the famed personages of historical operas – Nero, Emperor Titus, King Philip, President Nixon – actually appear to us onstage without the mediation of singers impersonating them. In *Hindenburg*, earlier opera is invoked during a scene in which we see the airship being built, by means of both animated cartoons and old footage of the construction project: quite appropriately Reich quotes the hammering of the Nibelungen in *Das Rheingold* both in the rhythm of the anvils and in a parodied recapitulation of their accompanying leitmotif.

A grim humor is achieved in the *Bikini* section when, after witnessing the evacuation of the natives from their atoll, we are shown an image of the Bikini bathing suit (hardly a suit, to be sure!) to remind us of the insensitivity of American consumers to the fate of the islanders. In *Hindenburg*, after we have seen actual footage of the burning blimp, we hear this sardonic comment from an aged German woman, Freya von Moltke, widow of one of the anti-Hitler conspirators of 1944: "Why have such a cigar, a huge silver cigar, in the sky?"

In *Dolly*, the voice of Cynthia Breazeal, creator of a robot, keeps repeating, "This gives me pause" in various pitches and rhythms, while her face is manipulated correspondingly. Similarly, Richard

Dawkins in *Dolly* keeps uttering the word *machine* again and again, as the chorus sing it and as we watch his face in various poses that suggest the complexity of his response. In *Hindenburg*, the captain of the ill-fated ship repeats, "I couldn't understand it. It couldn't have been a technical matter." And in *Dolly*, the phrase "intelligent machines" gets remixed in various combinations – textual, visual, audial – to the point that we are made to wonder what sort of intelligence there ever was behind the machines. The repetition of these words and lines throughout *Dolly* plant an accumulating apprehension about the potential effects of technology in the listener's mind. By the end of *Three Tales*, we feel that we have been at once irritated and mesmerized, which is likely what its creators intended us to be.

Fausts in the museum

Imagine entering a new, much-touted museum show entitled "The Faust Project." Although you are expecting something that evokes and/or represents some traditional images associated with the Faust legend, you are unprepared for an alienating combination of musical noises that you hear emanating from the room even before you enter. As you acclimate yourself to this new environment, you notice that what you took to be a museum guard is actually an actor playing a role in the show. At one corner you see a printing press in the style of around 1580; every half hour the guard, or actor rather, rolls out several pages of the *Faust Book* in German, that he then places in a rack for general distribution to museum visitors. Every quarter hour, a laser printer spews out a scientific paper on how some form of life, from birds and reptiles to human beings, can be cloned, and the actor then tacks these papers to the wall in between various art works (a few of them paintings but mainly prints) illustrating the Faust story. To make room for new papers, the actor removes the earlier printouts, which he then adds to a pile labeled "archive."

In another corner one finds a display of early editions of texts on the Faust story, from the *Faust Book* to Goethe's dramatic poem and thence down to the versions by Paul Valéry and Thomas Mann. In the center of the room is a segment of a modern laboratory in which a life-size effigy of a scientist, dressed in sixteenth-century costume, holds a test tube marked "Homunculus." Inside the test tube is a glowing light that, in the course of a few minutes, turns into a bright jewel and ultimately into the shape of a human infant, after which it returns to the glowing light. Six video monitors, each with a different program, allow six different musical embodiments of the Faust story to blast away at once: Liszt's *Faust* Symphony; Berlioz's *La Damnation de Faust*; Gounod's *Faust*; Boito's *Mefistofele*; the second movement of Mahler's Eighth Symphony; and Busoni's *Doktor Faust*. Other monitors behind and to the sides of these present scientists debating animal and human cloning, including the interviews in the *Dolly* section of the Korot/Reich *Three Tales*.

All of those practices that we call the arts are in effect brought together in this room – music, including opera and symphony, the visual arts from prints and painting to video, and literature – or I should say almost all the arts, for somehow dance never made it except for the dance sequences in the video of Gounod's *Faust*. These various arts in effect invade one another. The sounds of the musical versions of the Faust story, as well as of the interviews with scientists, make it difficult to concentrate on any single one. And these cacophonous sounds cause the viewing of the visual materials within the room to be difficult at best.

The border crossings we witness here take other forms as well. The high art of paintings and prints on the walls alternates with the social texts about cloning that are tacked up and alternated at regular intervals. The real world of live and moving, if also fictive, museum guards invades the sanctuary of the fixed art work that the room as a whole represents. One of the earliest printing presses, or at least a modern reproduction, is juxtaposed with a contemporary laser printer. Musical works in different period styles and different genres sound out at once. And the stable, set texts, represented by the painting, prints, the old *Faust Book*, and even by the competing musical performances, contrast with the changing texts about cloning and the improvisatory performance of the guard. The sixteenth-century effigy of Doctor Faustus has crossed over into a well-equipped modern lab. And the image in the test tube that changes from light to jewel to infant allows the violation of that traditionally sacred border separating the world of inert matter from the human. This violation of borders is of course the main point that this exhibit is making.

You may wonder where and when this exhibition took place. In fact, I have set up this scenario as a means of showing how opera might participate in a typically contemporary museum project in which all manner of borders are aggressively crossed. Any museum looking for a challenging new show is invited to stage this installation.

John Cage, *Europeras 1 & 2*

The earliest of these ten instances, Cage's *Europeras 1 & 2* is also the most radical.[24] Commissioned for performance at the Frankfurt Opera in 1987, the *Europeras* is a full-length opera for which Cage did not need to compose a single note. Rather, it is a collage of arias from earlier operas that the assigned singers themselves chose to perform. But the *Europeras* is not simply a concert of favorite arias. The cacophonic orchestral accompaniment uses the original scores for these arias, but scrambles them by means of computer-generated chance operations, with the result that fragments from Wagner appear with a Rossini aria and, in addition, with instruments different from those that the various composers stipulated. The opera is done without a conductor; instead, each musician is on his or her own, each watching a digital clock to keep within the time-brackets that the computer has determined for each segment.

Europeras 1 & 2 is as bizarre visually as it is musically. Singers were dressed up in various operatic costumes that had no relation to the particular character they were performing. Stage flats, based on

---

[24] For a detailed analysis of this work, see my chapter "John Cage's *Europeras 1 & 2*" in *Opera in History*, pp. 240–64.

images from operatic set designs of the past, changed regularly, with images of singers, composers, and animals (their appearance determined, as one might expect, by chance operations), in variously cropped forms, appearing from moment to moment. Singers and other stage personnel performed such actions as riding bicycles, climbing ladders, and contorting their bodies. The chance operations that likewise governed the stage lighting caused the stage to be lit up and darkened regardless of what actions were going on.

In its iconoclasm *Europeras 1 & 2* can be considered an assault on the traditional culture of opera, especially as it has existed in Europe, where the opera house in cities such as Paris, Vienna, and Berlin occupies a central site and has often served as the focus of social life. The work has not enjoyed much of an after-life – a few performances in a more modest, chamber form in several venues during the remaining years of Cage's life – but in the radicality with which it challenged our usual notions of what opera must be, Cage surely made his point.

Opera in the head

A psychiatric journal describes a hitherto uncharted disease to which it has attached the name "Opera-hallucinosis."[25] Symptoms were observed in a 74-year-old German mathematician who had studied the scores of numerous operas in the course of his life. Three days after emergency colon surgery he found himself unable to sleep and complained of being kept awake all night hearing the scores he knew from beginning to end, to the point that he lived in dread of hearing the start of an overture, for there seemed to be no way, as one can with a stereo or by simply strolling out of the opera house, of bringing the music to a stop.

Although brain tomography showed no evidence of abnormalities, and although his blood count was normal, the patient remained exhausted, irritable, and confused as a result of his unwilled operatic experiences. His doctors administered olanzapine, an anti-psychotic

[25] Rentrop, Knebel, and Förstl, "Opera-hallucinosis."

drug, after which, according to the report, "he regained his strength, became friendly, cooperative, and still appeared puzzled about the vivid orchestrations of his musical memory."[26]

The psychiatric report does not remark on whether or not he visualized any of these scores that he knew so well. But if he saw as well as heard these operas, one might ask how his hallucinatory mind managed to stage them: in the way to which he was accustomed to view them in the opera house in his youth, or in the innovative contemporary German way, which, if he had been able to keep some record for posterity, might have proved inspiring to a future opera director. And one also wonders if, after this debilitating experience, he ever cared to study or attend an opera again.

THE UPSHOT

As far as many longtime operagoers are concerned, opera clearly isn't what it used to be. After attending an opera performance in the United States, a touring older German couple expressed some relief that they could once more witness the traditional-style production they remembered from their early years. But iconoclastic, European-style productions have been creeping into some American opera houses – and with some repercussions, to be sure. When I attended the David Alden *film-noir Rodelinda* in San Francisco, I overheard some subscribers during intermission mumbling "Eurotrash," which has become a standard term for those disapproving of this type of production. And the formerly conservative Metropolitan Opera opened its 2009–10 season with a radically scaled-down *Tosca*, directed by Luc Bondy, which its audience, fondly remembering the sumptuous Franco Zeffirelli production, booed with considerable vehemence.

But the distinction between "traditional" and "innovative" productions is not as simple as adherents on both sides of the divide often take it to be. As David Levin reminds us in the theoretical groundwork he has mapped out for recent operatic innovations, new

---

[26] *Ibid.*, p. 432.

approaches have been practiced in opera production at various moments of history. One need only think of some of the productions created by Alfred Roller during the Mahler years at the Vienna State Opera or of the constructivist-inspired settings used by the Kroll Opera House in Berlin in the period immediately preceding the Nazi takeover. Moreover, Richard Wagner was not only an inventive stage innovator, but his arguments against the routinization that prevailed in German theaters of his day could be used by present-day directors to justify their attempts to shake up petrified traditions.[27] (Wagner's once-revolutionary stagings themselves became petrified at Bayreuth after his death.)

Yet insisting that innovation has a long history in a sense begs the question. The productions that have elicited the most controversy go back at best a single generation and, according to Levin, have their origin in the *Ring* that Patrice Chéreau staged for the Bayreuth centennial in 1976.[28] Most of them have been staged in European, especially German, opera houses, where state subsidies enable decisions on production style to be made with less regard for popular appeal than in countries, like the United States, which depend on box-office receipts and the biases of their local donors. Levin links this new mode of operatic production to the intellectual atmosphere created by figures such as Roland Barthes, Paul de Man, and Jacques Derrida, who raised questions about matters such as fidelity to the text and, indeed, about what a text constitutes in the first place.[29] Interpreting an opera is no longer simply the musical interpretation of a singer or conductor but something that demands the same concentration that goes into interpreting a difficult literary or philosophical text.

It is scarcely any wonder that this recent mode of opera production has created a high degree of controversy. A large part of any opera audience is unwilling and unprepared to follow the complex thoughts that an intellectually ambitious director has worked out about some familiar work. (What good would it do to advertise a

---

[27] Levin, *Unsettling Opera*, pp. 22, 44n, 40–43.   [28] *Ibid.*, pp. 17–22.
[29] *Ibid.*, pp. 11, 72.

Bohème deconstructed à la Derrida?) Indeed, for many people, going to hear one's favorite operas is akin to eating comfort food. How fair is it after all to make them shell out considerably more money than for a play or concert to then feel themselves inadequate to understand what is apparently expected of them?

To compound the problem, many contemporary directors seek to provoke their audiences in one way or another. They may ask their viewers merely to reconsider what an opera is all about, as the two *Rodelinda*s I discussed at the beginning of this essay sought to do; after all, the two types of film on which these productions were modeled can at least assume their audiences' familiarity with popular films of the past. But sometimes these productions are also politically provocative – and, one might add, more often from a leftist rather than from a neutral point of view. Since many American donors are unable to share these directors' politics, not to speak of their other intellectual commitments, it is scarcely any wonder that these donors have been known to threaten opera administrators with their intention to stop contributing funds. One must admit that many innovative productions – and I write here as someone generally sympathetic to directorial provocation – are not very effective: as with any interpretive project, sometimes the thing works and sometimes it clearly doesn't.

Yet directorial interventions, however controversial, are not likely to go away. Once the notion that fidelity to some earlier text – whether the "original" score or some long-standing tradition of how a particular opera has been staged – became open to question, there was no going back to interpretative innocence. The only way to recapture a composer's intentions is to study and memorize a score, as the postsurgical hallucinating patient, described earlier in this essay, had done avidly for many years. But of course a composer's intentions also include the latter's idea of some possible stage realization, an idea which, in many instances, was never spelled out in detail within the score. And even if spelled out, what if, except for the most traditional operagoers, this realization – for example, the Lohengrin swan or Tosca's candlesticks – would strike its audience as too clichéd today? (Some people, to be sure, find comfort in clichés.)

And then one must ask which version of a score one should feel faithful to. Since Verdi, for instance, revised a number of his operas for different productions occurring at different stages of his career – *Don Carlos* perhaps offering the greatest challenge – directors are forced to choose which of these texts they wish to perform.[30] If the hallucinator performed *Don Carlos* in his mind, he would have been hounded by whichever version he had studied long before. Given the fact that operas, like plays, are designed to be performed at different places and at different times, their texts are considerably more fluid than those of poems and novels: yet even such non-performance texts, if one considers the habit of writers such as Wordsworth, Henry James and Auden of revising their earlier work in the course of their lives, have caused considerable problems for their later editors trying to establish an appropriate text. Achieving fidelity is a tricky thing at best.

Opera productions seem iconoclastic only if their viewers measure them against some earlier notion they carry about what constituted a particular operatic text or style. Most of the examples of opera "by other means" that I cited earlier in this essay do not constitute new readings of established texts. The Korot/Reich *Three Tales* is not only an original text, but, given the technologies central to its creation, it could scarcely lend itself to a later re-creation. Likewise, Glass's imposition of an opera atop Cocteau's *La Belle et le bête* is one of a kind – though presumably Glass or any other composer could substitute an operatic text over any existing film. And *American Idiot* is a full-bodied staging of an album and concert that were already a goodly way along the road to opera.

Examples such as these suggest that opera has been participating in that active crossing of generic and media boundaries that has characterized the various arts during the past few decades. In Essay 7 I propose a category, "not-quite opera," to indicate the ways that

---

[30] See Levin's chapter on *Don Carlos* (*ibid.*, pp. 137–76) for an analysis of these choices and the consequences that each entails.

operagoers, whose experience was determined by the reigning nine-teenth-century repertory, perceived the new works that emerged in the course of the twentieth century. From *Pelléas et Mélisande* through *Saint François d'Assise*, what now count as the century's canonical works to many seemed pallid, fragmented, or not sufficiently outspoken, compared to the full-throttle operas from Rossini to Puccini that continued to dominate the opera-house repertory.

Yet in some respects twentieth-century opera retained a certain conservatism compared to such other forms as painting and dance. For one thing, operas continued throughout the century to tell stories. Even *Moses und Aron* and *Lulu*, despite their twelve-tone musical trappings, retain a narrative framework. Painting largely broke with representation early in the century and at particular moments sought total abstraction. The ballets developed by the Diaghilev troupe at the start of the century sometimes broke with narrative, and by mid century the defiantly anti-narrative ballets of George Balanchine had become the norm. By contrast, the new operas that have been commissioned in recent times have to a great degree been musicalizations of famous novels and plays (*The Great Gatsby, An American Tragedy, A Streetcar Named Desire*) or biographical narratives about celebrated figures (*X, Nixon in China, Doctor Atomic*). The Frankfurt Opera commission of Cage's *Europeras 1 & 2* is the exception that proves the rule: Heinz-Klaus Metzger and Rainer Riehn, the dramaturgs responsible for the commission, were themselves long-term spokesmen for the musical avant-garde in Germany, and, as far as I know, the work was never again performed either in Frankfurt or in any real opera house.

Yet Cage has spawned his own progeny outside the opera house. For example, pedestrians going through a Central Park tunnel in New York can hear a mélange of sounds recorded by John Morton, a Cage-influenced composer who recorded sounds that he heard in the park – whether conversation, animal sounds, or simply the wind – remixed these sounds by means of chance operations, and then reproduced them for all to hear in the acoustical chamber created by the tunnel.[31] Cage had long maintained that "the sounds of [people's] environment constitute a music which is more interesting than the music which they would hear if they went into a concert hall."[32] So why not gather sounds from the park and allow a park tunnel to serve as an opera house or concert hall?

The relative conservatism of opera, as I argue at various points in this book, is closely linked to the institutional nature of the traditional opera house. Whether in the subsidized European houses or in the donor-supported North American ones, the need for narrative has prevailed even when the music or the production took a radical turn. When Pierre Boulez in 1966 made his much-quoted remark about "blowing up the opera houses," he was expressing the frustration of experimental young composers in getting their work performed by German companies.[33] But even the more experimental work of older composers has not found its way into the ordinary repertory. Schoenberg's *Die glückliche Hand*, already a century old, is rarely performed in an opera house, nor are the defiantly non-linear but musically simple Stein/Thomson works, *Four Saints in Three Acts* and *The Mother of Us All*.

The institutional conservatism of the opera house, despite the occasional scandals set off by daring productions, becomes evident when we compare it with the path-breaking ways of museums, especially of those devoted to modernist and contemporary art. Although museum donors in the United States are often the same persons who serve as opera donors, they are also sometimes collectors, and in this role they feel it necessary to buy works that they deem "cutting edge." But the donor who has given a museum a Richard Serra sculpture or an installation by Louise Bourgeois may well be satisfied with a traditional production of some canonical opera. Attending the opera, one might say, demands a different frame of mind from visiting a museum. A museum visitor who feels baffled or outraged by some work of conceptual art, such as the

---

[31] Kennedy, "Sound Tunnel."
[32] Quoted in Kostelanetz, *Conversations with Cage*, p. 65.
[33] See Levin, *Unsettling Opera*, p. 18n, for the full quotation and its context.

imagined Faust installation I described earlier, can simply walk into another section of the museum and take a look at something more familiar or comforting. Operagoers commit themselves to several hours sitting through an event – whether a difficult new work or an in-your-face production of a beloved older one – that may cause them extreme discomfort. Moreover, even if the museum visitor decides to walk out of the building in disgust, the financial investment in admission fees is only a small fraction of the price of an opera ticket. When Kentridge, in a statement I quoted earlier, distinguished the ways he treated *Die Zauberflöte* at the Deutsche Guggenheim and in the opera house ("a colonial interpretation . . . would be pushing the opera into the service of an idea") he showed a keen sense of generic decorum, even though he later failed to resist introducing the killing of the rhinoceros into Sarastro's aria in his opera production.

In Essay 6 I shall sketch out a history of the shift from the rigorous guarding of generic boundaries in Sir Joshua Reynolds's theory of art to the systematic violation of these boundaries in the Wagnerian *Gesamtkunstwerk*. Yet a Wagner music-drama is itself a singular entity with its own generic identity and boundaries, as is evident in the long succession of works within this tradition down to the last operas of Richard Strauss. It remained for the twentieth century to attempt a more systematic crossing of boundaries: between genres, between media, between "high" and "low" art, between what we ordinarily classify as art and what we don't. With the introduction of so-called conceptual art during the 1960s, the museum became the favored site for boundary violations. The scenario for the Faust installation I suggested earlier demonstrates each of these forms of boundary-crossing. It is characteristic of museum installations in our time to try outdoing one another in the unexpected categories they can introduce into the world of art. In fact, just after drafting the last paragraph, I came across a newspaper article describing an installation at the Nordic Pavilion in the 2009 Venice Biennale in which a fictional real estate company hands out "goodie bags" to visitors as part of a supposed tour of a house; when these visitors returned to their hotels they found that each bag contained, among other items, a whole salami.[34] If the breakdown of traditional aesthetic categories is the chief criterion for innovation, then the museum has become the most radical place for experimentation.

By contrast the opera house operates with rigid rules and conventions that have accumulated over time: you arrive precisely on time or else stay in the lobby or go home; you sit in a darkened chamber (a convention dating back to Wagner's Bayreuth) and remain quietly, obediently in your seat for three to five hours; you keep your attention focused (or at least pretend to) on the stage goings-on. As mentioned earlier, the opera house until well into the nineteenth century was a none-too-decorous, often in fact raucous place. Moreover, nobody demanded that an operatic work remain intact: pieces from other works were interpolated at will (usually because of the desires of star singers), and, during the eighteenth century, a composite operatic genre called a "pasticcio" (examples of which Handel was happy to arrange) brought together works from various composers in a single evening. Indeed, as Lydia Goehr has shown, the notion that a musical composition possesses the individuality and integrity to which we give the name "work" did not take hold until the start of the nineteenth century.[35]

Conservative though it may be, the opera house has gradually absorbed some of the experimentation that has taken place at the fringe. Although Peter Sellars's once-controversial relocations of the Da Ponte/Mozart operas to modern-day New York were originally done for the Pepsico Festival and for video, many of his ideas have found their way into the work of later directors. Robert Wilson's characteristic style is equally evident in theatrical works like *The*

---

[34] Kennedy, "Artwork to Display." The Clark Institute in Williamstown, which regularly collects paraphernalia from the Biennale, has expressed fear that American customs authorities would not allow the salami to enter the country. But Maurizio Cattelan, the artist responsible for the goodie bags, offered to find a substitute in an American delicatessen if the authorities balk at the original. As in all the arts, the perceived need to get back to origins remains crucial.

[35] Goehr, *The Imaginary Museum of Musical Works*.

Black Rider and in such operas as *Alceste* and *Lohengrin* that he has been invited to stage. Although Kentridge's *Ulisse* and *Die Zauberflöte* were commissioned by the progressive Théâtre de la Monnaie, his reputation is now such that he was invited to stage Shostakovich's *The Nose* at the newly innovative Metropolitan Opera House.

Perhaps the most conspicuous new development in the opera house is the use of digital technology to create elaborate effects by means of lighting and projections. Audiences accustomed to the special effects possible in cinema today can marvel at the effects they can watch in live performances – especially for works that invite magic. Just as Venetian audiences of the mid seventeenth century thrilled to watch the gods descend by elaborate mechanical means, and Handel's audiences expected a similar stage-magic in his operas based on Ariosto and Tasso, so we now demand digital illusion for *Die Zauberflöte*, the various Faust operas, and Wagner's myth-centered narratives.

Opera will certainly not return to the conditions I remember from my earliest experiences watching touring companies: singers bringing in their own costumes regardless of the décor; the total absence of a stage director; backdrops flapping back and forth as the characters move about the stage; a ragged ensemble resulting from lack of rehearsal. Yet if, on occasion, you heard a genuinely great singer, it hardly mattered if she was corpulent, lacking in body movement, and oblivious to what went on around her. Indeed, such moments were truly divine. Opera has its paradoxes.

The affinities between opera and lyric are longstanding. During the seventeenth and eighteenth centuries in France, non-comic opera was distinguished from spoken drama by the term *tragédie-lyrique*. In Italian the word *lirico* is appended as an adjective to *opera* to form the generic term *opera lirica*, for the word *opera* can refer to a variety of things such as *work* or *action*. The term *lyric* has been preserved in the names of opera houses such as the *Théâtre-Lyrique*, which functioned in mid-nineteenth-century Paris, and in such present-day institutions as the Boston Lyric Opera and the Chicago Lyric Opera.

The word *lyric* derives from that ancient instrument, the lyre, which accompanied the recitation of poems. During the early modern period the word was revived to define shorter poems accompanied by plucked instruments supposedly descending from the lyre. In its early manifestations, opera demonstrated its affinity to lyric through the dominant role that these instruments – baroque harp, chitarrone, theorbo, and lute – played in the small chamber ensembles accompanying the singers. When we hear a performance of, say, *Il ritorno d'Ulisse in patria* or *La Calisto*, we are constantly aware of how conspicuously the various plucked instruments define the rhythms and the harmonies of the declamations uttered by the characters.

Plato's division of the literary genres, as mentioned at the end of Essay 3, was based on the role assumed by the voice narrating the events. In lyric poetry, which Plato exemplifies by the dithyramb used in Dionysian festivals, the poet claims to speak in his own voice. Epic is a mixed form in which the dialogue emanates from the various characters, with the narration coming from the poet himself. In drama, however, the poet's voice is suppressed in favor of the words coming from the personages whose dialogue he is imitating. Plato's concern in distinguishing the genres was, of course, the imitative nature of art: to the extent that lyric poetry represented the poet's own voice, it was imitative to a lesser degree than epic and drama. But since all art for Plato was suspect, even lyric poetry posed dangers for the ideal Republic whose health was central to the philosopher's argument.

The present essay proposes to define the relationship between opera and lyric by an approach to lyric that developed during the eighteenth century and, despite innumerable changes in poetic styles since that time, continued to dominate the way that lyric poetry was distinguished from other genres until at least the late twentieth century. I refer to the fact that poetry, which for centuries had been more closely associated with painting than with any other form, came to identify itself above all through its affinities with music. As M. H. Abrams, in his influential study *The Mirror and the Lamp*, has shown, poetry began to assume the non-mimetic, often undefinable qualities ascribed to music.[1] If a lyric poem was formerly linked to the lyre that supposedly accompanied it, poetry now came to embody music itself. Novalis expressed this new relationship between poetry and music in a memorable way with the question, "When one sets certain poems to music, why not set them to poetry [*Poesie*]?"[2]

And once this relationship had become established in readers' minds, poems were expected to convey emotion with the immediacy that listeners expected from the music they heard. The result was that lyric poems, just like musical works, became associated with intensity of experience. And since intensity could persist for at best relatively short periods of time, only brief poems could qualify for the honor of being called poetry. Edgar Allan Poe gave this notion its classic statement with the following words:

> A poem deserves its title only inasmuch as it excites, by elevating the soul. The value of the poem is in the ratio of this elevating excitement. But all excitements are, through a psychal necessity, transient.

[1] Abrams, *The Mirror and the Lamp*, pp. 50–52.
[2] Samuel, *Das philosophische Werk* II, p. 360. This quotation is used to serve another purpose in the next essay in this book.

That degree of excitement, which would entitle a poem to be so called at all, cannot be sustained throughout a composition of any great length. After the lapse of half an hour, at the very utmost, it flags – fails – a revulsion ensues and then the poem is, in effect, and in fact, no longer such.[3]

Poe goes on to argue that there is no such thing as a long poem, that works such as *Paradise Lost* and the *Iliad* are essentially a collection of short lyrics tied together by discursive passages not worthy of being called poetry.

The brevity and intensity that Poe demands in what we honor with the name of poetry becomes central to the way we approach the various arts in Walter Pater's exhortation to his readers that concludes his *Studies in the History of the Renaissance*:

We are all under sentence of death, but with a sort of indefinite reprieve . . . we have an interval, and then our place knows us no more. Some spend this interval in listlessness, some in high passions, the wisest . . . in art and song. For our one chance lies in expanding that interval, in getting as many pulsations as possible into the given time.[4]

Unlike Poe, Pater is not concerned here merely with the reading of poetry, but with our experience of all the arts. What both are celebrating is the intensity of our response to art, yet with the warning that this intensity comes at best in brief spurts.

I bring up these well-known passages in order to venture a theory of how we experience opera. As I shall argue in the course of this essay, opera is unique among the arts through its attempt to work up and sustain a level of high intensity – Pater's "as many pulsations as possible into the given time" – among its audiences. Moreover, each operatic style during the four centuries in which opera has flourished developed a distinct way of creating this intensity. Although the sustained intensity for which opera strives is shared by other forms of music, the sheer length of an opera, together with its use of visual

[3] Poe, *The Selected Poetry and Prose*, p. 383.   [4] Pater, "Conclusion," p. 1568.

and verbal effects, provides opportunities for intensity that other forms largely lack. Opera, in short, manages to extend the brief time that Poe allotted to a poem, as well as the interval that Pater asked his readers to expand, to create a full evening's pleasure.

To flesh out my theory, I turn to some studies in cognitive psychology and neuroscience of how music is processed within the human brain. In an earlier essay on the implications of recent experiments for our understanding of drama, painting, and music, I cited a number of scientific projects, beginning in 1980, that researched the way that music set off so-called "chills" in its listeners.[5] The first of these experiments, by the pharmacologist Avram Goldstein, employed the term "thrills," which, in studies by later researchers, gave way to "chills," defined as a distinct feeling of pleasure that is set off by listening to music and that takes such forms as goose-pimples or shudders down the spine.[6] In this early study, which, unlike later ones, did not measure reactions by means of devices such as positive emission tomography (PET) or functional magnetic resonance imaging (fMRI), the subjects brought selections of classical music that they had themselves selected and simply indicated to Goldstein at what points they experienced highs. Goldstein recorded the intensity, frequency, and duration of these moments and then, after administering naloxone, an opiate receptor antagonist, showed that the reported thrills were attenuated in some of his subjects. Music, he speculated, exercised effects analogous to drugs.

Subsequent research on how music induces "chills" considerably expanded the scope of the inquiry. The cognitive psychologist Jaak Panksepp examined reactions, by means of questionnaires, to short pieces of both classical and popular music and concluded, among other things, that music possesses clearly addictive effects; that sad songs elicited more powerful effects on listeners than happy ones; that female subjects reacted more strongly than males; that the degree of reaction varied for a subject in the course of a piece; and

[5] Lindenberger, "Arts in the Brain," pp. 19–22.
[6] Goldstein, "Thrills in Response to Music and Other Stimuli."

that subjects reacted more favorably to pieces that they themselves selected than to those chosen for them.[7]

Later papers by psychologists and neuroscientists have succeeded in locating particular networks that music sets off within the brain. A PET imaging study of 2001 by Anne J. Blood and Robert J. Zatorre showed particular places – in, for instance, the ventral striatum, thalamus, and insula – that became activated by pleasant music.[8] By the same token, activity within the amygdala, associated with fear (among other things), decreases as subjects react to pleasurable stimuli.[9] Like the earlier researchers on chills, Blood and Zatorre point out the addictive aspect of music, adding that not only does it affect the same brain areas as drugs but that these areas also react to food and sex. As mentioned in Essay 1 in the section on violence in opera, a study of 2005 by Vinod Menon and Daniel J. Levitin using the fMRI was able to locate still further areas, such as the nucleus accumbens and the ventral tegmental area, that, like the areas cited in Blood and Zatorre's paper, serve as part of the brain's reward system.[10] This study also demonstrated activation in the hypothalamus, which is associated with autonomic responses such as increases in heart rate and respiration. The researchers used only classical music selected by themselves, and they also tested their findings by playing scrambled, dissonant versions of these selections, with the result that the activations recorded earlier declined.

Oliver Grewe, as lead author of two articles on chills, has shown how these musical effects work to ratify a composer's artistic intentions. Using the same piece (the "Urlicht" movement from Mahler's Second Symphony) on all his subjects, Grewe and his team found

---

[7] Panksepp, "The Emotional Sources of 'Chills' Induced by Music."

[8] Blood and Zatorre, "Intensely Pleasurable Responses to Music."

[9] In this and other studies cited in this essay the amygdala is associated with fear and other negative emotions. But a recent review of research on the amygdala of monkeys shows that this segment of the brain has other functions, among them the ability to process and to reinforce awards. See Murray, "The Amygdala, Reward and Emotion."

[10] Menon and Levitin, "The Rewards of Music Listening."

that chills did not occur in a reflex-like manner, but instead correlated precisely with structural musical elements built into the score by the composer, with the conclusion that "strong emotions in response to music" are "a result of attentive, experienced, and conscious musical enjoyment."[11] The second article by Grewe as chief author correlates chills with such particular moments as the "violation of expectancies or beginning of something new," "the entry of a solo voice," and "special qualities in loudness."[12] As a result, the article concludes that "it is not so much the distinct musical feature, but the focus of attention on the music that is important for arousing chills." What helps focus attention is the "emotional communication system" within which listeners participate; this communication system, moreover, includes such features as listeners' familiarity with the style of a particular piece or their consciousness of "the feelings of the people we hear playing." Only rarely, according to this article, are chills aroused directly without the mediation of this communicative system: as an example of direct mediation, it cites the sudden fortissimo in Bach's *St. Matthew Passion* when the chorus screams the name of Barabbas.

What significance might these studies have for opera? After all, though occasionally an operatic aria may have shown up in one of the pieces selected by a research subject, or by researchers themselves, these experiments measure the responses of listeners to short selections of mainly non-operatic music, and sometimes even popular music. Yet they also tell much about the type of experience we have with any sort of music: that music affords satisfactions not different in kind from other, less prestigious stimuli that give us rewards; that the "highs" that listeners experience vary in length and intensity in the course of even a short piece; that familiarity with a particular piece or style affects the degree of satisfaction that listeners feel; that listeners are affected in distinct ways by different musical

---

[11] Grewe *et al.*, "How Does Music Arouse 'Chills'?" Quotation is on p. 448.
[12] Grewe *et al.*, "Listening to Music as a Re-Creative Process." Quotations are on pp. 312 and 313.

styles; that the social situation within which music is consumed helps shape listeners' responses; and that great composers, certainly without the help of recent scientific explanations, have always known where in the brain to aim their musical weapons.

Indeed, one can show how every particular style of opera developed its own means of creating and sustaining excitement among its listeners. Take, for instance, the style of *opera seria* during the eighteenth century. Any *opera seria* is predictably organized as a succession of intense individual arias and occasional duets, with at most only a few choral passages, all separated by long stretches of recitative in which the plot is narrated and enacted. Nobody expected to be rewarded with chills during the recitative, above all in those without orchestral accompaniment; indeed, as mentioned earlier, these stretches gave the patrons of opera-house boxes, within which much of the social life of eighteenth-century Italy took place, an opportunity to relax. Only in the aria and duet did listeners give the music their serious attention. The three sections of an *opera-seria* aria – or five sections, if one includes the repetitions within the first and the *da capo* sections – offered an opportunity for varying degrees of attention and excitement. The first section, often preceded by a long *ritornello* that we hear at predictable moments in the course of the piece, offers the initial excitement, but listeners are fully aware that this excitement will be heightened considerably in the final *da capo* section, in which the singer's capacity for elaborate ornamentation of the first section's musical material will be put to the test. And in between these is a middle section, usually in a different tempo, that will vary the emotional situation portrayed and communicated in the first section and, in effect, raise anticipations for whatever vocal pyrotechnics we await in the *da capo*.[13] From the point of view of the listener's emotional experience, an *opera seria* shares much of the structure of Poe's long poem: a series of intense lyrics, namely, its arias,

---

[13] For a vivid analysis of how the alternation of orchestral *ritornello* and solo singer create a "stimulus-response exchange between music-makers and listeners," see Feldman, *Opera and Sovereignty*, pp. 51–56. Quotation is on p. 51.

separated by long passages which, to the extent that listeners seek chills, would scarcely be deemed music.

Or take the two-section aria that dominated Italian nineteenth-century opera from Rossini to Verdi. Throughout the ordinarily slower first section, the listener is aware that the aria will culminate in a rousing cabaletta, designed to please singers who themselves seek to please the crowd with vocal tricks and, above all, with high notes that put these singers to the test. The two sections of the aria are separated by a recitative section, the so-called *tempo di mezzo* – sometimes with the singer in dialogue with another character – that sets the groundwork for the cabaletta about to come. If the first section poses an emotional dilemma, the cabaletta creates a resolution – both psychologically and musically – to this dilemma.

The excitement that audiences can experience in the transition from the first section to the cabaletta may gain some illumination from a paper investigating the crucial role of pauses within musical structures. A team headed by Devarajan Sridharan studied brain activations that occurred in the transitions between movements in symphonies by the eighteenth-century composer William Boyce.[14] These activations reached their peak as one movement was coming to a close and the next one was about to begin. "Movement transitions," as the authors put it, "are an important component of the natural music listening experience."[15] As the brain images reproduced in the article show, the activation is primarily on the right side of the brain, where music is generally lateralized.[16] Moreover, two distinct networks within the brain were activated during the transitions: before the pause between movements, according to this study, activation was concentrated in the ventral fronto-temporal network, but after the pause it took place in the dorsal fronto-parietal network. The latter, the authors state, "presumably performs a perceptual update of the transition in working memory."[17] The anticipation of an event and its ultimate assimilation are at once

---

[14] Sridharan *et al.*, "Neural Dynamics of Event Segmentation in Music."
[15] *Ibid.*, p. 528.   [16] *Ibid.*, p. 524.   [17] *Ibid.*, p. 530.

high points and also distinct moments in the way we hear music. As the authors put it, "Prediction and anticipation are truly at the heart of the musical experience."[18] Thus, in listening to a Verdi aria, we often experience heightened excitement as the first section draws to a close. Even the recitative of the *tempo di mezzo*, though it may not be of great musical interest in its own right, works to raise our feelings of anticipation for the oncoming cabaletta. As mentioned in Essay 1, we know from Verdi's letters that, in the course of his career, he grew increasingly embarrassed about the need to end his arias with cabalettas. Yet audiences, not to speak of singers, knew precisely where operatic excitement was to be found. An analogous excitement can be found in the transitions of the *opera-seria* aria. The orchestral *ritornello* that ends the first part of the aria and then returns at the start of the *da capo* raises feelings of anticipation for the vocal feats to be expected in this final section.

Wagnerian music-drama sought to even out the alternating highs and lows that characterized earlier opera. By creating what he called "infinite melody," Wagner intended to spread musical excitement across a whole lengthy work. Yet as every operagoer (except for the most avid Wagnerian) knows, there are stretches in Wagner – for example, Wotan's long narrative in the middle of the second act of *Die Walküre* – that offer considerably fewer musical thrills than others. To be sure, Wagner was often able to keep our musical brains in a heightened state for a goodly while – in my own experience, during the first acts of *Die Walküre* and *Tristan und Isolde*, in the former from Hunding's exit, in the latter from Isolde's narrative, to the end of each act. Wagner's organizing principle, the leitmotif, generally marks the high points. Varied as it is in its reappearances both in instrumentation and rhythm, the leitmotif, even in Wotan's narrative, works to remind us of thrilling earlier moments when it appeared, and to anticipate still later, hopefully even more thrilling, reappearances.

[18] *Ibid.*, p. 529.

It is clear that familiarity with an opera makes it more pleasing than it likely was at first hearing. Yet this is distinctly not the case with spoken drama: the same audiences who may be eager to see some new play that they know only from a newspaper review or by word of mouth ordinarily want the operas they attend to be thoroughly familiar. As a result, opera companies are more than generous with the *Carmen*s and *Tosca*s they offer, but stingy with the *Jenůfa*s, the *Lulu*s, and the *Poppea*s. The reader may object that for most of operatic history – certainly until the mid to late nineteenth century – impresarios offered mainly new fare. Yet earlier audiences were thoroughly familiar with the styles of the new operas, whether that of Monteverdi and Cavalli, or of Handel or Hasse, that they regularly heard. To cite a term used earlier, these audiences shared a common "emotional communication system."[19] Only a single style predominated at any one time in a particular national tradition; if you heard a new *opera-seria* aria in an unfamiliar opera, you still were familiar with the conventions governing the aria, and you could also get a special pleasure from whatever unexpected variations the composer (or, just as important, the improvising singer) gave to a particular type of aria.

To sustain musical excitement throughout a long work such as an opera, composers have found ways of varying the moods they seek to arouse. Behind *opera seria*, for example, there stands a theory of musical affect, by means of which a character expresses a particular emotional stance in each aria. Audiences easily recognized the difference, say, between a lament (Almirena's "Lascia ch'io pianga" from Handel's *Rinaldo*), a statement of constancy (Fiordiligi's "Come scoglio," Mozart's parody, from *Così fan tutte*, of an *opera-seria* constancy aria), or a demand for revenge (the title character's "Al lampo dell' armi" from *Giulio Cesare*). Wagner's leitmotifs also represent a variety of emotional stances, which vary, for instance, between Sieglinde's ecstatic cry, "O hehrste Liebe!" (later to become the misnamed "redemption through love" motif that concludes the

---

[19] Grewe *et al.*, "Listening to Music as a Re-Creative Process," p. 313.

Ring), the frightening potion motif in *Tristan*, and the plaintive *cor anglais* theme of the shepherd reminding the dying Tristan that Isolde's ship is not yet on the horizon.

The large variety of such musical stances has been reduced to two and to three by recent studies in neuroscience. A team headed by Martina T. Mitterschiffthaler used short pieces or excerpts of classical music that they classified as either "happy," "sad," or "neutral" to determine which sections of the brain could be activated by each.[20] Happy pieces included jaunty selections such as the Toreador Song from *Carmen* and the Blue Danube Waltz; sad, such conspicuously mournful selections as Max Bruch's "Kol Nidrei" and Solveig's song from *Peer Gynt*, while the term "neutral" was attached, among other pieces, to Debussy's "Clair de Lune" and the first-act prelude to *La traviata*. Although one might object that no piece of music is in itself emotionally neutral, the purpose of this division was to compare the effects on subjects of happy and sad pieces, respectively, to those of so-called neutral ones. The resulting study showed distinctly different sites of activiation for the happy and sad music. Whereas the former affected reward areas such as the ventral striatum, the latter evoked responses, as the researchers had surmised in advance, in the right-sided hippocampus/amygdala region among others, which, as they put it, is characteristic of mood disorders when "the amygdala [is] in a resting state, as well as during cognitive or affective challenges."[21] The pieces the group called neutral activated still other parts of the brain, the superior temporal gyrus and the insula. One wonders if the many other emotional stances used regularly in *opera seria* might be reflected individually in different areas of the brain.

It might be objected that one's definitions of what constitutes happy or sad or any particular emotion is too culturally restricted to tell us much about how the brain processes music. Yet a study has been published that shows two culturally unrelated groups in essential agreement on the emotional effects of music. A team headed by

[20] Mitterschiffthaler *et al.*, "A Functional MRI Study."   [21] *Ibid.*, p. 1158.

Thomas Fritz has demonstrated that Western listeners and also a culturally isolated group, the Mafa, who live in a remote, mountainous region in the northern part of Cameroon, were able to recognize the differences between happy, sad, and what the investigators name "scared/fearful" music.[22] The last-named consisted of what they call "spectrally manipulated" music, in which "three versions of the original excerpt were simultaneously audible in different keys."[23] Western and Mafa listeners were each able to recognize the differences between these three emotional effects in one another's music at what the investigators called "above chance level."[24] And both groups much preferred the consonant to the dissonant music. The cultural universal that this paper asserts is analogous, the authors claim, to earlier work showing a "largely universal recognition of human emotional facial expression."[25]

An earlier fMRI study by Stefan Koelsch and a team contrasted only two types of music, consonant, which they dubbed "pleasant," and dissonant, for which they did not employ actually composed music but, as with the previously cited study, scrambled samples of consonant music.[26] The consonant selections consisted of "joyful, instrumental dance-tunes"[27] – no "sad" music – with the result that this experiment made possible a stark contrast between what participants could find pleasing and uncomfortable. As in other studies, the dissonant music demonstrated activation in the amygdala as well as in such other, closely connected areas as the hippocampus and the parahippocampal gyri. The pleasant selections activated the ventral striatum and the anterior superior insula, among other areas. In another paper, a review by Koelsch of various studies on music and emotion, the author speculates that the activation of the amygdala during dissonant music may be due not to the generation of fear but rather may "reflect a mechanism activated to prevent the hippocampus from traumatization during the exposure to

---

[22] Fritz *et al.*, "Universal Recognition of Three Basic Emotions."
[23] *Ibid.*, p. 574.   [24] *Ibid.*, pp. 573 and 575.   [25] *Ibid.*, p. 575.
[26] Koelsch *et al.*, "Investigating Emotion with Music."   [27] *Ibid.*, p. 240.

potentially harmful stimuli."[28] One might ask at this point what results might be obtained if researchers, instead of employing electronically manipulated music to test the effects of dissonance (as in fact all the studies cited in this essay do), used such well-known non-tonal works as Berg's *Three Pieces for Orchestra* and Schoenberg's *Variations for Orchestra*; it may well be that subjects unaccustomed to difficult modern music would still have balked, while aficionados might have recorded an engaged and perhaps even "pleasant" reaction.

The 2006 paper by Koelsch and his team also discusses two phenomena that had not been noted in earlier studies. The first of these is the activation, during the pleasant, but not during the dissonant, music, of a particular area, the Rolandic operculum, that suggests movement in the larynx. In this paper the authors speculate that this movement may well be the result of mirror neurons[29] – a phenomenon first described scarcely a decade before – in which the subject's body mimics gestures it is observing in others.[30] Could it be, one might ask, that when we listen to music, whether instrumental, as in the Koelsch experiment, or vocal as well, we are unconsciously singing along? Everybody her (or his) own Callas!

The second phenomenon observed in this experiment is the fact that, in the course of listening to selections, activations increased over time both for the pleasant and unpleasant music.[31] Can this mean that when we hear longer musical works such as operas and oratorios, not to speak of long symphonies like those of Bruckner or Mahler, the intensity of our experience grows significantly during the period that we are engaged? And can this also mean that the recent tendency of opera companies to decrease the number of intermissions (*Il trovatore* or *La Bohème*, for instance, in two rather than four acts) not only saves

---

[28] Koelsch, "Investigating Emotion with Music: Neuroscientific Approaches." This quotation is on p. 416.

[29] Koelsch *et al.*, p. 247.

[30] See Rizzolatti *et al.*, "Resonance Behaviors and Mirror Neurons."

[31] Koelsch *et al.*, p. 248.

money in reducing personnel time (the presumed reason for this development) but also gives ticket holders a bonus in chills? And did not those chilling one-acters of the early twentieth century – *Salome, Elektra, Bluebeard's Castle, Erwartung, Eine florentinische Tragödie* – demonstrate a knowing sense, on the part of their composers, of how to manipulate the operagoer's brain?

A number of other studies have addressed themselves to the effects of music over time. A book-length investigation by Jerrold Levinson entitled *Music in the Moment* argued that, unlike literary narrative, for which we retain a memory of earlier incidents as we read, music is experienced only from moment to moment, and that only informed listeners such as trained musicians listen for structural elements.[32] Levinson grants some exceptions, for instance, Brahms's repetition, at the end of his Third Symphony, of the work's opening theme. By that standard, I might add, every Wagnerian music-drama opens the gates of remembrance because of the obvious repetition of leitmotifs. For Levinson, there is no Pateresque expansion of the individual moment, merely a succession of moments, as when, citing the first prelude from Book II of the *Well-Tempered Clavier*, he claims that we experience "only an absorption in the unfolding of each measure out of the preceding one, in the development, moment to moment, of each strand in the contrapuntal fabric."[33]

Although Levinson is a specialist in aesthetics, his thesis receives at least partial validation from an experiment led by Emmanuel Bigand demonstrating that listeners experience an emotional effect from the very first note of a piece.[34] Another study, by specialists in psychology and in music theory, of how we experience music in time contrasts the way it affects us from moment to moment with the way we afterwards remember it.[35] Testing their subjects with a number of mainly instrumental classical compositions, they find a considerable gap between these subjects' recorded reactions while

---

[32] Levinson, *Music in the Moment.*   [33] *Ibid.,* p. 88.

[34] Bigand, Filipic, and Lalitte, "The Time Course of Emotional Responses to Music."

[35] A. Rozin, P. Rozin, and Goldberg, "The Feeling of Music Past."

hearing each piece and their later memory of these reactions. "Listeners derive remembered experience primarily from the most intense moments of on-line experience," the authors claim; "the least intense moments . . . contribute relatively little to affective memory."[36] This study also postulates what it calls a "slope effect,"[37] defined as the tendency of composers to vary peak moments with passages of lower intensity and also to end a piece on an intense moment. "Without low points to provide contrast," they add, "high points would not pack the remembered punch that they otherwise would."[38] From the results of this study it would seem that Pater's desire to sustain peaks of intensity does not really work within the real world of art, at least not within music and other temporal arts, though the memories of our experience that we carry give us the illusion that the peak moments are the whole of this experience.

Thus far I have spoken of musical experience without reference to the role of language in vocal compositions. The studies I have used have been based largely on instrumental music, with only occasional selections drawn from vocal works, for example, the Toreador Song and the Lacrymosa from Mozart's *Requiem*. But opera, with which this essay and this book are centrally concerned, is a verbal as much as a musical art form. The tag "prima le parole e dopo la musica" has been a key issue within theories of opera since the form's beginnings, with influential statements to be found, above all, in the writings of Monteverdi, Gluck, and Wagner;[39] indeed, the question of whether words or music are primary within opera is the idea around which one of the more notable operas of the mid twentieth century, Strauss's *Capriccio*, revolves.

Recent brain research has demonstrated, as one article puts it, that "the linguistic and melodic components of songs are processed in interaction."[40] Since music is processed on the right side of the brain,

---

[36] *Ibid.*, p. 27.   [37] *Ibid.*, pp. 27–37.   [38] *Ibid.*, p. 37.
[39] See my discussion of these statements in *Opera: The Extravagant Art*, pp. 108–13.
[40] Schön, Gordon, and Besson, "Musical and Linguistic Processing." This quotation is on p. 79.

and language on the left, one might wonder if one side would dominate in song. The answer given by Daniele Schön and her group is not only that "phonological/lexical processing and pitch processing cannot be processed independently"[41] but that the right, or musical side, of the brain is dominant. When subjects were asked to pay particular attention to the linguistic component of a song, the language processing remained largely bilateral, but when they concentrated more on the music than on the text, the melodic processing was right lateralized.[42] To the extent that neural pathways favor the right side in song, one can proclaim "prima la musica" in opera, though of course the listener's actual experience of the finished musical product is unrelated to whatever primacy a composer or librettist may claim for either text or music.

Another experiment, conducted by two of the three researchers guiding the preceding experiment, showed that in one sense words and music are still processed independently, with words being processed faster, and thus earlier, than music.[43] Subjects were given excerpts from two nineteenth-century French operas, *Les Huguenots* and *Faust*, with each excerpt performed *a cappella* by a female singer, and with the final word of the excerpt sung in four different ways: (1) undistorted in either word or music; (2) the final word distorted but sung in tune; (3) the final word undistorted but sung out of tune; (4) both word and music distorted. In the last-named of these situations, the rapidity with which words were processed became especially clear.[44] In certain respects, then, one can still voice the formula "prima le parole." And one may also wonder if the ubiquity of supertitles in opera during the last two decades may affect the listener's experience, with the language areas of the brain gaining

---

[41] *Ibid.*, p. 78.

[42] Reviewing a number of scientific papers on brain lateralization, Irving Massey has concluded that "music invests [words] with a new quality. They assume the particular meaning conferred on them by the music." See Massey, *The Neural Imagination*, p. 128.

[43] Besson and Schön, "Comparison between Language and Music."

[44] *Ibid.*, p. 281.

primacy over the musical areas; if this should indeed be the case, those who object to supertitles on musical grounds can surely feel themselves vindicated.

The music theorist Fred Lerdahl has expressed some skepticism as to whether we can properly distinguish between language and music areas.[45] After a lengthy analysis of Robert Frost's poem "Nothing Gold Can Stay" as though it were a musical work, Lerdahl concludes that our mental representations of sounds, whether in poetry or music, "share a good deal more organization than has usually been supposed."[46] He goes on to predict that research will demonstrate the presence of "brain modules" that "process rhythm, contour, and timbral relationships" and that these modules "are the same in music and language while those that process purely pitch structures and purely linguistic structures occupy different parts of the brain."[47]

The relation of words and music may also differ according to the language being set. Aniruddh D. Patel, in a book surveying cognitive and neuroscientific studies of music and language, quotes an exchange between Richard Strauss and Romain Rolland on the considerable differences between setting German and French. Whereas Strauss insists on the composer's need to retain speech accent, Rolland asserts that in French "for a very large number of words, accentuation is variable, – never arbitrary, but in accordance with logical or psychological reasons."[48] Experienced operagoers, even if they do not understand these languages, would recognize the difference in effect between these languages when they are enunciated in music.

In another passage of his book, Patel cites an experiment done in Israel, where Wagner is not performed, to learn to what degree subjects can identify the semantic meaning of nine leitmotifs drawn from *Der Ring des Nibelungen*. The subjects were told to pretend that each leitmotif was a musical theme in a film and then to give the film a name. Only the love and death motifs were guessed correctly, but

---

[45] Lerdahl, "The Sounds of Poetry Viewed as Music."   [46] *Ibid.*, p. 426.
[47] *Ibid.*   [48] Quoted in Patel, *Music, Language, and the Brain*, p. 158.

Patel also reports "a remarkable amount of consistency for each leitmotiv."[49] One might object that even though the testing was done deliberately on subjects who would not have had access to Wagner in public performances, at least some of these subjects would have been familiar with the music and its supposed meanings by means of recordings.

Beyond whatever statements one can make about how listeners experience music separately from or together with the words it is setting, one must also consider the ways that the visual dimension of opera is tied to the musical experience. Anybody watching the *Ring* even without previous instruction about the plot would likely be able to identify such leitmotifs as the magic fire and the sword theme – at least when they first appear in visual form. But I know of no studies of opera that have put these matters to a test. There is, however, a study of the minuet movement from a Balanchine ballet, *Divertimento No. 15*, based on Mozart's music of that name.[50] The experimenters divided their subjects into three groups, one of which witnessed a video of the ballet without the music; a second heard the music without seeing the ballet; and a third experienced both the video and the music. Subjects were asked to note transitions to new sections and moments of tension and emotion. The results showed a high degree of correspondence among all three groups. Krumhansl and Schenck attribute this correspondence to the fact that Balanchine was notable for his attempt to tie music and choreography closely together. They admit that they would likely not attain a similar correspondence between music and dance with a choreographer such as Merce Cunningham, who "was known for creating marked oppositions between the two components."[51]

Concentrating on transitions and emotional high points renders only limited information about how music is integrated with visual elements. To speak anecdotally, whenever I hear an unfamiliar opera

---

[49] *Ibid.*, p. 329.
[50] Krumhansl and Schenck, "Can Dance Reflect the Structural and Expressive Qualities of Music?"
[51] *Ibid.*, p. 79.

on the radio and am unable (as I usually am) to make out most of the words, I should have a difficult time guessing what it is about, though I should likely know pretty quickly whether it is comic or tragic. Whatever emotional effect the music has on me would not be tied to specific content, though if I hear a non-musical sound such as a gun shot or a scream I would quickly be able to postulate some dramatic content (whether or not I am guessing correctly) in my mind. My ability to construct what is going on in the opera would likely be no more accurate than that of the Israeli subjects asked to guess the meaning of leitmotifs from the *Ring*.

The power of visual content to influence the emotional effect of music was explored in an experiment by a team led by Eran Eldar.[52] Subjects were shown film clips that the experimenters deemed of "neutral" emotional content. These clips were combined with both music they called neutral and with music of an emotionally "negative" character. Imaging with the fMRI showed activation of the amygdala and the anterior hippocampus when the negative music was combined with the film clips, but *not* when the music or the clips were experienced alone. As a result, the study concludes "that the brain exerts a preferential response to emotional stimuli when these are associated with concrete content."[53] This study suggests how powerfully music can manipulate one's emotional responses not only to a film, but also to any visual performance, whether an opera or a spoken drama.

It remains to be demonstrated empirically to what degree attending an opera differs from simply hearing the opera without visual cues. Much of one's knowledge of opera in our own time comes from simply listening to the music on recordings or on the radio. Yet the visual effect of different performances of the same work, whether conveyed live or electronically, can affect the way that listeners respond. At least such is the result of an experiment led by Bradley W. Vines on the effects of two clarinetists playing the

---

[52] Eldar *et al.*, "Feeling the Real World."   [53] *Ibid.*, p. 2835.

same pieces.[54] One clarinetist was visibly expressive, the other not. Both played the same pieces by Stravinsky and Poulenc. Although the musical performances could not be identical, the considerable differences in body movement between the two performers manifestly affected the subjects' responses. As the investigators conclude, "*Paralinguistic gestures* (such as head movements, eyebrow raising, and postural adjustments) convey a significant amount of information that reinforces, anticipates, or augments the auditory signal."[55]

In this study, participants had simply reported their reactions on a mechanical slider; a follow-up study attempted to replicate the results with electrodermal measurements.[56] A new group of subjects watched and/or heard the same clarinet performances. The two studies correlated most significantly among those who experienced both the audio and the visual performances. As the authors of this follow-up conclude, "The auditory signal that we so closely associate with music is in a physical gesture that has a visual counterpart." They go on to observe that in the early stages of primate evolution "seeing and hearing one another were part of the same event." The "visual dimension," they continue, "conveys important information about [a] musician's intention and interacts with the sound for the overall arousal state of the listener."[57]

Still another experiment on the relation of visual and auditory information has shown that even without hearing the notes listeners can identify changes of pitch from a singer's facial expressions (especially in the mouth and on the eyebrows) and head movement.[58] Subjects watching but not hearing three different female vocalists correctly judged pitch changes to a significantly high degree.

Every experienced operagoer is aware of the ability of individual singers to manipulate the emotions of listeners in their own way.

[54] Vines *et al.*, "Cross-Modal Interactions."
[55] *Ibid.*, p. 107 – italics the authors'.
[56] Chapados and Levitin, "Cross-Modal Interactions: Physiological Correlates."
[57] *Ibid.*, p. 646.   [58] Thompson and Russu, "Facing the Music."

A Maria Callas could often get away with poor singing through the power of her bodily presence. I myself heard a live broadcast of Act I of *La traviata* in London in June, 1958, together with two professional musicians, who winced in pain at her intonation and finally turned off the radio; next day, however, she got rave reviews in the press, though a few days later a distinguished senior music critic publicly chided his colleagues for ignoring musical values in favor of histrionic ones. By the same token, the distinguished singing of a Montserrat Caballé could be underestimated because what she offered visually, both in the size and the movements of her body, did not readily set her audience's emotions on fire.

The ability of visual matter to add to the emotional effect of opera goes well beyond the gestures and presence of individual singers. Since its beginnings, opera has cultivated elaborate settings, sometimes – as in the Venetian public theaters – at the expense of the orchestra, which remained minimal in size. Handel mounted fancy machines in his operas on magic themes. French grand opera of the 1830s sought to recapture the grandeur of the historical moments it was setting through sound effects and visual splendor. With the opening of his new festival house in Bayreuth in 1876, Wagner endowed his mythical stories with realistic settings, within which Rhinemaidens simulated swimming by means of wires and a dragon reared its ugly head before the hero could deflate it with his enchanted sword. And today the latest electronic gadgets available to stage directors for what we call "special effects" are providing a new lift for patrons in need of prodding to maintain their emotional highs among all-too-familiar operas.

Spectacle, in short, has served opera throughout its history to fill in where the music leaves off. Relatively few composers – Monteverdi, Handel, Gluck, Mozart, Beethoven, Rossini, Berlioz, Wagner, Verdi, Bizet, Puccini, plus a handful of moderns – have been able to sustain music of great communicative power throughout a work. And within the oeuvres of these composers certain works are more successfully sustained than others. It has been the task of singers, scenic designers and, in more modern times, conductors as well, to keep the arousal going for a full evening's fare.

Beyond the excitement afforded by scenic arrangements, the interest in plot and character that opera shares with fiction and spoken drama creates a continuity that can extend a viewer's tensions across a whole longer work. Yet the suspense of how a plot will play itself out, or how a character's fate may move us, is rarely as strong in an opera as it is in a play of comparable length. Operas are characteristically full of musical distractions – for example, orchestral and dance interludes, ceremonial scenes, arias that, whatever musical chills they may incite, encourage the singer to concentrate on sound at the expense of keeping the plot moving along – that interrupt the dramatic action in a way that spoken drama would not tolerate. The rules that forced an extraordinary tightness of plot in seventeenth-century French tragedy were considerably relaxed when these works were turned into opera: witness, for instance, the difference between the lean plotting of Racine's *Phèdre* and the looseness of Rameau's *Hippolyte et Aricie*.[59] Few operas could meet Aristotle's demand, in the *Poetics*, that plot must convey an illusion of probability and inevitability. Indeed, when one goes to the opera, one is rarely as curious about the work's outcome as one is with a spoken play; not only do operagoers find the synopsis in their programs, but the music, even in unfamiliar operas, serves to distract them from the intricacies of plot. Even Strauss's *Salome*, as tense and taut as opera ever gets, is interrupted to allow the audience to luxuriate in the orientalizing strains of The Dance of the Seven Veils.

Similarly, the empathy we are expected to feel for the plight of key characters in novels and plays does not play as central a role in opera as it does in non-musical forms.[60] In most periods of its history, opera presents us with characters who seem more mythical

---

[59] For a searching study of how the rules and practices of tragedy differ from those of *tragédie-lyrique*, see Kintzler, *Poétique de l'opéra français*.

[60] For an application of cognitive science to empathy in narrative fiction, see Keen, "A Theory of Narrative Empathy."

than real, considerably larger than life. It may well be that this mythical status is simply a consequence of the fact that they present themselves singing against a loud orchestra. Moreover, until the late nineteenth century the *dramatis personae* of non-comic opera generally consisted either of lofty historical figures or of characters drawn from traditional myths. Although we may feel powerfully moved by the music associated with particular operatic characters, we rarely grant these characters themselves much in the way of empathy. To the extent that opera constitutes a form of romance – to apply Northrop Frye's remark cited in Essay 3 – one should not expect empathy to function in opera any more than it does in literary romances such as *The Faerie Queene* or Gothic novels.

During the *verismo* period, to be sure, composers went out of their way to engage the sympathies of viewers for their distraught heroines. Even the most routine performances of *La Bohème* and *Madama Butterfly* set off conspicuous outbursts of tears as spectators witness the heroines' deaths. During other periods, a few characters have elicited audiences' empathy to an uncommon degree. One thinks, for instance, of Beethoven's Leonore and Florestan, who, as characters in a *Singspiel*, also function as characters in a spoken drama. One thinks as well of Wagner's Sieglinde, or of Brünnhilde and Wotan in the final act of *Die Walküre*, though distinctly not when the latter two re-appear in later portions of the *Ring*. And certainly some of Verdi's wronged fathers – notably Rigoletto, Simon Boccanegra, and Fiesco – manage to engage their audiences' empathy. At another extreme, the characters peopling *opera seria* are little more than a mosaic of the various affects defining their arias; to create a full characterization, if not necessarily to gain empathy, they demand a powerful singing actor as well as an imaginative stage director.

Is opera necessarily unique among longer musical forms in its ability to sustain emotional excitement for its consumers? Certainly the scenic dimension plays a central role in focusing and heightening their attention. But Handel's oratorios managed to hold audiences even without scenic embodiment – though today, of course, a number of these oratorios are being staged in the opera house.

One might add that, just as the expressive gestures of a clarinetist in the experiment I cited earlier added to listeners' excitement, so the visual presence of singers, orchestra, a large chorus, and, not least, an athletically engaged conductor, itself creates its own scenic embodiment. Similarly, the nineteenth-century symphony, beginning with Beethoven's Eroica, raised the emotional stakes for concert audiences, steadily increasing in length and in orchestra size, with the climactic moments, quite in contrast with the eighteenth-century symphony, held back until the final movement. Vocal-choral symphonies such as Mahler's Second and Eighth, not to speak of his early cantata, *Das klagende Lied*, offer much of the sound and the intensity of opera, though of course without stage representation.

It may well be that the emotional satisfactions experienced within the opera house were also possible within those extended performances designed over the centuries for sites of worship. The two great Bach passions, when performed on Good Friday in Leipzig's St. Thomas Church as part of the standard rituals, likely exerted a power over the local worshippers akin to the more secular pleasures of opera. Yet the chaste accoutrements of a Lutheran church could scarcely compare with the altogether more operatic milieu within which the mass had been celebrated for many centuries. The Catholic church, after all, knew how to integrate sight and sound long before opera impresarios learned their tricks.

Much earlier, that proto-*Gesamtkunstwerk* we call Greek tragedy brought together verbal text, scenic spectacle, dance movement, and a music whose actual sound and whose power to penetrate individuals we shall likely never know. In the foundation text of literary criticism, Aristotle described how the more cunning dramatists managed to awaken audience empathy with a striking blow in the gut, which, from recent inquiries in neuroscience, we now know actually took place in the brain.

6 | From separatism to union: aesthetic theorizing from Reynolds to Wagner

Consider the following statements, written within less than a decade of one another:

> I believe it may be considered as a general rule, that no Art can be engrafted with success on another art. For though they all profess the same origin, and to proceed from the same stock, yet each has its own peculiar modes both of imitating nature, and of deviating from it, each for the accomplishment of its own particular purpose. These deviations, more especially, will not bear transplantation to another soil.[1]

> It is a necessary and natural consequence of their perfection that, without any shifting of their objective boundaries, the different art forms are becoming increasingly similar to one another *in their effect on the mind* [*Gemüt*]. Music in its highest ennoblement must become form and move us with the quiet power of antiquity; plastic art in its highest perfection must become music and move us by means of its direct sensuous presence; poetry in its most perfect development must, like music, grip us powerfully but at the same time, like sculpture, surround us with quiet clarity. The perfect style belonging to each of the various art forms is shown in its ability to eliminate their specific limits without giving up their specific advantages.[2]

Each of these statements emanates from a figure who is at once a major theorist of art and a practitioner whose work retains its classical status today. Yet no two statements could be less alike in the circumstances under which they were voiced or in the roles we assign them within intellectual history. Sir Joshua Reynolds's warning to keep the various forms independent of one another was delivered in his capacity as president of the Royal Academy,

---

[1] Reynolds, *Discourses on Art*, p. 240.
[2] Schiller, *Über die ästhetische Erziehung des Menschen*, pp. 640–41.

and its recipients were art students assembled in 1786 for the annual distribution of prizes. Friedrich Schiller's words were written in the private study as part of a treatise in epistolary form that sought to establish a new rationale for art amid the political turmoil about which all Europe, and this author in particular, was fretting in 1793.

The first statement, like the various pronouncements about decorum and pictorialism in the annual prize-awarding addresses that make up what we call Reynolds's *Discourses*, represents an aesthetic that goes back to Renaissance humanism and that had not changed substantially in several centuries. The second statement, like many of the other observations in the *Aesthetic Letters* about the value and function of art, expresses a Utopian vision about a possible union of the arts that achieves significance for us by dint of historical hindsight, through our awareness of Wagner's notion of a *Gesamtkunstwerk* and, even more conspicuously, in our own, postmodern time, through our routine use of the term *multimedia* as a generic category. Not that the author of these prophetic words ever put them into practice: indeed, in his varying roles as philosopher, historian, dramatist, and lyric poet, Schiller observed the boundaries between genres and media as rigorously as Reynolds had done in his painting.

In fact, in a kind of "saving" clause at the start of this statement – "without any shifting of their objective boundaries" – Schiller protects his readers from any immediate threat to the traditional borderlines separating the arts. Yet the relationship between artwork and audience that emerges from this passage, unlike the one suggested by Reynolds, points to the future, for Schiller projects his union of the arts as something located, as he puts it with typographical emphases, *"in their effect on the mind."* The very title of Schiller's treatise, *On the Aesthetic Education of Man*, indicates that his is an affective theory of art concerned with the ways that consumers can experience art as a means of moral growth. Reynolds's defense of the separateness of the arts is based on the predominantly mimetic theory (note the phrase "modes of imitating nature") that dominates not only his own aesthetic but also most of the critical thought of the preceding centuries. Moreover, Schiller's repeated use of the words *perfect* and *perfection* to characterize the mission of art suggests that by the end of the eighteenth century the various arts were coming to occupy an ideal, autonomous, more privileged space transcending other forms of human activity.

The radically different ways in which the arts are related to one another in these two passages (as well as the distinctive theories of aesthetics that stand behind each statement) help confirm our contemporary notion that in numerous forms of discourse – political, economic, philosophical – the late eighteenth century constitutes a watershed in the history of western thought. This essay will center around some questions about the ways that the various arts came to be understood in relation to one another; opera will appear within this framework only as one art-form among many, but also as the one in which, through Richard Wagner's intervention, these relationships between the arts became reconfigured in a powerfully new way.

How can the move toward affective and expressive theories of art be connected with the breaking down of barriers that traditionally separated the various art forms? How can the diverse arts be said to function together as a system similar to other systems of thought? How were the arts classified and evaluated in relationship to one another? What new hierarchies emerged among the genres constituting a single art form? Was there really a move from the autonomy of individual arts to a union, as my juxtaposition of these statements may imply, or did this shift also imply a dominance of one or more arts within this supposed union?

And how is it that opera, a form that was at best peripheral within most discussions of aesthetics, became the site at which the union of the arts was to be theorized and put into practice? As a medium that, from its beginnings, drew upon a larger number of arts than any other, opera, despite the various so-called "reforms" along the way, remained a composite of diverse elements until Wagner, both in his theory and practice, attempted an integration of these elements in his new type of opera, eventually to be called music-drama and that advertised itself with that grand term *Gesamtkunstwerk*.[3]

DISPARITIES AMONG THE ARTS

Despite the traditional autonomy of the various arts that Reynolds reiterated in his *Discourses*, two media, poetry and painting, had been linked together steadily since the Renaissance.[4] This relationship was based upon what we today recognize as a misreading of Horace's dictum, in the *Art of Poetry*, that poetry is akin to painting.[5] Horace referred simply to the differing degrees of scrutiny one gave the two so-called "sister arts" according to the distance from which one viewed a painting, or to the degree of attention a particular literary or rhetorical genre demanded. For the Renaissance, however, his phrase *ut pictura poesis* provided not only a rationale for mutual imitation between the two art forms, but it also propagated what Rensselaer W. Lee has called "the theory of the learned painter,"[6] by means of which painting could lay claim to the high prestige that literature had traditionally enjoyed. It is significant that until well into the nineteenth century the most illustrious visual genre was history painting, which included not only what we label "history" today but virtually any form of public narrative, whether drawn from the Bible, mythology or political history. "Je suis peintre d'histoire, je ne suis pas portraitiste," Ingres protested during the early years of the nineteenth century when a prospective sitter asked to see "M. Ingres le portraitiste."[7] "The great work of the painter is

---

[3] What Wagner actually meant by the terms *music-drama* and *Gesamtkunstwerk* – as well as their relation to the term *opera* – has been a matter of argument over a long period of time. For a fine recent attempt to elucidate these terms and place them in historical context, see Goehr, "From Opera to Music Drama."

[4] For a classic account of the relations between poetry and painting from antiquity through the eighteenth century, see Hagstrum, *The Sister Arts*.

[5] For a convincing demonstration of what Horace actually meant in the passage, see Trimpi, "The Meaning of Horace's *ut pictura poesis*."

[6] See Lee, *Ut Pictura Poesis*, pp. 41–48.

[7] See Friedlander, *David to Delacroix*, p. 80.

the 'historia'," Leon Battista Alberti had written in 1435 in his influential treatise *On Painting*, adding that the function of "literary men" [*litterati*] was to "assist in preparing the composition of a 'historia'."[8] From the Renaissance onward, painting thus became a highly textualized art dependent upon literary precedents.

The sisterhood claimed by poetry and painting did not exist for poetry and music, even though the latter two were sometimes linked in ancient Greece.[9] As long as both poetry and painting were treated as imitative arts that represented actions or objects in the external world, they shared a common aim with one another. Music was treated as an imitative art only to the extent that composers sought sounds reflecting the words of a poem they were setting; otherwise, discussions of music concerned themselves with the effects that music could exert upon its listeners. The relative prestige of literature is revealed by the fact that at the inception and reformation of opera such major composers as Monteverdi and Gluck both insisted on the primacy of poetry over music.

The disparities evident between literature and the other arts on a theoretical level also manifest themselves on the social scale. For most of Western history, practitioners of the visual and aural arts counted as craftspeople. A large number of painters and musicians were themselves the children of practitioners who taught them their own crafts, or came from backgrounds too modest to assure them the degree of literacy – often including years spent studying classical languages – demanded of those who would call themselves poets. The disparity between music and poetry, even as late as the eighteenth century, was especially strong. Whereas Bach, Mozart, Beethoven, and Rossini were all sons of musicians, Handel the son of a barber-surgeon, Haydn of a wheelwright, and Gluck of a forester, writers ordinarily came from more socially elevated backgrounds or practiced occupations demanding a high degree of literacy: Voltaire's father, for instance, was a notary; Johnson's, a bookseller; Wordsworth's, a legal

---

[8] Alberti, *On Painting and on Sculpture*, pp. 71, 95, respectively.
[9] See Hagstrum, *The Sister Arts*, pp. 8–9.

agent for a landowner, Goethe's, a prominent official with the rank of "imperial counselor." Even the exceptions, when examined closely, affirm the relatively higher status of those calling themselves writer. Thus, as the orphaned and haphazardly educated son of a watchmaker, Rousseau made his role of outsider within the literary world central to his persona; indeed, early in his career, as Essay 9 will discuss in more detail, the public acknowledged him more readily as the composer of the opera *Le Devin du village* than as the writer of a provocative and ultimately far more influential text on the deleterious effects of civilization. If Sir Joshua Reynolds, as the son of a clergyman-schoolmaster, came from a more literate background than did painters such as Gainsborough and David, both of whom were sons of cloth merchants, this fact also helps explain the respect he commanded as a man of letters.

The disparity between literature and the other arts is evident as well in the relative success with which writing was transmitted over the ages. How much, after all, would we know of classical antiquity if its literary remains, fragmentary though they may be, had not come down to us? The music of antiquity has never been adequately reconstructed; the buildings, with rare exceptions, are in ruins; all but a few works of the legendary Greek sculptors are known only by later copies. Moreover, whereas the writings of authors deemed of classical status were easily available to literate persons from the Renaissance onward, most famous paintings could not be viewed directly but, until the recent development of public museums, solely by means of prints. Difficulties in the transmission of musical texts, together with constant changes in performing techniques, prevented the understanding and the revival of the musical past until quite recent times. Since nobody knew what the music used in Greek drama actually sounded like, it was easy enough for the Florentine Camerata to justify that not-yet-practiced form "opera" as the successor to ancient tragedy.[10] Gregorian

---

[10] For a new interpretation, influenced at once by social theory and intellectual history, of the role played by the Camerata in the foundation of opera, see Katz, *The Powers of Music*, especially the chapter entitled "The Camerata as Invisible College," pp. 49–75.

chant, institutionalized as it was within Roman Catholic liturgy, was the only musical form to maintain its identity and its canonical status over many centuries. Individual composers were often viewed more as performers (even of their own compositions) than as creators in the manner of poets. With the exception of Palestrina, whose compositions, like Gregorian chant, were performed in church, no composer achieved long-term canonical status until the rise of a movement in late-eighteenth-century England to perpetuate the work of earlier composers, above all of Purcell and Handel.[11] When William Cowper in *The Task* celebrated Handel as "the more than Homer of his age,"[12] he signaled the beginning of an attitude that would allow a composer of the past to be revered similarly to a classical writer.

The traditional primacy of literature, together with the relative autonomy of the various arts, is manifest as well in the academic study of the arts. Literature was the first of the arts to become a subject for formal investigation in the university, for it developed during the nineteenth century from the study of the history of the individual modern languages. The national, in fact nationalist, orientation that resulted from the nineteenth-century biases within literary study established differing schemes of periodization in particular countries: for example, whereas the term *Romanticism* generally encompasses the period 1798–1824 (from *Lyrical Ballads* to the death of Byron) in England, what the French name with this term does not begin for some literary historians until 1830 (the riots occasioned by *Hernani*), while in Germany the term refers to writing between 1796 and the 1820s (the heyday of the first and second Romantic schools) and has often been used so narrowly that it could not be applied to some of the greatest authors – Goethe, Schiller, Hölderlin, Kleist – of the age.[13] And the designation "Romantic opera" generally refers to a narrow body of German works from Weber through the early

---

[11] For a detailed account of this canonization process, see William Weber, *The Rise of Musical Classics*.

[12] Cowper, *Poetical Works*, p. 233 (book VI, line 647).

[13] For a survey of classification schemes in different countries, see Wellek, "The Concept of Romanticism in Literary History," in *Concepts of Criticism*, pp. 128–98.

Wagner. Moreover, art history and music history were relatively late, and also quite separate, developments within the university, and their period classifications are as independent of one another as those among the various national literary disciplines. Art historians classify painters from the late eighteenth through mid nineteenth centuries largely according to formal criteria, for example the "classic" David, Ingres, and Canova or the "Romantic" Delacroix, Friedrich, Turner, and Constable. Musicology, whose classifications derive from the development of German music, projects a classical style from Haydn through Beethoven and a relatively late-blooming Romantic style that starts with Schubert and for some historians goes on as late as the end of the nineteenth century. And since early musicology was rooted in the German university system, it is scarcely surprising that French and Italian music, let alone the operas produced outside Germany, were long classified – and also often disparaged – according to German practices.

No departmentally based academic discipline exists for the study of the various arts in relation to one another. In recent years the discipline calling itself comparative literature has encouraged university courses and symposia, as well as the compilation of bibliographies, on the subject it names "literature and the other arts." It goes without saying that the term perpetuates the primacy that literature has enjoyed for much of history over its various sister arts. Through librettos and their literary sources, moreover, the academic study of opera has increasingly found a second home outside musicology in departments of literature.

THE ARTS AS SYSTEM: TREATISES OF AESTHETICS

Though not an independent academic discipline, that branch of philosophy known by the term *aesthetics* has, since its inception in the mid eighteenth century, dedicated itself to theorizing the nature of art and the relation of the various arts to one another. Both the term and the discourse that it generated emerged from Alexander Baumgarten's treatise in Latin, *Aesthetica* (1750–58); independently of

Baumgarten, a rich literature comparing the arts and analyzing the effects of these arts developed in Great Britain in the course of the eighteenth century.[14] Down to our own time, the treatise of aesthetics has been a recognizable and continuing genre with its own set of conventions and with later examples building selfconsciously on their predecessors. In many instances the treatise has served as a means of filling out a larger philosophical system, as it did for Schelling and Hegel. Often the title by which we know a treatise contains the term originally used by Baumgarten (Jean Paul, Solger, Hegel, Croce), or the title may simply include the term *art* (Schelling, A. W. Schlegel, Nelson Goodman) to alert us at once to its genre and to the fact that its subject matter occupies a realm distinct from that treated in other modes of discourse.

Though it is to the full-blown aesthetic treatise – complete with definitions of the nature of art, justifications for its significance, and compendia of the various media and genres that make up the aesthetic realm – that we generally refer when we speak of a thinker's philosophy of art, many texts of more limited focus have contributed to the continuing discourse. For example, Burke's *Philosophical Enquiry into the Origin of Our Ideas of the Sublime and the Beautiful* (1757), though centered upon the terms indicated by its title, quickly made its way into the new aesthetic discourse, with an application of these terms forming a major component of Kant's own aesthetic inquiry. (The latter's *Critique of Judgment* [1790], though not overtly a philosophy of art but rather, like his earlier critiques, an examination of what can properly be stated about its particular area of investigation, still contains most of the elements to be found within aesthetic treatises.) Similarly, the terms in the title of Schiller's *On Naive and Sentimental Poetry* (1795) helped shape many later systems through their usefulness in distinguishing older, more "original," "immediate" examples of art from later, more selfconscious and imitative examples.

---

[14] For a detailed analysis of some of these British thinkers, see the chapter "Sense, Sensibility, Common Sense – the British Paradigm," in Katz and HaCohen, *Tuning the Mind*, pp. 183–241. The same authors have edited an anthology of the writings they describe, entitled *The Arts in Mind*.

Shelley's *Defence of Poetry* (1821), to the extent that the term *poetry* is extended to include art in general, indeed, even to the institutions of ancient Rome,[15] could be called a miniature aesthetic treatise. Some of the most telling contributions to aesthetic discourse have taken the even more miniature form of single paragraphs and sentences, most notably the so-called fragments that members of the early German school scribbled as part of their intense, ongoing discussions on art and its relation to other modes of knowledge. For example, Novalis's brief sentence, "When one sets certain poems to music, why not set them to poetry [*Poesie*]?"[16] – a sentence I quoted for another purpose in the preceding essay – at once rethinks the relations of aesthetic forms to one another and expands the conventional definition of what constitutes poetry. Even travel guides such as Thomas West's *Guide to the Lakes* (1778), to the extent that they instruct tourists at precisely which points to station themselves in order to experience "picturesque" scenery as though it were landscape painting, participate in and advance the new discourse of aesthetics.

Within the formal and larger treatises, the various art forms and their particular genres constitute a family whose network of interrelationships, however much these may differ from one treatise to another, is necessary to assure the cohesiveness of the system. Before the eighteenth century, that whole spectrum which we today classify as the various "arts" was not customarily discussed either systematically or in a comparative manner. During the Middle Ages, for instance, music, which was treated as one of the four mathematical arts called the quadrivium, belonged to a category different from the three verbal arts making up the trivium;[17] the visual arts, moreover,

---

[15] Reiman and Powers, *Shelley's Poetry and Prose*, p. 494.

[16] Samuel, *Das philosophische Werk* II, p. 360.

[17] See Curtius, *European Literature and the Latin Middle Ages*, pp. 36–39. For a comprehensive history of how those activities that, by the eighteenth century, came to be called the "fine arts" were classified during earlier periods, see Kristeller, "The Modern System of the Arts," in *Renaissance Thought and the Arts*, pp. 163–227.

did not qualify for the title "liberal" that was attached to the seven making up the trivium and quadrivium. To be sure, in his posthumously entitled *Paragone* (c. 1490), literally "comparison," Leonardo da Vinci had briefly surveyed most of the arts contained within the formal aesthetic treatises that emerged four centuries later. But his purpose was not, like that of the latter, a justification and explanation of the larger category of art, but rather a defense of his particular art, painting, which had usually been belittled as a mechanical craft in comparison with those arts that seemingly demanded more learning. To justify the superiority of painting against the other arts, Leonardo depreciates music for "fad[ing] away as soon as it is born"; poetry for being "often not understood, and requir[ing] many explanations"; sculpture for not "requir[ing] the same supreme ingenuity as the art of painting."[18]

Leonardo's remarks, brief though they may be, are notable at once for treating the arts as a group and for arguing, quite in contrast to theorists both before and after, for the superiority of painting. Even Sir Joshua Reynolds, despite his own professional stake in painting and in teaching young painters, maintains the traditional literary bias, with poetry being praised for its ability to engage the mind longer and more powerfully than painting.[19]

It was by means of the major aesthetic treatises of the last two hundred years that art received its legitimation, its identity, its aura. To assure art of its autonomy, these treatises were also forced to draw borderlines. A central method for creating these borders was to establish a transition zone between what the theorist deems artistic and what are clearly non-artistic activities. Thus, Kant distinguishes between the "purposive" and "non-purposive" arts, with the former belonging to that transition zone and, as a result, certifying the impregnability of the non-purposive arts. The verbal arts, for example, divide between non-purposive poetry and purposive

[18] See Vinci, *Paragone*, pp. 74, 60, 77, respectively. For a description of the relatively low status of the visual arts before Leonardo's time, see the introduction to this translation (pp. 12–14).

[19] Reynolds, *Discourses on Art*, pp. 145–46.

oratory; the plastic arts between sculpture and architecture; painting between painting proper and the purposive art of landscape gardening.[20] However different the particular systems of individual theorists, the more practically oriented arts play a similar role to insure the purity of the impractical ones. For example, Schopenhauer, in his long section on aesthetics in *The World as Will and Representation* (1818), places within his transition zone what he calls "the fine art of water-conduction," namely, the artificial waterfalls and fountains in the gardens of great houses, and, even lower in the zone, "the fine art of gardens" or landscaping.[21] August Wilhelm Schlegel, in contrast to most aesthetic theorists, seeks to raise the status of landscape gardening, which, in its finest examples, he compares to the art of major landscape painters; yet Schlegel also sets up his own lower forms – for example, Hogarth's art of caricature – to help validate the higher forms.[22]

Within the major treatises of aesthetics, a certain plenitude prevails by means of which art comes to constitute a world composed of a panoply of individual forms. Like the larger philosophical systems of which these treatises are sometimes a part, one notes an often elaborate array of categories parallel to and corresponding with one another, together with subcategories that are themselves subdivided into further categories. Sometimes these categories take the form of concepts such as symbol and allegory (central, for example, to the systems of Schelling and Solger),[23] the beautiful and the sublime (note, for instance, Kant's division of the latter into its "mathematical" and "dynamic" phases),[24] and sometimes these categories are simply the media (as well as the genres within a particular medium) that, taken together, are made to constitute the total world of art. "Niemand klassifiziert so gern als der Mensch, besonders der

---

[20] See Kant, *Critique of Judgment*, pp. 190–93.

[21] See Schopenhauer, *The World as Will*, vol. I, p. 264.

[22] See A. W. Schlegel, *Vorlesungen* pp. 341–46 and 364–65, respectively.

[23] See Schelling, *Philosophy of Art*, for example, pp. 45–50 and 147–52, and Solger, *Vorlesungen*, for example, pp. 129–45 and 260–61.

[24] See Kant, *Critique of Judgment*, pp. 103–23.

deutsche [nobody is so inclined to classify as man, especially a German]," Jean Paul wrote in his own quite elaborate, though also witty, treatise, *Primer of Aesthetics*.[25]

If concepts such as symbol and allegory, or beautiful and sublime, often come in twos within aesthetic systems, genres and media tend to appear in triplicate or quadruplicate. Since these genres and media are, in effect, the populace out of which the world of art is constituted, their presence in groupings larger than two serves to give this world a substantive grounding. By the end of the eighteenth century, literature had generally come to divide itself into the threefold pattern of epic, lyric and dramatic, a triad that, as Essays 3 and 5 pointed out, has its roots in Plato's attempt to evaluate these genres according to the degree to which each is imitative. Solger's treatise (finished before 1819), for example, divides the literary kinds into these three while dividing the other arts, namely sculpture, painting, architecture and music, into four.[26] Herder, in his early aesthetic treatise, *The Critical Woodlands of Aesthetics* (1769), suggests three senses – hearing, seeing, feeling – as central to aesthetic experience, to replace an earlier model that included only the first two of these senses.[27] Hegel, for whom thinking in triads was second nature, in his lectures of the 1820s proposed a distinct ordering of the arts for each of three periods of history: the symbolic (or pre-historic), the classical, and the romantic.[28] Wagner, in *The Artwork of the Future*, a work which, like the other aesthetic essays he wrote around 1850, serves at once to continue the theorizing of earlier treatises and to prepare the way for his own later practice as music-dramatist, derives art from precisely three forms: dance, music, and literature.[29] But Wagner's tie to dance is perhaps more motivated by a desire for theoretical completeness than by his practical needs as an artist: though he names dance as "the most real among all art forms"[30] and seeks to redefine it as gesture and

---

[25] Richter, *Vorschule der Ästhetik*, p. 67.   [26] Solger, *Vorlesungen*, pp. 257–67.

[27] Herder, *Die kritischen Wälder*, pp. 289–99.

[28] Hegel, *Aesthetics*, vol. I, pp. 76–81.

[29] Wagner, *Gesammelte Schriften*, vol. X, pp. 74–124.

[30] *Ibid.*, p. 78. By *real* Wagner means that dance is closer than other arts to the body.

movement, the degeneration into which he sees dance as having fallen on the modern stage prevented his giving this art much of a role in his own *Gesamtkunstwerke*, its role, in fact, being limited to the urban folk dances in *Die Meistersinger* and the formal ballet that, as Essay 9 will show in detail, he was forced to add to *Tannhäuser* to get this early work performed by the Paris Opéra.

Within the major aesthetic treatises, the various art forms often come to shape a universe of their own by means of mutual correspondences and by the fact that they combine with one another to create new forms or to renew older ones. Rousseau, though he left no systematic treatise on aesthetics, made many suggestive remarks on the interrelationship of the arts: for example, "The role of melody in music is precisely that of drawing in a painting."[31] In Schelling's tightly argued treatise, music, painting, and the plastic arts (the last in their most general sense) correspond, within the more limited realm of the plastic arts themselves, to architecture, bas-relief, and sculpture, respectively.[32] To illustrate this correspondence, Schelling, in an analogy apparently drawn from August Wilhelm Schlegel's theory and that achieved later notoriety, referred to architecture as "frozen music."[33] Jean Paul, in turn, called music "Romantic poetry through the ear."[34] Two arts are sometimes fused to create a new one. Thus, for Wagner, the Haydn symphony represents a fusion of dance with music, and Beethoven's Seventh Symphony, in what has since become a cliché in music criticism, represents the "apotheosis of the dance."[35] Sometimes analogies are drawn between contemporary works within different media, as when August Wilhelm Schlegel briefly suggests a relationship between the *Divine Comedy* and the Gothic cathedral.[36]

---

[31] Rousseau and Herder, *On the Origin of Language*, p. 53.
[32] Schelling, *Philosophy of Art*, p. 163.
[33] *Ibid.*, p. 165. On the history of the analogy, see Behler, "Schellings Ästhetik," pp. 138, 146.
[34] Richter, *Vorschule*, p. 466.
[35] Wagner, *Gesammelte Schriften*, vol. x, pp. 98 and 101, respectively.
[36] A. W. Schlegel, *Vorlesungen*, p. 321.

The complex relationships among the arts projected within these treatises include what are often highly evaluative judgments about how these arts and their various genres rank among one another. The bias in favor of literature discussed in the preceding section remains prevalent among most theorists, with some notable exceptions to be discussed later in this section. "Poetry [*die Poesie*] is the universal art," Solger writes at one point, though he later acknowledges that even the most universal art might not be able to exercise as powerful an influence as music or architecture within the intellectual climate in which he was writing.[37] For Schelling, poetry "can be viewed as the *essence* of all art, similar to the way the soul is viewed as the *essence* of the body."[38] But poetry during the Romantic period often means something more than that genre which we exemplify by a body of texts such as Shakespeare's sonnets and Keats's odes or even by literature as a whole. To the extent that it counts as the "universal" or model art form, it often seems to swallow up other art forms within its boundaries, as in the Novalis fragment quoted earlier about setting poems not to music but to poetry. As Lothario, one of the voices in Friedrich Schlegel's *Dialogue on Poetry* (1800), puts it, "Every art and every science that operates by means of discourse, if it is practiced for its own sake as art, and if it achieves the highest summit, is poetry [*Poesie*]." But one of Schlegel's other characters, Ludoviko, immediately expands the definition to encompass the non-verbal arts within the domain of poetry: "And every art that does not exercise its being in words has an invisible spirit [*Geist*], and this is poetry."[39] John Stuart Mill, distinguishing a "higher" form he calls "poetry" from a "lower" manifestation he calls "oratory," lumped together instances from all the major arts – Mozart's aria "Dove sono," Guido's madonnas, Greek statues of the gods, as well as a "real" poem, Burns's "My Heart's in the Highlands" – to exemplify the more prestigious term.[40] The word *poetry* became so

---

[37] Solger, *Vorlesungen*, pp. 259 and 267, respectively.
[38] Schelling, *Philosophy of Art*, p. 202.
[39] F. Schlegel, *Gespräch über die Poesie*, in *Kritische Schriften*, p. 492.
[40] Mill, "What is Poetry?" (1833), in *Essays on Poetry*, pp. 14–15, 17.

all-encompassing that by mid-century, John Ruskin, writing a book supposedly devoted to the understanding, indeed validation, of painting among the arts, subordinated painting to the higher term: "Painting is properly to be opposed to *speaking* or *writing*, but not to *poetry*. Both painting and speaking are methods of expression. Poetry is the employment of either for the noblest purposes."[41]

However narrow or all-encompassing the particular definition of poetry or literature in particular systems, the world of art that an individual theorist projects generally contains its own chain of being, by means of which various art forms exist in distinct hierarchical relations to one another. It is remarkable not only how long literature kept its place at or near the top of the hierarchy but also how persistently architecture and other "purposive" arts were kept near the bottom. When August Wilhelm Schlegel sought to raise the status of architecture, he did so by downplaying its practical uses and stressing instead its imitation of human and natural forms.[42] Still, one of the central facts about the relationships of the various arts between the mid eighteenth and mid nineteenth centuries is the rise in the status of music. As M. H. Abrams has pointed out, the ascent of music in the hierarchy was made possible by the shift from mimetic to expressive (and, I might also add, affective) theories of art.[43] As early as 1769, Herder, asking what the lost music of the ancient world was "expressing," called the poetry and music of antiquity the "inseparable sister arts" that once worked together to exert their effects.[44] Both here and in his essay on the origin of language (1772), Herder described song and speech as inextricably mixed in the sounds uttered by early man;[45] to the extent that origins help determine the stature of phenomena, music could claim a centrality in the history of culture that it had not known before.

[41] Ruskin, *Modern Painters*, vol. III (1911), p. 13.

[42] A. W. Schlegel, *Vorlesungen*, pp. 305–20.

[43] See Abrams's discussion, appropriately subtitled *"ut musica poesis,"* in *The Mirror and the Lamp*, pp. 88–94.

[44] Herder, *Die kritischen Wälder*, pp. 363–64.

[45] *Ibid.*, pp. 360–61, and Rousseau and Herder, *On the Origin of Language*, pp. 87–91.

Precisely the same year that Herder declared the sisterhood of poetry and music, Daniel Webb, in a treatise entitled *Observations on the Correspondence between Poetry and Music*, cited sonorous passages from poems, above all from the *Aeneid* and *Paradise Lost*, to point out the affinities between the two arts in arousing the passions.[46] Yet the groundwork that allowed a new significance to music was laid not so much in formal treatises as in the less formal essays and fragments of the early German Romantics: for instance, in the praise heaped by Wackenroder (in the guise of his alter-ego, the art-obsessed Josef Berglinger) upon that new genre, the symphony, for its ability to create "a beautifully developed drama" that remains a "pure poetic world" without the encumbrances of plot and character.[47] To the extent that Wackenroder resorts to literary analogy, indeed to a representational poetics, to make his point, the power of the literary model is still evident here; yet he insists that music does the job better than literature. Indeed, one can cite Wackenroder as the first in a long line of German writers who idealized music as being truer to their artistic perceptions than any other medium, including the literary medium within which they themselves were forced to work.

The first major treatise to treat music unambiguously as the highest of the arts was that of Schopenhauer, who ranked the arts according to their ability to objectify the will, that central principle within his system from whose "unrest and intensity" art supposedly protects the individual.[48] Although Schopenhauer gives a relatively high place to tragedy (since it accords with his bias toward the renunciation of the world), no art can emulate music, which expresses "the innermost essence of the world and of ourselves";[49] one of the central attributes that had long been used to argue for

---

[46] Webb, *Observations*.

[47] Wackenroder, *Sämtliche Werke*, vol. I, p. 244. For a searching study of the role played by instrumental music in Romantic theories of art, see Dahlhaus, *Die Idee der absoluten Musik*.

[48] Schopenhauer, *The World as Will*, vol. I, p. 265.

[49] *Ibid.*, pp. 302–03 and 306, respectively.

literature's superiority, namely its ability to provide a rational meaning to life, becomes, in Schopenhauer's anti-rational philosophy, the means for its dethronement in favor of music. But Schopenhauer's work remained unknown for a whole generation after it was published in 1819. Wagner's major aesthetic writings, completed before his discovery of the philosopher in 1854, still give priority to the verbal element in opera; only later, by means of his own musical practice and his (and Schopenhauer's) influence on his sometime disciple Nietzsche in *The Birth of Tragedy*, does music emerge as the supreme art.[50]

Within most treatises of aesthetics, even though illustrative examples of art-works may be drawn from different eras, the system, with its hierarchies and inward correspondences, exists in some timeless realm; indeed, the illusion of timelessness helps confirm the substantiality and autonomy that art possesses among human endeavors. It was of course Hegel's achievement among theorists of art to historicize the categories, with the result that the hierarchy of media and individual genres became relative to a particular age. Not that Hegel was the first to suggest the relativity of artistic value to a particular historical context: more than a half century before, Herder, whose anticipations of what later generations could take for granted often seem uncanny, had written: "There exists an ideal of beauty for every art, for every science, for good taste altogether, and it is to be found in peoples and eras and subjects and productions."[51] It was left to Hegel to work out this detailed

---

[50] For the early Nietzsche's use of Schopenhauer, as well as of the later Wagner, to argue for the supremacy of music, see *The Birth of Tragedy*, pp. 100–03; for an extreme statement by Nietzsche not only about the supremacy of music but about its independence from the texts that it purports to be setting, see his essay "On Music and Words," in Dahlhaus, *Between Romanticism and Modernism*, pp. 106–19. For a late statement by Wagner that revises the theory in his early aesthetic essays by stressing the role of symphonic music (above all Beethoven's) in shaping his music-dramas, see "Über die Anwendung der Musik auf das Drama" (1879) in Wagner, *Gesammelte Schriften*, vol. XIII, pp. 282–98.

[51] Herder, *Die kritischen Wälder*, p. 286.

historicization of the arts. Thus, architecture, relegated to the bottom of most systems, for Hegel landed at the top of the hierarchy during the symbolic or pre-historic period, in which the construction of massive buildings such as the tower of Babel and Egyptian temples becomes the means of bonding a people who have not yet reached the stage of selfconsciousness.[52] Sculpture, above all in Greek examples as mediated to German aesthetics by Winckelmann, becomes central to the next era, the classical age, which demands a form such as statues of the gods that objectify spirit but that can "still ignore the subjectivity of the inner life."[53] As selfconsciousness (for Hegel the defining characteristic of historical progress) increases, literary genres move up the hierarchy. During the last of his eras, the romantic (which encompasses the whole post-classical period), we move from painting to music to the literary genres, with epic, lyric and dramatic in ascending order. Since Hegel associates drama with "those epochs in which individual selfconsciousness has reached a high stage of development," it is not surprising, in view of the value that he places upon selfconsciousness, that this genre represents for him "the highest stage of poetry and of art generally" in the modern world.[54] For most readers today Hegel's historical method of ordering the arts doubtless makes his treatise appear more modern (however much these readers may differ with his ratings of particular art forms) than the more universalizing treatises of his time. After all, the historical perspective he introduced into European thought still so shapes our own thinking that it is difficult to treat these other treatises with the same seriousness we accord Hegel's.

The canons of particular artists from which the various treatises draw their examples vary considerably in the time-span that they cover. The problems of musical transmission were so great, as I indicated earlier, that most treatises can go back at most a generation to illustrate their points, though many speculate about what

---

[52] Hegel, *Aesthetics*, vol. II, pp. 638–9 and 644–8, respectively.
[53] *Ibid.*, p. 718.   [54] *Ibid.*, pp. 1179 and 1158, respectively.

the music of antiquity might have been like. Mozart and Rossini provide a surprisingly large proportion of the examples used, though earlier religious music (for example, Handel's), which generally had a longer performance life than that of secular music, receives attention as well. Schopenhauer, who usually avoids commending individual composers, was so taken by his contemporary Rossini's ability to use music to calm the unrelenting will that he claimed his operatic music "has no need of words at all" but "has its full effect even when performed with instruments alone."[55] Although Schopenhauer was smitten by Rossini's tunes despite his own anti-theatrical bias (an attitude that, as Essay 8 will show, helped shape some major modernist operas), he accommodated opera to his philosophy only by ignoring words, plot, and scenic embodiment.

The time-span for the visual arts in these treatises is obviously much longer than that for music. Ancient sculpture, presented usually by way of Winckelmann's interpretations, plays a central role in the treatises to a degree that painting does not. Indeed, the canon of painting in these treatises often starts with what we have since come to call the high Renaissance, with a surprisingly limited number of artists' names recurring from one analyst to the next. Michelangelo and Raphael count as the ultimate painters for most theorists of the late eighteenth and early nineteenth centuries with little if any mention of their *quattrocento* predecessors. When Hazlitt writes of the great painters of the past, "We are abstracted to another sphere . . . we enter into the minds of Raphael, of Titian, of Poussin, of the Caracci [*sic*], and look at nature with their eyes,"[56] his citation of the Carracci reminds us to what an extent tastes have changed since his time. At least as surprising as this mention of the Carracci brothers (whose centrality in the foundation of baroque style is still acknowledged in histories of art) is that of Correggio, whose name appears in an uncommon number of discussions of painting and whom Schelling, in a judgment quite typical of his time, calls "the

---

[55] Schopenhauer, *The World as Will*, vol. i, p. 312.
[56] Hazlitt, *Complete Works*, vol. x (1932), p. 7.

painter of all painters," a statement that was followed, also quite typically, with the reminder that "the highest and genuinely absolute essence of art appeared only in Raphael."[57]

By contrast with that of music and painting, the canon of litera-ture extends through the whole of Western culture. The disparity in time-span between literature and painting is evident in Hazlitt's list of what he called the "giant-sons of genius," whose literary exem-plars go back to Homer but in which painting starts only some three centuries before Hazlitt's own lifetime: "Homer, Chaucer, Spenser, Shakspeare, Dante, and Ariosto, (Milton alone was of a later age, and not the worse for it) – Raphael, Titian, Michael Angelo, Correggio, Cervantes, and Boccaccio, the Greek sculptors and tragedians, – all lived near the beginning of their arts – perfected, and all but created them."[58] As reshaped during the Romantic period, the literary canon to be found in aesthetic treatises of the time, as Hazlitt's list makes clear, is pretty much what it has remained to the present day, with Homer, the Greek dramatists (though with a certain disparagement of Euripides among German critics), Virgil, Dante, Ariosto, Cervantes, and Shakespeare looming as giants. If Calderón (and distinctly not Lope de Vega) plays an unexpectedly large role in German aesthetics, this is due to the recent rediscovery (and transla-tion) he had undergone in the work of the early Romantics.[59] Although the canon remains largely Western, it is not accidental, in view of the interest among the Romantics in Indo-European philology, that references to Sanskrit literature, for example the play *Shakuntala*, often appear.[60] And it is scarcely surprising that when

---

[57] Schelling, *Philosophy of Art*, p. 140.

[58] Hazlitt, *Complete Works*, vol. v (1930), p. 45.

[59] See, for example, the discussions of Calderón in Schelling, *Philosophy of Art*, pp. 273–76; Solger, *Vorlesungen*, pp. 319–20; and Hegel, *Aesthetics*, vol. i, pp. 405–07. Schelling and Hegel refer particularly to *La Devoción de la Cruz*, which counted as the exemplary Spanish play. But word of Calderón's special relevance also spread beyond Germany: note the reference to Calderón's sacred plays in Shelley's *Defence of Poetry* (in Reiman, *Shelley's Poetry and Prose*, p. 490).

[60] See, for example, Schelling, *Philosophy of Art*, p. 57, and Hegel, *Aesthetics*, vol. i, p. 339, and vol. ii, p. 1176.

recent writers are cited on the continent, these tend to be Goethe, Schiller, Byron, and Scott, while the other English poets, indeed most contemporary foreign writers, are notably missing in continental accounts.

INTERCHANGES AND ENCROACHMENTS

The late eighteenth and early nineteenth centuries mark not only the first sustained attempt to theorize the arts as a whole but also a systematic effort, continuing to our own day, to break down long-established borders between the various arts as well as borders between the individual genres constituting each art form. The power of *ut pictura poesis* was so great from the Renaissance onward that one might easily assume that borders – at least those between painting and poetry – were regularly broken throughout this earlier period. Yet in retrospect one can interpret the pictorialist tradition, by means of which each art form claimed to be drawing upon the resources of the other, as a means of securing rather than destroying the borders between them. As Christopher Braider has put it, "At the same time as it affirms what painters and poets have in common, *ut pictura* masks how far their respective arts are finally antithetical, locked in a contest from which neither escapes because neither can by itself ground or resolve it."[61] Once we see pictorialism as a means of guarding the integrity of individual art forms, we can read Lessing's *Laocoon* as an attempt to keep painters and poets from taking the doctrine so literally that they misunderstand the peculiar limits of their respective media. Thus, for Lessing, the recent poet Haller, in his long poem describing the Alps, had attempted a form of detailed, overly meticulous description suitable to painting but not to a temporally based verbal art form such as poetry.[62] Lessing of course was working out of a mimetic theory of art,[63] a theory that

---

[61] Braider, *Refiguring the Real*, pp. 221–22.   [62] Lessing, *Laokoon*, pp. 125–26.
[63] On the representational model common to Lessing and his predecessors Baumgarten and Mendelssohn, see Wellbery, *Lessing's "Laocoon,"* pp. 49–54.

was little different from the one motivating Reynolds's stricture, quoted at the start of this chapter, that "no art be engrafted . . . on another art."

Once the mimetic mode gave way to expressive and affective theories, the barriers separating the arts could more easily be challenged or ignored than before. If art was to be seen as the expression of genius, the major creators of the various arts were virtually interchangeable, as one notes in the following lines from Delacroix's journal, in which, advocating the importance of disproportion, the painter carefully includes representatives of all three major arts: "If we admire Mozart, Cimarosa, and Racine less because of the admirable proportion in their works, do not Shakespeare, Michelangelo and Beethoven owe something of their effect to the opposite quality?"[64] For Delacroix those who count as geniuses in the various arts constitute a community more vital than that between a major artist and lesser practitioners within the same medium.

With music, according to M. H. Abrams, "the first of the arts to be severed from the mimetic principle by a critical consensus,"[65] the interchanges between music and the other arts, above all literature, became a central concern for artists seeking new ways to practice their media. Beginning with the German Romantics, writers systematically sought to make language render the effects of music upon them. Wackenroder's character Berglinger not only describes these effects in discursive terms, as when, invoking the discourse of the sublime, he speaks of music "penetrating his nerves with quiet terror [*Schauer*]," but he also resorts repeatedly to similes to translate his experience into literary terms, for example, when he describes the progress of a melody as similar to that of "a brook . . . rushing through wild crags with frightening noise."[66] Wackenroder's

---

[64] Delacroix, *Journal*, vol. II, p. 42 (entry of 9 May 1853).

[65] Abrams, *The Mirror and the Lamp*, p. 92.

[66] Wackenroder, *Sämtliche Werke*, vol. I, pp. 132 and 134, respectively. For a detailed analysis of Wackenroder's method of achieving "verbal music," see Scher, *Verbal Music*, pp. 13–35.

attempt to make literature aspire to the condition of music stands at the beginning of a tradition that ultimately leads to Thomas Mann's detailed recreations of his composer-hero Adrian Leverkühn's compositions in *Doktor Faustus* (1947). It is especially appropriate that some of the model attempts to render music in verbal discourse should come from E. T. A. Hoffmann, whose own vocational affiliations encompassed musical and, in particular, operatic composition, literary and music criticism (not to speak of his role as bureaucrat), and, most distinguished of all from our present-day point of view, the writing of fiction. In his celebrated review of Beethoven's Fifth Symphony (1810), Hoffmann's contrast of Haydn and Mozart with Beethoven builds on Wackenroder's attempt at once to describe the effect of music and to suggest metaphorical equivalents for this effect. Whereas Haydn's symphonies "lead us into unbounded green woodlands, into a jolly, colourful crowd of happy people," in Beethoven's work "glowing rays shoot through the deep night of this realm, and we become aware of giant shadows that sway up and down, enclose us within increasingly narrow confines and destroy everything within us except for the pain of infinite longing [*Sehnsucht*]."[67] ·Hoffmann's analysis is notable not only for its attempt to find verbal equivalents for music but, in the very process of discovering this language, for demonstrating that a listener's experience with Beethoven is something different in kind from that with earlier composers.

By the end of the eighteenth century, above all in Germany, music was fast coming to displace painting as the central model or at least analogy for literature. Hoffmann's claim to find Romantic *Sehnsucht* in Beethoven's symphonic writing suggests the affinities a writer could feel with what a composer had accomplished. When Jean Paul labels chapters of his aesthetic treatise with such terms from church music as "Jubilate lecture" and "cantata lecture,"[68] he

---

[67] Hoffmann, "Beethoven, C-moll-Sinfonie (No 5)," p. 42. For a detailed study of musical description after Hoffmann, see Grey, "Metaphorical Modes," pp. 93–117.

[68] Richter, *Vorschule der Ästhetik*, pp. 398–456.

signals this shift, which he also illustrates in descriptions within his novels of the effects of hearing music. But the musical analogy also manifested itself in less overt but also more fundamental ways in certain formal experiments, for example, in Hölderlin's use of terms drawn from music to find a new mode of poetic organization by means of what he called "the alternation of tones,"[69] or in the volatile rhythmic and emotional shifts that mark the lyrics embedded in Tieck's narrative "Love story of the lovely Magelone" (1797), whose overtly musical style is foregrounded in the "real" music that Brahms later supplied in his Magelone song cycle (1861).[70]

The interchange between music and literature also worked in the opposite direction. Franz Liszt, in an essay (1855) on Berlioz's *Harold in Italy*, an instrumental work for viola and orchestra inspired by Byron's *Childe Harold*, suggested the role that literature was playing for composers of his time with the words, "The masterpieces of music are increasingly appropriating the masterworks of literature."[71] Music, one might say, was aspiring to the condition of a literature that was itself aspiring to the condition of music.

To be sure, the musical mimesis of texts goes back to earlier centuries, for example, to Monteverdi's distinctions between the "agitated," "soft," and "moderate" styles suitable to particular passages of poetry being set by a composer.[72] But imitations of this sort are local, often quite literal-minded attempts to make vocal music mimic writing. By contrast, that Romantic instrumental genre calling itself "tone poem," which continued to flourish until well into the twentieth century and which combines both art forms in its very name, is dedicated to recreating the larger idea of a literary work,

---

[69] See Ryan, *Hölderlins Lehre vom Wechsel der Töne.*

[70] On the musical character of these poems and their relation to Brahms's settings, see Frank, *Einführung in die frühromantische Ästhetik*, pp. 385–428.

[71] Liszt, "Berlioz und seine Harold-Symphonie," p. 58.

[72] Malipiero, *Claudio Monteverdi, Tutte le opere*, vol. VIII (1929), unnumbered page before p. 1. On the relation of Monteverdi's three styles to ancient Greek theories of musical imitation, see Hanning, "Monteverdi's Three Genera," pp. 145–70. See also the analysis of passages by Monteverdi embodying these styles in Tomlinson, *Monteverdi*, pp. 202–10.

sometimes even seeking, through the immediacy of musical effect, to outdo the famed literary original to which it feigns obeisance. The celebrated examples of musicalized literature give ample testimony about the prevailing literary canon at the times they were created: for instance, symphonies bearing titles such as *Harold in Italy*, the *Faust* and *Dante* of Liszt, or the *Manfred* of Tchaikovsky, tone poems such as Strauss's *Macbeth*, *Don Juan* and *Don Quixote*, or the settings of *Pelléas et Mélisande* variously by Fauré, Sibelius and Schoenberg, not to speak of innumerable concert overtures with titles the likes of *King Lear* and *Rob Roy* (Berlioz), *Faust* (Wagner), *Francesca da Rimini*, *Romeo and Juliet* and *Hamlet* (Tchaikovsky), or even, one might add, the not-so-celebrated *Manfred Meditation* for four-handed piano by that sometime composer, Friedrich Nietzsche. But composers did not simply go to established literary works to inspire and shape their works: they sometimes wrote programs of their own, for instance, Beethoven in his *Pastoral* symphony, Berlioz in his *Fantastic* symphony, and Mahler (who even kept rewriting his program after the completion of the work) in his *Resurrection* symphony. In each of these instances one suspects a need to "textualize" these instrumental compositions, as though the music needed the written word to be legitimized. One might add that these highly text-conscious musical works – what might be dubbed "operas without words" – can enjoy the prestige both of literature and of pure, if not quite precisely, absolute music. (To be sure, Liszt and Mahler never quite resisted the lure of adding words at the ends of their *Faust* and *Resurrection* symphonies.)

If I have concentrated thus far on mutual encroachments between music and literature, this does not mean that painting lost its tie to literature with the decline of the *ut pictura poesis* doctrine. Indeed, the imputed directive that one art should resemble the other may well have limited the possibilities of mutual interchange to surface imitation during earlier centuries. Yet when Keats, in "Ode on a Grecian Urn," and Mörike, in "Auf eine Lampe," write ecphrases on visual artifacts, they do not simply describe what they see, but they use these descriptions as a means to emulate the great aesthetic treatises of their time in acclaiming the autonomy of art.[73] Ruskin's attempt to communicate the nature and magnitude of Turner's achievement led him to develop a mode of composition as strikingly innovative as that of German writers, such as Wackenroder and Hoffmann, who had earlier sought to account for the effects of music. In a sentence such as the following, Ruskin, while discussing a Turner seascape, goes beyond traditional pictorialist description to stress the effect of the work upon the viewer, much as Romantic musical descriptions had sought to suggest what the listener could be imagining beyond what the picture actually shows: "But the surges roll and plunge with such prostration and hurling of their mass against the shore, that we feel the rocks are shaking under them."[74] Just as Liszt had boasted that music was appropriating literature, and just as Hoffmann in his role of author was appropriating music, so Ruskin, in innumerable passages of his art criticism, seeks to make his prose affect his reader in a mode analogous to those of the visual media he is describing.

But Turner was himself appropriating literature to the art of painting. As Ronald Paulson writes in a book on Turner and Constable significantly entitled *Literary Landscape*, "The art of Turner and Constable, however visual at the core . . . persists in asking verbal questions, and is incomprehensible without a consideration of its verbal aspect."[75] What Paulson argues in the course of his book is not that these two painters were "illustrating" literature in the pictorialist tradition (though Turner, unlike Constable, did his share of history paintings) but that, in their landscape painting, both created symbol systems that worked like literature without actually using or imitating literature. Indeed, as Paulson shows, the earnestness and largeness of scale that had traditionally marked history

---

[73] For classic interpretations of these poems as at once ecphrases and statements about art, see Spitzer, "The 'Ode on a Grecian Urn' or Content *vs.* Metagrammar," in *Essays*, pp. 67–97, and "Once Again on Mörike's Poem 'Auf eine Lampe.'" See also Jack, *Keats*, for an exhaustive investigation of how deeply Keats's poetry is suffused with his experiences viewing visual objects of art.
[74] Ruskin, *Modern Painters*, vol. I, p. 399.   [75] Paulson, *Literary Landscape*, p. 5.

painting became transformed in differing ways by Turner and Constable – and, in Germany, by the grand-style paintings of Caspar David Friedrich and Phillip Otto Runge – into the previously more circumscribed genre of landscape;[76] the epic quality of Constable's work is evident, for example, in the term "six-footer" given to his large later paintings of seemingly simple scenes within the Stour valley.

Even history painting (which retained its hold to the point that an artist as late as Degas practiced it in his youth) went through a certain transformation. Despite Ingres's boasting of his vocation of history painter, some of his most ambitious historical canvases are not actually scenes illustrating classic texts (though he also painted a number of these) but are primarily tributes to the power of artistic genius, as one notes from such titles as *The Apotheosis of Homer, Virgil Reading the Aeneid, Louis XIV and Molière, Luigi Cherubini and the Muse of Lyric Poetry*; as such they participate in a program similar to that of the aesthetic treatises of his time in demarcating a zone in which art achieves a quasi-religious status. Delacroix included a large number of scenes from literature among his subjects, and in this sense he continued the pictorialist tradition that had fed on literary texts (above all on the epic poems of Ariosto and Tasso) ever since the sixteenth century. Indeed, both Ingres and Delacroix left famous canvases depicting Ariosto's heroine Angelica.[77] Yet if one notes the large range of literary scenes that Delacroix reproduced – from texts as varied as the *Divine Comedy, Hamlet* (both Ophelia's death and the gravedigger scene), *Othello* (the last-named mediated by Rossini's opera), Byron's *Don Juan, Marino Faliero* and *Sardanapalus*, and Scott's *Ivanhoe* – one realizes that Delacroix sought something more than his pictorialist predecessors, that he aimed to replicate the literary canon in visual terms and, like Ingres (though more successfully), to make a larger statement about what he took to be the transcendent character of great texts.

---

[76] See *ibid.*, pp. 63–73, 108–09, 133–39.

[77] For a study of Angelica paintings from mannerist through Romantic artists, see Lee, *Names on Trees.*

The interchangeability of art forms is embodied in a rhetorical device, synaesthesia, by means of which the sense organ we use to experience a particular medium (for instance, hearing chords) is switched to a deliberately inappropriate medium (smelling colors). Although this device, like many others, goes back to Homer and the Bible, it was neither named nor used with great frequency until the nineteenth century. A brief passage from one of Hoffmann's musical writings proved seminal in literary history: the author's alter-ego, the bizarre musician Johannes Kreisler, in a reverie after listening to "much music," finds "colors, sounds, and odors coming together," with the smell of dark-red carnations mixing with the distant sound of a basset horn.[78] Baudelaire quotes this passage in his Salon of 1846 after complaining of the "lack of melody" in younger painters and praising the "plaintive colors" of Delacroix.[79] The passage further generated two programmatic sonnets: first, Baudelaire's own "Correspondances", which not only echoes Hoffmann's images but adds its own synaesthetic image with the "oboes green as meadows," and, second, Rimbaud's "Voyelles," which confounds sense experience even further than the earlier sonnet by assigning colors to vowels, creating a velvet jacket of flies, and endowing glaciers with lances.[80] In the wake of the experiments of Baudelaire and Rimbaud, literary language has come to assert its autonomy over whatever objects it earlier claimed to imitate. Moreover, by means of synaesthesia, literature again asserts its hegemony over the other arts, for, with the arbitrary signs it has at its command, it can scramble words associated with different media with an imperiousness that these other media cannot emulate.

[78] Hoffmann, "Kreisleriana," p. 56.

[79] Baudelaire, *Oeuvres complètes*, pp. 606–07.

[80] See *ibid.*, p. 85, and Rimbaud, *Oeuvres complètes*, p. 103. Baudelaire quotes the octave of "Correspondances" in his essay "Richard Wagner et *Tannhäuser* à Paris" as a means of introducing the visual images set off in his mind by the music of Wagner and Liszt (Baudelaire, *Oeuvres complètes*, p. 1043). Writing of Delacroix both in a review of his paintings (p. 700) and in his poem "Les Phares" (p. 87), he compares the effects of the painter's color to the composer Weber's fanfares.

The interchanges among art forms, indeed the encroachments of one art form upon another, during the Romantic period were mirrored by similar interchanges and encroachments among the various genres comprising each art form. As the classical system in place since the Renaissance broke down, transgressing the boundaries that had long separated the poetic genres became a practice analogous to crossing the boundaries between art forms. Within German Romantic theory, for instance, the novel emerged as the privileged site on which genres that had long gone their separate ways could mingle together at ease. "A novel [*Roman*] is a Romantic book," as one of the characters in Friedrich Schlegel's *Dialogue on Poetry* puts it, adding, "I cannot imagine a novel being anything other than a mixture of narrative, song, and other forms."[81] Not only did new generic combinations emerge, but the traditional hierarchy of genres underwent certain fundamental displacements. One can speak, for instance, of an elevation of lower genres to higher status. Thus, landscape painting, as I indicated above, assumed some of the functions, scope, and earnestness long associated with history painting, the noblest genre within its medium. A similar process of what one might call "heroicization" is evident within other art forms around 1800. The once lowly genre of the folk ballad took on massive proportions, both in length and philosophical scope, during the year 1798 in Goethe's and Schiller's ballads and in Coleridge's "Rime of the Ancient Mariner." Declaring his long poem *The Prelude* to be "in truth heroic argument,"[82] Wordsworth adapted the organization, the verse form, and the seriousness of tone associated with epic, the loftiest of literary genres, to package a landscape-obsessed autobiographical narrative. The symphony, previously taken to be a musical entertainment more unassuming in scope than, say, oratorio or *opera seria*, became heroicized literally at a single stroke by Beethoven's composition of the *Eroica* in 1803. And two years later, in *Fidelio*, Beethoven gave that light-weight form the *Singspiel* an

---

[81] F. Schlegel, *Kritische Schriften*, p. 515.
[82] Wordsworth, *The Prelude*, p. 100 (1805 version, book III, line 182).

earnestness and a heroic quality that, even with the precedent of *Die Zauberflöte*, it had not known before.

MUSIC-DRAMA, OR THE MYTH OF UNION

Behind the displacements and interchanges among genres and art forms there lurks a frequently articulated dream of union among the various arts. Schiller, in the quotation near the start of this chapter, expressed this desire without, of course, any design to put it into practice himself. A decade later, at the end of the university lectures posthumously published as his *Philosophy of Art*, Schelling projected a union of the arts that could conceivably come together in concrete form by means of theatrical performance: "The most perfect composition of all the arts, the unification of poesy and music through song, of poesy and painting through dance, both in turn synthesized together, is the most complex theatre manifestation, such as was the drama of antiquity." Despite his nostalgia for that union purportedly represented by Greek drama, he quickly recognizes the still-thriving descendant of this form: "Only a caricature has remained for us: the *opera*, which in a higher and nobler style both from the side of poesy as well as from that of the other competing arts, might sooner guide us back to the performance of that ancient drama combined with music and song."[83]

Though Wagner likely did not know these lectures, which had not yet been published when he theorized his so-called *Gesamtkunstwerk* around 1850, the task he set up for himself was to return that multimedia form which Schelling had termed a "caricature," namely opera, to the dignity it had supposedly known during its ancient days. It is notable, for example, that opera did not play a major role in the great aesthetic treatises of the late eighteenth and early nineteenth centuries. Unlike the symphony or the various literary genres, its mixed generic nature did not lead to easy classification. Even more important, the fact that for much of its history

---

[83] Schelling, *Philosophy of Art*, p. 280.

opera was less high-minded than popular easily led German theorists of the arts, such as Schelling, into disparaging it. A generation before Schelling's statement, J. G. Sulzer, in his much-circulated handbook *General Theory of the Fine Arts* (1771–74), had deprecated opera in similar terms: he saw the form as "capable of being the greatest, most important of dramatic forms because all the powers of the fine arts are united." But, as he adds, opera "has abandoned the path of nature . . . Contemptible as opera may be in its customary disfigure-ment . . . so important and honorable it might become."[84] (It is significant that this disparagement of opera among German theorists was still echoed, as Essay 3 demonstrated, in the anti-operatic remarks of Theodor Adorno.)

Moreover, since most operas of earlier centuries remained (unlike their librettos) unpublished and since they were rarely if ever revived, theorists of art had no ready access to the larger operatic canon. Hegel's few comments on opera in his *Aesthetics*, for example, are as disparaging as Schelling's, for in opera, as he puts it, there is "no real seriousness about the proper dramatic subject-matter, and [opera] puts us in the mood we have in reading one of the Arabian Nights."[85] Indeed, in one of the few moments of agreement between Hegel and his rival Schopenhauer, the former singles out Rossini for praise because he allows us "to abandon the subject-matter and take unhindered delight in the free inspirations of the composer."[86] By separating Rossini's music from the theatrical and verbal apparatus to which it was attached, both philosophers are able, in effect, to accommodate their beloved composer to that newly prestigious concept of absolute music.

---

[84] See Sulzer, *Allgemeine Theorie*, pp. 573, 583, 584, respectively. I place Schelling's and Sulzer's statements in a larger context in my chapter "Opera among the Arts – Opera among Institutions" in *Opera in History*, pp. 107–33. For a detailed discussion of the relative disparagement of opera at various times, see the section entitled "The Anti-operatic Prejudice" in *Opera: The Extravagant Art*, pp. 197–210.

[85] Hegel, *Aesthetics*, vol. II, pp. 1191–92.   [86] *Ibid.*, p. 949.

Wagner's attempt to make opera a serious form of art was dependent upon his finding a means, both in his theory and his practice, of bringing the various components of this mixed genre into union with one another. It was not enough, as it was for Hegel and Schopenhauer, to admire *Die Zauberflöte* or *Il barbiere di Siviglia* only for their music regardless of the antics onstage. Yet as one reads Wagner's aesthetic writings it is unmistakably clear that his projected union of the arts is not simply a mixture of various components but that it is a union focused upon a single medium, namely, drama. In *The Artwork of the Future*, while describing the procedures that the ideal future artist will use to create his work, Wagner writes: "The space in which this marvelous process is achieved is the *theater stage,* and the total art work [*das künstlerische Gesamtwerk*] that it brings to light is the *drama.*"[87] Wagner's theory can be seen above all as a theory of drama, more precisely of dramatic performance, in which the possibilities of various art forms are utilized to establish a particular relationship between the audience and the dramatic action enacted onstage. And to the extent that the various arts Wagner was bringing together became fused within a single genre – what was to be known as music-drama – he was not altogether violating Reynolds's "general rule," quoted at the start of this essay, "that no Art can be engrafted with success on another art."

Moreover, as someone who had lived in Paris during the heyday of *grand opéra* and had also toiled for years as a conductor in provincial German opera houses, Wagner had ample opportunity to note the form's frequent lack of dramatic seriousness. In the sense that Wagner favors a single genre, drama, his theory is not wholly different from that of Lessing, whose attempt to establish a rigorous separation of the arts arose from his desire to privilege the dramatic element latent in the two art forms, poetry and painting, upon which he focuses: Lessing's demands that the painter construct his scene around the "most pregnant moment" of his narrative,[88] and that the poet avoid excessive description in the interest of economy, attempt,

---

[87] Wagner, *Gesammelte Schriften*, vol. x, p. 167.   [88] Lessing, *Laokoon*, p. 117.

like Wagner's theory, to create what is essentially a dramatic encounter between audience and work. It is no accident, moreover, that these two theorists both sought success as practitioners of the theater.

I stress these underlying affinities between two theories that normally count as diametrical opposites as a means of questioning whether the watershed in the relations between the arts at the start of the nineteenth century was as extreme as it was taken to be during succeeding generations. Once we look back from our present vantage point, the disruptions that have occurred within the twentieth and early twenty-first centuries both among art forms and in the definition of art seem considerably more radical than what, despite the boasts of individual artists and theorists, took place earlier. However much Berlioz may have tried to appropriate Shakespeare or Scott, within his *King Lear* and *Rob Roy*, listeners who do not take their program notes too earnestly are likely to experience each of these pieces above all as the sort of concert overture with which an evening at the symphony hall often begins. However distinct, earnest, and difficult Wagner's style, the four works comprising *Der Ring des Nibelungen* belong recognizably to the same genre as, say, a work he much disdained, Meyerbeer's *Le prophète*, which, with its ice-skaters' ballet, even included an additional art form that Wagner subjected to his own generic transformation in the athletic feats of his gyrating Rhine maidens and of his Valkyries guiding their steeds among jagged peaks.

The unity that Wagner achieved by bringing the various art forms together under the aegis of music-drama was ultimately short lived. Soon after the start of the twentieth century, as the next essay will show, this unity was disrupted, sometimes violently, as generic forms were broken and redefined in hitherto unheard-of ways. And as the twentieth century came to its close, new and altogether fiercer questions emerged about the relations between individual art forms and genres and about what properly belongs to the domain of art. Note such typical challenges as the following: Robert Smithson's relocation of the boundaries between art and the natural world in "earthworks" such as the Great Salt Lake *Spiral Jetty* (1970); Merce Cunningham's refusal to integrate his dance with its "accompanying" music; John Cage's rethinking of the role of the creating artist in the "chance operations" he used to generate his music, his graphic art, and his written texts, including his collage opera *Europeras 1 & 2* (discussed in Essay 4); the continuing textual invasions of visual art-forms, from Picasso's and Braque's collages to Jasper Johns's number paintings down to Jenny Holzer's shifting electronic displays of her own writing; William Kentridge's use of puppets and film animation (described in Essay 4) to render a contemporary political commentary on top of an otherwise "musically authentic" performance of Monteverdi's *Il ritorno d'Ulisse in patria*; the introduction into the visual arts of new technologies – photography, film, video, neon signs – often mixed with one another, with traditional visual materials, or with elements of other media such as music and poetry, that, like the Faust museum installation I projected in Essay 4, flagrantly defy the classifications by means of which art once sought to claim stability. Indeed, it was not until the twentieth century, and above all in its closing decades, that Reynolds's stricture against "engrafting" one art upon another was fully, and also blatantly, overturned. Still, if the changes in the theory and practice of the arts that occurred during the early nineteenth century no longer seem quite as revolutionary as they once did, it may well be simply that recent revolutions strike us as more provocative than earlier ones. But with the hindsight of another few generations, we (or, more precisely, others) may also come to view these contemporary developments as predictable outgrowths of the dislocations among the arts that were initiated two centuries ago.

The terms we use to periodize opera are not necessarily the terms we use to characterize other forms of music. "Baroque opera," a label attached to well over a century of works from Monteverdi through the early Gluck, belongs to the same category we apply to all the arts. But although the music of Mozart and Haydn is classified as marking the so-called Classical style, we do not readily speak of *Don Giovanni* or *Die Zauberflöte* as Classical operas. Yet we *do* speak of Romantic opera, but this, as mentioned earlier, is a relatively narrow term that suggests Weber and his successors up to early Wagner, and it is most often applied to German examples. Yet how do we bring the Germans together with their contemporaries Rossini, Bellini, and Donizetti? Better perhaps to keep the Italians by themselves and speak of the Age of *Bel Canto*, a period concept intrinsic to opera and not transferable to other music, let alone the other arts.

Modernist opera, however, is a concept that seems to have caught on, if only because the operas we see as "modernist" emanate from composers whom we have already classified with this term. Unlike their nineteenth-century predecessors, the modernist composers of opera were not primarily "opera composers." Very few of the great nineteenth-century opera composers created significant oeuvres outside the opera house – the most notable exceptions being Beethoven, Berlioz, and Tchaikovsky. By contrast, the twentieth-century composers left their mark in genres such as symphony, chamber music, and song. Even Janáček and Britten, prolific though they were in opera, were almost equally successful in other musical forms. Modernist opera, in short, is intrinsically a part of modernist music. And it is also, as we shall see, an extension of modernism in all the arts, for the terms we use to characterize modernism – for example, shock, fragmentation, difficulty, disruption, irony, anti-realism, among many others – are as applicable to modernist opera as to any of the arts.

To the extent that operatic modernism participates in modernism as such, for the sake of argument let us for now assign it the same general dates as the larger movement of which it is presumably a part. Thus it is dominant throughout the first half of the twentieth century, from *Pelléas et Mélisande* (1902) to *The Rake's Progress* (1951). In a later section of this essay, I shall deal with the fortunes of operatic modernism during the second part of the century.

NOT-QUITE OPERA

Much operatic modernism consists of approximations of opera rather than what audiences have customarily viewed as full-blown opera. Concepts of what constitutes an opera, of what is properly operatic, have of course changed over the centuries. But for most of this time audiences (not to speak of composers) retained no memory of earlier concepts, for what they heard in the opera house was the prevailing operatic style of their own time.

It was not until the later nineteenth century, as mentioned earlier at several points, that a historical repertory was created. As a result, audiences formed a concept of opera encompassing their experiences of works from Mozart to *verismo*. Whether in the *bel canto* or French *grand-opéra* mode, the Verdian or the Wagnerian, opera came to mean a good-sized orchestra (increasingly so across the century), a chorus, historical period costumes, voices encompassing a well-distributed number of ranges, and, just as important, an extravagant theatricality combined with a limited array of plots that, however much sex or violence they might contain, carefully remained within certain predictable moral limits.

Seen against this notion of opera, modernist opera does not seem to measure up. Take for example *Pelléas et Mélisande*: with its slowness of movement, its refusal to sing out, it displays an anti-theatricality, an anti-operaticality that still, after more than a century, jars many conventional opera-goers, who keep waiting for the music to open up. As the next essay will develop in more detail, this anti-theatrical quality is central not only to *Pelléas* but also to a number of key modernist operas.

The refusal to sing out has manifested itself in some alternate modes of vocal expression. Schoenberg employed *Sprechstimme*, a mode hovering between speech and song, in the short opera *Die glückliche Hand* (1910–13) and in the song cycle *Pierrot lunaire* (1912). Or an opera can use a non-singing speaker like the Haushofmeister in the prologue to *Ariadne auf Naxos* (1916). Unlike the alternation of speech and song that comes to seem natural in the traditional *Singspiel* or in operetta, the Haushofmeister keeps interrupting the musical flow of Strauss's otherwise through-composed opera.

And note how *The Rake's Progress* from beginning to end under-cuts conventionally operatic poses. I happened to attend this opera at its first Viennese production soon after its Venice premiere – and without any preparation except for having heard some of Stravinsky's neoclassic ballet scores. Here, I thought, was a work that was more *about* opera than it was an opera in its own right. Anne Trulove's first-act aria, for instance, refused to give me the emotional satisfactions I was accustomed to demand of a soprano's grand solo piece. To be sure, I could see how the work's selfconsciousness about opera had been anticipated in Strauss's *Ariadne auf Naxos*, but Strauss somehow had managed to have his cake and eat it too: he could parody operatic convention while also, in the heroine's big aria and in the final duet, letting his characters sing out with full operatic passion.

There are other ways that modernist works are "not-quite opera." One way is to cultivate popular musical forms, as, say, *Mahagonny* (1930) and *Porgy and Bess* (1935) do, and thus to imply that the high-art status that had been granted opera in the late nineteenth century could no longer be upheld. It is as though the introduction of jazz or of instruments ordinarily associated with a world of night clubs returns opera to that earlier state in which, from the Venetian operas of the 1630s until at least the mid-nineteenth century, a distinction between high- and low-brow music had not yet been instituted.

Or the exact theatrical status of certain modernist operas may be uncertain. Although *Moses und Aron* ended up firmly operatic, it started out as an oratorio and retains some oratorio-like characteristics. Stravinsky's *Oedipus Rex* (1927) also hovers between opera and oratorio: part of Stravinsky's point was that the characters remain statuesquely static, whether they appear as operatically costumed figures or simply as soloists on the concert stage. If *Oedipus* is opera reduced to its bare essentials (which, with its succession of arias in a dead language interrupted by a speaking narrator, means it might no longer really be "opera"), what do we make of *Perséphone* (1934), whose heroine's words are spoken by an actress and intertwined with chorus and orchestra and tenor soloist, or how do we classify that much more minimal piece *L'Histoire du soldat* (1918)? In the latter there are no singers, only two actors, a dancer, and the narrator telling a tale that a small group of instrumental players (constricted by limitations imposed by World War I) then enacts musically. Kurt Weill, in fact, singled out *L'Histoire*, standing, as he put it "between play, pantomime and opera," as a model for the future of opera.[1] Shall we perhaps call this a "quasi-opera"? Indeed, once we introduce a generic category such as quasi-opera, all manner of pieces might find their way into the canon of modernist opera, *Pierrot lunaire*, for instance, or the Sitwell/Walton *Façade* (1926), both of which stage what are essentially song cycles (or, rather, *Sprechstimme* cycles) in a costumed and histrionic manner. It is clear that the concept of "opera by other means" that I suggested in Essay 4 to describe certain music-theater events of the past two decades can be applied as well to these bold experiments of the early twentieth century.

This not-quite status cannot hide the fact that much modernist opera is obsessed with the operatic past and, in fact, with the musical past in general. For modernist opera displays a historical consciousness rarely to be found in earlier opera. Before the end of the

---

[1] Weill, "Die neue Oper," in *Musik und musikalisches Theater*, p. 44.

nineteenth century, composers had begun to evoke earlier musical styles: for example, those reminders of eighteenth-century music inserted in Massenet's and Puccini's Manon operas and Tchaikovsky's *Pique Dame*, as though to render musical cues pointing to the time and place in which these operas are set.

The imitation and, as often as not, overt parody of earlier forms is central to such modernist works as *Ariadne auf Naxos* and *The Rake's Progress*. The prologue that Strauss added several years after the premiere of the former work presents the hero and heroine of this opera in the proverbial guise of the vain prima donna and tenor. In the opera proper Zerbinetta's aria selfconsciously parodies early nineteenth-century coloratura arias. In view of the seemingly anti-operatic frame that Hofmannsthal and Strauss later created, even the more overtly operatic sections of *Ariadne* – above all, the heroine's aria "Es gibt ein Reich" and the final duet – raise an audience's suspicions of an ironic undercurrent beneath these ecstatic moments.

The prime example of operatic selfconsciousness among modernist operas remains *The Rake's Progress*, whose deliberate distortion of earlier opera will be developed in more detail in the next essay. From beginning to end the audience feels teased into identifying which elements of the operatic past are being reproduced, whether by overt parody, imitation, or whatever term we choose to describe Stravinsky's appropriation of his predecessors. What early nineteenth-century Italian aria should Anne Trulove's first-act aria remind us of? Any particular one, or just what we might call the archetypal first-act soprano aria of the period? And surely the card scene must be alluding to the cemetery scene in *Don Giovanni*. Stravinsky has written about attending a two-piano performance of *Così fan tutte* with his librettist Auden while working on the opera, adding, in fact, that "the *Rake* is deeply involved in *Così*."[2] But the *Rake* is of course deeply involved in the whole history of opera.

Audiences adept at hearing modernist opera customarily have their historical antennae out for vestiges of the past. In the

---

[2] Stravinsky and Craft, *Memories and Commentaries*, p. 158.

understatedness of *Pelléas et Mélisande* they may hear at once the fullstatedness of Wagnerian music-drama and the halfstatedness of Wagner's final work, *Parsifal* (above all, its two outer "sacred" acts). And in Salome's final scene, as has long been commented upon, we hear a rewrite, as it were, of Isolde's *Liebestod*, with the perversity of kissing a severed head replacing the uncompromised transcendence that Wagner strove for. Listening to modernist operas, one is never surprised to find references to earlier opera, indeed to the history of music as a whole. In *Peter Grimes*, at one point, we hear what sounds like the Coronation Scene from *Boris Godunov* (1869), at another a group of women's voices intertwined like those in the final trio in *Der Rosenkavalier* (1911). Sometimes these references serve as a reminder that the operatic pretensions of an earlier time can no longer be sustained in the modern world, sometimes simply as a way of giving a new and unaccustomed twist to a memorable idea from the past. Whatever functions we may assign to these allusions, they also in a sense endow modernist opera with an operatic aura to compensate for its "not-quite" status.

MODERNISM, HARD AND SOFT

Let's define a "hard" modernist opera as one that audiences, at least its early ones, find forbidding, inaccessible, unfriendly to those who want to enjoy themselves listening to hummable tunes. Or even if it should offer such melodies, a modernist opera may be hard to take because it seeks to provoke its audience, often, in fact, to scandalize it.

Given this definition, it is not difficult to list a canon of hard-modernist operas. Almost any non-tonal opera would qualify. This canon would also include tonal operas strong on loudness and dissonance, most notably Strauss's *Salome* (1905) and *Elektra* (1909). And it would include as well operas that sharply undercut their audiences' notions of what an opera should be, like many of the not-quite-operas discussed in the preceding section: for example, Hindemith's *Cardillac* (1926), with its rigorous, seemingly unemotional baroque musical forms accompanying the unrelenting violence of the dramatic action; or, exactly contemporary with this opera, Stravinsky's *Oedipus Rex*, with its static, larger-than-life characters, or the two Stein/Thomson operas, *Four Saints in Three Acts* (1934) and *The Mother of Us All* (1947), whose music sets words with a minimum of referential content and whose plots, by any conventional narrative standards, seem to go nowhere.

The hard-modernist canon is conspicuously marked by a number of works that evoked outrage from segments of their early audiences or from political authorities in the locales in which they were performed. Strauss's *Salome* set a pattern that was repeated in one form or another in subsequent years. The original Wilde play was sufficiently blasphemous to prevent its realization on the British stage, but the less stringent moral standards in many German cities made possible a famous production by Max Reinhardt that Strauss witnessed, after which he quickly got to work on his operatic version. The work evoked strong responses from varying groups: the avant-garde-friendly young, including Arnold Schoenberg, hailed *Salome* for its musical progressiveness; Strauss's German-Jewish supporters showed approval of his portrayal of the five Jews, whose musical discourse clearly satirized Eastern European Jews, whom they saw as their cultural inferiors;[3] and of course there was ample room for the shock of ordinary opera-goers, who found the whole project sensational enough to flock in numbers that enabled the composer, as he liked to put it, to buy his famed villa in Garmisch-Partenkirchen.

The financial success of the opera was certainly not diminished by the fact that it was prohibited in Vienna, where even Mahler, then still director of the Vienna Opera, could not get it performed in his own house. Its belated Austrian premiere in Graz in 1906, as I shall describe in detail in Essay 9, enticed some of central Europe's most important cultural figures to travel to an event in a provincial house. *Salome*'s fortunes at the Metropolitan Opera two years after

---

[3] See Gilman, "Strauss and the Pervert."

its 1905 Dresden premiere illustrate the extra-musical considerations affecting many hard-modernist works. The soprano assigned the title role, the great Olive Fremstad, was publicized going to the New York City morgue to find out for herself what the head of a dead man likely weighed. The Met's boxholders were so shocked after the first performance that the opera was immediately withdrawn – not to be performed in the house again for several decades, though its later rival company, the Manhattan Opera, mounted a *Salome* within a couple of years.

In hard-modernist opera the moral element can never be fully separated from the musical. Had *Erwartung* (1909, performed 1924) and *Lulu* (1935; performed partially 1937, complete 1979) been heard widely soon after their composition, one wonders what strong reactions might have manifested themselves and what form their audiences' reaction might have assumed. The controversy surrounding *Mahagonny* at its Leipzig premiere in 1930 was more political than musical in nature, for the opera set off demonstrations by Nazis to the point that a number of productions scheduled in other German opera houses were canceled.

Of course the most celebrated scandal surrounding a modernist musical work was not occasioned by an opera at all, but was the rioting set off by the opening of *Le Sacre du printemps* in Paris in 1913. Yet this work's distance from opera is not that great, for the audience was reacting not only to the radicality of Stravinsky's musical style but at least as much to the boldness with which the music's primitivism was realized visually in the ballet's choreography. The sense of shock central to hard modernism, whether the medium is painting, poetry, or concert music, becomes all the more acute when spectators are gathered together to be bombarded both by the sounds and sights that surround them.

Or rather *were* gathered together, for shock wears off over time. *Salome* and *Elektra* can never exercise the same bite that their first audiences experienced. The usual way to return an opera such as *Salome* to its hard-modernist roots is by way of innovations in its stage production, providing, say, a head of John the Baptist still visibly bleeding or, as has been the usual formula, encouraging the heroine to shock audiences by way of her body. When I was a student in Vienna during the early 1950s, local rumor had it that the reigning Salome, Ljuba Welitsch, customarily ended her dance by baring her private parts to her various Herods at stage right (though decidedly not to the audience). Well before the end of the twentieth century it had become *de rigueur* (at least for those sopranos with sufficiently trim bodies) to denude themselves frontwise, if ever so briefly. The latest production I have witnessed, in October 2009, gave a new twist to the final scene when the heroine, lying on her back writhing, held the Baptist's bloody head firmly planted in her crotch.

Although the effects of most hard-modernist operas have softened with the years, not so the four Schoenberg operas, all but one of which remained unproduced until many years after their composition. *Erwartung*, composed over a century ago, for me at least remains powerfully disconcerting after repeated hearings. By contrast, many neoclassic operas that once proved formidable have acclimated themselves well. Although *The Rake's Progress*, as I indicated earlier, at first struck me as a bit academic in its examination of operatic conventions, many subsequent hearings and viewings have transformed this work for me, to the point that at certain moments, for example, Anne's deeply moving lullaby to the demented Tom, I experience an expressiveness of the sort one does not readily associate with Stravinsky.

One can also speak of a tradition of works that count as softmodernist from the start. I refer to the many operas that utilize techniques, both literary and musical, that had been pioneered in hard-modernist opera but that turned out to be less radically new and also less likely to scandalize, whether on moral or musical grounds. Let me insist at this point that I do not intend "hard" and "soft" as value judgments of particular works; rather, I use these terms to describe a phenomenon peculiar to modernism within the arts, namely, the fact that modernist art at certain moments assumed extreme positions to a degree scarcely discernible in earlier periods. These positions could not be sustained over long stretches of time: a musical dissonance can disturb for only so long until we absorb it, and a dramatic situation loses its power to disorient or to outrage in something of the same way.

Strauss's operatic career provides perhaps the most obvious instance of a composer's transition from hard to soft modernist. Whereas *Salome* and *Elektra* set a model for how radically modernist opera can provoke, his notorious shifting of compositional gears to the more easily digestible operas that followed *Elektra* – a retreat for which Schoenberg and the musical avant-garde never forgave him – did not actually represent an abandonment of modernism. *Der Rosenkavalier* (1911) and *Ariadne auf Naxos* (1912, 1916) could not have been composed a decade or two before. Each is innovative, both musically and dramatically, in its own way, as, for instance, in the bitonal moments in *Rosenkavalier* or in the theatrical selfconsciousness of *Ariadne*.

Yet the later Strauss operas display a certain musical timidity when viewed next to *Salome* and *Elektra*, not to speak of the works of Schoenberg and his school. Nor do they scandalize. The opening scene of *Der Rosenkavalier* showing the Marschallin and Oktavian in bed was little more than a tease compared to the final scene of *Salome*. Even the ecphrasis of an orgasm in the prelude to this opera remained discreet, for only in retrospect, after the curtain rises, would the viewer be aware of what Strauss was describing. Compare this ecphrasis to the one in Shostakovich's brashly hard-modernist *Lady Macbeth of Mtsensk* (1934), in which the orchestra tells us in no uncertain terms what is going on between the lovers onstage (though in some productions they retreat briefly to an alcove or neighboring room during this graphic musical interlude). Whether or not it was this particular scene that set off Stalin's ire when he attended a performance two years after the premiere, the official response to *Lady Macbeth* may well constitute the most devastating operatic scandal of the last century, if only because it discouraged Shostakovich from continuing his career as an opera composer.

Again, let me emphasize that my categories "hard" and "soft" are independent of my judgment of a work's greatness. To me at least

Der Rosenkavalier, Ariadne auf Naxos, and *Die Frau ohne Schatten* (1919) are just as important as the two Strauss operas that preceded them. Similarly, Benjamin Britten's operas, great though some like *Peter Grimes* (1945) and *Billy Budd* (1951) may be, belong to the soft-modernist category, for they live off certain modernist techniques developed earlier in the century. Nor did they scandalize in their time despite the homosexual themes that run discreetly through many of them; *Death in Venice* (1975), which treats this matter overtly, dates from a time in which the staging of these themes had become publicly acceptable. Yet at least one Britten opera, the relatively little known chamber opera *Curlew River* (1964), through its inventive instrumentation, its design for performance in church rather than in the opera house, and its mixture of Japanese Noh dramatic convention and Western medieval musical style, shows the distinct markings of a hard-modernist experiment.

If Poulenc's *Les Mamelles de Tirésias* (1947), in its surrealist madness and with its plethora of popular song types, is clearly hard-modernist, the later, more musically tame and ideologically pious *Les Dialogues des Carmélites* (1957) belongs to the soft-modernist genre. Janáček, with his insistent melodic repetitions and transformation of Czech speech rhythms into musical phrases, achieved a compactness and dramatic intensity that, from *Jenůfa* (1904) onwards, was hard-modernist to the core.

Yet what does one make of those twentieth-century composers who steadfastly refused the summons to make themselves into modernists? In the midst of drafting this essay, I read of the death, at 95, of Gian-Carlo Menotti, who, with a keen sense for theatrical effect, was able during the 1940s and 50s to give a certain musical pleasure to consumers intent on nothing more challenging than the early Puccini operas they loved. Menotti does not deserve the label "modernist" (even soft), a category he obviously shunned.

There is one great early twentieth-century opera that not only avoids any discernibly modernist musical style but actually allegorizes the dilemma of a composer who refuses to be caught up in the modernist bandwagon. I refer of course to Hans Pfitzner's *Palestrina*

(1917), whose hero insists on retaining the older polyphonic style against both the Counter-Reformation's demand for a simpler, more communicable style and the Florentine theorists advocating monody. *Palestrina* is in a late nineteenth-century idiom, Wagnerian in a sense but largely diatonic and in a voice distinctly Pfitzner's own. In the perversity and intransigence with which it defies the new aesthetic, *Palestrina* surely deserves the label "honorary modernist."

MODERNIST OPERA IN HISTORICAL PERSPECTIVE

Now that modernism is receding into the past, how does modernist opera look different to us from opera in earlier periods, and how innovative is it compared to other modernist music and other modernist art forms? I have already shown how modernist operas often seem diminished, sometimes distinctly unoperatic in relation to opera of the preceding century. And I have also indicated that certain key works created their modernist identity by provoking their audiences with new musical techniques and with controversial moral and political stances, often both at once.

I start with a factual observation: the major modernist composers have been conspicuously unproductive compared with their fore-bears. Whereas Handel and Rossini each composed around forty operas, Vivaldi supposedly a hundred (of which only a small percentage is extant), and Verdi close to thirty, the most productive modernists – Strauss, Prokofiev, Janáček, Britten – put out at best between half a dozen to a little over a dozen works. The two most celebrated modernist composers, Schoenberg and Stravinsky, each produced a single full-length opera (one not even completed) plus a few short operas. If Wagner, with the mere ten operas that comprise his mature canon, proved less productive than his contemporaries, this also indicates that his characteristic approach to operatic composition – the long gestation periods, the new styles he devised from one opera to the next, the difficulties he created for his audiences, as well as the obstacles he encountered getting his work produced – helped set up a model that later modernist composers would develop.

The decline in opera productivity can be attributed in one sense to the difficulties composers found making a living from opera – Strauss's commercial success, even with his most "difficult" operas, being a notable exception. Throughout most of operatic history, the major European cities possessed institutions – most often government-subsidized, though sometimes capitalist ventures as in seventeenth-century Venice – that offered composers and librettists (not to speak of singers, instrumentalists, and designers) a regular outlet to display their talents and make a living. And of course the public remained eager for new operas and rarely expected revivals of older ones. Each country to be sure differed in the way the opera industry, to use the term John Rosselli employed to describe the Italian system of the late eighteenth and early nineteenth centuries, was organized.[4] In nineteenth-century France, for example, the goal of any ambitious composer was to be produced at the Paris Opéra. The industry that Rosselli depicted was succeeded in the later nineteenth century in Italy by a system in which the music publishers, most notably Ricordi, brought together composer and librettist, arranged productions of new operas at the major theaters, and enjoyed the profits resulting from distribution of the scores. As long as new works were in vogue, the public could count on some way of getting them created and performed. But the economics of Italian opera at the turn of the twentieth century may well have encouraged a musical conservatism among Italian composers unlike the more adventuresome attitude prevalent among their French and German contemporaries.

By the start of the modernist period, older operas within the repertory had become the norm, and the demand for new ones, especially if they proved difficult at first hearing, was decreasing. Yet in Germany, at least, the presence of state-supported opera houses in cities large and small provided a venue for new work, even of a

---

[4] Rosselli, *The Opera Industry in Italy.*

forbidding character. Such challenging operas as Berg's *Wozzeck* (1925) and Schoenberg's *Von Heute auf Morgen* (1930) premiered in major houses, but, as with most hard-modernist operas, there were few subsequent performances; the former did not gain a real public until the 1950s, and the latter has never had much of a performance history. The Janáček operas were generally premiered in the provincial house in the composer's home town of Brno and did not even reach Prague, let alone the rest of Europe, until a good bit later. Britten's early operas were able to get produced by being attached to festivals – and eventually of course the composer created his own festival in Aldeburgh to help facilitate performances of his own works.

But the relative slowness of modernist composers in producing operas can be attributed not simply to economic conditions but also to the fact that the modernist aesthetic in all the arts demands that artists create their own styles independent of one another. However distinct the styles of, say, the so-called *bel canto* composers were, they each possessed a set of period conventions – for example, the particular shape of an aria, the distribution of arias and choruses – to fall back upon. Modernist composers, like modernist poets and painters, have to a great degree been forced to set up their own conventions (if we can even usefully employ the word *convention* in this period). Ezra Pound's celebrated command to his fellow poets, "Make it new," stands as a tag applicable to modernism in general – and of course Pound even tried his hand (twice!) at composing modernist opera.[5] Moreover, many modernists have felt it incumbent upon themselves to recreate their styles, sometimes several times over, in the course of their careers. Stravinsky's *Nightingale* (1914, and itself straddling two distinct stages in the composer's career) is worlds apart from *The Rake's Progress*, Prokofiev's *Love of Three Oranges* (1921) from *The Gambler* (1929), and the latter

---

[5] Pound used this phrase throughout his life to keep himself and his fellow modernist writers on track. He also used it as the title of a collection of essays (1934). Pound's operas, both of which reflect his literary interests, are *Le Testament* (1926), based on François Villon, and *Cavalcanti* (1933).

just as far removed from *War and Peace* (1946). Yet the Janáček operas, by contrast, are all of a piece.

It is characteristic of a modernist opera that, both because of its small public and the difficulty of preparing adequate performances, there is often a time lag between its completion and first staging. *Pelléas et Mélisande* waited some seven years (although Debussy put off finishing the full orchestral score until he was assured of a production); *Wozzeck* waited three years; Prokofiev's *Fiery Angel* waited virtually thirty years, during which time several proposed productions failed to materialize. By contrast the ink on the scores of some of the most famous operas of past centuries was scarcely dry by the time their first curtains went up.

Since modernist opera shares what one might call an aesthetic of difficulty with the other modernist arts, one might ask at what point its avant-garde breakthroughs came about in comparison with these other arts. The most radical development in twentieth-century music – at least from the point of view of a long-resisting public – remains Schoenberg's break with tonality in 1908, specifically with the third movement of his second string quartet. This was one year after Picasso's *Les Demoiselles d'Avignon*, generally considered the start of Cubism; and it is three years after the Fauve experiments with color. More relevant to Schoenberg's own milieu is the development of Expressionist painting, both the composer's own paintings and those of his friend Kandinsky. Schoenberg ultimately chose not to pursue painting, and his work never became abstract as Kandinsky's later did. But Kandinsky's work does not abandon representation until his paintings of late 1913, and even then, as in the supposedly non-representational *Composition VII* (November, 1919), a recent analyst has located "figurative relics of religious subject matter (motifs of salvation)."[6]

Within German poetry the first radical experiments with language were those of August Stramm and, more successfully, of Georg Trakl. These took place several years after Schoenberg's break with

[6] Hoberg, "Vasily Kandinsky," p. 30.

tonality. Trakl's first linguistically distorted poems, which date from late 1912, resulted from the poet's reading a German translation of Rimbaud, whose own experiments in *Illuminations* of 1872 can count today as the earliest examples of modernism in literature from a stylistic point of view.[7] Mallarmé's experiments with poetic form followed soon after, but I know of no poetry in the other European languages before the second decade of the twentieth century that played with language as radically as Trakl's did.[8] And at very much the same time as Schoenberg's break with tonality, Gertrude Stein was rethinking the language and structure of narrative in *The Making of Americans* (1906–11, not published until 1925).

The abandonment of tonality affected operatic composition in a particular way. Without a system for organizing a composition, Schoenberg felt forced to write relatively short pieces. But setting texts gave him a crutch, as it were, to sustain a piece. Schoenberg's two short operas, *Erwartung* and *Die glückliche Hand*, were considerably longer, by dint of their being based on texts, than his individual instrumental writings of the early atonal period, for example, the Opus 11 piano pieces (1909) and the Five Pieces for Orchestra (1909). Similarly, Berg's full-length *Wozzeck*, sustained as it was by the play on which it was based, allowed the composer to create a structure much vaster than that of his instrumental works. By the early 1920s, of course, Schoenberg had evolved his twelve-tone system, which encouraged him and Berg (though distinctly

---

[7] For a detailed discussion of how Trakl turned Rimbaud's breakthrough into a new way of conceiving poetry in German, see my chapter "The Discovery of a Style" in Lindenberger, *Georg Trakl*, pp. 58–80. On Rimbaud's and also on Gertrude Stein's significance in the history of modernist poetry in English, see Perloff, *The Poetics of Indeterminacy*, pp. 45–66 (on Rimbaud), 67–108 (on Stein).

[8] Trakl's linguistic radicalism was matched by the musical radicalism of Anton von Webern, who was much drawn to Trakl and who, in the years following the poet's death, set seven of his poems to music. As Anne C. Shreffler puts it in her book-length study of Webern's Trakl songs, "By distorting traditional images and dissociating them from one another, Trakl produces something very much like atonality in music." See Shreffler, *Webern and the Lyric Impulse*, p. 29.

not Webern, who remained committed to the short piece) to undertake longer instrumental pieces.

If Schoenberg's two early operas stand at the forefront of modernist experimentation during the first years of the twentieth century, several operas composed nearly two decades later are key representatives of that phase of modernism within the arts that we call the classicism, or neoclassicism, of the 1920s. I refer to works such as Busoni's *Doktor Faust* (1925), Hindemith's *Cardillac* (1926), and Stravinsky's *Oedipus Rex* (1927). What holds these operas together is a disdain for Wagnerian music-drama, indeed, for the whole Romantic tradition. All use elements drawn from baroque style as a means of foregrounding artifice over overt expressiveness. And each is organized as a number opera, in contrast to the unencumbered flow of music-drama; indeed, much of the energy exerted by these number operas derives from their self-conscious defiance of the Wagnerian tradition.

Just as Schoenberg's early operas share the radical distortions of traditional forms with the paintings and poetry of their time, so the neoclassical operas of the 1920s find their parallels in, say, Picasso's neoclassical paintings of the early 1920s or in Joyce's *Ulysses* (1922), each of whose episodes, drawn as they are from the *Odyssey*, cultivates a distinctly different literary style. Or one might also cite T. S. Eliot, whose anti-romantic fervor manifested itself in an anti-subjective theory and practice of poetry, together with proclamations of his allegiance to classicism. Even *Wozzeck*, despite its standing as a music-drama in the Wagnerian tradition, manifests its own form of classicism through the fact that each of its short scenes is modeled after a traditional musical form.

POSTMODERNIST OPERA, PERHAPS?

I took a stab at defining postmodern opera over two decades ago when assigned a berth in a collection called "Post-Modern Genres," mine being the only piece that did opera.[9] The term *postmodern* was

[9] Lindenberger, "From Opera to Postmodernity."

much in the air at that time, and critics representing the various art forms were intent on locating the particular traits that separated postmodern from modernist within these forms. In architecture one could point to the echoing of various past styles (often several styles in a single building) in, say, Michael Graves or the later Philip Johnson, who practiced a mode of artifice contrasting sharply with the clean lines of the modernist International Style. Or in painting there was that move from the subjectivity associated with Surrealism and Abstract Expressionism to such anti-subjective, often also anti-elite-art postmodernist movements as Pop Art, Op Art, Minimalism, and Conceptual Art.

But what could I do with postmodernist opera? Opera, I quickly realized, is a relatively conservative form, and, despite the powerful hard-modernist breakthroughs in the early part of the twentieth century, there was little comparable in opera during the latter part of the century. I spent a good bit of my essay comparing the art museum and the opera house, as I did again in Essay 4 of the present book, as well as trying to account for the greater welcome that greeted daringly new forms in the museum. To be sure, I came up with a few operatic examples, most notably John Adams's *Nixon in China* (1987), which sent some controversial recent political figures to the operatic stage singing against pulsating minimalist rhythms; or the Wilson/Glass *Einstein on the Beach* (1976), which stretched the limits of opera through its use of electronic media and its absence of individual singing voices. My primary example of a postmodern approach to opera was not the creation of new works but rather the re-creation of familiar old operas by iconoclastic directors who challenged a conservative opera public by giving these works unexpected settings and often a new social message to boot.

When I adapted this essay for a collection of my own essays in 1990, I was able to add a few examples not available three years before – for instance, Peter Sellars's resettings of the Da Ponte/Mozart operas in seemingly improbable contemporary American settings; or John Cage's *Europeras 1 & 2* (1987), whose aleatory method and improvisational contributions by its singers accord easily with what counts as postmodern in other arts (as they well should since Cage helped institute these procedures in mid century).[10]

Yet in the intervening years I began to wonder how useful the term *postmodern* is in describing opera. For one thing, as Daniel Albright has shown in his searching study of operatic and other theatrical experiments of the 1920s and 30s, many elements I took to be postmodern had been anticipated decades before.[11] Moreover, the most radical pieces I described in my essay have not been developed much further at this point. After their Frankfurt run, Cage's various versions of *Europeras* have been performed – and in diminished form – only under the aegis of Cage and his disciples. Glass's operatic career after *Einstein on the Beach* has moved in a more conventional direction, notable for the nearly two dozen operas (a productivity more typical of nineteenth-century composers) that, unlike *Einstein*, use real singers and could best be classified as soft-modernist works. What would easily count as postmodern demands a different kind of performance space – and one not dependent on subscribers intent on hearing operatic voices and symphonic orchestras. Generically, postmodern opera, like many postmodern artifacts within that larger realm we call the arts, belongs to that classification "mixed media" used by museums to designate items not confined to such traditional materials as oil, graphite, or charcoal.

OPERATIC MODERNISM IN RETROSPECT

If we place the recent works I treated in Essay 4 as "opera by other means" within a category related to but also different from opera – a turn-of-the-twenty-first-century version, say, of that category "not-quite opera" – it is possible to look back at the last century as a period of continuing modernism that achieves much of its identity through its dialogue with nineteenth-century opera. Consider the

---

[10] Lindenberger, *The History in Literature*, pp. 163–88. On *Europeras 1 & 2*, see my discussion in Essay 3 as well as my chapter about this work in *Opera in History*, pp. 240–64.

[11] Albright, *Untwisting the Serpent*.

nature of nineteenth-century opera: from Rossini through Verdi, from Meyerbeer through Massenet, from Weber through Wagner, whatever the differences in national styles, here was a period that distinguished itself from the preceding two centuries of opera in certain conspicuous ways. For one thing, opera at the start of the nineteenth century became considerably louder than it had ever been before, with larger, more full-bodied voices, an increasingly larger orchestra, more massive choral forces, and above all a largeness of conception encapsulated in the French term *grand opéra*. Even the innovations brought about by Wagnerian music-drama, however much it distanced itself from other operatic traditions, participated fully in this development. And most significant nineteenth-century opera remained in the tragic mode; after Rossini, Italian comic opera, which had flourished during the eighteenth century, became increasingly rare. Indeed, as we now look back at four centuries of opera, nineteenth-century opera, compared with what came before and after it, stands out above all for its grandeur and its solemnity.

In its dialogue with its nineteenth-century predecessor, modernist opera plays upon some crucial similarities and differences. When it goes loud, as in *Salome* and *Elektra*, it does so with a violence and a perversity unheard and unheard of earlier. When it goes florid, as in *Cardillac* and *Oedipus Rex*, it eschews earlier notions of vocal beauty to produce sounds that seem deliberately strained, even grotesque. When it seeks tragic effect, as in *Wozzeck* and *Katya Kabanova*, it does so with a concision and an unbearable intensity rarely equaled earlier. When it undertakes what seems a traditional operatic plot, as in *Pelléas et Mélisande* and *Doktor Faust*, it does so with understatement or irony.

Impressive as the canon of modernist opera looks today, it is a fact that few, if any, hard-modernist works are performed with the frequency (or are embraced as heartily by the opera-house audience) that marks some twenty or more operas of the preceding century as well as the Mozart operas. Perhaps only *Salome* comes close. Among what I have called soft-modernist operas, only *Der Rosenkavalier* belongs in this category. Much though one may admire and also love *Mahagonny*, *Lulu*, and *The Rake's Progress*, nobody expects crowds to flock their way, the way they do to *Il barbiere di Siviglia*, *Rigoletto*, and *Carmen*. (To be sure, a run of *Lulu* sold out in San Francisco in 1989, but largely, one suspects, for extra-musical reasons.)

The relative lack of opera-fan enthusiasm for modernist opera has by no means deterred the composition of new operas. Most twentieth-century composers of stature have produced at least one opera, even Steve Reich, who, as Essay 4 explains, has produced two examples of what I call "opera by other means." During the first half of the twentieth century a goodly proportion of new operas – for instance, Zandonai's *Francesca da Rimini* (1914) or Braunfels's *Die Vögel* (1920), not to speak of those Puccini operas composed during the new century – could not be called modernist so much as derivations of late nineteenth-century opera. This was also the period that witnessed the significant hard-modernist operas, very few of which date from the later part of the century – with the notable exception of that uncompromisingly austere work, Messiaen's *Saint François d'Assise* (1983), which I shall discuss in detail in the next essay.

Yet composers and impresarios have remained endlessly optimistic about producing new operas in full knowledge of the resistance audiences feel toward unfamiliar works. Still, the past couple of decades have witnessed a resurgence of operatic commissions by major companies. The formula for success usually includes these elements: famous singers to attract an audience; a director chosen to provide the work with theatrical flair; music drawing on one or more earlier modernist styles; and, more often than not, a plot deriving from some well-known book, play, or film familiar to the audience. To cite several American examples, note such operas as the following: André Previn's *A Streetcar Named Desire* (drawn from the play and movie), San Francisco Opera, 1998; John Harbison's *The Great Gatsby* (drawn from the novel), Metropolitan Opera, 1999; Jake Heggie's *Dead Man Walking* (drawn from a non-fiction book and movie), San Francisco Opera, 2000; William Bolcom's *A View from the*

Bridge (drawn from the play), Chicago Lyric Opera, 1999, and *A Wedding* (drawn from the Robert Altman movie), Chicago Lyric Opera, 2004. All of these were reasonably accessible, classically soft-modernist works, and all gained a goodly amount of national attention. Most have gone on to productions at other opera houses, but of course it is too early to tell whether any of these works has the staying power to attract audiences over the years.

I end this retrospect with a prospect, or rather a set of questions, about the operatic future. Might we be entering a new era of opera different from modernism, without its shock effects, whether moral or musical? Is it conceivable that any of the acknowledged high points of modernist opera – for example, *Oedipus Rex*, *Wozzeck*, *Mahagonny* – may at some point gain a following comparable to that of the nineteenth-century warhorses? Or is the opera house, like the symphony hall, destined to become largely a museum for pre-modernist and perhaps also classical modernist works, with the more controversial operas relegated to special performance places, like those museums devoted to the most contemporary art? Will operatic composers meld Western and non-Western forms of music, as I suggested in Essay 3 by way of Tan Dun's *First Emperor* (Metropolitan Opera, 2006), which not only adds some Chinese instruments to the orchestra but also makes vocal music out of Chinese speech inflections? Will works such as *Einstein on the Beach* and *The Cave*, with their absence of operatic voices, provide models for mixed-genre events that call themselves something like "performance pieces" or "musical entertainments"? As the population that grew up on rock music becomes dominant in our society, could the venues developed for popular music provide an institutional framework for these forms? Indeed, will rock operas like The Who's *Tommy* and Green Day's *American Idiot* come to seem mainstream? Might the older repertory languish for want of interest and, consequently, funds? Through its vigorous pursuit of other means, might opera as we have known it these past four centuries finally lose its identity?

An anti-theatrical opera would seem to be a contradiction in terms. Theatricality, after all, suggests an exaggerated perspective on what we take to be reality, a certain inauthenticity that, as Jonas Barish argued in *The Antitheatrical Prejudice*, has been an issue within Western thought since its beginnings. The term *operatic* implies the exaggeration of a theatrical stance already assumed to be exaggerated. Thus, an opera that questions the nature and value of theatricality would seem to put enormous constraints on composers and performers, not to speak of audiences eager to experience the enactment of those high emotions that they would not dare to reveal in their everyday lives.

Yet many of the operas that we now see as central to the twentieth-century canon display an anti-theatricality similar to what Barish, in his final chapter, describes in such major dramatists of the century as Chekhov, Pirandello, Brecht, and Beckett. Pirandello, as he puts it, poses "a challenge to the theater as an expressive medium, a rebuke to its age-old claim to be able to instruct us about our true natures," while Beckett initiates "a new radicalism" in which "the tissue of plausible event is stripped away" and "character is scraped down to the bone of consciousness." For Barish, the revolutionary innovations of twentieth-century theater have worked to "burn down the ornate, overloaded theater of the past in the hope that a purified theater will rise from its ashes."[1]

The task of the present essay is to demonstrate the differing ways that four operas cutting across the twentieth century – Debussy's *Pelléas et Mélisande* (1902), Schoenberg's *Moses und Aron* (1932), Stravinsky's *The Rake's Progress* (1951), and Messiaen's *Saint François*

---

[1] Barish, *The Antitheatrical Prejudice*, pp. 453, 457, 464, respectively.

d'Assise (1983) – express an anti-theatricality analogous to what Barish explores in the drama of the same period. But unlike Barish, who considers modern drama in the light of a 2,500-year debate about the theater, I am principally concerned with the ways in which modernist works, whether spoken or musical, respond to what their creators and audiences would have viewed as peculiarly theatrical in the writing of the past. Thus, Brecht's use of a multitude of devices to break the theatrical illusion, or Beckett's insistent repetitions and his refusal to work toward what once counted as a dramatic resolution, play upon their audiences' knowledge and often too-willing acceptance of the conventions governing the so-called well-made play. In this form, whether the "serious" drama of an Ibsen or the boulevard plays of a Scribe, the need for a constantly forward-moving plot and for characters who could pass for real-life persons provided a model that twentieth-century drama worked fervently to undo.

Similarly with opera. Just as the model for what counts as theatrical was rooted in the writing of the preceding century, so, as I argued in Essay 7, the model for what is peculiarly operatic derived from the works with which audiences have been most familiar, namely the canonical operas of the mid and late nineteenth century. What we see as "operatic" has, of course, changed in the course of history: what would have seemed operatic in the Venetian public theaters of the mid seventeenth century is something quite different from what was deemed operatic in the heyday of *opera seria* during the eighteenth century.[2]

For twentieth-century audiences, who until recent years rarely heard operas earlier than those of Mozart, the operatic canon, as mentioned earlier, occupied a relatively small segment of musical history. Despite differences in national styles, some key operas of the

---

[2] In an earlier discussion of what I called "operatic discourse," I postulated a scale ranging from "operatic" to "verbal" to encompass the differences between what I am here calling "theatrical" and "anti-theatrical." (See *Opera: The Extravagant Art*, pp. 75–95.) Whereas the earlier account remained largely on a theoretical level, I here seek to contextualize these extremes by distinguishing between a "theatrical" nineteenth century and an "anti-theatrical" twentieth century.

1850s display an extreme of what subsequent operagoers could perceive as operatic: in Italy, *Il trovatore* (1853); in Germany, *Tristan und Isolde* (1859); in France, *Faust* (1859). In *Il trovatore*, as Essay 1 stressed, we experience a melodramatic plot in which crises follow one another at a dizzying pace until the final catastrophe; an unrelenting extravagance of gesture, as in Leonora's putting a stop to the duel fought by her two would-be suitors, or the gypsy's flamboyant narrative about her exchange of babies; and a frenzied piling up of the arias, duets, and ensembles that take the formal conventions of early nineteenth-century opera to their limits. In *Tristan*, what we come to see as operatic derives from the large orchestra that defines and underlines the overwhelming emotions of the lovers; from the extraordinary length to which individual high points – the second-act love duet, Tristan's last-act feverish monologue – are sustained; from the sheer volume demanded of the voices throughout. In *Faust*, the operatic manifests itself in the single-minded earnestness into which Goethe's theatrically selfconscious and sometimes comic text has been transformed; in the shamelessly sweet arias and duets assigned to the tenor and soprano; in the dramatic exuberance of its grand ensembles, such as the Walpurgisnacht ballet, the death of Valentin, and the death of Marguerite.

If these and other operas of their time later seemed to hit a highwater mark of operatic theatricality, the final works by two of their composers show a clear retreat from this extreme.[3] In *Falstaff* (1893), for instance, Verdi allows arias and ensembles to be fragmented and truncated, as though questioning the authenticity with which he spoke out operatically some forty years earlier. The most histrionic and also the most fully worked out aria, Ford's "È sogno?," is actually a parody of the revenge arias endemic in earlier Italian opera. Indeed, *Falstaff* parodies such other elements of traditional opera as the wooing duet, the serenade, and the conspiracy scene.

---

[3] My use of *Falstaff* and *Parsifal*, in the following pages, as transitions from a highly theatrical nineteenth-century mode to a more muted twentieth-century one, was suggested by Linda and Michael Hutcheon's essay on Verdi's and Wagner's late style, "'Tutto nel mondo è burla.'"

Although parody is a common enough device within the comic genre to which *Falstaff* belongs, it is also significant that during the mid-nineteenth century comic opera had virtually ceased to exist in Italy. In its finale, *Falstaff*, like *Don Giovanni* (1787) a century before and like *The Rake's Progress* half a century later, draws its characters out of the action to allow them, like spectators in the theater, to comment upon it.

Wagner's *Parsifal* tests the limits of nineteenth-century theatricality in ways that anticipate the anti-theatrical moves that I shall point out in operas of the next century. Note, for example, the sharp distinction between the "secular" middle act, the only act in which audiences traditionally have applauded, and the two outer "religious" acts, whose conclusions are acknowledged with awed silence. Wagner has carefully segregated what we are to view as theatrical and what supposedly transcends theater.

In contrast to the two spiritual acts, *Parsifal*'s middle act is clearly the music-drama's single operatic act. What we experience as operatic in this act – the flower maidens exercising their charms in Klingsor's magic garden, Kundry's role as love goddess – we are also to see as bogus, as dangerous and as inauthentic as anything that the anti-theatrical polemicists from Plato onwards, as Barish presents them in his book, found in earlier drama. The encounter between Parsifal and Kundry that should have brought the "love" interest to a climax in Act II becomes instead a proud repudiation of sexual love. Parsifal's loud exclamation, "Amfortas! Die Wunde!"[4] is an operatic gesture that also works to forestall the consummation of love. Indeed, once Parsifal has rejected Kundry's overtures, she loses her theatrical power and is gradually reduced, in the final part of the act, to the passive, virtually silent creature that she remains throughout Act III. In *Tristan und Isolde*, by contrast, the discovery of the lovers in Act II, though it prevents immediate consummation as well as a musical closure to the love duet, simply postpones the inevitable consummation, which Isolde, returning with full

---

[4] Wagner, *Parsifal*, ed. Voss, p. 148.

vocal power in her "Liebestod," brings about at the end of the opera on a higher, non-earthly level.

Gurnemanz, the central figure of the two anti-theatrical acts of *Parsifal*, also has the longest role in this music-drama, and, in view of his understated, unlyrical style, his is also the least "operatic" role. His discourse remains relatively close to speech rhythms; when Wagner's characters in earlier music-dramas – Loge, Mime, and Beckmesser, for instance – speak this way, they are comic, ironic, grotesque, and they speak rapidly. But Gurnemanz speaks his lines slowly and with utter earnestness (he is, after all, the most knowing character of the opera) and only occasionally sings out to accompany the orchestra in one of the leitmotifs.

To be sure, each of *Parsifal*'s two presumably anti-theatrical acts ends on a distinctly theatrical note with the temple rituals – especially the final act, which culminates in Parsifal's proclamation of his triumph. Yet, as Wagner's generic designation for *Parsifal, Bühnenweih-festspiel* ("sacred festival play"), suggests, the composer, like Calderón in his *autos sacramentales*, has it both ways, with a highly charged theatricality contained within a religious framework that maintains at least the pretense of having transcended its theatrical roots.

From the anti-theatricality of *Parsifal*'s Gurnemanz scenes, it is a small but quite significant step to *Pelléas et Mélisande*. Wagner's approximation of speech rhythms, the frequent understatedness of both the words and the music, and the attempt to conjure up a sense of mystery unfamiliar within earlier opera: all these helped lay the groundwork for Debussy. But the crucial element behind this most anti-theatrical of operas was the dramaturgy of the play by Maurice Maeterlinck (1892) from which Debussy drew his text. The play itself was an attempt to apply Symbolist theory to drama, with the result that, in his plays of the 1890s, the Symbolist disdain for explicitness and its advocacy of suggestiveness and understatement challenged the overt theatricality central to popular nineteenth-century drama.

Few dramatists have risen or fallen in esteem as fast as Maeter-linck. Little performed today, he lives on through Debussy's opera and, just as importantly, through his anti-theatrical legacy, which, as a recent book on Maeterlinck has argued, was picked up half a century after his heyday by dramatists such as Beckett, Ionesco, and Pinter.[5] Note the following exchange from Maeterlinck's play as Golaud asks his child, Yniold, to observe his wife, Mélisande, through a window as she talks with his brother, Pelléas:

GOLAUD: De quoi parlent-ils?

YNIOLD: De moi; toujours de moi.

GOLAUD: Et que disent-ils de toi?

YNIOLD: Ils disent que je serai très grand.

GOLAUD: Ah! misère de ma vie! ... Pelléas et petite-mère ne parlent-ils jamais de moi quand je ne suis pas là?

YNIOLD: Si, si, petit-père; ils parlent toujours de vous.

GOLAUD: Ah! ... Et que disent-ils de moi?

YNIOLD: Ils disent que je deviendrai aussi grand que vous.

[GOLAUD: What are they talking about?

YNIOLD: About me; always about me.

GOLAUD: And what are they saying about you?

YNIOLD: They're saying I'll be very big.

GOLAUD: How miserable for me! ... Don't Pelléas and Mommy ever talk about me when I'm not there?

YNIOLD: Yes, yes, Daddy.

GOLAUD: Oh! ... And what are they saying about me?

YNIOLD: They're saying I'll turn out to be as big as you.][6]

The inconsequentiality of this exchange, in which a jealous Golaud desperately seeks information about his wife's relations with his brother, is emblematic of the difficulties that audiences must have faced in making theatrical sense out of this play. The most urgent questions here receive typically childlike, *non-sequitur* responses.

The music to which Debussy set these words reacts to earlier operatic discourse much as these lines react to earlier theater.[7] Both

---

[5] See McGuinness, *Maurice Maeterlinck*, pp. 86–87, 155, 161, 170, 198–203, 213–16, 226, 228–29, 234–35.

[6] Maeterlinck, *Théâtre*, vol. II (1929), pp. 83–85.

[7] Debussy, *Pelléas et Mélisande*, pp. 227–30.

the text and the music go against our usual expectations. In Debussy's setting of the lines before the first ellipsis, the orchestra creates a sinister effect to suggest Golaud's jealousy, which scarcely seems justified by Yniold's innocent reply that the lovers are discussing his future height. It builds to a climax that, it turns out, does little more than express Golaud's frustration that Yniold's replies tell him nothing.

The first ellipsis omits part of a speech in which Golaud reproaches himself. When the questioning begins again, the orchestral response is minimal, with no climax, no strong emotions suggested. It is as if the new set of questions, though little different from the earlier ones, can no longer evoke emotion, not even frustration, but simply suggest a certain enervatedness in the dramatic action. The lines I have quoted are the same in both the play and the opera, for the play contained all the elements that Debussy needed to achieve the anti-theatrical effects he sought. Among the works in that genre that the Germans dub *Literaturoper*, few operas keep as closely and fully to their literary sources as does *Pelléas*. Except for the elimination of four short scenes, including two in which the servants of the house comment upon the action, as well as the cutting down of some speeches, the libretto remains pretty much Maeterlinck's original play. Removing the servant scenes renders the opera even more elusive than the play. The elusiveness for which this opera is celebrated (or, by some listeners, condemned) is located most conspicuously in its heroine. Mélisande's elusiveness is not simply an aspect of the *fatalité* that she shares with a multitude of her contemporaries in literature, opera, painting, and dance. Knowing as little as we do about her (where is she from? what motivates her? what causes her death?) is necessary for the aura of untheatricality that both Maeterlinck and Debussy sought to achieve. Endowing her with better-defined contours or placing her actions within a cause-and-effect sequence would have given her a conventional theatricality that it was her creators' need to avoid at all costs.

A synopsis of the play or the opera would not in itself reveal its anti-theatrical quality. In fact, the story would look like a typical nineteenth-century opera plot about adultery and revenge on the part of the wronged mate. We are unaware of its unconventional quality until we read the actual dialogue or listen to the music. This quality is particularly evident if we compare the final love scene (Act IV, Scene iv) between Pelléas and Mélisande, culminating as it does in Golaud's killing of his rival, with its implied model, the love duet of *Tristan und Isolde*, which too is interrupted by the jealous husband's appearance and the mortal wounding of the illicit lover.

Whereas Wagner's scene builds steadily, inexorably toward its grand climax, with the lovers singing in unison as it nears its end, Debussy's remains for the most part restrained, with occasional moments of agitation and passion punctuating the quiet atmosphere. His lovers' acknowledgment of their love, quite in contrast to Wagner's high-volume declarations, is spoken virtually in a whisper, with minimal orchestral accompaniment. And whereas Wagner's lovers, oblivious of Brangaene's warnings, are taken by surprise by the husband's entrance, Debussy's become aware of Golaud lurking nearby in the forest and then remain passive as he kills his brother and wounds his wife. While Wagner's love-night culminates in a long series of recriminations, Debussy's ends abruptly after Golaud's action, to be followed by the anticlimactic final act, at the beginning of which we learn – in an undermining of cause-and-effect relationships typical of Maeterlinck and Debussy – that Mélisande's wound was not in itself serious enough to kill her. Few if any last acts in opera are as anticlimactic as that of *Pelléas*, but then few climactic scenes are as restrained as the love duet immediately preceding it.

Even a century after its premiere, *Pelléas et Mélisande* has not fully acclimated itself for operagoers. My own experience attending many productions of *Pelléas* over the years has taught me to avoid conversing during intermissions with fellow subscribers, for the latter, having come to the theater with expectations nurtured by the standard repertory, often complain that everything they treasure about opera – full-throated song, high drama, forward-thrusting music – is missing here.

When Mélisande, almost midway through the opera, sings from the balcony about her long hair ("Mes longs cheveux descendent")[8] we think we have finally been granted an aria. Yet in the context of any earlier nineteenth-century opera her song would not even count as an aria – indeed, it would scarcely compel an audience's attention. As Debussy was reported saying long before he even conceived this opera, "In the opera house they sing *too much*. One should *sing* only when it is worthwhile and hold moving lyrical expression in reserve."[9] The mode of vocal discourse that Debussy invented for this, his only completed opera, was, of course, a deliberate attempt to undo what he took to be an overwrought, antiquated operatic language. As he put it in his brief statement, "Why I Wrote *Pelléas*," "I ... tried to obey a law of beauty that seems notably ignored when it comes to dramatic music: the characters of this opera try to sing like real people, and not in an arbitrary language made up of worn-out clichés. That is why the reproach has been made concerning my so-called taste for monotonous declamation, where nothing seems melodic."[10] Earlier in this note Debussy, after mentioning his own "passionate pilgrimages to Bayreuth" in his youth, had complained of Wagner as "a great collector of formulae."[11] What has made *Pelléas* difficult for operagoers ever since its premiere is precisely its avoidance of easy formulae, whether Wagnerian or Italian.

The anti-theatrical quality of Debussy's declamation appears "undramatic" only when measured by what its audiences were most familiar with. It is significant, for instance, that the first performances of Monteverdi's operas since the seventeenth century took place within two years after the premiere of *Pelléas et Mélisande* and that the critic Louis Laloy, a fervent Debussy admirer, wrote that "the criticisms aimed at the *Orfeo* ... resemble those aimed at *Pelléas*. The two works should displease the same spirits."[12] Moreover, French

---

[8] *Ibid.*, pp. 153–54.

[9] Quoted in Orledge, *Debussy and the Theatre*, p. 49 (emphases Debussy's).

[10] Lesure, *Debussy on Music*, p. 75. [11] *Ibid.*, p. 74.

[12] Louis Laloy, "Schola Cantorum – 26 février."

opera before the nineteenth century had been marked by a mode of discourse far closer to speech than to the mode that had characterized Italian opera since the eighteenth century and that also dominated opera in France during the nineteenth. What we see as anti-theatrical, as I have been arguing, is what challenges and violates the theatrical conventions with which we are most immediately familiar.

The anti-theatricality of Schoenberg's *Moses und Aron* takes a quite different form from that of *Pelléas*. Its non-tonal method is not in itself an indication of anti-theatricality. After all, vocal music, including opera, was long a central concern for Schoenberg and his followers. Schoenberg's first operatic venture, the mini-opera *Erwartung* (1909), composed directly after his break with tonality, seems thoroughly theatrical despite its iconoclastic musical technique. Atonal music, both during its free phase and after Schoenberg had developed the twelve-tone method in the early 1920s, lent itself particularly well to creating strong theatrical effects, especially the depiction of extreme psychological states, as in the sustained hysteria of *Erwartung* or the visions and the violence portrayed in the title character of Alban Berg's *Wozzeck* (1925).

A similar theatricality distinguishes *Moses und Aron*, which in one sense looks like the most theatrical of major twentieth-century operas. Although Schoenberg was never able to set the final act of the libretto he had himself written, the work as it stands is a grand-scale post-Wagnerian music-drama with a huge orchestra, large choruses, dances, and spectacular scenic effects, above all in the scene depicting the Hebrews worshipping the Golden Calf.

To cite only a few of the opportunities that *Moses und Aron* has granted its stage directors and scenic designers, this scene includes such elements as a group of old men killing themselves before the Calf; the crazed crowd of worshippers killing a youth who, in the name of the Hebrew God, challenges polytheism; a drunken dance; four naked maidens who are embraced by priests as the latter are about to knife them to death as sacrifices; and, to bring this scene to a climactic end, an action in which the men tear off their clothes, denude the women, and stage an orgy at the altar. No Hollywood Biblical extravaganza is likely to outdo Schoenberg's script.

And yet the extreme theatricality that Schoenberg realizes in this opera is thoroughly challenged by the role that Moses undertakes. As in *Parsifal*, the anti-theatrical is defined for us through the presence of strongly theatrical elements. While *Parsifal* is divided between overtly theatrical and anti-theatrical scenes, *Moses und Aron* presents its two antithetical figures at once, sometimes, indeed, in duet with one another. These two figures are depicted from the beginning as representing contradictory views about theatrical performance. Whereas Aron is willing to grant the unruly crowd its desire to participate in the ceremonies associated with its traditional gods, Moses stands resolutely for the interdiction against such rituals imposed upon them by the monotheistic God whose message he is trying to convey. Schoenberg, in this opera, is in fact dramatizing that long-standing conflict about representation within the Judeo-Christian tradition that Barish's book has portrayed.

For Moses, the one God must remain unrepresentable: indeed, the word *"unvorstellbar"* [unrepresentable], echoed innumerable times in his speeches, is doubtless the most memorable word in the opera. But Moses is also depicted from the outset as a man without verbal skills, and he depends upon his slickly articulate brother to convey his message to the crowd. In Act II, once Moses has ascended Mount Sinai to receive the Ten Commandments, Aron finds himself having to deal with the crowd, and he allows it to go its own, theatrically inclined way by enacting its traditional polytheistic rituals. Aron has already demonstrated his theatrical ways in Act I when, to impress the crowd, he temporarily transformed Moses' staff into a serpent and cured his brother's leprous hand.

The conflict between the brothers manifests itself in musical terms through the sharply contrasting modes of vocal discourse associated with each. Whereas Aron's role is assigned to a tenor who sings his lines in a smoothly lyrical manner, Moses's part is not even sung but is uttered in the *Sprechstimme* mode that Schoenberg had devised early in his atonal period.[13] Although musical pitches are recorded for the singer, these notes are uttered in a way much closer to speech than to song. Moreover, the contrast we hear between Moses's austere, harsh bass voice and Aron's slick tenor, with both of them often singing in duet, dramatizes the opera's essential conflict at every point in the most conspicuous manner possible. At the end of Act II, which is as far as Schoenberg got in the musical setting of his three-act text, Moses returns from the mountain to condemn Aron's and the crowd's conduct in uncompromising terms. The opera thus culminates in a thorough repudiation of the theatricality we have been witnessing throughout.

The debate about theatricality central to *Moses und Aron* can be interpreted allegorically in at least two ways: the first political, the second aesthetic. In view of the fact that Schoenberg was working on his opera in Berlin during the later 1920s and early 1930s, any listener – indeed, any reader of the libretto – finds it difficult not to connect Aron's manipulation of the anarchic crowd with Hitler's similar endeavors during these, the crucial years in his rise to power. When we hear these words spoken by Aron to please the crowd after its demand for its older gods, it is difficult to resist detecting their resemblance to Hitler's rhetoric:

> Deine Götter geb ich dir wieder
> und dich ihnen;
> wie es dich verlangt. …
> Ihr spendet diesen Stoff,
> ich geb ihm solche Form:
> Alltäglich, sichtbar, faßlich
> in Gold verewigt. …
> Ihr sollt glücklich werden!
>
> [I'm returning your gods to you
> and you to them,
> as you have demanded. …

---

[13] On the history of Schoenberg's use of this mode, see Stadlen, "Schoenberg's Speech-Song."

You are providing the content,
I shall give it a form:
common, visible, graspable
eternalized in gold. . . .
You will be happy.][14]

Moses und Aron also invites a second set of political meanings. During the mid-1920s, before he had composed the opera's libretto, Schoenberg wrote a non-musical drama, *Der biblische Weg*, in which two modern embodiments of Moses and Aron appear as conflicting sides of a single figure, a scarcely veiled portrait of Theodor Herzl, the founder of Zionism. The play itself is a highly theatrical representation of the political difficulties that Herzl encountered through his inability to reconcile the "theatrical" needs of everyday political dealings with his "untheatrical" need to maintain his integrity.

But Schoenberg's opera suggests still another set of meanings, this one within the realm of aesthetics. As the leader of the central European musical avant-garde, Schoenberg, like his older contemporary Sigmund Freud, felt a keen identification with Moses. From Schoenberg's point of view, the break with tonality and the later development of the twelve-tone scale were inevitable stages in the history of musical form. Like Moses, he viewed himself as chosen to lead others into new and unfamiliar territory. And also like Moses, he saw himself as a lonely figure, one who was in fact persecuted by those unwilling to undergo the hardships (for Moses, life in the desert; for Schoenberg, hearing difficult music in the concert hall) that he demanded of them. Within Schoenberg's imaginative world, audiences were all too ready to turn to the Arons of contemporary music, that is, toward the traditionally tonal, more readily digestible composers who could offer them the easy listening of a quick musical fix. Only by enduring the untheatrical rigors he demanded of them could audiences hope to enter the musical promised land.[15]

---

[14] Schoenberg, *Moses und Aron*, pp. 189–94.
[15] For more detailed discussions of the political and aesthetic contexts of *Moses und Aron*, see my essay "Arnold Schoenberg's *Der biblische Weg* and *Moses und*

The untheatricality we experience in Stravinsky's *The Rake's Progress* is quite different in kind from that of either *Pelléas et Mélisande* or *Moses und Aron*. Whereas the latter two operas expect their audiences to accept the aesthetic illusion they create, Stravinsky's encourages audiences to distance themselves from the onstage action. For Stravinsky and his librettists, W. H. Auden and Chester Kallman, *The Rake's Progress* project provided an opportunity selfconsciously to re-examine the conventions of opera, in both their verbal and musical aspects. Enjoyable though the resulting music and the stage action may be, the opera's creators have made it impossible for a viewer simply to sit back unthinkingly. The opera's untheatricality thus lies in the fact that, in keeping us from being trapped by the stage illusion, it forces us to think seriously about the history and nature of operatic conventions.

To be sure, many earlier operas undermined the aesthetic illusion and played explicitly with convention. Stravinsky's epilogue, in which the characters return to comment on their actions, was, as I mentioned earlier, anticipated by *Don Giovanni* and *Falstaff*. Offenbach's and Gilbert and Sullivan's operettas provide innumerable spoofs of easily recognizable operatic conventions. And the Strauss/Hofmannsthal *Ariadne auf Naxos* juxtaposes *opera seria* with *commedia dell'arte* to expose the limitations and the underlying meanings of each of these forms.

But *The Rake's Progress* pursues its examination of the past with a seriousness and a rigor unique in the history of opera. For all its toying with stage illusion, *Ariadne auf Naxos* culminates in the most thoroughgoingly imaginable illusion, in which the once-despairing heroine is rescued by a hero with whom she engages in an ecstatic and unashamedly operatic love-duet. Moreover, Stravinsky had made the examination of the musical past central to many compositions of

Aron," and my chapter entitled *"Moses und Aron, Mahagonny,* and Germany in 1930" in *Opera in History,* pp. 191–239. For the political and religious contexts of *Der biblische Weg,* see Mäckelmann, *Arnold Schönberg und das Judentum.* The play, which remained unpublished in German until the 1990s, is available in both German and English (see Arnold Schoenberg, *Der biblische Weg,* pp. 162–329).

his neoclassical period: for example, *Pulcinella* (1920), which reworks Pergolesi and his contemporaries, and *Le Baiser de la fée* (1928), a rewriting of various Tchaikovsky pieces.

The Rake's Progress is the last major work of this period. Unlike the pieces I mention above, it re-examines not a single composer or period but, rather, the very nature of opera. Not that Stravinsky directly evokes the Wagnerian tradition, which remains present for us through its deliberate absence. For *The Rake's Progress* resolutely brackets this tradition, against which he polemicized throughout his career, to pursue the form and conventions of the pre-Wagnerian number opera, with its predictable succession of recitatives, cavatinas, cabalettas, and larger ensembles.[16] Those familiar with the operatic past keep hearing snippets from earlier number operas – or, at least, they think they hear something familiar, for Stravinsky has hidden his traces and also distorted his sources with telling dissonances.

As an early commentator on this work put it, "The whole genre of opera itself serves as model," and allusions to the operatic past have proved readily discernible.[17] Since Auden and Kallman happened to be avid opera listeners, the whole project displays a thorough knowingness about the medium built in from the beginning. Note, for instance, the disposition of the various roles, which follows the system of early- to mid-nineteenth-century Italian opera: the rash tenor lover (Tom Rakewell); his bland lyric-soprano beloved (Anne Trulove); the bass patriarchal father (Trulove); the baritone villain (Nick Shadow); the mezzo-soprano pushy other woman (Baba). And note the genealogy of Nick Shadow, who looks back to the devil figure in the various Faust/Mephistopheles operas as well as to the multiple villains of *Les Contes d'Hoffmann* (1881).

The *Rake*'s closeness to operatic tradition lies not only in its larger plan but, above all, in its individual segments. For example, Anne

---

[16] See Stravinsky and Craft, *Memories and Commentaries*, pp. 167–76.

[17] See Kaufmann, "Ausverkauf der alten Oper," quotation on p. 290, allusions on pp. 292–95. For more allusions, see Griffiths, *Igor Stravinsky*, pp. 96–98.

Trulove's long and elaborate solo scene at the end of Act 1 parallels Violetta's similar scene closing the first act of *La traviata*.[18] In each case the librettists have rigorously organized their material to make the plot fit the conventions governing a soprano's Act 1 aria: the opening recitative that defines the character's dilemma; the ensuing andante, in which she seems to have made up her mind; the *tempo di mezzo*, in which she displays some second thoughts about her earlier resolution; and, finally, the glittering, showpiece cabaletta, where she makes her resolution once and for all (for Violetta, to maintain her freedom; for Anne, to go after Tom in London). Both the music and the words, "I go, I go to him," of this last section have the characteristic forward thrust of the Italian cabaletta.[19] In each scene, moreover, the character is temporarily rendered indecisive by an external voice (for Violetta, her lover's; for Anne, her father's). And each cabaletta, after a good bit of florid singing, culminates in a triumphant high *c* (or, in the case of *La traviata*, an *e* flat for those sopranos brave enough to try).

Despite the high artifice of *The Rake's Progress*, Stravinsky provides a number of moments in which we are at least briefly taken in by the illusions and even moved – above all in the madhouse scene as Anne sings a simple lullaby to her dying, demented lover.[20] But as soon as this scene ends, the composer cunningly breaks the illusion with the epilogue.

Audiences unfamiliar with opera may well take *The Rake's Progress*, with its auctioning off of the bearded "other woman" and its bordello and madhouse scenes, as a thoroughly theatrical romp. But its theatricality is so overt and outrageous that it also forces us to reflect upon what this is all about – as, indeed, its characters do in the epilogue. The ironic distance that it encourages was, in fact, present already in the caricatured poses of the Hogarth series of paintings upon which the libretto is based. After Stravinsky happened to see

---

[18] See, respectively, Stravinsky, *The Rake's Progress*, pp. 112–30, and Verdi, *La traviata*, ed. Della Seta, pp. 80–107.

[19] Stravinsky, *The Rake's Progress*, pp. 127–29.   [20] *Ibid.*, pp. 383–85.

these paintings in Chicago during a touring exhibition in 1947, he recognized that he now had the subject for what was to be his only full-length opera. And he must doubtless have sensed a kinship between Hogarth's sense of irony and his own.

If *The Rake's Progress* achieves its untheatricality by encouraging us to rethink the very nature of theatricality, Messiaen's *Saint François d'Assise* makes no bones about its refusal even to appear to be theatrical. Until the Paris Opéra's director, Rolf Liebermann, persuaded the composer in 1975 to undertake this project, nobody, including Messiaen himself, would have imagined an opera coming out of this pious figure, whose *oeuvre* consisted mainly of keyboard and instrumental work, much of it specifically Roman Catholic in nature.

Messiaen himself acknowledged the implausibility of his becoming an opera composer. For one thing, he did not feel he possessed the gift for operatic composition. Nor was he interested in the medium from a theatrical point of view. Indeed, according to his own account, he accepted the invitation only after Liebermann ordered him to "write an opera for the Opéra de Paris" in the presence of the then-president of France, Georges Pompidou, during a state dinner. Messiaen's statements on opera generally express disdain – of fans "who wait for the tenor's high B-flat" and of others who "come only for the spectacle." The majority of operas, for him, fall into two categories: those "that are good theater and bad music and those that are good music and bad theater."[21]

But Messiaen also showed immense respect for a select few operas whose music he revered and which he analyzed regularly in his classes, most notably, to judge from references in his writing, *Pelléas et Mélisande, Tristan und Isolde, Boris Godunov,* and *Wozzeck.* Indeed, the first of these played a special role in his life, for, as he declared in an interview shortly before his death, studying the score of *Pelléas* at age ten made him decide to become a composer;[22] as he

---

[21] Messiaen, *Music and Color*, pp. 207–08.

[22] Marti, "'It's a Secret of Love'," pp. 24–25.

had put it in an earlier interview, *Pelléas* had the effect of "a revelation, love at first sight. ... That was probably the most decisive influence I've received – and it's also an opera, isn't it?"[23] It is significant that this most untheatrical of composers should be shaped by so anti-theatrical an opera – to the point that he jokes about whether it really is an opera in the first place!

But once Messiaen had consented to write an opera, he was careful to set limits on its theatricality. Composing a saint's life – and particularly one whose story, unlike those of saints who suffered martyrdom, lacked sensational elements – inhibited any temptation to be overtly dramatic. To avoid undue artifice, Messiaen based his libretto on the known sources about Francis's life and, as much as possible, on the saint's own writings; the *Canticle of the Sun*, for example, is quoted nearly in full, though it is spread out among several scenes. In addition, Messiaen sought to avoid many operatic conventions: "There's no overture," he boasted, "no interludes between the various scenes, no symphonic numbers that can be played separately ... there are neither arias nor vocal ensembles."[24] He viewed the chorus as the only traditional operatic convention that he retained. And much of the opera's verbal content consists of theological discussion, prayer, and the enunciation of exempla.

Messiaen's fear of ordinary theatricality motivated him to discard some well-known episodes from St. Francis's life. For example, Francis's meeting with St. Clare found no place in the opera because of posthumous rumors of "a love affair between the two saints."[25] Francis's conflict with his father was omitted for fear of setting up an Oedipal drama ("I loathe psychoanalysis," Messiaen said).[26] The saint's taming of the Wolf of Gubbio, a central element in Franciscan iconography, could not be accommodated because the animal might look as ridiculous onstage as the "grotesque dragon in *Siegfried*,"[27] and his dispute with Assisi town officials was unsatisfactory because

---

[23] Messiaen, *Music and Color*, pp. 110–11.   [24] *Ibid.*, p. 223.
[25] *Ibid.*, p. 213.   [26] *Ibid.*   [27] *Ibid.*

it would have necessitated "other characters with period costumes."[28] The closest Messiaen came to introducing an operatic
villain ("sin isn't interesting, dirt isn't interesting")[29] is the unpleasant,
bureaucratically minded Frère Élie.

So what was left in the story to shape an opera? Certainly some
famous incidents passed the composer's rigorous screening test: for
example, St. Francis's curing of the leper, his communication with
the birds, and his receiving the stigmata. Still, by ordinary operatic or
theatrical standards *Saint François d'Assise* is conspicuously short on
incidents. It is a slow-progressing spectacle with some four hours of
music (not counting its two intermissions) in eight scenes, each one
of them built around a single incident involving relatively few
characters, with the saint present in all but one.

Messiaen concocted a form of musical discourse unlike that of any
earlier opera. Instead of singing arias the characters chant in a
declamatory style, which, though influenced by the speech rhythms
of *Boris Godunov* and *Pelléas*, creates a thoroughly original effect
because of the relative slowness of the music and, even more
important, because the orchestra remains subdued during the
speeches. Orchestral and choral commentary, instead of accompanying the characters' declamation, tends to occur between phrases and
speeches. Messiaen's declamatory style, moreover, evokes a medieval modal world, which, as one commentator puts it, creates a
"contrast between archaic musical converse among the characters
and continuous surprise from the orchestra."[30]

Much of this orchestral commentary consists of birdsongs that
Messiaen himself transcribed outdoors and that are central to much
of his other music. But the birdsongs have a special function in *Saint
François d'Assise*, not only in the scene with the birds, which includes
both a "small" and a "grand" concert of the birds, but also in defining
the characters of the opera. Each character is, in fact, associated with
one or more particular birds. During the two so-called *concerts
d'oiseaux* Messiaen even labels his birds and their respective countries

---

[28] *Ibid.*, p. 215.   [29] *Ibid.*, p. 213.   [30] Griffiths, *"Saint François d'Assise,"* p. 505.

of origin in his score.[31] Through the often strange sounds of these birdsongs, together with the huge chorus and orchestra Messiaen demands for the opera, the composer creates a powerful sonic experience that achieves its own, unique form of theatricality. Moreover, the unfamiliar instruments he insists upon – three *ondes Martenots*, the geophone, and all manner of exotic percussion devices – may well cause listeners to re-evaluate what precisely they mean by the term "theatricality." Within the terms of this essay, the characters' slow and stately dialogue, like the *Sprechstimme* in which Schoenberg's Moses speaks, can be viewed as an anti-theatrical extreme against which the loud and dissonant orchestral outbursts, similarly to those of Schoenberg, define their theatricality through the sharp contrast they offer between opposing modes of discourse.

And despite Messiaen's disdain for ordinary theater, he expresses pride in what at one point he even called the "theatricality" of the leper scene,[32] which, after St. Francis has kissed the leper, culminates in the latter's "jumping and dancing like a madman."[33] Since this moment of high action comes at the end of a slowly developing, half-hour-long scene, the dramaturgy that Messiaen is practicing in this work is one that contrasts conspicuously with the high-pitched drama characteristic of nineteenth-century opera.

But so also does the dramaturgy of the other three works I have discussed in detail. Both Debussy and Messiaen, for instance, despite a leisureliness that seems to defy an earlier concept of theatricality, create hypnotic effects for their audiences that define a new mode of theatricality. (Hypnosis, by its very nature, demands a slowing down.) Schoenberg, by confronting theatrical and anti-theatrical characters within a single work, and Stravinsky, by inviting his audience to join him in anatomizing the conventions of earlier opera, force us to reconsider what theatricality is all about in the first place.

---

[31] Messiaen, *Saint François d'Assise*, vol. VI (1988), pp. 183–98, 282–318.
[32] Messiaen, *Music and Color*, p. 209.
[33] Messiaen, *Saint François d'Assise*, vol. III (1988), p. 129.

The anti-theatricality I have located in these four works should not obscure the fact that many great twentieth-century operas remain securely within a traditional theatrical mode. Certainly the operas of Puccini and Strauss, who, though born in the mid-nineteenth century, composed most of their operas during the twentieth, seem theatrical to the core – this despite Strauss's occasionally exposing the theatrical illusion, as in *Ariadne auf Naxos* and in his final opera, *Capriccio* (1942). Alban Berg's two operas, however innovative their musical style, perpetuate the dramatic method of post-Wagnerian music-drama. Benjamin Britten moved directly from his grand-operatic *Peter Grimes* (1945) to his small-scale, anti-theatrical chamber opera *The Rape of Lucretia* (1946), whose static quality (with a corresponding paucity of dramatic action in which even the rape scene remains understated) is guaranteed by the fact that the roles of the two narrators are about as long as those of the characters within the story. And again, like many anti-theatrical operas, and certainly including the Schoenberg and Messiaen operas I have discussed above, *The Rape of Lucretia* invokes a religious aura – in this instance, Christian stoicism – to establish its distance from ordinary theatricality.

Many twentieth-century operas have manifested a similarly static quality, to the point that critics often call them "oratorio-like." One thinks, for instance, of John Adams's *The Death of Klinghoffer* (1991) but also, for that matter, of *Saint François d'Assise*. And one might remember that Schoenberg first conceived *Moses und Aron* as an oratorio but was persuaded by his publisher to use the material for an opera instead.

"Opera" and "oratorio," moreover, have been used as opposing terms since the early eighteenth century. Though Handel's oratorios today seem at least as "operatic" as his *opere serie* (some, like *Theodora* and *Semele*, even achieving considerable success on the stage), they defined themselves in their time, as mentioned in Essay 2, by means of their contrast with opera: religious rather than secular, bourgeois rather than aristocratic, native rather than foreign. From the point of view of the present essay, it is significant that, in the course of the twentieth century, the opera–oratorio dichotomy no longer seems as absolute as before, that, in fact, seemingly static, oratorio-like operas have proved their power to excite audiences.

Within the last two to three decades, a number of musical dramas (whether or not one chooses to call them operas) explored the possibilities of anti-theatricality even more radically than the four on which this article has focused. In some of the examples I took up in Essay 4, a number of works I labeled "opera by other means" have challenged their audiences as to whether even to label them "opera" in the first place. What one might call anti-operaticality, a special manifestation of anti-theatricality, is evident, for example, in the ways that works such as Reich's *The Cave* and *Three Tales* steadfastly resist operatic vocal style, or that Cage's *Europeras 1 & 2* literally distorts beloved classic works by scrambling their orchestration and their décor. There were, of course, some notable experiments in anti-theatrical opera during the first half of the twentieth century, many of them collaborations between major modernist writers, designers, and composers. One thinks, for instance, of the Cocteau/Picasso/Satie *Parade* (1917), the Stein/Thomson *Four Saints in Three Acts* (1933), and the Apollinaire/Poulenc *Les Mamelles de Tirésias* (1947). What distinguishes these works from more recent anti-theatrical experiments is that the former tended to be of a more occasional and "scandalous" nature, while the latter can often get performed in opera houses – indeed, are sometimes even commissioned by opera companies.[34]

The last thirty years or more have also, above all in Europe, constituted the age of so-called *Regieoper*, in which directors such as Patrice Chéreau, Hans Neuenfels, and Peter Sellars have radically rethought (some would even say dismembered) a good bit of the traditional canon. Through the unexpected visual effects they project – for example, a medieval potentate in black tie, or TV monitors displaying multiple images of a character singing her aria downstage – or

---

[34] For detailed discussions of these three earlier works within their historical context, see Albright, *Untwisting the Serpent*, pp. 185–97, 311–63, 297–308.

through the changes in décor that they have instituted, most notoriously, perhaps, introducing the Rhine Maidens as prostitutes tending a dam during Wagner's own time or Don Giovanni operating among gangs in the South Bronx, they have, in effect, destabilized and retheatricalized works whose unselfconscious theatricality had never before been in doubt. And Sellars, one might note, in 1992 directed a production of Messiaen's opera for the Salzburg Festival with a full panoply of TV monitors.

By now it should be clear that the term *anti-theatricality* I have used to characterize some significant twentieth-century operas is not monolithic in meaning but covers a range of stances: the slow, hypnotic approach of *Pelléas et Mélisande* and *Saint François d'Assise*; the outrageous staginess of *The Rake's Progress*, which forces audiences to think about the nature of operatic convention; and the stark dichotomy of anti-theatrical and theatrical discourses that marks the titular figures of *Moses und Aron*. Yet, in their differing ways, all these stances depend upon their audiences' recognition that these operas have broken with the unselfconscious theatricality that marked most operas of the preceding century.

It may well be that these twentieth-century forms of anti-theatricality have worked to initiate a new mode of theatricality quite different from the nineteenth-century form against which it originally defined itself. After all, today's audiences, at least in the major operatic centers, retain little if any memory of the melodramatic acting and staging routines that once dominated operatic interpretation. Can it be that works such as *Saint François d'Assise* or *Einstein on the Beach*, or radical reinterpretations of *Il trovatore* or *Die Meistersinger*, will emerge as exemplars of operatic norms? And will the dichotomy between the theatrical and the anti-theatrical upon which this essay is predicated soon come to seem irrelevant?

It is easy enough to imagine doing a history of opera based on a succession of musical texts, or librettos, or, what is much more usual, a combination of these. A history of opera can also, as is frequently the case these days, consist of a history of performers and performing practices. But what about a history of how members of the audience engaged, or may have engaged, with what they heard and saw? As a preliminary sketch toward this sort of history, consider the following significant moments, each roughly a half century apart.

MONTEVERDI, *LA FAVOLA D'ORFEO*, MANTUA, DUCAL PALACE, FEBRUARY 24, 1607

What must they have thought, those noblemen of Mantua, as they witnessed the first performance of Monteverdi's *Orfeo*? Surely they were not aware that they were observing the birth of a new art form, one that would continue and evolve for at least four more centuries. Strictly speaking, however, this was not exactly the birth of opera, for several works – all of them attempts, in one way or another, to activate the theories about the rebirth of Greek drama enunciated by the Florentine Camerata – had been performed during the preceding decade. But Monteverdi's was something different from these earlier operas, whose continuous recitative strikes us as ultimately boring when we hear it revived today. For Monteverdi not only gave his recitative a dramatic intensity largely lacking in that of Caccini and Peri (who had both set to music this same ancient myth), but he also found a means of varying degrees of intensity with choruses and with lyrical outbursts that looked forward to what would later come to be called operatic arias.

What frames of reference might this audience have had for what they were witnessing? If any had attended these earlier operas, would they have noted the difference in Monteverdi's use of this new medium? Would they, for instance, have heard the ways that the composer adapted the style of his madrigals – especially those of Books IV and V, published a few years before the opera – to create the lyrical interludes interrupting the recitative? And would they have seen the work primarily as a new embodiment – this one with continuous music instead of simply interspersed musical interludes – of that genre called pastoral drama, of which Tasso's *Aminta* and Guarini's *Il pastor fido* would have been most familiar? Or would they have seen it as similar to those myth-inspired musical spectacles called *intermedi* that characteristically were inserted between the acts of spoken plays during the preceding century? The day before the performance, a Mantuan, Carlo Magno, in a letter to his brother in Rome, expressed the uniqueness of the occasion when he wrote, "It [*Orfeo*] should be most unusual, as all the actors are to sing their parts."[1] On that same day, in fact, a traditional play with *intermedi* had been performed as part of the carnival festivities.

It may well be that some in the all-male audience, composed of members of the local intellectual and social establishment, the Accademia degli Invaghiti, had attended one of the few earlier opera performances, perhaps the Rinuccini/Peri *Euridice*, which had been mounted in 1600 at the Pitti Palace in Florence to celebrate the wedding of Maria di Medici and King Henry IV of France. It is known that Duke Vincenzo Gonzaga of Mantua, the sponsor of Monteverdi's *Orfeo*, had been present on that occasion. Indeed, many early operas were commissioned to celebrate specific events such as weddings, as was Monteverdi's succeeding (and largely lost) opera, *Arianna*, composed for the wedding of Vincenzo's son Francesco and Margherita of Savoy a year after the *Orfeo* performance. Indeed, since many of the earliest operas were, like *Euridice* and *Arianna*, prepared

---

[1] See Fenlon, "Correspondence Relating to the Early Mantuan Performances," p. 170.

for ceremonial occasions, *Orfeo* is exceptional for being planned simply as an entertainment for the local academy to celebrate the carnival season. To be sure, it received a second performance six days later so that it could be heard by the ladies of Mantua. And unlike most early operas, which were rarely repeated after their initial performances, *Orfeo* had a brief afterlife, including performances as far away as Salzburg – and with its original tenor, Francesco Rasi – a decade later. But soon after that it disappeared from the stage until the early twentieth century.

Yet much about those first *Orfeo* performances of 1607 remains uncertain. We happen to know a good bit about the difficulties of hiring a soprano castrato to sing some of the female roles, because Duke Vincenzo's two sons happened to correspond with one another at the time – the younger son, Ferdinando, residing in Pisa at the time, while his older brother Francesco was in Mantua helping plan the performance. The cast was to be all male: not, to be sure, a requirement in Mantua as it was in Rome, nor was this a policy during the following year when an outstanding female singer, Virginia Andreini, created the title role in *Arianna*. Evidently the number of adequate castrati in the Mantuan choir was not sufficient for the new opera, and Francesco, as one learns from the correspondence, depended on his brother to arrange the loan of a castrato from the grand duke of Florence, with whom the Gonzagas maintained close relations.[2] We know about this singer from the letters: he was named Giovanni Gualberto Magli; he sang La Musica and at least one other female character of whose identity we cannot be absolutely certain; and he initially was slow in learning his music, though ultimately he was praised for his performances.

Although the other singers were drawn from the ducal *concerto*, only one other can be identified with a particular role: this was Rasi, who, as a result of his success as Orfeo, might well count as the first opera star. Rasi was capable of doing quite elaborate ornamentation,

---

[2] The correspondence between the brothers is reprinted, in both Italian and English, in *ibid.*, pp. 167–72.

as is evident from the ornaments indicated for Orfeo's third-act plea, "Possente spirto," in Monteverdi's published score; one might note, in fact, that the score also contains an unornamented vocal line for this aria on which singers less talented than Rasi could base their renditions. Otherwise, a number of the probable singers and instrumentalists can be identified, even if their particular roles remain in doubt. From a study of the voice ranges for individual parts, one can make reasonable guesses as to how these parts were doubled.[3]

Another mystery surrounding the *Orfeo* performance is where precisely it took place. When I visited the ducal palace in 1958, the guide took tourists up to the so-called Hall of Mirrors, which he identified as the site of this now-legendary event. I remember trying to imagine the first audience as it listened to passages familiar to me. But alas, recent excavations in the palace have unearthed another Hall of Mirrors that more accurately deserves that name, and, moreover, from other evidence it turns out that the *Orfeo* performance took place in still another part of the palace, though the exact room is not known with certainty.[4]

Yet the most teasing mystery surrounding the opera concerns the work's conclusion. The happy and thoroughly Christianized ending in which the hero's father Apollo leads him up to heaven to be reunited with his dead wife appears only in the score that Monteverdi published two years after the first performance. And since this score remains our only evidence for the music, it is this ending that must perforce be heard in the theater. Yet Alessandro Striggio's libretto, which had been published in time for the initial performance so that the audience, like people watching electronic supertitles today, could follow the words, ends tragically – with the Bacchantes, following Virgil's narration in the *Georgics*, cornering

---

[3] For an exhaustive analysis of what parts were doubled and who likely sang which roles, see Carter, "Singing *Orfeo*." Carter also reproduces some enthusiastic accounts of Rasi's performances in various concerts and *intermedi* (*ibid.*, pp. 83–85).

[4] For a discussion of the evidence surrounding the Hall[s] of Mirrors and of the room in which the opera was likely performed, see Besutti, "Spaces for Music."

the hero in order to kill him in response to his condemnation of all women except for Euridice.[5]

How, one asks, did Monteverdi and his librettist come to change the ending as radically as they did? What must the violent initial ending have sounded like musically in comparison with the relatively tame conclusion that we know? Did generic considerations play a role? After all, the famed pastoral plays of Tasso and Guarini had counted as generically controversial since they occupied a middle ground between tragedy and comedy – indeed, the term *favola* used in the opera's title was sometimes applied to these works. Or was the ending changed between the two performances in Mantua to better suit the tastes of the ladies invited to the second one?[6] Or, as has been speculated, was it changed for an intended third performance in 1607 to celebrate the visit (later canceled) of the Duke of Savoy – in which case the *deus ex machina* in the happy ending might have motivated an elaborate staging more appropriate for entertaining a distinguished visitor?[7] Or might one see the Christianized ending, as Karol Berger has argued, as an allegory of music history, as a reassertion of the *prima prattica*, the sacred polyphonic mode that Monteverdi, in a famous controversy a few years earlier, had rejected in favor of his own, dissonance-rich, monodic "second practice"?[8] In view of the musical power that this work still exerts on us, it keeps teasing us to fill in the uncertainties with speculations.

CAVALLI, *LA CALISTO*, VENICE, TEATRO S. APONAL, NOVEMBER 28, 1651

Though among the most frequently performed seventeenth-century operas today, *La Calisto* failed badly in its first, brief run and, as far as

---

[5] A translation of Striggio's libretto for Act v can be found in Whenham, *Claudio Monteverdi: Orfeo*, pp. 36–41.

[6] See Carter, *Monteverdi's Musical Theatre*, p. 121.

[7] Steinheuer, "*Orfeo* (1607)," p. 123, and Besutti, "Spaces for Music," *ibid.*, p. 86.

[8] Berger, *Bach's Cycle, Mozart's Arrow*, pp. 39–42.

is known, had no later performing history until well into the twentieth century. Since newspaper reviews did not yet exist, and since word of mouth rarely resulted in written records, one can only speculate about the opera's initial failure. A recent book suggests that the absence of the lead alto castrato (who, in fact, died shortly after the premiere) discouraged attendance.[9] A study of gender in Venetian opera of the period suggests that *La Calisto* "distorted" its audience's "generic expectations," for after teasing it "with a musical language that represents explicit female pleasure," the opera is resolved in favor of "spiritual enlightenment," while the spectators are left with "unfulfilled erotic yearnings."[10]

There is, in fact, a good deal of guess-work necessary to understand that considerable body of work composed after the opening of the public operas houses in Venice beginning in 1637. Since the music (unlike the librettos) was not ordinarily published, the survival of Cavalli's and other composers' operas was dependent on the fact that certain patricians, most notably Marco Contarini, established collections of manuscript scores that have come down to us today.[11] Much of the knowledge we have of the circumstances surrounding the production of Cavalli's operas, and of *La Calisto* in particular, comes from the discovery of the papers of Marco Faustini, the impresario of *La Calisto* and a number of his later operas.[12] Faustini was also the brother of Giovanni Faustini, the librettist of *La Calisto* and several of his earlier operas; as it turned out, this was the last work on which they collaborated, for Giovanni Faustini died of a fever at thirty-six, just before the brief run of this opera concluded.

Although we have no evidence of how the early audiences reacted to *La Calisto*, Marco Faustini's papers, as well as other documents, provide considerable details about the performances.

---

[9] B. L. Glixon and J. E. Glixon, *Inventing the Business of Opera*, p. 309.

[10] Heller, *Emblems of Eloquence*, p. 219.

[11] On the Contarini collection of Cavalli's scores, see Glover, *Cavalli*, pp. 66–72.

[12] Faustini's notebook, as well as other archival sources, supplies much of the detail documented in B. L. Glixon and J. E. Glixon, *Inventing the Business of Opera*.

We know the names of the cast (including the castrato who canceled), the investors, the choreographer, and the designers of the scenery, machines, and costumes.[13] We even have counts of audience attendance for this opera and other Cavalli works: whereas the few performances of *La Calisto* average barely 100 out of a potential 450 each night,[14] the other Cavalli operas did much better, many even getting performed in distant places such as Palermo and Naples, not to speak of various northern Italian cities;[15] indeed, Cavalli's fame was so great that in 1660 he was invited to France by Cardinal Mazarin to compose the opera celebrating the marriage of Louis XIV and Maria Teresa of Spain.

Especially telling are the records discovered in Marco Faustini's account books on the expenses devoted to different aspects of his productions. Since *La Calisto* moves between heaven and earth, with gods ascending and descending frequently during the action, we find directions for objects such as "chariot of Diana, which goes up the mountain, that ascends and descends," or "descent of Jove and of Mercury, that should also have three different façades; to ascend with three persons, and should also serve for the descent of Iris."[16] As in much Baroque theater throughout Europe, audiences craved the spectacles that stage machines could create, and the *Calisto* plot, with its various gods going back and forth between realms, offered especially fertile opportunities.

Just as expense was evidently not spared on the visual effects, impresarios during the period were able to keep their costs in line by maintaining small instrumental ensembles. (By contrast the sizable orchestra that a court opera such as Monteverdi's *Orfeo* boasted was not viable in a profit-oriented institution.) Thus, Marco Faustini's account book for the 1651–52 season, during which *La Calisto* was performed, reveals payments to the first keyboard player (the composer himself), a presumed second keyboard player, a theorbist, and

[13] *Ibid.*, p. 326.   [14] *Ibid.*, p. 353.
[15] See the list venues in Glover, *Cavalli*, pp. 160–62.
[16] B. L. Glixon and J. E. Glixon, *Inventing*, p. 264.

three string players.[17] Skimpy by later standards, surely, but with good singing and exciting staging, this must have sufficed for mid-seventeenth-century audiences – as it does again today for the authentic-music consumer and as exemplified by the William Kentridge production of Monteverdi's *Il ritorno d'Ulisse in patria* discussed in Essay 4.

Whatever the reasons that *La Calisto* was less appreciated than most of Cavalli's other operas, it speaks to our present-day taste in an uncommon way. Note, for example, how Giovanni Faustini has rewritten and eroticized Ovid's brief account of the title character's rape by Jupiter. In both accounts, Jupiter disguises himself as Diana, to whose band Ovid's Callisto belongs, in order to get hold of his prey. Yet Ovid maintains a gentle irony throughout the tale: Callisto is embarrassed and rattled by the experience, and the real Diana, noticing that her nymph has been violated, throws her out of the group. Faustini and Cavalli, by contrast, exploit the situation's comic possibilities, even to the point of grossness: Jupiter in drag raises his baritone voice to the soprano register (it is unknown whether the original singer used falsetto or had the real Diana sing his part); Calisto thoroughly enjoys Jupiter's act, expressing her gratitude to the real Diana – quite graphically, in fact – for the sexual excitement that the latter has supposedly given her; and Diana, not understanding what has happened to her charge, rebuffs her for her forwardness. The jealous Juno's eventual entrance complicates the comic plot even further, while the Satyr who circulates among the various characters adds *commedia dell'arte* tricks to undercut whatever pretences they may voice.

But Faustini and Cavalli have added even more complications by introducing the romance between Diana and Endimione, and, as though that were not enough, by adding the god Pan as still another of Diana's suitors. Yet the farcical elements are counterbalanced throughout by the most high-flown lyricism. Endimione's music in particular has a ravishing effect on the listener even when the latter

---

recognizes the absurdity of his pleas. The predictably serious Diana is counterbalanced in turn by her nymph Linfea – performed in drag by a low-voiced male – who expresses her sexual longings with comic frankness.

Throughout the opera, the raunchy coexists with the serious in a way that communicates easily with audiences of our own time, as it likely would not have (even if the score had been known) during the intervening centuries. Yet the ideas on gender voiced in *La Calisto* and in many other mid-seventeenth-century operas can be found in Venetian discourses of the period: for instance, those of Giovanni Francesco Loredano, who at one point, as Wendy Heller puts it, "justifies rape (or at the very least vigorous seduction) as a male prerogative."[18] The amoral stance often attributed to Busenello and Monteverdi's *L'incoronazione di Poppea* finds parallels in the writings of the Accademia degli Incogniti, whose ideas permeate many librettos of the period.[19]

The balance of comic and serious, characteristic of *La Calisto*, is echoed as well by the balance of recitative and aria in this and other Cavalli operas of the early 1650s. By the end of his long career (he composed some forty operas) audiences had started to demand a higher proportion of vocal display, with the result that the aria came to dominate Italian opera, as it would for the following two centuries and more. But in *La Calisto* arias remain short, and, though their texts are different metrically from the intervening recitative, the latter does not sound as musically distinct from aria as it would later be in the form we call *opera seria*. In this opera the drama seems to flow in a seamless manner, with Cavalli's fertile musical imagination moving easily between the explanatory recitative and the lyrical effusions continually interrupting it.

---

[18] Heller, *Emblems of Eloquence*, p. 54.

[19] See the chapter entitled *"Bizzarrie feminile,"* ibid., pp. 48–81. Heller also shows how the nun Arcangela Tarabotti countered many of the antifeminist ideas emanating from the Accademia (pp. 57–68). On *Poppea* and the Accademia, see also Fenlon and Miller, *The Song of the Soul*, and Rosand, *Monteverdi's Last Operas*, pp. 333–37 and 373–75.

But *La Calisto* represents still another kind of historical moment, for in the Venetian public opera of its time Italian theater most closely approximates the Elizabethan theater and that of the Spanish so-called Golden Age: all these legendary theatrical periods are characterized by an inclusiveness of various elements: of comic and serious, of class diversity within the audience,[20] of an unselfconscious ease with which the supernatural world intersects with the mortal one. In Italy as well as in France, musical drama was exempt from the classical strictures that shaped spoken drama. It remained, to be sure, a brief moment, for opera was soon to adopt a new set of conventions in which, for better and worse, the comic and serious were to go their separate ways and in which audiences as well were to segregate themselves by money and class.

HANDEL, *RINALDO*, LONDON, QUEEN'S THEATER, FEBRUARY 24, 1711

If generations of English majors have come to believe that opera is a ridiculous art, this may well result from their reading of those much-anthologized remarks by Addison in *The Spectator* following the first performance of *Rinaldo*. Addison's famous attack is aimed not at the music but, first, at the Italian text, which he finds "florid" and full of "tedious Circumlocutions" and, second, at the elaborate theatrical spectacle, which he labels "Childish and Absurd."[21]

Addison scores his most telling attack on the opera in an incident regarding the sparrows that were released on the stage. Seeing an "ordinary Fellow carrying a Cage full of little Birds upon his Shoulder" on the street, he asks "what Use he would put them to," only to learn "he had been buying Sparrows for the Opera." After the

---

[20] On the audience makeup in the Venetian public theaters, see B. L. Glixon and J. E. Glixon, *Inventing*, pp. 295–322. Although not as diverse as those in Elizabethan England or Golden Age Spain, Venetian audiences included the middle class as well as the nobles who rented the tiers of boxes.

[21] Addison and Steele, *The Spectator*, vol. 1, pp. 23, 26. For Steele's quite similar take on *Rinaldo*, see *ibid.*, pp. 63–65.

fellow's friend, "licking his Lips," asks if they "are to be roasted," he is told "No, no, . . . , they are to enter towards the end of the first Act, and to fly about the Stage."[22] As it turns out, although the birds perform their stunt as scheduled, the audience, Addison tells us, is actually being tricked by the sounds supposedly emanating from them. These sounds are nothing more than a deception or, to use a contemporary term, they are the result of "special effects," for they come from "a Consort of Flagellets and Bird-calls which was planted behind the Scenes."[23]

Despite Addison's gleeful exposure of this illusion, the audiences who flocked to *Rinaldo* were wildly appreciative. Although this was Handel's first of some forty operas composed for London, *Rinaldo* enjoyed more performances over the years than any other of his operas, with revivals each year for the following four years, productions in Naples and Hamburg, and a much-revised London version in 1731.[24] Indeed, the special effects around which Addison's satire centered account for much of the work's popularity. Spectacle was something that audiences in Italy had demanded – often at the expense of other elements, above all of the orchestra – ever since the beginnings of public opera in Venice during the 1630s. But though Italian opera was still relatively new to England when *Rinaldo* was produced, spectacle had been central to English theater from the Jonsonian masque to Purcell's so-called "semi-operas."

The choice of text for this opera was motivated by the opportunities it offered for spectacle. Though named after its hero, it is centered equally around its major female character, Armida, whose magical powers allowed the producer, Aaron Hill, to conjure up a multitude of effects, both of a theatrical and vocal nature. The visual effects include an amazing variety of situations: characters suddenly disappearing into thin air or being transformed into other characters; the heroes being met by monsters with lit torches; flames, smoke,

[22] *Ibid.*, p. 24.   [23] *Ibid.*

[24] For a list of performances, see Kubik, *Händels Rinaldo*, pp. 18–21. After 1731 there is no record of any performances until 1946. Indeed, after Handel's own time none of his operas was revived until about 1920.

and thunder rising from a chasm; Armida singing as she flies through the air in a chariot drawn by two dragons. Armida, whose music ranges from the seductiveness with which she entices Rinaldo to the rage she displays once he has abandoned her, enjoyed almost a century and a half of popularity on the operatic stage in the hands, successively, of such major composers as Lully (1686), Gluck (1777), Haydn (1784), and Rossini (1817) – with Dvořák offering a belated footnote in his little-performed version of 1904. Some twenty-four years after *Rinaldo*, Handel was able to resurrect Armida's magical properties, as well as her emotional range, in the figure of Alcina, the Ariosto character whom Tasso had imitated for his *Gerusalemme liberata*, from which Hill drew his scenario. Both Ariosto's and Tasso's epics counted for audiences as popular romance, much as science fiction movies do today. Addison, after mentioning the opera's "Thunder and Lightning, Illuminations, and Fireworks," displayed his highmindedness by citing "Monsieur Boileau, that one Verse in *Virgil*, is worth all the *Clincant* or Tinsel of *Tasso*."[25]

Entertaining though Addison's attack on *Rinaldo* and, in effect, on Italian opera in general may be, readers of *The Spectator* were also likely aware of a certain special interest on the part of both Addison and Steele. Addison was still disappointed by the failure of his English opera *Rosamonde* in 1707, and Steele was known for having a financial interest in a rival theater and had rented a concert room to promoters who could only be hurt by Handel's success. Charles Burney, in his *General History of Music* of 1789, by which time Addison and Steele had come to count as classic writers, devotes more than half his discussion of *Rinaldo* to these conflicts of interest: "We should not forget," Burney admonishes his readers, "who were the authors of the Tatlers and Spectators, nor how they were circumstanced."[26]

At the time *Rinaldo* was first produced, Italian opera – not to speak of Handel himself – was still a novelty in London. Although

[25] Addison and Steele, *The Spectator*, vol. I, pp. 25–26.
[26] Burney, *A General History of Music*, vol. II, p. 675.

Italian singers had been performing there for half a decade, they usually sang in intermezzos between the acts of plays. The first full-length opera known to have been sung entirely in Italian, *Almahide*, dates from only a year before *Rinaldo*.[27] By the time *Rinaldo* was produced, the two London theaters had divided their missions to assign Italian opera to the Queen's Theater in the Haymarket and English drama to Drury Lane. Unlike most of Handel's later ventures, in which the composer served as entrepreneur and manager of his own productions, the *Rinaldo* project was wholly in the hands of Aaron Hill, who hired an Italian librettist, Giacomo Rossi, to turn his scenario into verse and organize it according to the conventions of *opera seria*. Handel, not yet the great cultural icon he was to become over the years in London, was still a hired hand, at this point known mainly for the fact that he had had some success working in Italy during the preceding years and had recently been appointed music director by the Elector of Hanover, who, as the London public was quite aware, was waiting in the wings for the death of Queen Anne, whose successor he was scheduled to be.

Handel was still so little known to the public that Rossi, in his introduction to the libretto, which members of the audience, like our own contemporaries reading supertitles, customarily bought in order to follow the words (printed in both Italian and English), sought to bolster the composer's reputation by referring to him as the "Orpheus of our Age," a phrase that gave Addison the opportunity for another pot-shot when he dubbed the composer with the German moniker "Minheer *Hendel*" and then made fun of the librettist for claiming, "in the same Sublimity of Stile, that he [Handel] Composed this Opera in a Fortnight."[28]

Although Addison had nothing to say about the music as such, the rapid composition of *Rinaldo* may well have been due to the fact that, since Handel was playing to an audience unacquainted with his work in Germany and Italy, he could draw from his large store of

---

[27] See Kubik, *Händels Rinaldo*, p. 44.
[28] Addison and Steele, *The Spectator*, p. 26.

earlier music. As a result, a large proportion of the opera consisted of revisions of arias and instrumental movements from earlier operas, cantatas, oratorios, sonatas and the like. Although he continued to borrow from his German and Italian work throughout his career (as well as from other composers!), no Handel opera contains as much of his earlier work as *Rinaldo*.[29] One aria, for example, Almirena's "Bel piacere," is almost identical, in both words and music, to an aria for Poppea in Handel's preceding opera, *Agrippina*, composed for Venice little over a year before; most of the other arias and duets, to be sure, were given substantial revisions. (One might note that originality did not emerge as a serious aesthetic criterion until a few decades later.)

Yet even if the audience had been aware of these borrowings, this fact would surely not have diminished the opera's success, for people had attended *Rinaldo* largely for two reasons: the spectacle and the virtuoso singers, above all, the great castrato Nicolini in the title role. And Handel's role as composer may have been less in the minds of this audience than his improvisations at the harpsichord, especially, as Burney tells us, at the end of Act II when Handel, according to Burney, "must have captivated by the lightness and elasticity of his finger."[30] And this audience must also have applauded the thoroughly happy ending that Hill arranged when the evil sorceress Armida and her lover, the Muslim king of Jerusalem, Argante, not only get married but also convert to Christianity – a resolution that even the pious Tasso chose not to pursue in his poem. But then, as Addison reminds us at the start of his attack on *Rinaldo* (and as recent experiments in neuroscience, as I point out in Essay 5, suggest of music in general), an opera's "only Design is to gratify the Senses, and keep up an indolent Attention in the Audience."[31]

[29] Handel, *Rinaldo*, introduction by David R. B. Kimbell, p. XII. For a comprehensive list of Handel's borrowings in *Rinaldo*, see Kubik, *Händels Rinaldo*, pp. 103–05.

[30] Burney, *A General History of Music*, vol. II, p. 674.

[31] Addison and Steele, *The Spectator*, vol. I, pp. 22–23.

ROUSSEAU, *LE DEVIN DU VILLAGE*, FONTAINEBLEAU, OCTOBER 18, 1752

What we know about *Le Devin du village* comes mainly from the composer's mouth. Rousseau was above all a verbal being, familiar to us today in his diverse roles as political theorist, philosopher, polemicist, memoirist, and novelist. Throughout his life, however, he considered his official profession that of a musician; in particular, of a music copyist. And for a few years during the 1750s he was best known for his brief opera *Le Devin du village*, which, though regularly performed in Paris until well into the nineteenth century, is familiar today not through its music but from its composer's detailed description of its genesis and first performance in his *Confessions*.[32] Up to then the only literary work that had brought him attention was the so-called First Discourse, which, published less than two years before the opera's premiere, startled his contemporaries by contending that the development of the arts and sciences had proved detrimental to humanity.

The premiere of *Le Devin du village* took place at the royal castle of Fontainebleau in the presence of the king and queen and their entourage. The composer makes a point of his awkwardness, his inappropriate dress, and his general lack of ease in this company; as always throughout his life, he was the outsider who had managed to charm his way into circles far beyond his assigned place in a closed social world. And yet the opera in both its text and music, like the discourse he had published earlier, argues against artifice and social hierarchies in favor of simplicity and naturalness. With its village characters it belongs to the tradition of pastoral drama, yet these are supposedly "real" country folk in contrast to the mythical characters peopling such earlier works as Tasso's *Aminta* and Monteverdi's *Orfeo*. Rousseau's plot revolves around the conflict of love and social class, for the heroine, Colette, seeks out the local soothsayer, to help her win back her suitor, Colin, who has been tempted by a woman of a higher social order.

---

[32] See Rousseau, *The Confessions*, pp. 344–61 (Book Eight).

Simplicity in all forms – a simple story about simple people singing simple tunes set against simple harmonies – dominates *Le Devin du village* throughout. Despite its popularity, it has invited little but disparagement from musical scholars. As a recent study of Rousseau's music puts it, "The harmonic construction is rather banal, the keys employed are few."[33] And certainly if one compares this opera to Mozart's *Bastien et Bastienne*, composed to a text that parodied *Le Devin du village*, one quickly recognizes that Mozart's musical sophistication, even at twelve, the age at which he wrote his version of this pastoral tale, went considerably beyond Rousseau's. But it is easy enough to disparage philosophers who also try to compose music: the compositions of Rousseau, Nietzsche, and Adorno, however modest their place within the history of music, remain eminently listenable – indeed, Gustav Mahler once felt the need to call Nietzsche "a far better composer than was generally acknowledged."[34]

Whatever the limitations of Rousseau's harmonic palette, his melodies have proved infectious. Louis XV is known to have hummed tunes from the opera in a croaky voice the day after the performance; he even invited the composer for an audience, though Rousseau refused, partly because he feared being embarrassed by his chronically irritable bladder, and also because he dreaded becoming obligated to the monarch if the latter, as he expected, offered him a pension.

The infectiousness that the opera's first listeners at Fontainebleau experienced was felt throughout the musical world of Paris once it opened at the Opéra on March 1, 1753. (I myself can testify to this phenomenon: ever since I heard a recording of *Le Devin du village* over fifty years ago, two melodies – Colette's plangent entrance aria and Colin's rousing "Quand on sait aimer et plaire" – have continued to pester my brain.) The insidiousness of Rousseau's tunes can be attributed partly to the style that he had adopted for this opera, for he

---

[33] Collisani, *La musica*, p. 112.
[34] See De La Grange, *Gustav Mahler*, vol. III (1999), p. 399n.

was imitating the manner of Italian comic opera, whose tunefulness was still foreign to French ears, accustomed as they were to the harmonic complexities of Lully and Rameau.

Rousseau had first experienced Italian music while serving as secretary to the French ambassador to Venice some nine years before, when he quickly overcame what he called his "national prejudice against Italian music."[35] And it is also possible that he attended a performance of Pergolesi's *La serva padrona* when this opera was brought to Paris by an Italian troupe in 1746. Soon after *Le Devin du village* he wrote his "Letter on French Music," which, besides arguing that the Italian language is more suitable for musical setting than French, insists on the primacy of melody over harmony.[36] This letter, together with *Le Devin du village*, became a central text in the so-called Guerre des Bouffons, which followed the controversial visit of an Italian troupe from 1752 to 1754 that performed a series of Italian comic operas, among them *La serva padrona*, which excited the public far more than during its earlier run.

"All Paris divided into two camps," Rousseau writes, with the advocates of French music "made up of the great, the rich and the ladies," while those in the Italian camp, to which Rousseau and his opera belonged, included "true music lovers, talented people, and men of genius."[37] Rousseau tells us that they even had party names, the "King's corner" (for the French advocates) and the "Queen's corner" (for those who sided with Italian opera) that derived from the fact that each party sat under either the king's or the queen's box at the Opéra. The Guerre des Bouffons is an early example of those operatic wars which, like that between the advocates of Gluck and Piccinni during the late 1770s, and between Wagner and Verdi a century after that, allowed national and personal biases to play out in bloodless verbal battles over musical and dramatic style.

---

[35] See Rousseau, *The Confessions*, p. 294.
[36] See O'Dea, *Jean-Jacques Rousseau*, pp. 26–33.
[37] Rousseau, *The Confessions*, p. 358.

However shrill Rousseau may have sounded in his advocacy of Italian over French music, *Le Devin du village* remains a recognizably French opera. After all, despite his rejection of French as a language for musical setting, he chose to write his text in his native language. And although nobody would mistake it for, say, the music of Rameau, Rousseau's manner at times sounds more French than Italian. The overture is distinctly in the French style, and after the Fontainebleau performance Rousseau added a typically French *divertissement* at the end for the performances at the Opéra. Moreover, this *divertissement*, with its celebration of villagers coming together communally, anticipates some of the great and characteristic scenes in Rousseau's later writing: for example, the country festivities in *La Nouvelle Héloïse* and the vision of celebrating free citizens in which the *Letter to D'Alembert* culminates.[38]

The ease with which *Le Devin du village* communicated musically with its early listeners can be related to the way the characters are made to communicate with one another. The soothsayer, by dint of his ability to look into the hearts of the two lovers, illustrates a key tenet of Rousseau's: that sympathy allows us to look into the psyche of others and to identify with their plight.[39] Through the infectiousness of the music, one might add, the audience quickly becomes involved in the world of the characters, to whom it grants its sympathy.

In retrospect, however, the pastoralism of *Le Devin du village* may not seem quite as natural as it once did. In its time it helped establish Rousseau as the great prophet of nature, whose later writings, together with his real-life "back-to-nature" sojourns, have nourished a long series of revolts against civilization such as the Utopian movements of the nineteenth century and the hippiedom of the 1960s.

From a later vantage point, the simple shepherd's life that Colin and Colette lead has less in common with what we today see as

---

[38] See Collasini, *La musica*, pp. 106–09.
[39] Thomas applies Rousseau's notion of sympathy to *Le Devin du village* in *Aesthetics of Opera*, pp. 206–14.

natural than it has with that more theatrical form of shepherding that Marie Antoinette and her court pursued in the *hameau* that the queen constructed at Versailles. With their country costumes and buildings imitating those of real villages, these last representatives of the *ancien régime* could play-act what they had witnessed in paintings and in Rousseau's little opera.

Just as the operas of Lully long outlived the court of Louis XIV for which they were created, so *Le Devin du village* maintained its place in the repertory of the Opéra long after the world that first cheered it had been replaced by a succession of new political orders. The end came suddenly when, in 1829, after well over 500 performances and just a year before the Restoration came to a close, somebody tossed a powdered wig onto the stage.[40] This *coup de grâce* was a reminder that this opera now appeared to be just another artifact of the *ancien régime* – a neat irony in view of the key role that Rousseau had played in undermining that very regime.

ROSSINI, *TANCREDI*, VENICE, TEATRO LA FENICE, FEBRUARY 6, 1813

It contains what is likely the most insidiously obsessive tune in all opera, the "Di tanti palpiti" with which the *en travesti* hero brings his/her entrance aria to its rousing conclusion. Now that *Tancredi* gets but rarely performed, other operatic tunes are doubtless more familiar, *Rigoletto*'s "La donna è mobile," for example, or the *Carmen* habañera (which made its way into children's TV programs), or the two-women duet from Delibes's otherwise little-performed *Lakmé*, whose cunningly orientalist tune was used in British Airways commercials to lure listeners into making exotic travel arrangements. But for the few decades during which *Tancredi* held the stage, "Di tanti palpiti" had become the stuff of legend, with gondoliers supposedly using it to serenade their tourists through Venetian canals, or with courtroom trials interrupted by humming spectators; while in

---

[40] See Prod'homme, "Les dernières représentations."

subsequent years it continued in instrumental arrangements by various composers,[41] until a new opera aesthetic – represented, in their differing ways, by Verdi and Wagner – brought Rossini into eclipse, with the *coup de grâce* administered by the wicked parody in the tailors' chorus during the final scene of *Die Meistersinger*. Yet once this persistent tune enters the mind it assumes the characteristics of what Oliver Sacks, writing as a neurologist, calls a "brainworm,"[42] as I myself can testify, for it has plagued me day and night throughout the time I have been preparing this section.

Yet *Tancredi* is notable for much more than this lilting cabaletta, for the opera was Rossini's first major success. Though the tenth of his operatic works (some, to be sure, were less than a full evening's fare), it quickly made its way from one opera house to another and imprinted the Rossini style, with its high volume and its brash rhythms, in the minds of the international opera public. The famous opening lines from Stendhal's *Life of Rossini*, "Napoleon is dead, but a new conqueror has already shown himself to the world; and from Moscow to Naples, from London to Vienna, from Paris to Calcutta, his name is constantly on every tongue,"[43] not only indicates the hold he exerted on his listeners but also presents him in the guise of a military conqueror – scarcely an accident, for *Tancredi* was Stendhal's favorite among Rossini's many operas, and Tancredi himself is a conquering hero.

In eighteenth-century *opera seria* a heroic figure such as Tancredi would have been performed by a castrato, but by Rossini's time the castrato had become a dying breed. Later, during the same year as *Tancredi*, the composer actually wrote a part for a castrato, namely, the Arsace in *Aureliano in Palmira*, performed by Giambattista Velluti, who is now seen as the last of the major castrato opera singers. The memory of these singers lingered in Rossini's mind, as it did for most members of his audience. Though written for the low female voice,

---

[41] See Hadlock, "*Tancredi* and *Semiramide*," p. 157.

[42] Sacks, *Musicophilia*, pp. 41–48 (see Essay 1 for another example).

[43] Stendhal, *Life of Rossini*, p. 3.

the role of Tancredi, like that of many later *en travesti* roles, was surely meant to awaken these memories for its listeners. Indeed, when, many years back, I saw Marilyn Horne come onstage – sword in hand and clothed in full battle regalia – for Tancredi's entrance aria, I told myself that this was the closest I should ever get to experiencing what I fancied must be the castrato voice. As Tancredi declared his love for Amenaide and built toward the irresistible "Di tanti palpiti" in which the aria culminates, Horne sang with the vocal power, and also with the unbelievable agility, that called to mind what I had read about the famed castrati.

When Stendhal wrote his book on Rossini a decade after the *Tancredi* premiere, the composer had just finished his last Italian opera, *Semiramide*, before launching into his brief career as a composer of French opera. For Stendhal none of the works after *Tancredi* exudes the special charm of this early opera, which he characterizes with terms such as "entrancing," "refreshing," "lilting," "delightful," and "youthful."[44] The later operas, though full of things he finds praise for, also are problematic for him. The differences he notes between *Tancredi* and its successors are reminiscent of the distinction that Friedrich Schiller had made some three decades before Stendhal's book between "naïve" and "sentimental" art, between that which is created with unselfconscious ease and that which is more labored.[45] Stendhal, moreover, associates the problematic quality of the later Rossini operas with the composer's supposedly growing dependence on German harmony, which he contrasts with the happy simplicity of Italian melody.[46] Needless to say, our own tastes today would scarcely make this distinction in Rossini's work, since the great comic operas we have come to prize, as well as the *opere serie* that have enjoyed a major revival in recent years, all came after *Tancredi*. Staunch liberal that he was, Stendhal, one might add, had also sought to link the military heroics of *Tancredi* with the

---

[44] *Ibid.*, pp. 52, 55, 62, 68.

[45] Note Isaiah Berlin's use of Schiller's distinction to characterize Verdi as a "naïve" artist (in Essay 1, section entitled "Quoting").

[46] Stendhal, *Life of Rossini*, pp. 63, 68.

composer's early-childhood memory of French republican troops liberating his home territory in 1796.[47] Moreover, Stendhal's experience of this opera was mediated through the singing of the great Giuditta Pasta, whom he heard in the title role on numerous occasions and about whom – especially in the entrance aria – he waxed eloquent.[48]

Despite the popularity of *Tancredi*, the first impersonator of the title role, Adelaide Malanotte, spurned "Di tanti palpiti," with the result that Rossini composed an alternative aria, "Dolci d'amor parole," considerably more elaborate vocally than the original, which she apparently had not found substantial enough.[49] Yet once she became aware of how much the public demanded "Di tanti palpiti," she was willing to alternate the original with the alternative one in her performances. Malanotte also participated in another alternative – this one not an aria but a whole new ending to the opera that did not come to light until the 1970s. Her lover, Count Luigi Lechi of Brescia, prepared the text for a conclusion that, closely following Voltaire's tragedy *Tancrède*, allowed the hero to die as a result of a battle wound, but not before discovering that his beloved Amenaide had not been disloyal to him after all. The opera's original libretto, by Gaetano Rossi, had faithfully followed the long-standing operatic convention demanding a happy end, in which hero and heroine are reunited after all misunderstandings have been cleared up.

But the new tragic version, performed in Ferrara soon after the Venice premiere of the original version, was a failure and remained in manuscript until Count Giacomo Lechi, a descendant of Luigi Lechi, made it available for the critical edition of Rossini's works.[50]

---

[47] *Ibid.*, p. 65. For a detailed analysis of Stendhal's *Life of Rossini* and its relation to the world of the Restoration, see Walton, *Rossini in Restoration Paris*, pp. 24–67.

[48] Stendhal, *Life of Rossini*, pp. 52, 56, 58.

[49] This alternative aria, written for different words but also including the phrase "tanti palpiti" (though to new and less catchy music) is included in the critical edition. See Rossini, *Tancredi*, vol. II, p. 610–47. It has also been recorded by Marilyn Horne together with alternative arias for other Rossini operas.

[50] For the music and text of the tragic ending, see *ibid.*, vol. II, pp. 648–716.

As a journalist at the time had remarked, "The death of Tancredi, which was introduced here [Ferrara] and which did not care to adapt itself to the public, did not please."[51] Scarcely surprising, for tragic endings were extremely rare during the first two centuries of opera. It is as though audiences assumed different mind-sets for opera and for spoken drama. If you were attending Voltaire's *Tancrède*, you were prepared from the start to feel moved by the sad fate of the tragic hero. But at the opera (assuming that the same patrons attended musical and spoken drama) you sought above all to be sensuously diverted by the virtuoso singing and the spectacle. In opera an ending in which all the characters rejoice seems to follow naturally – even if, when one knows the *Tancredi* libretto alone, the conclusion seems merely tacked on. A few years later, Rossini broke with convention to create a tragic ending for *Otello*; but for Rome, whose audiences were thought incapable of stomaching a catastrophe in the opera house, he provided an alternative happy ending, which, as it turned out, never caught on (though Shakespeare was still little known in Italy, it is hard to imagine anybody approving of Otello and Desdemona reconciled).[52]

Soon after the Ferrara ending was published, I heard the tragic finale in the single live performance of *Tancredi* I have attended. As someone obviously long accustomed to operas culminating in their chief characters' deaths, it seemed to follow as naturally for me as the *lieto fine* had for Rossini's audiences. Indeed, it turned out to be moving in a way that one does not ordinarily expect from Rossini. The hero's final cavatina eschews all vocal fireworks and instead cultivates a manner closer to that of Gluck than to its actual composer.[53] Indeed, living in an age in which, far more than in Rossini's time, one expects one's expectations to be challenged, it was surely a

[51] Quoted in Gossett, *The Tragic Finale*, p. 30.
[52] For a description of the changes made for Rome, see Rossini, *Otello*, vol. 1, p. xxxvii.
[53] For descriptions of the music for this ending, see *ibid.*, p. 32, and Gossett, *Divas and Scholars*, p. 152.

treat to move (and with Marilyn Horne to boot!) from the rollicking "Di tanti palpiti" to the simple pathos of the conclusion.

WAGNER, *TANNHÄUSER*, PARIS, OPÉRA, MARCH 13, 1861

The usual explanation for the *Tannhäuser* riots is that the composer broke the rules about where the mandatory ballet was to be inserted. By long-standing Parisian convention the ballet was staged during a middle act, about the hour, 10 P.M., that the Jockey Club members were ready to arrive and ogle the female dancers, after which they felt free to go backstage and arrange to meet them privately. The proper moment for the *Tannhäuser* ballet was the second act, precisely when the song contest on the Wartburg was to be held. But how could Wagner have accommodated dancers in this setting – above all, in the presence of the pious Elisabeth (and what self-respecting male would want to ogle a Wagnerian soprano?). The only logical place for dancing was the Venusberg scene, which, though it allowed ample opportunity for sensual display, had to come at the start of the opera when the prospective oglers were still at dinner. (Had Wagner lived in our own, less chronologically rigid age, he could easily have reversed the events, with the Venusberg appearing in mid evening as a flashback right after Tannhäuser's paean to Venus in the song contest.)

Rioting over the violation of convention was itself a convention in Parisian aesthetic politics: witness the fuss made in 1830 at the opening of Hugo's *Hernani* when the author provoked his audience by moving the alexandrine's caesura two syllables in each direction and, perhaps even worse, when he allowed a royal personage to violate decorum by asking so mundane a question as to what time it is. But the flouting of convention on such seemingly technical matters as the vocabulary of poetry or the order of scenes in an opera is actually a ruse for larger political and social matters. Standing behind the eruptions at the *Hernani* opening were conflicts between the self-proclaimed adherents of the new Romanticism and those who held on to classicist views; between republicans and monarchists; between the young and those who, whatever their actual age, counted as old. Baudelaire, in his defense of *Tannhäuser* written only a few days after the first Paris performance, made a connection between these events when he compared the violent reaction to Wagner's opera with the initial resistance to Hugo's dramas and Delacroix's paintings.[54]

Certainly the absence of a ballet at the right moment played a central role in the opera's failure in Paris. Although Wagner had been warned by the management many months before the premiere that the ballet was crucial to ensuring a successful run, he remained defiant, insisting instead that the bacchanal he was adding to the first scene would have to suffice. Even Berlioz, who rarely hesitated to challenge the conventions of French musical life, inserted the expected dances smack in the middle of each of the two parts of *Les Troyens*. (Even this conciliatory gesture did not succeed in getting him a production at the Opéra, and he had to rest content with the less prestigious Théâtre Lyrique, which, two years after the *Tannhäuser* premiere, was able to put on only the second of the two parts.) Wagner himself, in his two accounts of the *Tannhäuser* affair – the first a newspaper article written right after the incident, the second his autobiography many years later – stressed the role of the Jockey Club in setting off the incident.[55]

What, beyond the absence of a ten o'clock ballet, stood behind the *Tannhäuser* squabble? For one thing, both in his theory and his practice, Wagner violated the principles to which the French musical establishment and, above all, the newspaper critics, adhered. As one hostile reviewer, Oscar Comettant, put it, "What one wants to find in the theater is a gripping drama, with a lucid exposition, a well-managed plot, a forceful denouement, one that allows the musician to take wing freely – not to indulge idiosyncratic reveries that can affect no one but himself, but to express genuine, well-characterized

[54] Baudelaire, "Richard Wagner et *Tannhäuser* à Paris," *Oeuvres complètes*, p. 1065.
[55] See "Bericht über die Aufführung des 'Tannhäuser' in Paris," reprinted in Csampai and Holland, *Tannhäuser: Texte*, pp. 199–209, and Wagner, *Mein Leben*, vol. II, pp. 190–223.

emotions."[56] What the reviewers obviously demanded of an opera was a continuation of the tradition of *grand opéra* à la Meyerbeer, Halévy, and Auber.

Let us look at what actually took place at the Opéra when Wagner, hoping and expecting to enjoy a major international triumph – one that would pave the way for a Paris production of the still unproduced *Tristan und Isolde* – experienced the worst fiasco of his career. At the first of the three performances the opening scene seemed to go well – at least there were no interruptions. Laughter erupted with the shepherd's song (apparently not well performed) that served as transition between the first two scenes. And the second scene was ruined not because of the audience but because the Landgraf's hunting dogs drowned out the music with their howling and barking.

The worst trouble at the premiere came near the end of Act II when Tannhäuser decides to go to Rome as a penitent. This was precisely the time that the ballet should have taken place, and the Jockeys expressed their dismay by blowing their whistles to the accompaniment of a screaming and hissing crowd. At this point, as Paul Lindau (who obtained a ticket by joining the house claque) described the performance in his memoir, "The battle was lost beyond saving."[57] The second intermission witnessed both verbal and physical abuse in the corridors. And the final act, as Lindau put it, "resembled nothing so much as the uninterrupted desecration of a corpse," which the spectators "dismembered and mutilated to the sounds of their braying and howling."[58]

The two succeeding performances, on March 18 and March 24, fared even worse. Wagner was forced to accept cuts in the second performance because of the administration's vain hope that a shorter opera might better please the public. At this second performance the

---

[56] Reprinted, together with another hostile review by Paul Scudo, in Grey, *Richard Wagner*, pp. 347–71. The above quotation is on p. 356.

[57] Lindau, "The 'Tannhäuser' Scandal," p. 17. The preceding details are drawn from Lindau's account (pp. 3–22).

[58] *Ibid.*, p. 18.

whistles and hisses emanating from the Jockeys did not get going until the middle of Act II, but, together with the noise from the audience as a whole, the disruption was evidently even worse than at the premiere. The third performance fared no better. Wagner had asked for a Sunday, which, since it was not a subscription night, would, he hoped, allow more seats to become available for his supporters; but it hardly mattered. This time the Jockeys started whistling from the start of the opera, and confusion reigned throughout. The music often stopped for a quarter hour at a time before a calm moment could be found for the singers to resume. Wagner, who refused to attend this performance, demanded that further performances be canceled, with the result that he had to forgo the profits he had counted on to pay his ongoing debts, not to speak of the prestige he had sought from being performed in what then counted as the world's opera capital.

But the aggressiveness of the Jockeys was only one factor in the opera's failure in Paris. Through the many months of negotiations and rehearsals for the *Tannhäuser* premiere, everything that was going on was reported – often in the most negative light – in the press and by word of mouth. The circumstances under which the work was chosen to be performed were themselves controversial: Princess Pauline Metternich, the young wife of the Austrian ambassador and herself a fervent Wagner fan, had so successfully worked her charms on Napoleon III at a social gathering that he authorized the production by imperial decree. As a result, a number of operas that were waiting in line for productions were postponed. These included *Les Troyens*, which as mentioned above, never even made it to the Opéra. Berlioz, who, as a fellow musical renegade, should have been Wagner's ally and who is known to have admired much of Wagner's music, chose not to come to his aid at a time when his voice might have made a difference. When asked to review *Tannhäuser* for the influential *Journal des débats*, Berlioz simply declined. After the premiere he wrote to an anti-Wagnerian friend, "As for the horrors, they were hissed splendidly," and after the second performance, he expressed his *Schadenfreude* to his son with the words, "The press is unanimous in wiping him out. As for me, I am cruelly avenged."[59]

If Berlioz had turned into an enemy, it goes without saying that the established opera composers and their adherents were scarcely ready to accept the new aesthetic that Wagner exemplified as blatantly as he did. Wagner had excoriated his one-time benefactor Meyerbeer, who still commanded a loyal public, in *Das Judentum in der Musik*. Even the relatively unvengeful Rossini, always prepared to speak of food, supposedly described Wagner's music as "lacking melody like a roast without sauce."[60] Anecdotes such as this one floated around Paris throughout the rehearsals and performances. A new verb, *tannhauser*, playing on the participle *tannant* (fatiguing, wearisome), made the rounds. It goes without saying that the climate for a successful production was scarcely favorable.

Moreover, the composer's own observed demeanor did not ingratiate him to potential adherents. His intransigence about the placement of the ballet typified his attitude toward everybody connected with the production. After all, foreign composers such as Donizetti and Verdi readily complied when they wrote for the Opéra – but then Wagner would scarcely have cared to compare himself to them. Throughout the rehearsals, for example, he waged an ongoing public battle with the assigned (and also admittedly incompetent) conductor, Pierre Louis Philippe Dietsch. As one of Wagner's most level-headed biographers, Martin Gregor-Dellin, put it, "Wagner committed the worst mistake one can make in a closed society: he conducted himself arrogantly."[61]

But out of a debacle there can also emerge martyrdom and subsequent sanctification. It remained for Baudelaire, who had no stake in the outmoded aesthetic to which the almost universally hostile reviewers were tied, to lay the groundwork for these

---

[59] Quoted in Cairns, *Berlioz*, vol. II, p. 662. For a searching review of the often tortured relationship between these two leaders of the new music of the mid nineteenth century, see Kolb, "Flying Leaves."

[60] Gregor-Dellin, *Richard Wagner*, p. 465. [61] *Ibid.*, pp. 464–65.

developments in his influential pamphlet. He flatly declares it "intolerable" that the Jockey Club should sacrifice a serious work of art in order "to enjoy the luxury of finding mistresses among the dancers at the Opéra."[62] To make his case, Baudelaire reviews Wagner's whole oeuvre, both the musical and the theoretical works, to portray him as a revolutionary who is challenging the foundations of earlier drama and music, indeed, of the arts as a whole. Significantly, Baudelaire in this essay quotes the octave of his programmatic sonnet "Correspondances," whose celebration of synaesthetic experience illustrates his own responses to Wagner's music, in which, referring specifically here to the overture to *Lohengrin*, he professes to feel "a *large diffuse light . . . the intensity of light* crossing with such rapidity that the nuances supplied by the dictionary would not suffice to express *this excess constantly being reborn of ardor and whiteness* [italics Baudelaire's]."[63] The Wagner who emerges in these pages is the guiding spirit of what came to be known as *Wagnérisme* in France, the inspiration for Symbolist poetry, indeed, if we note Baudelaire's stress on the composer's aesthetic theories, the father of the modernist arts.

A final note: in 1895, a long generation after its Paris premiere, *Tannhäuser* enjoyed a belated triumph at the Opéra. That same year H. Fiérens-Gevaert published a series of interviews in successive issues of the *Journal des débats* with surviving singers and other participants connected with the original production. Among his subjects was the Prince de Sagan, a Jockey-Club member who had found the noise to which he had contributed so deafening that he remembered nothing of the music. The prince now professed a love for Wagner, whose music "causes [him] to experience new sensations" similar to those he feels when he "contemplates a pretty woman."[64] Wagner by now was safely canonized, and the prince may well have reached an age in which music provided a satisfactory substitute for actual assignations.

---

[62] Baudelaire, *Oeuvres complètes*, p. 1069.   [63] *Ibid.*, p. 1043.
[64] Quoted by Fiérens-Gevaert, "Tannhaeuser."

STRAUSS, *SALOME*, GRAZ, STADT-THEATER, MAY 16, 1906

If we look at who attended and what effects the performance had on them, the Graz *Salome* was considerably more important than the opera's actual premiere in Dresden the preceding December. This was in fact the fourth production of an opera that was fast circulating among the German opera houses and, soon after, among major foreign ones as well. But this was the first Austrian production, and Graz became at best a provincial substitute for the Vienna Court Opera, which, despite the pleas of its director, Gustav Mahler, was prevented from producing it by the official Hapsburg censor, who found the subject matter inappropriate for a house sponsored by a Christian emperor.

Yet the Graz premiere drew a large proportion of what we today see as the greatest living composers. To be sure, Debussy and Ravel were not there, nor was the young Stravinsky, still ensconced in Russia, but Puccini made a special trip from Italy – though not to the premiere itself but to the next day's performance. "The most extraordinary thing, terrible cacophony," he wrote to a composer friend, Ervin Lendvai; "there are some very beautiful feelings in the orchestra, but in the end it wears you out."[65] Puccini was not the only person to complain of being worn out: so did the composer himself, who was conducting the work for the first time and, in a letter to his wife, besides expressing his general satisfaction with the orchestra and the singers, explained that he had not expected the job of keeping the orchestra together to be as taxing as it was.[66]

The other composers present at the Graz premiere included Mahler and his wife Alma, whose promising composition career had ended, at her husband's insistence, at the time of their marriage; Arnold Schoenberg, together with his brother-in-law Alexander von Zemlinsky (one-time teacher not only of Schoenberg but also of Alma Mahler, whom he had once courted); Schoenberg's student Alban Berg, though his other talented student, Anton von Webern,

---

[65] Quoted in Phillips-Matz, *Puccini*, p. 160.
[66] Grasberger, *Der Strom der Töne*, p. 168.

did not come along. Another Strauss was present as well, namely, the widow of Johann Strauss (no relation, as music dictionaries customarily remind us).

The performance left significant effects on all the composers who had congregated in Graz: some of these effects artistic, others of a more personal nature. It is hard, to be sure, to pin down any direct influence of *Salome* on Puccini's subsequent work: cacophony was surely not his thing, and violence had already been present in *Tosca*, though one wonders if *Salome* might have helped motivate his choice of the story of Turandot, a similarly cold woman with a penchant for head-chopping.

The effect of the performance on Mahler was profound. Still reeling from his defeat at the hands of the Vienna censor, Mahler, on the train back to Vienna from Graz, used the occasion for a remark about the nature of fame. In conversation with the popular writer Peter Rosegger, the composer expressed his astonishment at the Graz audience's enthusiasm when, as Alma put it in her memoirs, "we were convinced that not one in a hundred really understood the music." Rosegger replied that "the voice of the people was the voice of God," after which the Mahlers asked "whether he meant the people here and now or the people as posterity."[67] Soon after, in an interview, Mahler compared himself with Strauss, whom he called a man of his time ("Zeitgemässer"), whereas he himself was not of his time ("Unzeitgemässer") – this being an allusion to the title of one of Nietzsche's books.[68] As it turned out, Mahler was correct: by the late twentieth century he had reached a higher place in the pantheon of composers than his more consumer-oriented colleague.

As for the opera itself, both Mahlers were generally admiring, though Alma less so than her husband. As one can infer from a letter by Mahler to her, they both objected to the unevenness of the score, and both came down hard on the music of Salome's dance. Although Mahler refers to the opera as "a work of 'virtuosity' in a

---

[67] A. Mahler, *Gustav Mahler*, p. 98.
[68] De la Grange, *Gustav Mahler*, vol. III, p. 399.

bad sense," he also chides Alma for "under-valuing what is, after all, a very significant work."[69]

The effect of *Salome* on the other composers present in Graz was something less complex than that on the Mahlers. Zemlinsky went on to conduct the opera on innumerable occasions, both as director of the German opera in Prague and at other houses. As one of the great derivative composers of the early twentieth century, Zemlinsky displays the traces of both Strauss and Mahler. Moreover, his one-act shocker, *Eine florentinische Tragödie*, is an obvious attempt to reproduce something of *Salome*'s effect.

Alban Berg, twenty-one years old at the time and already an active composer, displayed his enthusiasm for *Salome* by attending it repeatedly soon after the Graz performance. After traveling to Dresden to hear it at a music festival, he heard six performances given by a Breslau traveling company at the Vienna Volksoper, which was not subject to the censorship that had been exercised at the Court Opera. The affinity that Berg felt for the opera is evident, for instance, in the grotesque elements prominent in both of his own operas, *Wozzeck* and *Lulu*. And it goes without saying that his character Lulu is clearly a sister of Salome. (Had Debussy chosen to come to Graz, might he have recognized Strauss's heroine as a sister of his Mélisande?) Still, ten years later, well after he had ceased being a tonal composer and well after Strauss had left cacophony behind, Berg decided he no longer found either *Salome* or *Elektra* of interest.[70]

Since Webern did not join his teacher and fellow student in Graz, one can at best guess what his reaction might have been. One of Webern's own students reported that he "had no good words for Strauss," but another quoted him as saying "Die 'Salome' bleibt [*Salome* will survive]."[71] Among twentieth-century composers, the

---

[69] A. Mahler, *Gustav Mahler*, p. 275. See also Mahler's remark about "uneven" artists such as Titian and Sir Francis Bacon, p. 287.

[70] See Carner, *Alban Berg*, p. 6.

[71] See H. Moldenhauer and R. Moldenhauer, *Anton von Webern*, pp. 505 and 685n respectively.

austere Webern appears at the furthest possible remove from the sumptuous Strauss.

Although Schoenberg admired *Salome* for its musical adventurousness and continued to express this admiration for some years, by 1914 Schoenberg, like Berg, was expressing nothing but disdain for the earlier composer. "From an artistic point of view he [Strauss] no longer interests me," Schoenberg wrote in a letter; "what I once seem to have learned from him, I luckily misunderstood."[72] Moreover, his attitude toward Strauss was motivated at least as much by the way the elder composer treated him as by the music that the latter produced. Strauss, impressed by Schoenberg's early work, had opened doors for him in Berlin well before the *Salome* performance. But Schoenberg's abandonment of tonality two years after the premiere alienated Strauss to the point that he refused Schoenberg's request for help in arranging a performance of the latter's Five Pieces for Orchestra. And doubtless Strauss would not have recognized Schoenberg's *Erwartung* as an intensification of at once the musical language and the hysteria of *Salome*. As Schoenberg, in his still imperfect English, put it near the end of both their lives, "Though he [Strauss] was helpful to me in my youth, he has later changed his attitude toward myself. I am sure that he does not like my music and in this respect I know no mercy: I consider such people as enemies."[73]

There was still another major composer at the Graz performance, though no record of his presence can be found in the sources that I consulted. His later works *Doktor Fausti Weheklag* and *Apokalipsis cum figuris* may well be the greatest music that was never either composed or performed. I refer to Adrian Leverkühn, the central character of Thomas Mann's novel *Doktor Faustus*, whom his creator sent to Graz to attend *Salome*. As a figure of the representative avant-garde composer of the early twentieth century, Leverkühn displayed a distinctly mixed reaction to *Salome*, calling it an "auspiciously

---

[72] Schoenberg, *Briefe*, p. 48. [73] Auner, *A Schoenberg Reader*, p. 317.

revolutionary work," yet one "whose aesthetic sphere in no way attracted him."[74] This reaction may well be what Mann took to be Schoenberg's response to the opera – or at least what Mann's musical mentor Theodor Adorno thought to be Schoenberg's response. But the performance plays a major role in the development of the novel, for Leverkühn, directly after attending *Salome*, travels to Pressburg (now Bratislava) to seek out the prostitute Esmeralda, from whom he had shied away when he first met her in a Leipzig brothel some time before.[75] He now knowingly allows himself to be infected with venereal disease, which in the logic of the narrative leads to his pact with the devil, who grants him twenty-four years of intense creativity.[76]

In closing I cite still another visitor, this one a real-life person – a true enthusiast of music though not by any means a composer. Yet he was also destined to become a performer, not, to be sure, on the operatic but on the world stage. The seventeen-year-old Adolf Hitler had begged money from relatives to make the pilgrimage to Graz – or so we know from his having told Strauss's son Franz of the trip many years later while both were attending the Bayreuth Festival.[77] In retrospect, one wonders what seeds might have been planted in the adolescent's mind as he heard Strauss's musical translation of the five Jews' Yiddish-sounding speech patterns – patterns totally unrelated to the way that the Jews of Herod's

---

[74] Mann, *Doktor Faustus*, pp. 153–54 (Chapter 19).

[75] Serenus Zeitblom, the narrator of the novel, remains ambiguous about whether the visit to Pressburg actually took place before or after the performance, or if the composer actually went to Graz after all (p. 154). What is central to the story is the narrative link that Mann establishes between the opera and the visit to Esmeralda.

[76] See the discussions of this closely connected series of events in two essays by Vaget, "Thomas Mann und Richard Strauss," pp. 78–79, and "The Spell of *Salome*," pp. 50–52.

[77] See Strauss's letter to his nephew, the conductor Rudolf Moralt, in Wilhelm, *Richard Strauss persönlich*, p. 124. The occasion for the letter was the fact that in 1939 Nazi cultural officials in Graz forbade further performances of *Salome* at the site of its Austrian premiere, their grounds being, according to the composer, that it was a "Jewish ballad."

time spoke.[78] Could the future Führer have felt that people of that sort deserve to be obliterated? And might he have fantasized a more efficient way of accomplishing this than cutting people's heads off one at a time?

BERG, *WOZZECK*, VIENNA, THEATER AN DER WIEN, JUNE 16, 1953

Modernism was never much liked by the Viennese public, and this despite the fact that their city, together with Paris, was the center from which much of the modernist energy in all art forms emanated. The Viennese modernist past remained ignored – indeed, often suppressed – not only after the Nazis took over but for a goodly number of years after World War II. Vienna just after the war was an impoverished city, its Jewish cultural elite either in exile or obliterated, its remaining population battered down since the early 1930s by one ideological construct after another. What had once counted as an international cultural capital was now reduced to a provincial town.

When I spent a student year there in 1952–53 preparing my dissertation on the great Austrian modernist poet Georg Trakl, my desire to experience modernist music at the site of its creation could not be realized – neither in chamber-music or symphony concerts nor at the opera. No Webern, no Schoenberg, and very little Berg, except for a couple of *Wozzeck* performances in the course of the year. (Webern, in fact, had set to music a number of my dissertation subject's poems.) It seemed ironic that the so-called Second Viennese School (the first, of course, consisting of Haydn, Mozart, and Beethoven) was little known even to this supposedly music-minded public. To be sure, Strauss's two great modernist operas, *Salome* and *Elektra*, were immensely popular and much performed. But the many modernist operas that had once circulated among the

---

[78] On Strauss's imitation of the so-called *Mauscheln* of Eastern European Jews, see Gilman, "Strauss and the Pervert," pp. 320–22.

germanophone opera houses were as good as lost. No *Mahagonny* or *Three-Penny Opera*; no Busoni, Hindemith or Krenek, or even the once-beloved though scarcely modernist Korngold. Similarly, the great visual art that had been produced in Vienna early in the century was little displayed or talked about – neither the decorative work of the Wiener Werkstätte nor the paintings of Klimt and Schiele. Even Mahler had been forgotten: I do not remember a single symphony of his being done by either of the two major orchestras that season – though Wilhelm Furtwängler conducted the *Lieder eines fahrenden Gesellen* cycle on one occasion with what had once been the composer's own orchestra, the Vienna Philharmonic.

The Viennese opera repertory, much like that in other countries during the mid-twentieth century, remained stale: a collection of warhorses in conventional productions that could upset nobody except for those few who sought adventure. As elsewhere, singers were contracted to the local company and rarely sang in other houses. They were, in fact, so accustomed to one another that they could create a beautifully integrated ensemble, something evident in the often sublime performances of the Mozart and Strauss operas, occasionally of *Fidelio*, rarely of Wagner (never a favorite in Vienna), while the Italian, French, and Russian repertory, always sung in German (as was still the custom before the emergence of international, jet-traveling stars), was usually done routinely at best.

When I asked early in the season if I might expect to hear *Wozzeck*, people told me that this would have to wait until Karl Böhm came to Vienna for his brief conducting stints. Though once one of Hitler's favored conductors, he also had a weakness for a composer who had counted as "degenerate" within the Nazi pantheon. Böhm's first *Wozzeck* of the season was scheduled for late in the autumn on a regular subscription night. Since the dollar enjoyed an uncommonly favorable exchange rate in those days, I could afford a good seat, which meant that I was surrounded by the subscribers. It was clear even before the first-act curtain went down that the people around me were unresponsive – or at least refusing to be responsive – to what they heard.

The only real applause at the end of the act came from the young people in standing room far behind me. In fact, they cheered wildly in clear defiance of their elders. I joined the cheering, only to find that the older folk in my section were trying to silence me, as though I had broken some taboo. "Wir haben keine Komponisten mehr [We no longer have any composers]," I overheard one woman mutter to her husband in disgust. "Pardon me," I interjected, "but Alban Berg has been dead for all of seventeen years." Although I remember the performance as powerful, above all the Marie of Christl Goltz, I also remained aware throughout the evening of a cold hostility emanating from much of the audience.

But the June 16 performance was something else again. Since it took place during the period annually demarcated as the *Wiener Festwochen*, the audience was not dominated by the subscribers – though I don't remember much cheering either. Still, the fact that a modernist work was part of the festival lent a certain festiveness to the occasion, a festiveness that was reinforced for me when the composer's widow, Helene Berg, walked slowly down the aisle shortly before the performance began. She was escorted by an American conductor, William Strickland, who had devoted himself to keeping Berg's name alive. Appropriately enough, for the Second Viennese School was at that time better known in foreign countries, especially the United States, than in the city of its origin.

I was made aware of who she was by my companions, a couple well acquainted with the circle around Alma Mahler and the Bergs. As I stared at Frau Berg, the husband whispered to me, "Whom does that long face remind you of?" I couldn't for the life of me find a response, until he asked me if it reminded me of Velázquez's portraits of the Spanish royal family. Indeed, it did, for she possessed the elongated face that, over the centuries, had persisted among the Hapsburgs. "She is the last of the known illegitimate offspring of Emperor Franz Josef," my friend revealed with a knowing smile.

Then the opera began, and my experience of the music was now colored by the presence of this dignified, aging lady, long known for the devotion she had shown to her distinguished husband and for the piety, after his early death, with which she guarded his memory. And here was a readily recognizable member (if not quite legally acknowledged) of one of the great European dynasties. As I looked downstairs admiringly during the performance from my seat in the first row of the balcony, I saw the devoted muse who had enabled her equally devoted spouse to create this drama of betrayal and revenge.

Little could I have known at the time that the external facts helping shape my experience that evening were altogether false. Soon after Helene Berg died over a quarter century later, the truth of her supposedly ideal marriage would be revealed: during his final decade, and beginning with an early performance of *Wozzeck*, Alban Berg's passion had been directed not toward Helene but toward Hanna Fuchs-Robettin, Alma Mahler's sister-in-law.[79] And he had even encrypted their love in his *Lyric Suite* by means of themes suggested by their initials and by an allusion to *Tristan und Isolde*. Indeed, Frau Berg's stubborn refusal, during her lifetime, to allow the not-fully-orchestrated final act of *Lulu* to be performed did not, as had long been thought, derive from the loyalty she expressed toward defending her late husband's intentions but, far more likely, from whatever revenge she could exercise for his disloyalty toward her. Here, indeed, was the *Wozzeck* story as reenacted on a higher, more civilized social level.

By the time of Frau Berg's death in 1979, Vienna had begun to recover its modernist past. The establishment, a few years before, of a major ensemble named the Arnold Schoenberg Choir suggests a new fashionability to a name and a movement that had long inspired contemptuous feelings. The architecture, decorative art, and painting of modernist Vienna, by the final decades of the twentieth century, became the rage both in their home town and throughout the world. And the music of Berg, if not quite that of Schoenberg and Webern, now came to assimilate itself to earlier musical tradition. As I look back to the *Wozzeck* performances I heard in Vienna

---

[79] For a book-length study of Berg's relationship to Fuchs-Robettin, see Floros, *Alban Berg and Hanna Fuchs*.

well over half a century ago, I recognize that they posed a challenge for me that they no longer do. This challenge, indeed, was insepar-able from the power they exercised over me. While writing this section, I accessed *YouTube*, on which I just watched the *Wozzeck* murder scene from a recent Berlin production. It now seemed as easy listening as Strauss.

WAGNER, *TRISTAN UND ISOLDE*, NEW YORK, METROPOLITAN OPERA, MARCH 28, 2008

It was the last of six scheduled performances, of which the first five had all been marred by bad luck. Bad luck in opera means the cancellation of major singers – something far worse in the eyes of fans than, say, the scenery collapsing or the lighting going awry. The motive behind this run of *Tristan und Isolde* was the Met's success in scheduling the two currently reigning Wagnerians, Deborah Voigt and Ben Heppner, together in these roles for the first time.

During its century-and-a-half life, *Tristan und Isolde* has gone through three distinct stages in its relation to its audiences. In the early years of its performance history this so-called music-drama disturbed listeners through its sheer difficulty, above all its refusal to resolve – at least until its end many hours later – the notorious chord that appears in the work's first phrase. By the turn of the twentieth century, *Tristan* had become a site for erotic bonding, as Alban Berg had once bonded to its music both with his wife Helene and (through his cryptic allusion in the *Lyric Suite*) with his later beloved, Hanna Fuchs-Robettin; or as the tuberculous adulter-ous lovers in Thomas Mann's story "Tristan" had bonded while the heroine, Frau Klöterjahn, played the music on the piano. By our own time the *Tristan* score presents few difficulties for listeners, and other, more strident forms of music have replaced it as a convenient means for bonding. Today we go to this now familiar opera to thrill to those big, steely voices – during any single decade never more than one or two Isoldes, at best a single, if any, Tristan – that can cut cleanly through Wagner's large, lush orchestra.

But cancellations of these few voices can badly compromise anybody's *Tristan* experience. During the New York run it was Heppner who missed the most performances – the first four, in fact, and due, it was reported, to some medical misdiagnosis. One substitute tenor after another was engaged to fill in – none of these, according to the reviews I saw, really up to par. Voigt was present for these four performances, but in the fourth she bowed out before the end because of a reported digestive mishap – and what is called her "cover" quickly took over. Finally, Heppner made it for the fifth performance (and triumphantly so, I read), but Voigt was still indisposed, though her cover was favorably reviewed.

Some six months before, knowing I should be in the East for a few days in early spring, I purchased a ticket for the last *Tristan*. But well before I arrived, I recognized that my chances of hearing the scheduled singers remained small. The New York *Times*, after having reported the cancellations and substitutions regularly, announced the morning before the last performance that the originally scheduled singers would be on hand that evening. While busy that day with my usual museum-going during my brief trips to New York, I prepared myself for the forthcoming evening with the same dedication that I assumed the great stars themselves felt during the day. But I also exercised some skepticism: who knows what new digestive problem (the soprano had, after all, undergone a much-publicized gastric operation) or drug reaction (something known to afflict the tenor) would develop in the course of the day (or even of the performance)?

As I approached the opera-house entrance I noted that no new names had been plastered over Voigt's and Heppner's on the large poster near the door. Things looked hopeful. As I entered the lobby I overheard people chatting nervously about whether they were going to be singing after all. Strangers encouraged one another that this would surely be true. But just before the curtain went up a management representative appeared on the stage. This was surely a sign of bad news, as operagoers had long learned to assume. As the New York *Times* reviewer recorded, "The audience erupted with groans, hisses and cries of 'No!' "[80] But the dreaded man on the stage quickly reassured us all that he had come simply to announce a replacement for the Brangaene – and, as it turned out, somebody I had heard before in this role and much admired. We sighed collectively in relief.

And what about the performance? Obviously it was thrilling – at least that's the way one had to experience it, for I'm sure that what I took to be my experience was mediated by the knowledge that this was to be seen as a memorable event. Although I rarely depend on the judgment of critics, I could only agree with the *Times* when it spoke of Heppner's "maximum expressivity, utter honesty and visceral power" or of Voigt's "gleaming phrases soaring over the orchestra." Even though Voigt failed to land quite securely on her pianissimo *f* sharp at the end of the "Liebestod" and cut the whole-note noticeably short, I recognized that such minor flaws merely confirm the fact that I was never so carried away that I lost my ability to discern what was going on musically.

Certainly those neural circuits in my brain that respond to music – and especially to a score as seductive and overpowering as *Tristan und Isolde* – would have lit up furiously if I, as well as the others around me, had been wired to an fMRI. The *Times* reviewer stressed the risk-taking that Voigt and Heppner encouraged one another to engage in, and this contrasted strikingly with an earlier moment, nine years before, in which I had heard Heppner during his first run of *Tristans*, when, though singing beautifully, he had also appeared hesitant, even choosing to cut much of the taxing final act to make sure he would not lose his endurance (after all, the first Tristan, Ludwig Schnorr von Carolsfeld, had died of pneumonia only weeks after he had created the role in 1865). And this reviewer in his enthusiasm compared the whole occasion to a night in 1974 when Birgit Nilsson and Jon Vickers, the reigning Wagnerians of that era, had done the opera together for the one and only time at the

---

[80] Tommasini, "A 'Tristan und Isolde' Well Worth the Wait."

Metropolitan – an event I could appreciate at best from afar, though I had had a ticket for the two of them doing it in San Francisco three years before only to find Vickers having to cancel after his throat had collided with a guy-wire in his garden!

Such is opera! How many events such as the March 28 *Tristan* does the avid opera consumer after all experience in the course of a lifetime? In the succeeding months, whenever I mentioned having been present at this performance, I found myself congratulated for my good luck, not only by the Wagner fans I knew but also by anti-Wagnerian operagoers and even non-opera people who had read about this production's fate in the media. Being witness to a significant operatic event amounts to a badge of honor among those who take opera seriously. Indeed, great performers you have heard in person are like trophies you collect, and this applies not simply to opera or classical music but to any form of music, and to sports, for that matter. Getting to that *Tristan* performance was like catching Bob Dylan going "electric" at the 1965 Newport Festival or watching the USA beat Russia in ice hockey at the 1980 Olympics. My own trophies include serving as a page boy in the NBC studios for Toscanini's 1947 *Otello*; hearing both Joan Sutherland and Leontyne Price in minor roles when they were still unknown to me as well as to the general public; or hearing Deborah Voigt herself during her student days, when I told myself that this was a voice I would be following in later years; or attending one of Glenn Gould's last public concerts during the early 1960s (though not, alas, the very last). Of course, I should love to have boasted of hearing Maria Callas in the flesh, but she canceled both the performances for which I had purchased tickets (the excuses she gave were later exposed as utter lies!), and she remains the only generally acknowledged great singer of my lifetime whom I never heard in person.

So how do I account for this greed to experience the musically great? After all, I remain wholly indifferent to whatever charisma may emanate from pop artists, sports heroes, and film stars. Doubtless it all derives from the household culture within which I was raised. My mother boasted of attending the first production (though not quite the premiere) of *Der Rosenkavalier* in Dresden. My father spoke repeatedly of hearing Geraldine Farrar when, at eighteen, she made her debut in Gounod's *Faust* in a Berlin performance that granted her immediate international renown; catching the young Chaliapin while on business travel in Russia; hearing Caruso in any number of roles in several different cities; and making it to one of Adelina Patti's annual farewell concerts.

But seeking out, remembering, and boasting of having caught great singers at their height (and often, to be sure, when they were already over the hill, as were Beniamino Gigli and Lauritz Melchior on the only occasions I heard them) is something that goes back to near the beginnings of opera, to the ascendancy of Anna Renzi as the first acknowledged star.[81] Over the centuries, diaries, letters, memoirs, and newspaper reviews, even poems, novels, and films, attest to the near-divinity status attached to names such as Renzi, Farinelli, Malibran, Pasta, Melba, Caruso, and Callas. The young Richard Wagner claimed he underwent a transformative experience when he heard Wilhelmine Schröder-Devrient as Leonore in *Fidelio*, and later composed several roles in his own early operas for her.[82]

Good ensemble productions of certain works such as *Le nozze di Figaro* and *La bohème* can satisfy audiences even without major voices. *Pelléas et Mélisande* and certain modernist operas can make

---

[81] Renzi, called by Rosand "the first diva of the Italian operatic stage," created the role of Ottavia in Monteverdi's *L'incoronazione di Poppea*, as a result of which a volume of poetry by diverse hands, *Le glorie della Signora Anna Renzi romana* (1644) was addressed to her. See Rosand, *Opera in Seventeenth-Century Venice*, p. 385, as well as the discussion of Renzi's career (pp. 228–35).

[82] Modern research has demonstrated the probability that this experience occurred while he heard her as Romeo in Bellini's *I Capuleti e i Montecchi*, and that he changed the claim to *Fidelio* in order to establish a genealogy extending from Beethoven to himself. Wagner admitted that his transformation owed more to her stage presence than to her voice, which showed considerable flaws. See Deathridge and Dahlhaus, *The New Grove Wagner*, p. 7.

do with performers who are better actors than they are singers, as long as they are supported by a good orchestra. The mechanical marvels of opera in the seventeenth and early eighteenth centuries could excite audiences regardless of the singers on stage, as do the corresponding digital marvels we witness today. But the ability occasionally to transform an individual's soul rests squarely in the lungs and throats of great singers.

WHY (WHAT, HOW, IF) OPERA STUDIES?

INTERLOCUTOR: Your title alone portrays you on the defensive. Why all those questions? If it's a new field you're seeking to institute, your hesitancy is not likely to win converts.

AUTHOR: Don't get me wrong. I don't want to persuade anybody to institute still another field, of which the modern university boasts more than it needs. I just want to deal with the practical institutional problems we face studying a phenomenon such as opera, which, as it happens, straddles a number of distinct fields.

INTERLOCUTOR: But the moment I hear the term *studies* attached to an area, I sense a political agenda guiding you: think of those other fields that have imposed themselves on universities in recent years: feminist studies, Afro-American studies, Chicano studies, gay and lesbian studies, disability studies, animality studies and any number of others that, in the future, will be seeking a place in the academic sun.

AUTHOR: So everything calling itself *studies* has to be politically motivated? What about film studies? Surely this would be the appropriate analogy to opera studies. Like film studies, opera studies is dedicated to the understanding of a particular genre or, more properly, a medium. Except, of course, that opera encompasses four times as many years of history and impinges on a larger number of other disciplines: musicology, obviously, but also theater history, art history, and every one of the literature fields in those countries where opera has thrived.

INTERLOCUTOR: But don't all those so-called *studies* cross disciplines? Certainly film studies demands some knowledge of art history and, in particular, the history of photography – not to speak of the nineteenth-century novel out of which the earliest films emerged. Can't you just say that making any sort of new knowledge these days demands being interdisciplinary?

AUTHOR: Of course. But what I'm concerned with here is the difficulties we face trying to be interdisciplinary. Each of the disciplines upon which opera studies draws has its own peculiar history, its own set of rules and conventions, even a particular mind set that colors the personalities of its practitioners.

INTERLOCUTOR: Surely you can make too big a thing of small differences. After all, we're talking about the people who constitute humanities faculties. One can easily grant them their differences from natural and even social scientists, but why quibble about what distinguishes professors dedicated to the understanding of the various art forms? As the least-respected, lowest-paid body within the modern university, all of them should be busy bonding with one another. People doing opera studies, like those in film and the overtly political movements labeled *studies*, could surely use this opportunity to proclaim their solidarity as fellow workers in the humanities.

AUTHOR: That would all be very nice, especially if it had anything to do with institutional realities. My point is that every discipline functions as an institution unto itself. It's ironic, isn't it, that whereas opera has been an ongoing institution for over four hundred years, opera studies is in effect an orphan that cannot claim a natural home in any one of the existing humanistic disciplines.

INTERLOCUTOR: But how, in view of the enormous differences in national styles over the centuries, can you even think of opera as an institution?

AUTHOR: I suspect that it's the enormous complexity of operatic creation and production that has given opera its institutional character. Whatever the differences in the national styles you mention, opera has maintained its home in the opera house, whether in the form of court theater or commercial theater or, as so often in its history, in some combination of these two. And it's not just the venue within which opera is performed: since its origin, opera has organized itself institutionally around a predictable crew of characters – impresario, librettist, composer, stage designer, singers, instrumentalists, chorus, dancers. What other art form can boast such continuity?

INTERLOCUTOR: Most of them, I suspect. Think of the way painting was regulated for centuries by the various art academies.

AUTHOR: Regulated, perhaps, yes. But think as well of all the great art that developed in defiance of these academies. Since opera has characteristically needed considerable financial resources plus a team of diverse talents to flourish at all, the possibility of an operatic *salon des rejetés* seems ridiculous. It's hard to think of any opera in the standard repertory that did not get its start in a real opera house, even if it had to be in the provinces. The long-neglected Janáček at least had an opera house in his home town of Brno that was willing to put on his work. And the famous avant-garde operas of the twentieth century – *Salome, Wozzeck, Saint François d'Assise,* for example – all emerged out of the opera-house system, sometimes, as with Messiaen's difficult work, even with advance commissions. If *Moses und Aron* seems to defy this rule, that's because the composer, thinking it unfinished, withheld it; had he composed that missing third act in 1930, it would surely have gone the rounds of the German opera houses. Who knows? Even some of those recent concoctions I called "opera by other means" in Essay 4 were commissioned by opera houses – progressive ones, to be sure, like the Frankfurt Opera and the Théâtre de la Monnaie.

INTERLOCUTOR: All right, I'm willing to believe that, among the arts, opera is a well-organized form, maybe even the most intricately organized of them all. But remember the differences in national tradition. How can you speak of what you call a single institution when – and this was especially true in the nineteenth century – the composers, librettists, and singers followed their own national styles? Think of how different the repertory of the Théâtre Italien in early nineteenth-century Paris was from that of the Opéra in the same town.

AUTHOR: Different yes, but all these national styles had a common ancestor in Florentine theory and early seventeenth-century Italian practice. All the descendants can easily trace their genealogies back there. Still, no matter how different the product in different countries during later centuries, a composer was able to move back and forth between styles. From Gluck through Verdi there's a whole series of composers who could write in the Italian, the German, and the French mode depending on who commissioned him.

INTERLOCUTOR: We've got somewhat off the track, since we're no longer talking about opera studies but about opera itself.

AUTHOR: It's you who questioned my notion of opera as an ongoing institution. But whether or not you buy this idea, I was simply drawing a contrast between opera as an artistic form and the academic study of this form. If you look at the particular disciplines within which opera has been examined, you'll see that each one has, as I started to say, pursued its own agenda.

INTERLOCUTOR: One would think that bringing all these perspectives to bear would enrich the understanding of opera.

AUTHOR: In a sense, perhaps. But in reality the practitioners of these disciplines have all too often talked past one another and also, I might add, chosen to misunderstand and undermine one another's efforts. Their loyalty is less to the pursuit of knowledge than to the guild that regulates a particular discipline; or perhaps I should say that their idea of what constitutes knowledge is what they think will please other members of their guild.

INTERLOCUTOR: If you're so bothered by conflicts within the academic realm, think of the conflicts between librettist and composer – or between impresario and both of these – that are so central to operatic history.

AUTHOR: Although musicians and writers come from different enough worlds, the institutional power wielded by the opera house has forced them to come together, not just with each other, but with the other diverse artists needed to produce an opera. But let's turn now to the differences between the academic entities within which opera can be studied. Before we even get to musicology, we'll look at what separates the various disciplines supposedly concerned with literature. Ever since literary study became an academic discipline in the nineteenth-century European university, it's been fragmented into departments devoted to understanding each particular national literature. This situation of course derived from the nationalist biases characteristic of that century, but these divisions prevailed within academic institutions long after what motivated them ideologically was no longer an issue. As a result, specialists in, say, French and Russian are as likely to speak different critical languages as they do different real languages.

INTERLOCUTOR: And of course the same differences prevail between the different schools of national opera, as they were called during that arch-nationalist century. For every composer you can name who crossed national borders to obtain a foreign commission (which usually meant composing for Paris, where the money and the prestige in those days were located), I can cite others, like Smetana and Janáček or like Weber and Lortzing, who were perceived as so narrowly national that it took years for their work to become acclimated, if it was at all, in foreign opera houses.

AUTHOR: But the differences between scholars in the various national literatures involve more than their national commitments, for each of these fields developed according to its own rhythms, with its own methodologies and its own perceptions of what constitutes literature. Yet there was one thing they generally had in common when they began: in their early days in the university they all pursued what has been called the positivistic mode, which meant that their chief concern was to create accurate editions of those texts they deemed central to the national literary tradition as well as to gather the historical facts surrounding these texts and their authors.

INTERLOCUTOR: If all these national disciplines were doing this, why do you make so much of their differences?

AUTHOR: When they started, they were all motivated not just by their particular nationalist needs but also by their desire to achieve intellectual respectability within an institution increasingly dominated by natural scientists. Since science was forced to justify itself by laboratory experiments that could be replicated, literary study too sought some form of replicability, which meant that you limited yourself to what you might be able to prove in a courtroom. And this, in turn, meant that you studied matters such as a work's sources, or its discernible influence on later works, or its textual history, or what its creator said about his or her intentions. You didn't "analyze" the work's structure or make value judgments about it: this was considered "criticism," an activity appropriate to journalists but scarcely thought worthy of a university researcher.

INTERLOCUTOR: In view of what goes on in literature departments today, it's hard to believe anybody ever thought that way.

AUTHOR: They haven't for a long time, but the various fields within the humanities gave up the positivistic model at varying times – or at least they supplemented this model with others of a distinctly unscientific cast. Some people in every field have kept on doing the editorial work and the source hunting, though the newer models influenced the ways this work was later done. German was probably the first field to break with the positivistic model – perhaps because it had been the first to establish this model in the mid-nineteenth century. By the start of the twentieth century an alternative model called *Geistesgeschichte* had emerged in German studies. French, on the other hand, held on to the old model until late in the last century: most of the exciting developments in French literary theory since the 1960s took place in institutes outside the university. And English made its break in mid-century with the advent of the New Criticism, in which a work's formal elements could be analyzed and evaluated regardless of its historical roots.

INTERLOCUTOR: But what has all this to do with operatic study?

AUTHOR: Since the various fields within which opera can be studied broke with the positivistic model at sharply divergent times, there was no method that seemed "natural" to the form. But of course until recently, opera was located pretty much within the province of musicology (except when there was some great librettist like Metastasio or Hofmannsthal who "belonged" to the Italianists or the Germanists). And musicology, together with art history and classics, held on rigidly to the positivistic method long after it had come to seem *passé* within the other humanities areas.

INTERLOCUTOR: But what about music analysis? That's always been welcome within the field.

AUTHOR: A number of fields developed formal modes that followed sufficiently rigid rules so they weren't taken to be inappropriate within the positivistic model. French specialists practiced *explication de texte*; art historians did Wölfflin-inspired studies of a picture's composition; and musicologists, especially in America, did Schenkerian analyses to locate the *Ursatz* rooted within any given work. None of this seemed to threaten the larger model guiding each field, though this was not true of the New Criticism, which from the start situated itself polemically against positivism. The result was that English, at least within the anglo-phone world, opened up possibilities that were realized consider-ably later by its neighboring disciplines.

INTERLOCUTOR: So how did what you see as the backwardness of musicology affect the study of opera?

AUTHOR: You got lots of often fine historical studies of individual composers and their work – as well as of the ambiance within which they flourished – many of which I've found useful for their factual information (as, indeed, I have throughout this book), just as I've always turned to the older positivistic studies in literature. But I'd learned to be on my guard for the hidden ideological biases that colored these literary studies. And I found that traditional musicology harbored many of these same biases.

INTERLOCUTOR: What sorts of biases?

AUTHOR: Among the most powerful of these is the nineteenth-century notion – still held by many until late in the twentieth century – that an art form and its various genres develop over time something like a biological organism. The result is an image of opera, above all among German musicologists and their American heirs, as the development of music-drama from Gluck to, say, Alban Berg. And note as well the nationalist bias here, something more overt in the various national-literature disciplines, which portrayed a country's literary history as the evolution (note the Darwinian coloring) of national consciousness.

INTERLOCUTOR: But how can you call musicology nationalistic? Unlike your literary disciplines, it studies music globally – or at least within the European orbit.

AUTHOR: It's not overt, as I said, and I suspect most musicologists never even thought they had a national bias. But German music, above all the evolution of its formal elements from Bach to the Second Viennese School, has been the central measuring stick. This is all quite understandable when one recognizes that musicology, like the other humanistic disciplines, has its roots in the German university; but it's up to us today to get beyond these biases. They've been detrimental to the understanding of those operas that don't fit the peculiarly German image of music-drama: Rossini ends up a country bumpkin; Handel, German though he originally was, gets short shrift as an opera composer since he doesn't fit the music-drama model; and Verdi for long was taken seriously only for his final two operas. But there was another, just as fundamental problem with the positivistic model: in order to reassure itself that it was not straying from provable fact, all too frequently musicological studies of opera got lost in minutiae without much concern for larger questions.

INTERLOCUTOR: Questions such as what?

AUTHOR: Such as: What makes opera unique among the dramatic genres? How does it relate to other artistic forms at particular times in history? Given the circumstances under which it is created and produced, how does it function as what is essentially a collaborative form? And what is its relationship to the social and political contexts within which it is created and transmitted in time?

INTERLOCUTOR: So what propelled you as a literary person to write about opera?

AUTHOR: Precisely those questions, which I felt needed asking.

INTERLOCUTOR: Did it seem odd to you to undertake a long-term project on opera?

AUTHOR: It's certainly not what people in literature were doing then. But by the time I started work on *Opera: The Extravagant Art* I'd finished five books on literature and didn't need to care much what others might think. Furthermore, I was identified with comparative literature, within which studying the interrelationship of literature with other art forms was a longstanding tradition.

INTERLOCUTOR: In practical terms, what got you to do this book?

AUTHOR: During the early 1970s I was scheduled to teach in Stanford's program in Florence, and all of us teaching overseas were expected to develop new courses relevant to the local setting. As somebody with a longstanding interest in opera, I proposed Italian opera for one of my courses. Without this impetus, it would never have occurred to me to make opera part of my teaching.

INTERLOCUTOR: And how did you prepare yourself for it?

AUTHOR: Given my background in comparative literature rather than in any single national tradition, I was accustomed to taking on exploratory projects. And I'd already included a few passages on how opera represents history in the book I was then completing, *Historical Drama*. But working up this course still meant doing the usual spade work in the library; and while it was easy enough to get the background I needed from standard musicological sources, I was also struck by the fact that the larger questions I suggested above – questions that had become standard within literary scholarship – had not been addressed by musicologists.

INTERLOCUTOR: But what about Kerman's *Opera as Drama*? Surely here was a classic book by an eminent musicologist that proposed a whole new theory of opera.

AUTHOR: I certainly agree, and it was the one book I was able to assign as a required text for the course. But I also saw this book as thoroughly literary and, I might add, out of date in its method and biases. As I explained in detail in Essay 3, it derived its method from the most advanced model available in literature during the early 1950s, namely the New Criticism and, in particular, the work of the Scrutiny group in Britain. Just as F. R. Leavis, the leader of this group, was able to name no more than five or so great British novelists, so Kerman could cite only a few opera composers worth studying. "The significant operatic canon is not large," he wrote, "Monteverdi, Purcell, Gluck, Mozart, Verdi, Wagner, Debussy, Berg, Stravinsky, and a few others."[1]

INTERLOCUTOR: So your own project in *Opera: The Extravagant Art* was perhaps not as new as you implied.

AUTHOR: Since I started writing more than two decades after Kerman, his models, literary or otherwise, were obviously no longer viable.

INTERLOCUTOR: What models did you choose?

AUTHOR: Whatever seemed new in the seventies and, in particular, what seemed relevant to that strange, hybrid, and often recalcitrant art form we call opera.

INTERLOCUTOR: What particular models, may I ask?

AUTHOR: Bakhtin, certainly, but also Foucault, Barthes, and, though to a lesser extent, deconstruction. And besides, I could build on my own book, *Historical Drama*, which, as I mentioned in the prologue to the present book, provided me with a model for a genre study. All of this was pretty far removed from what musicologists were then doing, and, as a result, *Opera: The Extravagant Art* nearly failed to get published.

INTERLOCUTOR: How is that?

AUTHOR: The refereeing system by which a university press needs to assure itself of quality control makes for difficulties when you're doing a book straddling academic fields – fields that, as I explained earlier, have developed in differing ways and at different rates. Here I was using the latest literary theory, and yet I had to be

---

[1] Kerman, *Opera as Drama*, p. 251.

judged by musicologists for whom my models must have aroused suspicion and hostility.

INTERLOCUTOR: Couldn't you have packaged your work as a literary project?

AUTHOR: I tried; in fact I told the three university presses to whom I sent the manuscript to please send it to literary scholars who also had a good knowledge of music. Perhaps there weren't enough of these, or the presses didn't trust them, so each press sent it to at least one musicologist. The result was that my work, influenced as it was by some rather heady literary theory, was being judged within a field that, at the time, was still committed to a positivistic method.

INTERLOCUTOR: Your referees must have felt baffled.

AUTHOR: If they were they didn't let on. One reader was reasonably polite, saying the book made for pleasant enough reading – "journalistic," it was put – but was not "rigorous" enough to count as scholarship ("rigor" was a key criterion for value within the positivistic model). Another, decidedly less polite (so impolite, it turned out, that the publisher, instead of sending me the report, simply summarized it on the phone to me), declared he would never allow his Verdi seminar to read my book. The result was that two of these presses could not in good conscience publish me even though they had solicited the manuscript. The third one was about to turn me down as well, until I begged for a third reading and insisted that they send it to a literary person. Since the press's director had been showing interest in the manuscript for some years, he went along with this request, and the last reading – by a literary scholar, luckily for me – was enthusiastic enough to get the book through the press board. If this hadn't worked out, I would seriously have considered giving up on the manuscript.

INTERLOCUTOR: So what do you conclude from this experience?

AUTHOR: What I said earlier, namely, that interdisciplinary work is hampered by the differing rules and conventions within the individual disciplines. And besides that, the guild mentality I described earlier treats those who invade a new territory as poachers who need to be deported back to their own domains. I never recommend interdisciplinary projects to the untenured.

INTERLOCUTOR: But you still went ahead with two more books on opera.[2]

AUTHOR: The first of these came out a decade and a half later, and by then I could claim the authority of my preceding book on the topic. Times, moreover, had changed. By the late 1990s music, art history, and even classics had shed many of their positivistic biases and, in fact, were doing some of the same things – gender studies, cultural studies, and the like – that people in literature were cultivating. Younger musicologists, I found, seemed quite friendly to what I had written.

INTERLOCUTOR: So disciplines in the humanities are coming together. Are you more sanguine now about interdisciplinary work?

AUTHOR: There's always the guild mentality, which is not limited to the academic community but has to do with the way people behave within groups. Anybody doing a project on opera outside a music department will still have to justify it within the precincts of his or her own field. When I got a fellowship to do *Opera: The Extravagant Art* I went through the comparative-literature competition at the National Endowment for the Humanities and presented the proposal as thoroughly literary in character, which I suppose it was to the extent that it made use of current literary theory. And when I applied a few years ago to start regular sessions on opera at the Modern Language Association conventions, I did not call the project "opera studies" but rather "opera as a literary and dramatic form." The association, after all, sees its mission to lie within what it calls "language and literature" and would likely have balked if I hadn't presented it that way. Even though I had recently been the association's president, I still had to follow guild rules.

---

[2] These two books are Lindenberger, *Opera in History* and the present volume.

INTERLOCUTOR: It sounds as though you need to engage in subterfuge to pursue your agenda.

AUTHOR: That's simply a fact of life when you cross disciplines. Every guild has its particular policies, and you learn to package your work accordingly. But I *was* able to use the term "opera studies" some years ago when I applied to the Stanford Humanities Center to start a workshop on opera for faculty and graduate students in diverse fields. The center had asked specifically for interdisciplinary proposals.

INTERLOCUTOR: Did you invent the term for that purpose?

AUTHOR: I don't really know when or where the term got going, though I suspect that this was the first time I used it. There's a book series, after all, called Princeton Studies in Opera that goes back to 1991, and the Cambridge Studies in Opera that started soon after. I may have got the term from there or I may have picked it up from others.

INTERLOCUTOR: If there are book series, that must mean opera studies has arrived.

AUTHOR: It's a start toward institutionalization. That's one way you lay claim to intellectual territory: through a book series and also through journals like the *Cambridge Opera Journal*, which was founded in 1989 to promote interdisciplinary work in opera. And then think of the various recent books on opera by people who, as I mentioned in Essay 2, were based in fields such as history, English, political science, and sociology, while a number of musicologists have been using some of the same theoretical tools as literary scholars to approach opera. To be sure, even when we're trying to be interdisciplinary, we often write in differing styles according to the conventions of our individual disciplines. The present book, for instance, is full of personal anecdotes about my own experiences with opera over the years. There are many who will likely find this indecorous.

INTERLOCUTOR: Or narcissistic.

AUTHOR: It all depends where you are coming from. In anglophone modernist literary studies, where I've done much of my

teaching, the first person pronoun is quite acceptable, but the further you get away from this area – say, German literature, musicology, and certainly the social sciences – the more unseemly this style must seem.

INTERLOCUTOR: With all those barriers separating disciplines, could you ever imagine a Ph.D. program in opera studies like those that are flourishing in film studies?

AUTHOR: I can *imagine* it and I could even conceptualize a curriculum, to include not only training in music and literature but in art and theater history and even in sociology. But even if we could overcome the various disciplinary barriers I have mentioned, I could scarcely advocate the production of Ph.D.s in opera studies. It just doesn't make sense in a bad academic job market such as we've endured for the past forty years.

INTERLOCUTOR: But why Ph.D.s in film studies and not in opera?

AUTHOR: Not that there are even that many in film studies. But film courses are so popular these days – with the opportunity in a few places even to do a concentration in film – that they enjoy an economic base within the university. You can't ask somebody to do a Ph.D. in something that doesn't have the economic support to create a job.

INTERLOCUTOR: Then how can you advocate research in opera studies without establishing a venue within which this research can take place?

AUTHOR: I should hope that this could be located in already established departments, even if those performing this research would have to engage in some of the subterfuge you accuse me of. Yet I *would* advocate an interdisciplinary minor in opera studies that students doing the usual Ph.D. in the various humanities fields could undertake. This minor might also be offered as a master's degree for students not intending to go on for the Ph.D. Ideally these programs would be housed in some entity independent of the participating departments.

INTERLOCUTOR: How do you justify this when you're so dead set against a Ph.D. in opera?

AUTHOR: It's far less threatening to the standard disciplines, and above all it wouldn't involve having to create academic employment in an area where there isn't ever likely to be an undergraduate degree program. What this *would* make possible is an integrated series of courses – in music, literature, and the other fields relevant to opera – that would train people, whatever their central discipline, to offer well-informed courses on opera when they go off to their own jobs in these disciplines. These courses have proliferated in recent years, and they draw undergraduate students, not of course in the numbers that film courses do but enough so that a solid knowledge of opera might make a new Ph.D. look good to a prospective employer. There's a big difference between walking into a course with a real background in the area and just being an opera enthusiast, as I suspect many people who offer these courses are.

INTERLOCUTOR: Don't tell me you're ready to run down a teacher's enthusiasm. How do you expect students ever to want to listen?

AUTHOR: Enthusiasm without knowledge is not enough. To do a good opera course, even at the most elementary level, you need to show students a whole variety of things: for example, the conventions governing the organization of arias at any particular moment of operatic history; or the history of performing practices; or how some famous literary work and, just as likely, some third-rate boulevard play were transformed to meet the needs of operatic performance; or how the social changes after some revolution led librettists and composers to create a particular image of history on the stage. You need to store data from a goodly number of disparate sources to understand opera properly.

INTERLOCUTOR: And all this just to present the topic on the elementary level?

AUTHOR: Undergraduates don't like to feel insulted by instructors who can't offer them substance. But the audience seeking information about opera goes considerably beyond the undergraduate population. Opera's become so popular a form in recent years that there's a hunger among the educated public for informed discussion. A person who's been well trained – even with the relatively small number of courses that would constitute what I called an opera-studies minor – could perform a real service for this public through such activities as writing program notes and presenting those pre-performance lectures that are fast becoming ubiquitous in the serious performing arts. In my own experience, these notes and lectures have all too often been full of scarcely relevant details, like the composer's romantic attachment at the time that he conceived the opera or the unanalyzed fact that the history being depicted on stage has little or nothing to do with what happened in real-life history.

INTERLOCUTOR: I challenge you to demonstrate the irrelevance of these things.

AUTHOR: It's not that they are irrelevant in themselves but that their relationship to the opera in question may be far more complex than the interpreter lets on. Let's say the composer really *did* have a passionate relationship with somebody just as he was starting the opera and that he was even imagining the lady's body as he composed the big love-duet – as Wagner likely visualized Mathilde Wesendonck while doing the big *Tristan* duet. But it may also be much more relevant to a particular opera to discuss the conventions of love-duets, and of duets in general at the time; and even more relevant to show how he undercut these conventions and thoroughly surprised, or even irritated, his audience. And then there's the problem of accounting for a composer's particular style, especially during those periods in which scores were not ordinarily published but exist only in manuscript in some obscure archive – or are no longer extant at all. And yet a Handel or a Mozart or even a Verdi was likely shaped by music of which his current interpreters, whether scholars or musicians, are little aware. By contrast, a literary scholar can easily recapture what a Fielding or a Wordsworth read, since the writers on whom they were building, even if these seem obscure today, have always been available in multiple libraries. And as for the image of history presented in an operatic work, it's not enough to show that real history was different from this image. Much may have happened between the historical event and the later opera: say there's a chronicle written soon after the original event, then, two centuries later, a historical novel, then a popular drama based on this novel, then an earlier opera preceding the present opera; and this earlier work has a totally unhistorical character who was inserted at the insistence of a soprano who happened to be sleeping with the impresario; and the later librettist, after consulting the earlier opera, retains this character even though the original soprano is long since retired. And with every new text about the original historical event, the point of view has changed, not only because of the differing generic conventions of chronicle, novel, drama, and opera, but also because the ideology prevailing at the time the opera was composed is wholly different from that which stood behind the earlier texts representing this event.

INTERLOCUTOR: You make it seem very complicated indeed.

AUTHOR: Knowledge is a complicated thing.

INTERLOCUTOR: I see you're projecting a vast reservoir of information to be gathered, studied, and interpreted by a new elite of experts whom you hope to see empowered to dispense the results in a clear and concise way to college students and opera audiences – and with the proper enthusiasm to boot!

AUTHOR: That's how new fields get started, after all.

Abbate, Carolyn, *In Search of Opera* (Princeton University Press, 2001).

Abbate, Carolyn, *Unsung Voices: Opera and Musical Narrative in the Nineteenth Century* (Princeton University Press, 1991).

Abrams, M. H., *The Mirror and the Lamp: Romantic Theory and the Critical Tradition* (New York, NY: Norton, 1958).

Adams, John, *Hallelujah Junction: Composing an American Life* (New York, NY: Farrar, Straus and Giroux, 2008).

Adams, Nicholson B., "A Spanish Romanticist Parodies Himself: *Los Hijos del Tío Tronera*," *Proceedings of the Modern Language Association*, **45** (1930), pp. 573–77.

Addison, Joseph, and Richard Steele, *The Spectator*, Donald F. Bond (ed.), 5 vols. (Oxford: Clarendon Press, 1965).

Adorno, Theodor W., *Beethoven: The Philosophy of Music*, Rolf Tiedemann (ed.), Edmund Jephcott (trans.) (Stanford University Press, 1998).

Adorno, Theodor W., "Bourgeois Opera," David J. Levin (trans.), in David J. Levin (ed.), *Opera Through Other Eyes* (Stanford University Press, 1993), pp. 25–43.

Adorno, Theodor W., *Gesammelte Schriften*, Gretel Adorno and Rolf Tiedemann (eds.), 20 vols. (Frankfurt am Main: Suhrkamp, 1970–).

Adorno, Theodor W., *Introduction to the Sociology of Music*, E. B. Ashton (trans.) (New York, NY: Continuum, 1988).

Adorno, Theodor W., "Rede über Lyrik und Gesellschaft," in *Noten zur Literatur*, 3 vols. (Frankfurt: Suhrkamp, 1958), vol. I, pp. 73–104.

Alberti, Leon Battista, *On Painting and on Sculpture: the Latin Texts of "De pictura" and "De statua,"* Cecil Grayson (ed. and trans.) (London: Phaidon Press, 1972).

Albright, Daniel, *Untwisting the Serpent: Modernism in Music, Literature, and Other Arts* (University of Chicago Press, 2000).

Auerbach, Erich, *Mimesis: The Representation of Reality in Western Literature*, Willard R. Trask (trans.) (Princeton University Press, 1953).

Auner, Joseph, *A Schoenberg Reader: Documents of a Life* (New Haven, CT: Yale University Press, 2003).

Bakhtin, Mikhail, *The Dialogic Imagination: Four Essays*, Michael Holquist (ed.), Caryl Emerson and Michael Holquist (trans.) (Austin, TX: University of Texas Press, 1981).

Baldini, Gabriele, *The Story of Giuseppie Verdi: "Oberto" to "Un ballo in maschera"*, Roger Parker (trans. and ed.) (Cambridge University Press, 1980), pp. 217–18.

Barish, Jonas, *The Antitheatrical Prejudice* (Berkeley, CA: University of California Press, 1981).

Basevi, Abramo, *Studio sulle opere di Giuseppe Verdi (1859)*, Ugo Piovano (ed.) (Milan: Rugginente, 2001).

Baudelaire, Charles, *Oeuvres complètes*, Y.-G. Le Dantec (ed.) (Paris: Gallimard, 1951).

Bauman, Thomas, *W. A. Mozart: "Die Entführung aus dem Serail"* (Cambridge University Press, 1987).

Behler, Ernst, "Schellings Ästhetik in der Überlieferung von Henry Crabb Robinson," *Philosophisches Jahrbuch*, **83** (1976), pp. 133–83.

Benjamin, Walter, *Illuminations*, Harry Zohn (trans.) (New York, NY: Schocken, 1969).

Berger, Karol, *Bach's Cycle, Mozart's Arrow: An Essay on the Origins of Musical Modernity* (Berkeley, CA: University of California Press, 2007).

Berlin, Isaiah, "The Naiveté of Verdi," *Hudson Review*, **21** (1968), pp. 138–47.

Besson, Mireille, and Daniele Schön, "Comparison between Language and Music," in Isabelle Peretz and Robert J. Zatorre (eds.), *The Cognitive Neuroscience of Music* (Oxford University Press, 2003), pp. 277–93.

Besutti, Paola, "Spaces for Music in Late Renaissance Mantua," in John Whenham and Richard Wistreich (eds.), *The Cambridge Companion to Monteverdi* (Cambridge University Press, 2007), pp. 76–94.

Bigand, Emmanuel, and Suzanne Filipic, and Philippe Lalitte, "The Time Course of Emotional Responses to Music," *Annals of the New York Academy of Sciences*, **1060** (2005), pp. 429–37.

Blood, Anne J., and Robert J. Zatorre, "Intensely Pleasurable Responses to Music Correlate with Activity in Brain Regions Implicated in Reward and Emotion," *Proceedings of the National Academy of Sciences*, **98/20** (2001), pp. 11818–23.

Bokina, John, *Opera and Politics: From Monteverdi to Henze* (New Haven, CT: Yale University Press, 1997).

Bourdieu, Pierre, *Distinction: A Social Critique of the Judgment of Taste*, Richard Nice (trans.) (Cambridge, MA: Harvard University Press, 1984).

Bourdieu, Pierre, *Homo Academicus*, Peter Collier (trans.) (Stanford University Press, 1988).

Bourdieu, Pierre, *The Rules of Art: Genesis and Structure of the Literary Field*, Susan Emanuel (trans.) (Stanford University Press, 1996).

Braider, Christopher, *Refiguring the Real: Picture and Modernity in Word and Image, 1400–1700* (Princeton University Press, 1992).

Budden, Julian, *The Operas of Verdi*, 3 vols. (New York, NY: Oxford University Press, 1973–78).

Burney, Charles, *A General History of Music: From the Earliest Ages to the Present Period (1789)*, Frank Mercer (ed.), 2 vols. (New York, NY: Harcourt, Brace, 1957).

Cairns, David, *Berlioz*, 2 vols. (Berkeley, CA: University of California Press, 2000).

Carner, Mosco, *Alban Berg: The Man and the Work* (London: Duckworth, 1975).

Carter, Tim, *Monteverdi's Musical Theatre* (New Haven, CT: Yale University Press, 2002).

Carter, Tim, "Singing *Orfeo*: on the Performers of Monteverdi's First Opera," *Ricercare*, **11** (1999), pp. 75–118.

Chapados, Catherine, and Daniel J. Levitin, "Cross-Modal Interactions in the Perception of Musical Performances: Physiological Correlates," *Cognition*, **108** (2008), pp. 639–51.

Christov-Bakargiev, Carolyn, *William Kentridge* (Brussels: Société des Expositions du Palais des Beaux-Arts de Bruxelles, 1998).

Chusid, Martin, "A New Source for *El Trovador* and Its Implications for the Tonal Organization of *Il trovatore*," in Martin Chusid (ed.), *Verdi's Middle Period: 1849–1859: Source Studies, Analysis, and Performance Practice* (University of Chicago Press, 1997), pp. 207–25.

Collisani, Amalia, *La musica di Jean-Jacques Rousseau* (Palermo: L'Epos, 2007).

Conati, Marcello (ed.), *Encounters with Verdi*, Richard Stokes (trans.) (Ithaca, NY: Cornell University Press, 1984).

Conati, Marcello, "Higher than the Highest, the Music Better than the Best," Jonathan Keates (trans.), in *Verdi, Il trovatore, English National Opera Guide, No. 20* (London: John Calder, 1983), pp. 7–14.

Cowper, William, *Poetical Works*, H. S. Milford (ed.), 4th edn. (Oxford University Press, 1934).

Crisp, Deborah, and Robert Hillman, "Verdi in Postwar Italian Cinema," in Jeongwon Joe and Rose Theresa (eds.), *Between Opera and Cinema* (New York, NY: Routledge, 2002), pp. 156–63.

Crutchfield, Will, "Vocal Ornamentation in Verdi: the Phonographic Evidence," *19th Century Music*, 7 (1983), pp. 3–54.

Csampai, Attila, and Dietmar Holland (eds.), *Tannhäuser: Texte, Materialien, Kommentare* (Hamburg: Rowohlt, 1986).

Curtius, Ernst Robert, *European Literature and the Latin Middle Ages*, Willard R. Trask (trans.) (New York, NY: Pantheon, 1953).

Dahlhaus, Carl, *Between Romanticism and Modernism: Four Studies in the Music of the Later Nineteenth Century*, Mary Whittall (trans.) (Berkeley, CA: University of California Press, 1980).

Dahlhaus, Carl, *Die Idee der absoluten Musik* (Kassel: Bärenreiter, 1978).

Dean, Winton, and John Merrill Knapp, *Handel's Operas: 1704–1726*, rev. edn. (Oxford: Clarendon Press, 1995).

Deathridge, John, and Carl Dahlhaus, *The New Grove Wagner* (New York, NY: Norton, 1984).

Debussy, Claude, *Pelléas et Mélisande* (New York, NY: Dover, 1985).

Delacroix, Eugène, *Journal*, André Joubin (ed.), 3 vols. (Paris: Plon, 1932).

De La Grange, Henri-Louis, *Gustav Mahler*, 4 vols. (Oxford University Press, 1995–).

Della Seta, Fabrizio, "Gli esordi della critica Verdiana – a proposito di Alberto Mazzucato" in Sieghart Döhring and Wolfgang Osthoff (eds.), *Verdi-Studien: Pierluigi Petrobelli zum 60. Geburtstag* (Munich: G. Ricordi, 2000), pp. 59–73.

De Van, Gilles, *Verdi's Theater: Creating Drama through Music*, Gilda Roberts (trans.) (University of Chicago Press, 1998).

Dent, Edward J., *Mozart's Operas: A Critical Study* (New York, NY: McBride, Nast, 1913).

Doody, Margaret Anne, *The True History of the Novel* (New Brunswick, NJ: Rutgers University Press, 1996).

Eldar, Eran, and Ori Ganor, Roee Admon, Avraham Bleich, and Talma Hendler, "Feeling the Real World: Limbic Response to Music Depends on Related Content," *Cerebral Cortex*, **17** (2007), pp. 2828–40.

Feldman, Martha, *Opera and Sovereignty: Transforming Myths in Eighteenth-Century Italy* (University of Chicago Press, 2007).

Fenlon, Iain, "Correspondence Relating to the Early Mantuan Performances," in John Whenham (ed.), *Claudio Monteverdi: Orfeo* (Cambridge University Press, 1986), pp. 167–72.

Fenlon, Iain, and Peter N. Miller, *The Song of the Soul: Understanding 'Poppea'* (London: Royal Musical Association, 1992).

Fiérens-Gevaert, H., "Tannhaeuser," *Journal des débats*, **107** (May 2, 1895), p. 3.

Floros, Constantin, *Alban Berg and Hanna Fuchs: The Story of a Life in Letters*, Ernest Bernhardt-Kabisch (trans.) (Bloomington, IN: Indiana University Press, 2008).

Frank, Manfred, *Einführung in die frühromantische Ästhetik* (Frankfurt am Main: Suhrkamp, 1989).

Freud, Sigmund, "Trauer und Melancholie," in *Studienausgabe*, 11 vols. (Frankfurt am Main: S. Fischer, 1969–75), vol. III, pp. 197–212.

Freyhan, Michael, *The Authentic* Magic Flute *Libretto: Mozart's Autograph or the First Full-Score Edition?* (Lanham, MD: Scarecrow Press, 2009).

Friedlander, Walter, *David to Delacroix*, Robert Goldwater (trans.) (New York, NY: Schocken, 1968).

Fritz, Thomas, and Sebastian Jentschke, Nathalie Gosselin, Daniela Sammler, Isabelle Peretz, Robert Turner, Angela D. Friederici, and Stefan Koelsch, "Universal Recognition of Three Basic Emotions in Music," *Current Biology*, **19** (2009), pp. 573–76.

Frye, Northrop, *Anatomy of Criticism: Four Essays* (Princeton University Press, 1957).

Fulcher, Jane F., "Shifting the Paradigm from Adorno to Bourdieu," in Victoria Johnson, Jane F. Fulcher, and Thomas Ertman (eds.), *Opera and Society in Italy and France from Monteverdi to Bourdieu* (Cambridge University Press, 2007), pp. 312–29.

García Gutiérrez, Antonio, *El Trovador (drama); Los hijos del tío Tronera (sainete)*, Jean-Louis Picoche (ed.) (Madrid: Alhambra, 1979).

Gilman, Sander L., "Strauss and the Pervert," in Arthur Groos and Roger Parker (eds.), *Reading Opera* (Princeton University Press, 1988), pp. 306–27.

Glixon, Beth L., and Jonathan E. Glixon, *Inventing the Business of Opera: The Impresario and His World in Seventeenth-Century Venice* (Oxford University Press, 2006).

Glover, Jane, *Cavalli* (London: B. T. Batsford, 1978).

Goehr, Lydia, "From Opera to Music Drama: Nominal Loss, Titular Gain," in Thomas S. Grey (ed.), *Richard Wagner and His World* (Princeton University Press, 2009), pp. 65–86.

Goehr, Lydia, *The Imaginary Museum of Musical Works: an Essay in the Philosophy of Music*, rev. edn. (New York, NY: Oxford University Press, 2007).

Goldstein, Avram, "Thrills in Response to Music and Other Stimuli," *Physiological Psychology*, **8** (1980), pp. 126–29.

Gossett, Philip, *Divas and Scholars: Performing Italian Opera* (University of Chicago Press, 2006).

Gossett, Philip, *The Tragic Finale of Rossini's* Tancredi (Pesaro: Fondazione Rossini, 1977).

Gossett, Philip, "Verdi's Ideas on Interpreting His Operas," in Fabrizio Della Seta, Roberta Montemorra Marvin, and Marco Marica (eds.), *Verdi 2001*, 2 vols. (Florence: Olschki, 2003), vol. I, pp. 399–407.

Grant, Mark N., *The Rise and Fall of the Broadway Musical* (Boston, MA: Northeastern University Press, 2004).

Grasberger, Franz (ed.), *Der Strom der Töne trug mich fort: Die Welt um Richard Strauss in Briefen* (Tutzing: Hans Schneider, 1967).

Gregor-Dellin, Martin, *Richard Wagner: Sein Leben, Sein Werk, Sein Jahrhundert*, 2nd edn. (Munich: Piper, 1991).

Grewe, Oliver, and Frederik Nagel, Reinhard Kopiez, and Eckart Altenmüller, "How Does Music Arouse 'Chills'?: Investigating Strong Emotions, Combining Psychological, Physiological, and Psychoacoustical Methods," *Annals of the New York Academy of Sciences*, **1060** (2005), pp. 446–49.

Grewe, Oliver, and Frederik Nagel, Reinhard Kopiez, and Eckart Altenmüller, "Listening to Music as a Re-Creative Process: Physiological, Psychological, and Psychoacoustical Correlates of Chills and Strong Emotions," *Music Perception*, **24/3** (2007), pp. 297–314.

Grey, Thomas S., "Metaphorical Modes in Nineteenth-Century Music Criticism: Image, Narrative, and Idea," in Steven Paul Scher (ed.), *Music and Text: Critical Inquiries* (Cambridge University Press, 1991).

Grey, Thomas S. (ed.), *Richard Wagner and His World* (Princeton University Press, 2009).

Griffiths, Paul, *Igor Stravinsky: The Rake's Progress* (Cambridge University Press, 1982).

Griffiths, Paul, *"Saint François d'Assise,"* in Peter Hill (ed.), *The Messiaen Companion* (London: Faber, 1995), pp. 488–509.

Hadlock, Heather, *"Tancredi* and *Semiramide,"* in Emanuele Senici (ed.), *The Cambridge Companion to Rossini* (Cambridge University Press, 2004), pp. 139–58.

Hagstrum, Jean, *The Sister Arts: The Tradition of Literary Pictorialism and English Poetry from Dryden to Gray* (University of Chicago Press, 1958).

Handel, George Frideric, *Rinaldo: opera seria in tre atti*, David R. B. Kimbell (ed.) (Kassel: Bärenreiter, 1993).

Hanning, Barbara Russano, "Monteverdi's Three Genera: a Study in Terminology," in Nancy Kovaleff Baker and Barbara Russano Hanning (eds.), *Musical Humanism and Its Legacy: Essays in Honor of Claude V. Palisca* (Stuyvesant, NY: Pendragon Press, 1992), pp. 145–70.

Harris-Warrick, Rebecca, "Lully's On-Stage Societies," in Victoria Johnson, Jane F. Fulcher, and Thomas Ertman (eds.), *Opera and Society in Italy and France from Monteverdi to Bourdieu* (Cambridge University Press, 2007), pp. 53–71.

Hazlitt, William, *Complete Works*, P. P. Howe (ed.), 21 vols. (London: Dent, 1930–34).

Head, Matthew, *Orientalism, Masquerade and Mozart's Turkish Music* (London: Royal Musical Association, 2000).

Hegel, G. W. F., *Aesthetics: Lectures on Fine Art*, T. M. Knox (trans.), 2 vols. (Oxford: Clarendon Press, 1975).

Heller, Wendy, *Emblems of Eloquence: Opera and Women's Voices in Seventeenth-Century Venice* (Berkeley, CA: University of California Press, 2003).

Hepokoski, James, *"Ottocento* Opera as Cultural Drama: Generic Mixtures in *Il trovatore,"* in Martin Chusid (ed.), *Verdi's Middle Period: 1849–1859: Source Studies, Analysis, and Performance Practice* (University of Chicago Press, 1997), pp. 147–96.

Herder, Johann Gottfried, *Die kritischen Wälder der Ästhetik*, in Martin Bollacher (ed.), *Werke*, 10 vols. (Frankfurt am Main: Deutscher Klassiker Verlag, 1985–2000), vol. II (1993), *Schriften zur Ästhetik und Literatur*, ed. Gunter E. Grimm, pp. 9–442.

Hoberg, Annagret, "Vasily Kandinsky: Abstract, Absolute, Concrete," in *Kandinsky* (New York, NY: Guggenheim Museum, 2009), pp. 23–57.

Hoffmann, E. T. A., "Beethoven, C moll-Sinfonie (No. 5)," in Georg Ellinger (ed.), *Werke*, 15 vols. (Leipzig: Deutsches Verlagshaus Bong, n.d.), vol. XIII, pp. 40–56.

Hoffmann, E. T. A., "Kreisleriana," in Georg Ellinger (ed.), *Werke*, 15 vols. (Leipzig: Deutsches Verlagshaus Bong, n. d.), vol. I, pp. 33–71.

Horkheimer, Max, and Theodor W. Adorno, *Dialektik der Aufklärung: Philosophische Fragmente* (Frankfurt am Main: Fischer, 1988).

Hutcheon, Linda, and Michael Hutcheon, *Opera: Desire, Disease, Death* (Lincoln, NE: University of Nebraska Press, 1996).

Hutcheon, Linda, and Michael Hutcheon, "'Tutto nel mondo è burla': Rethinking Late Style in Verdi (and Wagner)," in Fabrizio Della Seta, Roberta Montemorra Marvin, and Marco Marica (eds.), *Verdi 2001*, 2 vols. (Florence: Olschki, 2003), vol. II, pp. 905–28.

Jack, Ian, *Keats and the Mirror of Art* (Oxford: Clarendon Press, 1967).

Janssen, Theo, and Ralph Quinke (dirs.), *"The Black Rider" Documentary* (Ralph Quinke Filmproduktion, 1990).

Jauss, Hans-Robert, *Toward an Aesthetic of Reception*, Timothy Bahti (trans.) (Minneapolis, MN: University of Minnesota Press, 1982).

Jefferson, Alan, *Elisabeth Schwarzkopf* (London: Victor Gollancz, 1996).

Johnson, Samuel, "Hughes" in Roger Lonsdale (ed.), *Lives of the Most Eminent English Poets*, 4 vols. (Oxford: Clarendon Press, 2006), vol. III, pp. 39–42.

Kant, Immanuel, *Critique of Judgment*, Werner S. Pluhar (trans.) (Indianapolis, IN: Hackett, 1987).

Katz, Ruth, *The Powers of Music: Aesthetic Theory and the Invention of Opera* (New Brunswick, NJ: Transaction Publishers, 1994).

Katz, Ruth, and Ruth HaCohen, *The Arts in Mind: Pioneering Texts of a Coterie of British Men of Letters* (New Brunswick, NJ: Transaction Publishers, 2003).

Katz, Ruth, and Ruth HaCohen, *Tuning the Mind: Connecting Aesthetics to Cognitive Science* (New Brunswick, NJ: Transaction Publishers, 2003).

Kaufmann, Harald, "Ausverkauf der alten Oper: Notizen zu Strawinsky (1961)," in Attila Csampai and Dietmar Holland (eds.), *Bertolt Brecht/Kurt Weill,* Die Dreigroschenoper; Igor Strawinsky, The Rake's Progress: Texte, Materialien, Kommentare (Hamburg: Rowohlt, 1987), pp. 289–95.

Keen, Suzanne, "A Theory of Narrative Empathy," *Narrative*, **14/3** (2006), pp. 207–36.

Kennedy, Randy, "Artwork to Display, or to Enjoy With Eggs," *New York Times*, July 3, 2009.

Kennedy, Randy, "Sound Tunnel: Avant-Garde Park Portrait," *New York Times*, July 6, 2009.

Kentridge, William, *Black Box* (Berlin: Deutsche Guggenheim, 2005).

Kentridge, William, *Flute*, Bronwyn Law-Viljoen (ed.) (Johannesburg: David Krut Publishing, 2007).

Kerman, Joseph, *Opera as Drama* (New York, NY: Knopf, 1956).

Kintzler, Catherine, *Poétique de l'opéra français, de Corneille à Rousseau* (Paris: Minerve, 1991).

Koelsch, Stefan, "Investigating Emotion with Music: Neuroscientific Approaches," *Annals of the New York Academy of Sciences*, **1060** (2005), pp. 412–18.

Koelsch, Stefan, and Thomas Fritz, D. Yves v. Cramon, Karsten Müller, and Angela D. Friederici, "Investigating Emotion with Music," *Human Brain Mapping*, **27** (2006), pp. 239–50.

Koestenbaum, Wayne, *The Queen's Throat: Opera, Homosexuality and the Mystery of Desire* (New York, NY: Poseidon Press, 1993).

Kolb, Katherine, "Flying Leaves: Between Berlioz and Wagner," *19th-Century Music*, **23** (2009), pp. 25–61.

Kostelanetz, Richard, *Conversations with Cage* (New York, NY: Limelight Editions, 1988).

Kreuzer, Gundula, "*Zurück zu Verdi*: The 'Verdi Renaissance' and Musical Culture in the Weimar Republic," *Studi Verdiani*, **13** (1998), pp. 117–54.

Kristeller, Paul Oskar, *Renaissance Thought and the Arts: Collected Essays*, 2nd edn. (Princeton University Press, 1990).

Krumhansl, Carol L., and Diana Lynn Schenck, "Can Dance Reflect the Structural and Expressive Qualities of Music?: A Perceptual Experiment on Balanchine's Choreography of Mozart's Divertimento No. 15," *Musicae Scientiae*, **1/1** (1997), pp. 63–85.

Kubik, Reinhold, *Händels Rinaldo: Geschichte, Werk, Wirkung* (Neuhausen-Stuttgart: Hänssler-Verlag, 1982).

Laloy, Louis, "Schola Cantorum – 26 février," *La Revue musicale*, **6** (March 15, 1904), p. 170.

Laurence, Dan H. (ed.), *Shaw's Music*, 3 vols. (New York, NY: Dodd, Mead, 1981).

Lawton, David, "Ornamenting Verdi's Arias: The Continuity of a Tradition," in Alison Latham and Roger Parker (eds.), *Verdi in Performance* (Oxford University Press, 2001), pp. 49–78.

Lawton, David, "*'Le Trouvère'*: Verdi's Revision of *Il trovatore* for Paris," *Studi Verdiani*, **3** (1985), 79–119.

Leavis, F. R., *The Great Tradition: A Study of the English Novel* (Garden City, NY: Doubleday, 1954).

Leavis, F. R., "The Novel as Dramatic Poem (I): 'Hard Times'," *Scrutiny*, **14** (1946–47), pp. 185–203.

Leavis, F. R., "The Novel as Dramatic Poem (III): 'The Europeans'," *Scrutiny*, **15** (1947–48), pp. 209–21.

Leavis, F. R., and Q. D. Leavis, *Dickens: The Novelist* (London: Chatto and Windus, 1970).

Leavis, Q. D., *Fiction and the Reading Public* (London: Chatto and Windus, 1932).

Lee, Rensselaer W., *Names on Trees: Ariosto into Art* (Princeton, NJ: Princeton University Press, 1977).

Lee, Rensselaer W., *Ut Pictura Poesis: the Humanistic Theory of Painting* (New York, NY: Norton, 1967).

Lerdahl, Fred, "The Sounds of Poetry Viewed as Music," in Isabelle Peretz and Robert J. Zatorre (eds.), *The Cognitive Neuroscience of Music* (Oxford University Press, 2003), pp. 413–29.

Lessing, Gotthold Ephraim, *Laokoon*, in Wilfried Barner (ed.), *Werke und Briefe*, 12 vols. (Frankfurt am Main: Deutscher Klassiker Verlag, 1985–2000), vol. v, part 2 (1990), pp. 11–321.

Lesure, François (ed.), *Debussy on Music*, Richard Langham Smith (trans.) (New York, NY: Knopf, 1976).

Levin, David, *Unsettling Opera: Staging Mozart, Verdi, Wagner, and Zemlinsky* (University of Chicago Press, 2007).

Levine, Lawrence W., *Highbrow Lowbrow: The Emergence of Cultural Hierarchy in America* (Cambridge, MA: Harvard University Press, 1988).

Levinson, Jerrold, *Music in the Moment* (Ithaca, NY: Cornell University Press, 1997).

Lindau, Paul, "The 'Tannhäuser' Scandal in March 1861," Daphne Ellis (trans.), *Wagner*, **24** (September 2003), pp. 3–22.

Lindenberger, Herbert, "Arnold Schoenberg's *Der biblische Weg* and *Moses und Aron:* On the Transactions of Aesthetics and Politics," *Modern Judaism*, **9** (Feb. 1989), pp. 55–70.

Lindenberger, Herbert, "Arts in the Brain; or, What Might Neuroscience Tell Us?" in Frederick Aldama (ed.), *Toward a Cognitive Theory of Narrative Acts* (Austin, TX: University of Texas, 2010), pp. 13–35.

Lindenberger, Herbert, "From Opera to Postmodernity: On Genre, Style, Institutions," *Genre*, 20 (1987), pp. 259–84.

Lindenberger, Herbert, *Georg Trakl* (New York, NY: Twayne, 1971).

Lindenberger, Herbert, *Historical Drama: The Relation of Literature and Reality* (University of Chicago Press, 1975).

Lindenberger, Herbert, *The History in Literature: On Value, Genre, Institutions* (New York, NY: Columbia University Press, 1990).

Lindenberger, Herbert, *On Wordsworth's* Prelude (Princeton University Press, 1963).

Lindenberger, Herbert, *Opera: The Extravagant Art* (Ithaca, NY: Cornell University Press, 1984).

Lindenberger, Herbert, *Opera in History: From Monteverdi to Cage* (Stanford University Press, 1998).

Liszt, Franz, "Berlioz und seine 'Harold-Symphonie'," in L. Ramann (ed.), *Gesammelte Schriften*, 6 vols. (Leipzig: Breitkopf und Härtel, 1880–83), vol. IV (1882), pp. 1–102.

Lonardi, Gilberto, *Il fiore dell'addio: Leonora, Manrico e altri fantasmi del melodramma nella poesia di Montale* (Bologna: Il Mulino, 2003).

Lord, Albert Bates, *The Singer of Tales* (Cambridge, MA: Harvard University Press, 1960).

Luppert, Pauline, "*American Idiot* and the Road to Berkeley Rep," *The Berkeley Rep Magazine*, (2009–10) no. 1, pp. 13–18.

Mäckelmann, Michael, *Arnold Schönberg und das Judentum: der Komponist und sein religiöses, nationales und politisches Selbstverständnis nach 1921* (Hamburg: Karl Dieter Wagner, 1984).

Maeterlinck, Maurice, *Théâtre*, 3 vols. (Paris: Bibliothèque-Charpentier, 1925–29).

Mahler, Alma, *Gustav Mahler: Memories and Letters* (New York, NY: Viking Press, 1969).

Malipiero, G. Francesco (ed.), *Monteverdi, Claudio, Tutte le opere*, 16 vols. (Asolo: n. p, 1926–42).

Mann, Thomas, *Doktor Faustus* (Frankfurt: Fischer Taschenbuch Verlag, 1971).

Marti, Jean-Christophe, "'It's a Secret of Love': An Interview with Olivier Messiaen," Stewart Spencer (trans.), *liner notes, Saint François d'Assise* (Deutsche Grammophon, 1999), pp. 17–29.

Marvin, Roberta Montemorra, "Verdian Opera Burlesqued: A Glimpse into Mid-Victorian Theatrical Culture," *Cambridge Opera Journal*, 15 (2003), pp. 33–66.

Massey, Irving, *The Neural Imagination: Aesthetic and Neuroscientific Approaches to the Arts* (Austin, TX: University of Texas Press, 2009).

McGuinness, Patrick, *Maurice Maeterlinck and the Making of Modern Theatre* (Oxford University Press, 2000).

Menon, Vinod, and Daniel J. Levitin, "The Rewards of Music Listening: Response and Physiological Connectivity of the Mesolimbic System," *NeuroImage*, **28** (2005), pp. 175–84.

Messiaen, Olivier, *Music and Color: Conversations with Claude Samuel*, E. Thomas Glasow (trans.) (Portland, OR: Amadeus Press, 1986).

Messiaen, Olivier, *Saint François d'Assise*, 8 vols. (Paris: Alphonse Leduc, 1988–1992).

Mill, John Stuart, *Essays on Poetry*, F. Parvin Sharpless (ed.) (Columbia, SC: University of South Carolina Press, 1976).

Mitterschiffthaler, Martina T., and Cynthia H. Y. Fu, Jeffrey A. Dalton, Christopher M. Andrew, and Steven C. R. Williams, "A Functional MRI Study of Happy and Sad Affective States Induced by Classical Music," *Human Brain Mapping*, **28** (2007), pp. 1150–62.

Moldenhauer, Hans, and Rosaleen Moldenhauer, *Anton von Webern: A Chronicle of His Life and Work* (New York, NY: Knopf, 1979).

Montale, Eugenio, *Mottetti: Poems of Love*, Dana Gioia (trans.) (St. Paul, MN: Greywolf Press, 1990).

Montale, Eugenio, *L'opera in versi*, Rosanna Bettarini and Gianfranco Contini (eds.) (Turin: Giulio Einaudi, 1980).

Montale, Eugenio, *Selected Poems*, Jonathan Galassi, Charles Wright, and David Young (trans.) (Oberlin, OH: Oberlin College Press, 2004).

Moor, Paul, "Horsing Around with a Classic," *International Herald Tribune*, April 3, 1996.

Moretti, Franco, "Conjectures on World Literature," *New Left Review*, Ser. 2, **1** (January-February 2000), pp. 54–68.

Moretti, Franco (ed.), *The Novel*, 2 vols. (Princeton University Press, 2006).

Mossa, Carlo Matteo (ed.), *Carteggio Verdi-Cammarano (1843–1852)* (Parma: Istituto Nazionale di Studi Verdiani, 2001).

Murray, Elisabeth A., "The Amygdala, Reward and Emotion," *Trends in Cognitive Science*, **11/11** (2007), pp. 479–97.

Nietzsche, Friedrich, *The Birth of Tragedy and The Case of Wagner*, Walter Kaufmann (trans.) (New York, NY: Random House, 1967).

O'Dea, Michael, *Jean-Jacques Rousseau: Music, Illusion and Desire* (New York, NY: St. Martin's Press, 1995).

Orledge, Robert, *Debussy and the Theatre* (Cambridge University Press, 1982).

Osthoff, Wolfgang, "'Pianissimo, benché a piena orchestra' – Zu drei Stellen aus *Trovatore, Traviata* und *Otello*," in Sieghart Döhring and Wolfgang Osthoff (eds.), *Verdi-Studien: Pierluigi Petrobelli zum 60. Geburtstag* (Munich: G. Ricordi, 2000), pp. 213–37.

Panksepp, Jaak, "The Emotional Sources of 'Chills' Induced by Music," *Music Perception*, **13/2** (1995), pp. 171–207.

Parker, Roger, "In Search of Verdi," in Fabrizio Della Seta, Roberta Montemorra Marvin, and Marco Marica (eds.), *Verdi 2001*, 2 vols. (Florence: Olschki, 2003), vol. II, pp. 929–35.

Parker, Roger, *Leonora's Last Act: Essays in Verdian Discourse* (Princeton University Press, 1997).

Parker, Roger, *Remaking the Song: Operatic Visions and Revisions from Handel to Berio* (Berkeley, CA: University of California Press, 2006).

Patel, Aniruddh D., *Music, Language, and the Brain* (Oxford University Press, 2008).

Pater, Walter, "Conclusion" to *Studies in the History of the Renaissance*, in M. H. Abrams (ed.), *Norton Anthology of English Literature*, 5th edn. 2 vols. (New York, NY: Norton, 1986), vol. II, pp. 1565–68.

Paulson, Ronald, *Literary Landscape: Turner and Constable* (New Haven, CT: Yale University Press, 1982).

Pavel, Thomas, *La Pensée du roman* (Paris: Gallimard, 2003).

Perloff, Marjorie, *The Poetics of Indeterminacy: Rimbaud to Cage* (Princeton University Press, 1981).

Phillips-Matz, Mary Jane, *Puccini: A Biography* (Boston, MA: Northeastern University Press, 2002).

Phillips-Matz, Mary Jane, *Verdi: A Biography* (Oxford University Press, 1993).

Plato, *The Dialogues of Plato*, Benjamin Jowett (trans.), 2 vols. (New York, NY: Random House, 1937).

Poe, Edgar Allan, *The Selected Poetry and Prose*, T. O. Mabbott (ed.) (New York, NY: Random House, 1951).

Potter, Keith, *Four Musical Minimalists: La Monte Young, Terry Riley, Steve Reich, Philip Glass* (Cambridge University Press, 2000).

Pound, Ezra, *Make It New: Essays* (London: Faber and Faber, 1934).

Prod'homme, J. G., "Les dernières représentations du 'Devin de village' (Mai-Juin 1829)," *La Revue Musicale*, **7** (August 1926), pp. 118–25.

Reich, Steve, *Writings on Music: 1965–2000*, Paul Hillier (ed.) (New York, NY: Oxford University Press, 2002).

Reich, Steve, and Beryl Korot, *"A Theater of Ideas: Steve Reich and Beryl Korot on Three Tales," record liner for Three Tales* (New York, NY: Nonesuch Records, 2003).

Reiman, Donald H. and Sharon B. Powers (eds.) *Shelley's Poetry and Prose* (New York, NY: Norton, 1977).

Rentrop, M., and C. Knebel, and H. Förstl, "Opera-hallucinosis," *International Journal of Geriatric Psychiatry*, **24** (2009), pp. 432–33.

Reynolds, Joshua, *Discourses on Art*, Robert R. Wark (ed.) (San Marino, CA: Huntington Library, 1959).

Richter, Jean Paul, *Vorschule der Ästhetik*, Norbert Miller (ed.), in *Werke*, 7 vols. (Munich: Carl Hanser, 1960–64), vol. v (1963), pp. 7–514.

Rimbaud, Arthur, *Oeuvres complètes*, Roland de Renéville and Jules Mouquet (eds.) (Paris: Gallimard, 1951).

Rizzolatti, G., L. Fadiga, L. Fogassi and V. Gallese, "Resonance Behaviors and Mirror Neurons," *Archives Italiennes de Biologie*, **137** (1999), pp. 85–100.

Robinson, Paul, *Opera and Ideas: From Mozart to Strauss* (New York, NY: Harper and Row, 1985).

Rosand, Ellen, *Monteverdi's Last Operas: A Venetian Trilogy* (Berkeley, CA: University of California Press, 2007).

Rosand, Ellen, *Opera in Seventeenth-Century Venice: The Creation of a Genre* (Berkeley, CA: University of California Press, 1991).

Rosen, David, "Meter, Character, and *Tinta* in Verdi's Operas," in Martin Chusid (ed.), *Verdi's Middle Period: 1849–1859: Source Studies, Analysis, and Performance Practice* (University of Chicago Press, 1997), pp. 339–92.

Rosselli, John, *The Opera Industry in Italy from Cimarosa to Verdi: The Role of the Impresario* (Cambridge University Press, 1984).

Rossini, Gioacchino, *Otello ossia il more di Venezia*, Michael Collins (ed.), 2 vols. (Pesaro: Fondazione Rossini, 1994).

Rossini, Gioacchino, *Tancredi*, Philip Gossett (ed.), 2 vols. (Pesaro: Fondazione Rossini, 1984).

Rousseau, Jean-Jacques, *The Confessions*, J. M. Cohen (trans.) (Harmondsworth: Penguin, 1953).

Rousseau, Jean-Jacques, and J. G. Herder, *On the Origin of Language*, John H. Moran and Alexander Gode (trans.) (New York, NY: Frederick Ungar, 1966).

Rozin, Alexander, Paul Rozin, and Emily Goldberg. "The Feeling of Music Past: How Listeners Remember Musical Affect," *Music Perception*, **22/1** (2004), pp. 15–39.

Rumph, Stephen, "Mozart's Archaic Endings: A Linguistic Critique," *Journal of the Royal Musical Association*, **130/2** (2005), pp. 159–96.

Ruskin, John, *Modern Painters*, 5 vols. (London: George Allen, 1901–11).

Ryan, Lawrence, *Hölderlins Lehre vom Wechsel der Töne* (Stuttgart: Kohlhammer, 1960).

Sachse, Georg, *Sprechmelodien, Mischklänge, Atemzüge: Phonetische Aspekte im Vokalwerk Steve Reichs* (Kassel: Gustav Bosse Verlag, 2004).

Sacks, Oliver, *Musicophilia: Tales of Music and the Brain* (New York, NY: Knopf, 2007).

Salzman, Eric, and Thomas Desi, *The New Music Theater: Seeing the Voice, Hearing the Body* (New York, NY: Oxford University Press, 2008).

Samuel, Richard (ed.), *Das philosophische Werk* II, in *Novalis Schriften: die Werke Friedrich von Hardenbergs*, Paul Kluckhohn and Richard Samuel (eds.), 6 vols. (Darmstadt: Wissenschaftliche Buchgesellschaft), vol. III (1968).

Schelling, F. W. J., *Philosophy of Art*, Douglas W. Stott (ed. and trans.) (Minneapolis, MN: University of Minnesota Press, 1989).

Scher, Steven Paul, *Verbal Music in German Literature* (New Haven, CT: Yale University Press, 1968).

Schiller, Friedrich, *Über die ästhetische Erziehung des Menschen*, in Rolf-Peter Janz (ed.), *Theoretische Schriften* (Frankfurt am Main: Deutscher Klassiker Verlag, 1992).

Schlegel, August Wilhelm, *Vorlesungen über Ästhetik I*, Ernst Behler (ed.) (Paderborn: Ferdinand Schöningh, 1989).

Schlegel, Friedrich, *Kritische Schriften*, Wolfdietrich Rasch (ed.) (Munich: Carl Hanser, 1964).

Schoenberg, Arnold, *Der biblische Weg*, Moshe Lazar (trans.), *Journal of the Arnold Schoenberg Institute*, **17** (1994), pp. 162–329.

Schoenberg, Arnold, *Briefe*, Erwin Stein (ed.) (Mainz: B. Schott's Söhne, 1958).

Schoenberg, Arnold, *Moses und Aron* (Mainz: Schott, 2000).

Schön, Daniele, and Reyna Leigh Gordon, and Mireille Besson, "Musical and Linguistic Processing in Song Perception," *Annals of the New York Academy of Sciences*, **1060** (2005), pp. 71–81.

Schopenhauer, Arthur, *The World as Will and Presentation*, Richard E. Aquila and David Carus (trans.), 2 vols. (New York, NY: Pearson/Longman), vol. 1 (2008).

Senici, Emanuele, "'Se potessimo tornare da capo'," in Fabrizio Della Seta, Roberta Montemorra Marvin, and Marco Marica (eds.), *Verdi 2001*, 2 vols. (Florence: Olschki, 2003), vol. II, pp. 937–43.

Sheppard, W. Anthony, "Blurring the Boundaries: Tan Dun's *Tinte* and *The First Emperor*," *Journal of Musicology*, **26** (2009), pp. 285–326.

Shreffler, Anne C., *Webern and the Lyric Impulse: Songs and Fragments on Poems of Georg Trakl* (Oxford: Clarendon Press, 1994).

Solger, K. W. F., *Vorlesungen über Ästhetik*, K. W. L. Heyse (ed.) (Darmstadt: Wissenschaftliche Buchgesellschaft, 1962).

Spitzer, Leo, *Essays on English and American Literature*, Anna Hatcher (ed.) (Princeton University Press, 1962).

Spitzer, Leo, "Once Again on Mörike's Poem 'Auf eine Lampe'," Berel Lang and Christine Ebel (trans.), *Proceedings of the Modern Language Association*, **105** (1990), pp. 427–34.

Sridharan, Devarajan, and Daniel J. Levitin, Chris H. Chafe, Jonathan Berger, and Vinod Menon, "Neural Dynamics of Event Segmentation in Music: Converging Evidence for Dissociable Ventral and Dorsal Networks," *Neuron*, **55** (2007), pp. 521–32.

Stadlen, Peter, "Schoenberg's Speech-Song," *Music and Letters*, **62** (1981), pp. 1–11.

Steinberg, Michael P., and Susan Stewart-Steinberg, "Fascism and the Operatic Unconscious," in Victoria Johnson, Jane F. Fulcher, and Thomas Ertman (eds.), *Opera and Society in Italy and France from Monteverdi to Bourdieu* (Cambridge University Press, 2007), pp. 267–88.

Steinheuer, Joachim, "*Orfeo* (1607)," in John Whenham and Richard Wistreich (eds.), *The Cambridge Companion to Monteverdi* (Cambridge University Press, 2007), pp. 119–40.

Stendhal, *Life of Rossini*, Richard N. Coe (trans.) (New York, NY: Orion Press, 1970).

Stravinsky, Igor, *The Rake's Progress* (London: Boosey and Hawkes, 1951).

Stravinsky, Igor, and Robert Craft, *Memories and Commentaries* (Berkeley, CA: University of California Press, 1959).

Sulzer, J. G., *Allgemeine Theorie der Schönen Künste*, 2nd edn. (Leipzig: Weidmannsche Buchhandlung, 1792).

Thomas, Downing A., *Aesthetics of Opera in the Ancien Régime, 1647–1785* (Cambridge University Press, 2002).

Thompson, William Forde, and Frank A. Russu, "Facing the Music," *Psychological Science*, **18/9** (2007), pp. 756–57.

Till, Nicholas, *Mozart and the Enlightenment: Truth, Virtue and Beauty in Mozart's Operas* (London: Faber and Faber, 1992).

Tomlinson, Gary, *Metaphysical Song: An Essay on Opera* (Princeton University Press, 1999).

Tomlinson, Gary, *Monteverdi and the End of the Renaissance* (Berkeley, CA: University of California Press, 1987).

Tommasini, Anthony, "A 'Tristan und Isolde' Well Worth the Wait," *New York Times*, March 30, 2008.

Toye, Francis, *Verdi: His Life and Works* (New York, NY: Knopf, 1931).

Trimpi, Wesley, "The Meaning of Horace's *ut pictura poesis*," *Journal of the Warburg and Courtauld Institutes*, **37** (1973), pp. 1–34.

Vaget, Hans-Rudolf, "The Spell of *Salome*: Thomas Mann and Richard Strauss," in Claus Reschke and Howard Pollack (eds.), *German Literature and Music: An Aesthetic Fusion – 1890–1989* (Munich: Fink, 1992), pp. 39–60.

Vaget, Hans-Rudolf, "Thomas Mann und Richard Strauss: Zeitgenossenschaft ohne Brüderlichkeit," *Thomas Mann Jahrbuch*, **3** (1990), pp. 50–85.

Verdi, Giuseppe, *La traviata*, Fabrizio Della Seta (ed.) (University of Chicago Press, 1996).

Verdi, Giuseppe, *Il trovatore*, David Lawton (ed.) (University of Chicago Press, 1992).

Vinci, Leonardo da, *Paragone: a Comparison of the Arts*, Irma A. Richter (trans.) (London: Oxford University Press, 1959).

Vines, Bradley W., and Carol L. Krumhansl, Marcelo M. Wanderley, and Daniel J. Levitin, "Cross-Modal Interactions in the Perception of Musical Performance," *Cognition*, **101** (2006), pp. 80–113.

Visconti, Luchino. *Two Screenplays: La Terra Trema, Senso*, Judith Green (trans.) (New York, NY: Orion, 1970).

Wackenroder, Wilhelm Heinrich, *Sämtliche Werke und Briefe*, Silvio Vietta and Richard Littlejohns (eds.), 2 vols. (Heidelberg: Carl Winter, 1991).

Wagner, Richard, *Gesammelte Schriften*, Julius Kapp (ed.), 14 vols. (Leipzig: Hesse und Becker [1914]).

Wagner, Richard, *Mein Leben*, Eike Middell (ed.), 2 vols. (Bremen: Carl Schünemann Verlag, 1986).

Wagner, Richard, *Parsifal*, Egon Voss (ed.) (Mainz: Schott, 1973).

Walton, Benjamin, *Rossini in Restoration Paris: The Sound of Modern Life* (Cambridge University Press, 2007).

Watt, Ian, *The Rise of the Novel: Studies in Defoe, Richardson and Fielding* (Berkeley, CA: University of California Press, 1957).

Webb, Daniel, *Observations on the Correspondence between Poetry and Music* (1769), in Ruth Katz and Ruth HaCohen (eds.), *The Arts in Mind: Pioneering Texts of a Coterie of British Men of Letters* (New Brunswick, NJ: Transaction Publishers, 2003), pp. 255–324.

Weber, William, *The Rise of Musical Classics in Eighteenth-Century England: A Study in Canon, Ritual, and Ideology* (Oxford: Clarendon Press, 1992).

Weill, Kurt, *Musik und musikalisches Theater: gesammelte Schriften mit einer Auswahl von Gesprächen und Interviews*, Stephen Hinton and Jürgen Schebera (eds.), rev. edn. (Mainz: Schott, 2000).

Wellbery, David, *Lessing's "Laocoon": Semiotics and Aesthetics in the Age of Reason* (Cambridge University Press, 1984).

Wellek, René, *Concepts of Criticism*, Stephen G. Nichols, Jr. (ed.) (New Haven, CT: Yale University Press, 1963).

Whenham, John (ed.), *Claudio Monteverdi: Orfeo* (Cambridge University Press, 1986).

Wiesmann, Sigrid, "'Eine verlachte Liebe ist die ehrgeizigste Liebe, die es gibt' – Anmerkungen zu Werfels Nachdichtungen von *La forza del destino, Simon Boccanegra* und *Don Carlos*," in Sieghart Döhring and Wolfgang Osthoff (eds.), *Verdi-Studien: Pierluigi Petrobelli zum 60. Geburtstag* (Munich: G. Ricordi, 2000), pp. 281–89.

Wilhelm, Kurt, *Richard Strauss persönlich: Eine Bibliographie* (Berlin: Henschel, 1999).

Williams, Bernard, "Naïve and Sentimental Opera Lovers," in Edna and Avishai Margalit (eds.), *Isaiah Berlin: A Celebration* (London: Hogarth Press, 1991), pp. 180–92.

Wordsworth, William, *The Prelude*, Jonathan Wordsworth, M. H. Abrams, and Stephen Gill (eds.) (New York, NY: Norton, 1979).

Abbate, Carolyn, 27, 52, 53
Abrams, M. H., *The Mirror and the Lamp*, 116, 154, 161
Abstract Expressionism, 191
Accademia degli Incogniti, 227
Adams, John, 78, 80, 99
  A Flowering Tree, 78
  Doctor Atomic, 78, 110
  El Niño, 78
  Hallelujah Junction, 78
  Nixon in China, 78, 110, 191
  The Death of Klinghoffer, 78, 216
Addison, Joseph, 2, 228–32
Adorno, Theodor, 54, 65, 69, 252
  as composer, 234
  Beethoven: The Philosophy of Music, 69
  Berg: Der Meister des kleinsten Übergangs, 69
  "Bourgeois Opera," 67–69, 170
  disparagement of opera, 31, 58, 73, 77, 169
  "Fantasia sopra *Carmen*," 69
  Introduction to the Sociology of Music, 58
  "Lyric and Society," 44
  "Sakrales Fragment: Über Schönbergs *Moses und Aron*," 69
Adorno, Theodor (with Max Horkheimer), *Dialectic of the Enlightenment*, 68
Alberti, Leon Battista, *On Painting*, 143
Albright, Daniel, 192, 217
Alden, David, 85, 106
Almahide (pasticcio), 231

Altman, Robert, *A Wedding*, 195
André, Johann, 48
Andreini, Virginia, 221
Anne, queen of Britain, 231
Anti-theatricality, 2, 7, 158, 176, 196–218
Apollinaire, Guillaume, *Les Mamelles de Tirésias*, 217
Ariosto, Ludovico, 114, 159
  Orlando furioso, 166, 230
Aristotle, *Poetics*, 37, 67, 136, 138
Armstrong, Billie Joe, 96
Auber, Daniel, 244
Auden, W. H., 109, 178, 209, 210
Auerbach, Erich, *Mimesis*, 65, 66, 71
Auric, Georges, 95
Austen, Jane, 63, 73

Bach, Johann Sebastian, 143, 270
  Passions, 61, 120
  Well-Tempered Clavier, 128
Bacon, Sir Francis, 250
Bakhtin, Mikhail, 54, 71–72, 73, 74, 75, 272
Balanchine, George, 110
  Divertimento No. 15, 132
Baldini, Gabriele, 36
Balzac, Honoré de, 65
Bardare, Emanuele, 37
Barish, Jonas, *The Antitheatrical Prejudice*, 196, 197, 199, 206
Barthes, Roland, 107, 272
Bartok, Bela, *Bluebeard's Castle*, 128
Basevi, Abramo, 36
Baucardé, Carlo, 11

Baudelaire, Charles
"Correspondances," 167, 247
"Les Phares," 167
"Richard Wagner et *Tannhäuser* à
Paris," 167, 243, 246–47
"Salon of 1846," 167
Bauman, Thomas, 47, 48–51
Baumgarten, Alexander, *Aesthetica*,
146–47, 160
Bavarian State Opera (Munich), 85
Bayreuth festival, 57, 61, 107, 113, 135,
204, 252
Beckett, Samuel, 196, 197, 201
Beecham, Sir Thomas, 89–90
Beethoven, Ludwig van, 21, 135, 143,
146, 156, 161, 174, 253, 261
Eroica Symphony, 138, 168
Fidelio, 69, 79, 137, 168, 254, 261
Fifth Symphony, 38, 162
Pastoral Symphony, 164
Seventh Symphony, 152
Sonata, Op. 26, 19
Behler, Ernst, 152
Beijing opera, 80
Bel canto opera, 29, 67, 77, 174, 175, 187
Bellini, Vincenzo, 7, 28, 29, 35
I Capuleti e I Montecchi, 261
Benjamin, Walter, 89, 91
Berg, Alban, 98, 189, 255, 272
and tradition of music-drama, 216, 270
attitudes toward Richard Strauss,
248, 250, 251
Lulu, 69, 110, 124, 194; Adorno on, 68;
as example of "hard modernism,"
181; delayed in being produced
complete, 256; heroine as akin to
Salome, 250
Lyric Suite, 256, 257
relations with Hanna
Fuchs-Robettin, 256

relations with Helene Berg, 255, 256
Three Pieces for Orchestra, 127
Wozzeck, 69, 188, 190, 193, 195, 250,
253–57, 265; Adorno on, 68;
as example of "hard modernism,"
187; Messiaen's admiration for, 212;
its theatricality, 205; structure of, 189
Berg, Helene, 255–56
Berger, Karol, 223
Bergman, Ingmar, *Virgin Spring*, 81
Berlin, Isaiah, 34, 239
Berlin Staatsoper, 105
Berlioz, Hector, 45, 174, 245–46
Fantastic Symphony, 164
Harold in Italy, 163
King Lear Overture, 164
La Damnation de Faust, 103
Les Troyens, 243, 245
Rob Roy Overture, 164
Bernstein, Leonard, *Candide*, 79
Besutti, Paola, 222
Bible, 65, 142, 167
Bigand, Emmanuel, 128
Bizet, Georges, 135
Carmen, 39, 41, 69, 79, 124, 125, 129,
194, 237
Bjoerling, Jussi, 18
Blood, Anne J., 119
Blythe, Stephanie, 42
Boccaccio, Giovanni, 159
Böhm, Karl, 254
Boito, Arrigo, 30
Mefistofele, 52, 103
Bokina, John, 52
Bolcom, William
A View from the Bridge, 194–95
A Wedding, 195
Bondy, Luc, 106
Boston Lyric Opera, 115
Boulez, Pierre, 111

Bourdieu, Pierre, 3
    Distinction, 55
    Homo Academicus, 55–56
    Rules of Art, 54
Bourgeois, Louise, 111
Boyce, William, 122
Brahms, Johannes
    "Die schöne Magelone," 163
    Third Symphony, 128
Braider, Christopher, 160
Brandeis, Irma, 32
Braque, Georges, collages, 173
Braunfels, Walter, *Die Vögel*, 194
Breazeal, Cynthia, 101
Brecht, Bertolt, 93, 196, 197
Bretzner, C. F., 47, 50
Britten, Benjamin, 174, 184, 185, 187, 216
    Billy Budd, 184
    Curlew River, 184
    Death in Venice, 184
    Peter Grimes, 179, 184, 216
    The Rape of Lucretia, 216
Brontë, Charlotte, *Jane Eyre*, 67
Brontë, Emily, *Wuthering Heights,* 63
Browning, Elizabeth Barrett, 75
Bruch, Max, "Kol Nidrei," 125
Bruckner, Anton, 127
Budden, Julian, 10, 14, 15, 21, 43
Buffet, Bernard, 55
Burke, Edmund, *The Sublime and
    the Beautiful*, 147
Burney, Charles, 230, 232
Burns, Robert, 153
Burroughs, William, *The Black Rider*,
    93, 94
Burton, Robert, *Anatomy of Melancholy*, 72
Busenello, Gian Francesco, 227
Busoni, Ferruccio, 254
    Doktor Faust, 103, 190
Byron, George Gordon, Lord, 145, 160

Childe Harold's Pilgrimage, 163
Don Juan, 166
Manfred, 94
Marino Faliero, 166
Sardanapalus, 166

Caballé, Montserrat, 135
Caccini, Giulio, 219
Cage, John, 110–11, 173
    Europeras 1 & 2, 104–5, 110, 173,
        191–92, 217
Calderón, Pedro, 159, 200
    La Devoción de la Cruz, 159
Callas, Maria, 4, 15, 26, 67, 127,
        135, 260, 261
Cambridge Opera Journal, 275
Cambridge Studies in Opera, 275
Camerata, Florentine, 144, 185, 219, 266
Cammarano, Salvatore, 9, 13, 14, 15, 17, 42
Canova, Antonio, 146
Carner, Mosco, 250
Carracci family, painters, 158
Carter, Tim, 222, 223
Caruso, Enrico, 15, 261
Castrati, 3, 59, 85, 221, 224, 225, 232,
        238–39
Cattelan, Maurizio, 113
Cavalli, Francesco, 124, 224, 225, 227
    La Calisto, 115, 223–28
Cavour, Conte di Camillo Benso, 25
Cervantes, Miguel, 159
Chaliapin, Fyodor, 261
Chamisso, Adelbert von, *Peter
    Schlemihl*, 94
Chapados, Catherine, 134
Chaucer, Geoffrey, 76, 159
Chekhov, Anton, 196
Chéreau, Patrice, 40, 107, 217
Chicago Lyric Opera, 115, 195
Chomsky, Noam, 82

Chusid, Martin, 19

Cimarosa, Domenico, 161

Clark Institute, 113

Cocteau, Jean
  La Belle et le bête, 94–96, 109
  Parade, 217

Coleridge, Samuel Taylor,
  "Rime of the Ancient Mariner,"
  168

Collisani, Amalia, 234

Commedia dell' arte, 209, 226

Commetant, Oscar, 243

Conceptual Art, 191

Conrad, Joseph, 63

Constable, John, 146, 165–66

Constructivism, 107

Contarini, Marco, 224

Corelli, Franco, 17, 37

Corneille, Pierre
  Cinna, 50
  Pertharite, 84

Correggio, Antonio da, 158, 159

Cossotto, Fiorenza, 42

Cowper, William, *The Task*, 145

Crisp, Deborah, 26

Croce, Benedetto, 147

Crutchfield, Will, 29

Cunningham, Merce, 132, 173

Curtius, Ernst Robert, 148

Cuzzoni, Francesca, 84, 85

Da Ponte, Lorenzo, 50, 113, 191

Dahlhaus, Carl, 155, 156, 261

Daltrey, Roger, 97

Dante [Alighieri], 159
  Divine Comedy, 65, 152, 166

Darwinism, 270

David, Jacques-Louis, 144, 146

Davis, Anthony, *X*, 110

Davis, Miles, *Kind of Blue*, 73

Dawkins, Richard, 101, 102

Deathridge, John, 261

Debussy, Claude, 248, 250
  "Clair de Lune," 125
  Pelléas et Mélisande, 7, 67, 95, 175–76,
    179, 188, 193, 196, 200–05, 209, 214, 215,
    261, 272; hypnotic effects of, 218;
    its anti-theatricality, 7; its influence
    on Messiaen, 212–13; its speech
    rhythms, 96
  "Why I Wrote *Pelléas*," 204

Defoe, Daniel, 64

Degas, Edgar, 166

Delacroix, Eugène, 146, 161, 166,
  167, 243

De La Grange, Henri-Louis, 234, 249

Delibes, Léo, *Lakmé*, 237

Della Seta, Fabrizio, 16

De Man, Paul, 107

Dent, Edward J., 47

Derrida, Jacques, 107, 108

Deutsche Guggenheim, 90, 91

Deutsche Oper, Berlin, 40

De Van, Gilles, 36

Diaghilev, Sergei, 110

Dickens, Charles, 64, 67, 76
  Hard Times, 63, 64, 70

Dietsch, Pierre Louis Philippe, 246

Dionysian festival, 115

Donizetti, Gaetano, 35, 174, 246
  Lucia di Lammermoor, 18–19

Doody, Margaret, 75

Drury Lane Theater, 231

Dryden, John, 64

Dumont, Margaret, 24

Dvořák, Antonin, *Armida*, 230

Eldar, Eran, 133

Elector of Hanover (later King
  George I), 231

Eliot, George, 63
   Middlemarch, 69
Eliot, T. S., 190
Empathy, 136–37, 138
Euripides, 159

Farinelli (Carlo Broschi), 261
Farrar, Geraldine, 261
Farrell, Eileen, 18
Fauré, Gabriel, *Pelléas et*
   Mélisande, 164
Faust Book, 102, 103
Faustini, Giovanni, 224, 226
Faustini, Marco, 224–26
Feldman, Martha, 57, 121
Fenlon, Iain, 220, 227
Fielding, Henry, 64, 65, 278
Fiérens-Gevaert, H., 247
Film studies, 263–64, 276, 277
Flaubert, Gustave, 65
   L'Education sentimentale, 54
   Madame Bovary, 62
Floros, Constantin, 256
Forster, E. M., 70
Foucault, Michel, 53, 54, 272
Frank, Manfred, 163
Frankfurt Opera, 104, 110, 192, 265
Franz Josef, Emperor of Austria, 255
Fremstad, Olive, 181
Freud, Sigmund, 208
   Mourning and Melancholy, 90
Freyhan, Michael, 72
Friedlander, Walter, 142
Friedrich, Caspar David, 146, 166
Fritz, Thomas, 126
Frost, Robert, "Nothing Gold Can
   Stay," 131
Frye, Northrop, 71, 72–73, 76, 137
Fuchs-Robettin, Hanna, 256, 257
Furtwängler, Wilhelm, 254

Gainsborough, Thomas, 144
García Gutiérrez, Antonio
   El Trovador, 8, 9, 11–13, 29, 30, 42
   Los hijos del tío Tronera, 29–30
   Simón Bocanegra, 29
Garibaldi, Giuseppe, 40
George I, king of Britain, 231
Gershwin, George
   Porgy and Bess, 176
   Rhapsody in Blue, 55
Gesamtkunstwerk, 4, 15–16, 112, 138,
   140, 142, 152, 169, 171
Gigli, Beniamino, 33, 261
Gilbert, W. S., 209
Gilman, Sander L., 180, 253
Glass, Philip, 99, 109
   Einstein on the Beach, 94, 191, 192,
   195, 218
   La Belle et le bête, 94–96
Glixon, Beth L., 224–26, 228
Glixon, Jonathan E., 224–26, 228
Glover, Jane, 224
Gluck, Christoph Willibald, 135, 143,
   174, 235, 241, 266, 272
   Alceste, 94, 114
   and tradition of music-drama, 270
   Armide, 230
   Iphigénie en Aulide, 45
   Iphigénie en Tauride, 48, 49
   Orfeo ed Euridice, 45, 77
   theories of, 129, 143
Glyndebourne Opera, 85
Goehr, Lydia, 113, 142
Goethe, Johann Wolfgang, 144, 145, 160
   ballads, 168
   Faust, 94, 102, 198
Goldstein, Avram, 118
Goltz, Christl, 255
Gonzaga, Ferdinando, 221
Gonzaga, Francesco, 220

Gonzaga, Vincenzo, Duke of
  Mantua, 220
Goodman, Nelson, 147
Gossett, Philip, 11, 29, 36, 241
Gothic novel, 94, 137
Gould, Glenn, 260
Gould, Stephen Jay, 101
Gounod, Charles
  Faust, 45, 94, 103, 130, 198, 261
  Mireille, 77
Graham, Martha, 93
Grand opéra, 42, 135, 171, 175, 193,
  216, 244
Graves, Michael, 191
Graz Stadt-Theater, 180, 248–53
Green Day, *American Idiot*, 96–99, 195
Gregor-Dellin, Martin, 246
Gregorian chant, 144–45
Grewe, Oliver, 119–120
Grey, Thomas S., 162
Grieg, Edvard, *Peer Gynt*, 125
Griffiths, Paul, 210, 214
Guarini, Giambattista, *Il pastor fido*,
  220, 223
Guerre des Bouffons, 235

HaCohen, Ruth, 147
Hadlock, Heather, 238
Hagstrum, Jean, 142, 143
Halévy, Fromenthal, 244
  La Juive, 19
Haller, Albrecht von, 160
Handel, George Frideric, 60, 77, 124,
  135, 143, 145, 185, 278
  Agrippina, 232
  Giulio Cesare, 124
  longtime neglect of his operas,
    67, 84, 270
  oratorios, 57, 61, 79–80, 137, 158, 216
  pasticcios of, 113

Rinaldo, 124, 228–32
Rodelinda, 84–86, 106, 108
Semele, 216
staging of his "magic" operas, 114, 135
Theodora, 216
Handspring Puppet Company, 87
Hanning, Barbara Russano, 163
Harbison, John, *The Great Gatsby*, 110, 194
Hardy, Thomas, 70
  Jude the Obscure, 73
  Tess of the d'Urbervilles, 67
Harris-Warrick, Rebecca, 45, 124
Hasse, Johann, 124
Haydn, Joseph, 143, 146, 152, 162, 174, 253
  Armida, 230
Hazlitt, William, 158–59
Head, Matthew, 48, 49
Hegel, G. W. F., 69, 147, 151, 156–57,
  159, 170–71
Heggie, Jake, *Dead Man Walking*, 194
Heller, Wendy, 227
Henri IV, king of France, 220
Hepokoski, James, 19
Heppner, Ben, 257–59
Herder, Johann Gottfried, 151, 154–55, 156
Herero massacre, 90–91
Herzl, Theodor, 208
Hill, Aaron, 229, 230, 231
Hillman, Robert, 26
Hindemith, Paul, 254
  Cardillac, 179, 190, 193
Hitler, Adolf, 207, 252–53, 254
Hobert, Annagret, 188
Hofer, Josepha, 11
Hoffmann, E. T. A.
  "Beethoven, C-moll-sinfonie," 162, 165
  "Kreisleriana," 167
Hofmannsthal, Hugo von, 178, 209, 269
Hogarth, William, 150, 211–12
Hölderlin, Friedrich, 145, 163

Holzer, Jenny, 173
Homer, 76, 145, 159, 167
　The Iliad, 117
　The Odyssey, 190
Horace, *Art of Poetry*, 142
Horkheimer, Max, 68, 91, 92
Horne, Marilyn, 239, 240, 242
Hugo, Victor, 8
　Hernani, 145, 242–43
　Le Roi s'amuse, 42
Hutcheon, Linda, 31, 52, 198
Hutcheon, Michael, 31, 52–53, 198

Ibsen, Henrik, 34, 197
　Peer Gynt, 94
Ingres, J. A. D., 142, 146, 166
Ionesco, Eugène, 201

Jack, Ian, 165
James, Henry, 63, 66, 70, 109
Janáček, Leoš, 174, 184, 185, 187, 188,
　265, 267
　Jenůfa, 124, 184
　Katya Kabanova, 193
Jauss, Hans-Robert, 50
Jean Paul (J. P. F. Richter), *Primer of*
　Aesthetics, 147, 150–51, 152, 162–63
Jockey Club, Paris, 242–47
Johns, Jasper, 173
Johnson, Philip, 191
Johnson, Samuel, 1, 2, 64, 143
Jonson, Ben, masques, 229
Joseph II, emperor of Austria, 46, 47, 54
Joyce, James
　Finnegans Wake, 73
　Ulysses, 190

Kalidasa, *Shakuntala*, 159
Kallman, Chester, 209, 210
Kandinsky, Vasily, 55, 188

Composition VII, 188
Kant, Immanuel, *Critique of Judgment*,
　147, 149–50
Katz, Ruth, 144, 147
Kaufmann, Harald, 210
Keats, John, 165
　odes, 153, 164, 165
Kennedy, Randy, 111, 113
Kentridge, William, 86–92, 112, 114,
　173, 226
　Black Box, 90–92
Kerman, Joseph, 21, 66–68, 70, 73,
　77, 271–72
Khomeini, Ayatollah, 51
Kimbell, David R. B., 232
Kipnis, Alexander, 90
Kleist, Heinrich von, 145
Klimt, Gustav, 254
Koelsch, Stefan, 126–27
Koestenbaum, Wayne, 53
Kolb, Katherine, 246
Korngold, Erich, 254
Korot, Beryl, 100–1
Krenek, Ernst, 254
Kreuzer, Gundula, 22
Kristeller, Paul Oskar, 148
Kroll Opera House, 107
Krumhansl, Carol, 132
Kubik, Reinhold, 229, 232
Kunju opera, 80
Kurzweil, Ray, 101

La Fenice, 25, 237
Lacan, Jacques, 53
Laloy, Louis, 204
Lawrence, D. H., 63
Lawton, David, 10, 14, 28
Leavis, F. R., 63–65, 66, 67, 69, 70,
　71, 72, 76, 272
Leavis, Q. D., 64, 65

Lechi, Count Giacomo, 240
Lechi, Count Luigi, 240
Lee, Rensselaer W., 142, 166
Legge, Walter, 90
Lehar, Franz, *Die lustige Witwe*, 79
Lendvai, Ervin, 248
Leonardo, see Vinci, Leonardo da
Lerdahl, Fred, 131
Lessing, G. E., *Laocoon*, 160–61, 171–72
Levin, David J., 40, 106, 107, 109
Levine, Lawrence W., 22
Levinson, Jerrold, 128
Levitin, Daniel J., 38, 119
Licitra, Salvatore, 11
Liebermann, Rolf, 212
Lindau, Paul, 244
Liszt, Franz, 165, 167
    "Berlioz und seine Harold
        Symphonie," 163
    symphonies, 103, 164
Literary study
    comparative literature in, 52, 53, 76,
        146, 269, 272, 274
    cultural studies in, 54
    deconstruction in, 53, 107, 272
    explication de texte in, 269
    Geistesgeschichte in, 268
    nationalist biases in, 267, 270
    New Criticism in, 268, 269, 272
    New Historicism in, 54
    positivism in, 55, 267–68
Literaturoper, 202
Lonardi, Gilberto, 32, 33
Lope de Vega, 159
Lord, Albert, 76
Loredano, Giovanni Francesco, 227
Lortzing, Albert, 267
Louis XIV, king of France, 45, 49,
    56, 225, 237
Louis XV, king of France, 234

Lully, Jean-Baptiste, 45, 49, 235, 237
    Armide et Renaud, 230
    Le Bourgeois Gentilhomme, 49
Lyric (generic category), 44, 70, 74,
    83, 115, 121, 151, 157

Mäckelmann, Michael, 209
Maeterlinck, Maurice, *Pelléas et
    Mélisande*, 95, 200–2, 203
Magli, Giovanni Gualberto, 221
Magno, Carlo, 220
Mahler, Alma, 248–50, 255, 256
Mahler, Gustav, 107, 127, 180, 234,
    248–50, 254
    Das klagende Lied, 138
    Lieder eines fahrenden Gesellen, 254
    Second Symphony, 119, 138, 164
    Eighth Symphony, 103, 138
Malanotte, Adelaide, 240
Malibran, Maria, 261
Mallarmé, Stéphane, 189
Manhattan Opera, 181
Mann, Thomas
    "Tristan," 257
    Doktor Faustus, 103, 162, 251–52
Margherita of Savoy, 220
Maria di Medici, 220
Maria Theresa, queen to Louis XIV, 225
Marie Antoinette, queen to
    Louis XVI, 237
Martinelli, Giovanni, 17
Marvin, Roberta Montemorra, 30
Marx Brothers, *A Night at the Opera*,
    23–25
Massenet, Jules, 193
    Manon, 33, 178
Massey, Irving, 130
Mayer, Michael, 97
Mazarin, Cardinal, 225
Mazzucato, Alberto, 16

McGuinness, Patrick, 201
Melba, Nellie, 261
Melchior, Lauritz, 261
Mendelssohn, Moses, 160
Menon, Vinod, 38, 119
Menotti, Gian-Carlo, 184
Messiaen, Olivier, 212–13
    Saint François d'Assise, 110, 194,
        212–15, 216, 218, 265; austerity of,
        60; its anti-theatricality, 196
Metastasio, Pietro, 269
Metropolitan Opera, 23, 41, 180–81, 194,
    195, 257–60
Metternich, Princess Pauline, 245
Metzger, Heinz-Klaus, 110
Meyerbeer, Giacomo, 68, 193, 244, 246
    Le Prophète, 42, 172
    Les Huguenots, 130
    Robert le Diable, 19, 94
Michelangelo (Buonarroti), 158, 159, 161
Mill, John Stuart, "What Is Poetry?", 153
Miller, Peter N., 227
Miller, Philip, 91
Milton, John, 159
    Paradise Lost, 117, 155
Minimalism, 96, 191
Mitterschiffthaler, Martina T., 125
Modernist opera, 31, 77, 158, 174–95,
    198–218, 253–57, 261
Moldenhauer, Hans, 250
Moldenhauer, Rosaleen, 250
Moltke, Freya von, 101
Montale, Eugenio, 7, 31–34
Monteverdi, Claudio, 80, 124, 135, 174
    Arianna, 220, 221
    L'incoronazione di Poppea, 124, 227, 261
    La favola d'Orfeo, 53, 67, 204,
        219–23, 225, 233
    Il ritorno d'Ulisse in patria, 86–88, 99,
        114, 115, 173, 226

role in operatic canon, 77, 204, 272
    theories of, 129, 143, 163, 223
Moor, Paul, 40
Moralt, Rudolf, 252
Moretti, Franco, 73–74
Mörike, Eduard, "Auf eine Lampe," 164
Morton, John, 110
Mozart, Wolfgang Amadeus, 135, 143,
    158, 161, 162, 174, 253, 254, 272, 278
    Bastien et Bastienne, 234
    Così fan tutte, 124, 178
    Die Entführung aus dem Serail,
        46–52, 54, 61
    Die Zauberflöte, 11, 50, 69, 72, 112, 114,
        169, 171, 174; alternate version of,
        72; as *Singspiel*, 79; Kentridge
        production of, 88–92
    Divertimento No. 15, 132
    Don Giovanni, 45, 153, 174, 178, 199,
        209, 218
    "Eine kleine Nachtmusik," 38
    Idomeneo, 47
    La clemenza di Tito, 50
    Le nozze di Figaro, 67, 261
    Requiem, 129
    role in operatic canon, 175, 193,
        197, 272
    Sonata in A major, K. 331, 48
Murray, Elizabeth, 119
Musicology
    nationalist biases in, 270
    positivism in, 55–56, 268–70, 274
Musorgsky, Modest, *Boris Godunov*, 179,
    212, 214
Muti, Riccardo, 10

Napoléon III, emperor of France, 245
Neuenfels, Hans, 40, 217
Neuroscience and music, 3, 4, 38–39,
    60, 83, 118–34

Newport Festival, 260
Nicolini (Nicolò Grimaldi), 232
Nietzsche, Friedrich, 234, 249
  The Birth of Tragedy, 68, 156
  Manfred Meditation, 164
  "On Music and Words," 156
Nilsson, Birgit, 259–60
Noh drama, 81, 82, 184
Novalis (Friedrich von Hardenberg),
  116, 148, 153

O'Dea, Michael, 235
Obratzova, Elena, 42
Offenbach, Jacques, 209
  Les Contes d'Hoffmann, 95, 200–2
Op art, 191
Opera buffa, 78
Opéra comique, 22, 78
Opera-hallucinosis, 105–6, 108–9
Opera lirica, 115
Opera seria, 53, 78, 168, 197, 209
  affect in arias of, 85, 124, 125, 137
  audiences in, 3, 57
  modern productions of, 84
  Handel and, 216, 231
  Mozart and, 47, 54
  Rossini and, 35, 238
  structure of aria in, 98, 121–22, 123, 227
Opera studies, 1, 52–61, 263–75
  interdisciplinary approaches to,
    53–54, 264, 277
Oratorio, 79–80, 127, 168, 177, 216, 217
Osthoff, Wolfgang, 19
Ovid, *Metamorphoses*, 226

Pacific Operaworks, 87
Palestrina, 145
Panksepp, Jaak, 118–19
Paris Opéra, 105, 152, 186, 212, 236,
  242–47, 265

Parker, Roger, 19, 31, 37
Parry, Milman, 76
Pärt, Arvo, *Tabula Rasa*, 73
Pasta, Giuditta, 240, 261
Patel, Aniruddh, 131–32
Pater, Walter, *Studies in the History of
  the Renaissance*, 117–18, 128, 129
Patel, Aniruddh D., 131–32
Patti, Adelina, 261
Paul, grand duke of Russia, 46, 48
Paulson, Ronald, 165–66
Pavarotti, Luciano, 17
Pavel, Thomas, 75
Peony Pavilion, see Tang Xianzu
Pepsico festival, 113
Pergolesi, Giovanni Battista, 210
  La serva padrona, 235
Peri, Jacopo, *L'Euridice*, 53, 219, 220
Perloff, Marjorie, 189
Pfitzner, Hans, *Palestrina*, 184–85
Phillips-Matz, Mary Jane, 248
Picasso, Pablo
  collages, 173
  Les Demoiselles d'Avignon, 188
  neoclassical paintings, 190
  Parade, 217
Piccinni, Niccolò, 235
Picker, Tobias, *An American
  Tragedy*, 110
Pinter, Harold, 201
Pirandello, Luigi, 196
Plato, 83, 115–16, 151, 199
Poe, Edgar Allan, "The Poetic
  Principle", 116–17, 121–22
Pol Pot, 91
Pompidou, Georges, 212
Ponnelle, Jean-Pierre, 39
Pop art, 191
Postmodernism, 82, 140, 172–73,
  190–92

Poulenc, Francis, 96, 134
  Les dialogues des Carmélites, 184
  Les mamelles de Tirésias, 184, 217
Pound, Ezra, 187
  Cavalcanti, 187
  Le testament, 187
Poussin, Nicholas, 158
Previn, André, *A Streetcar Named Desire*, 110, 194
Price, Leontyne, 35, 37, 260
Princeton Studies in Opera, 275
Prod'homme, J. G., 237
Prokofiev, Sergei, 185
  The Fiery Angel, 188
  The Gambler, 187
  The Love of Three Oranges, 187
  War and Peace, 188
Puccini, Giacomo, 39, 82, 110, 135, 184, 194, 216, 248, 249
  La bohème, 39, 73, 108, 127, 137, 261
  Madama Butterfly, 33, 39, 137
  Manon Lescaut, 178
  Tosca, 33, 39, 41, 67, 106, 108, 124, 249
  Turandot, 39, 77, 249
Purcell, Henry, 145, 229, 272
Pushkin, Alexander, *Evgeny Onegin*, 71–72, 75

Queen's Theater, Haymarket, 231

Rabelais, François, 71, 72
Racine, Jean, 161
  Phèdre, 136
Rameau, Jean-Philippe, 235, 236
  Hippolyte et Aricie, 136
Raphael (Raffaello Sanzio), 158, 159
Rasi, Francesco, 221–22
Ravel, Maurice, 96, 248
  L'Enfant et les sortilèges, 55
Regieoper, 217

Reich, Steve, 77–78, 99, 100–2
  The Cave, 77, 100, 195, 217
  Three Tales, 77, 100–2, 103, 109, 217
Reinhardt, Max, 180
Reni, Guido, 153
Renzi, Anna, 261
Reynolds, Sir Joshua, 112, 139–41, 142, 144, 149, 161, 171, 173
Richardson, Samuel, 64
Richter, Irma A., 149
Ricordi (Casa), 186
Riehn, Rainer, 110
Rimbaud, Arthur
  "Voyelles," 167
  Illuminations, 189
Rinuccini, Ottavio, *L'Euridice*, 220
Robbins, Jerome, *Moves*, 81
Robinson, Paul, 16, 42, 52, 53
Rock music, 59, 60, 96–99
Rolland, Romain, 131
Roller, Alfred, 107
Romantic opera, 8, 40, 145, 174
Rosand, Ellen, 227, 261
Rosegger, Peter, 249
Roselli, John, 186
Rossi, Gaetano, 240
Rossi, Giacomo, 231
Rossini, Gioacchino, 35, 104, 110, 135, 143, 158, 174, 185, 193, 240
  Armida, 230
  Aureliano in Palmira, 238
  disparagement of, 270
  extravagance of his *opere serie*, 59
  Il barbiere di Siviglia, 39, 171, 194
  on Wagner, 246
  ornamentation in, 29
  Otello, 166, 241
  Schopenhauer's praise of, 158, 170
  Semiramide, 239
  structure of aria in, 122

Tancredi, 237–42
Rousseau, Jean-Jacques, 144, 152
  Letter on French Music, 235, 236
  Letter to d'Alembert, 236
  Confessions, 233
  *Discourse on the Sciences and the
    Arts*, 144, 233
  La Nouvelle Héloïse, 62, 236
  Le Devin du village, 144, 233–37
Rumph, Stephen, 47
Runge, Phillip Otto, 166
Ruskin, John, *Modern Painters*, 154, 165
Ryan, Lawrence, 163

Sacks, Oliver, 9, 10, 238
Sagan, Prince de, 247–48
Said, Edward, 51
St. Francis, *Canticle of the Sun*, 213
Salzburg festival, 218
San Carlo Opera company, 1
San Carlo, Naples, 59
San Francisco Museum of Modern
    Art, 88
San Francisco Opera, 17, 23, 28,
    85, 194
  audience resistance at, 23, 39, 106
  Callas's cancellations at, 260
  operas commissioned for, 194
Satie, Erik, 217
Savoy, Duke of, 223
Schelling, F. W. J., 147, 150, 152, 153,
    158–59, 169, 170
Schenck, Diana Lynn, 132
Schenker, Heinrich, 269
Scher, Steven Paul, 161
Schiele, Egon, 254
Schiller, Friedrich, 145, 160
  ballads, 168
  On Naïve and Sentimental Poetry,
    34, 147, 239

*On the Aesthetic Education of
    Man*, 139–41, 169
Schlegel, August Wilhelm, 147, 150,
    152, 154
Schlegel, Friedrich, *Dialogue on
    Poetry*, 69, 153, 168
Schnorr von Carolsfeld, Ludwig, 259
Schoenberg, Arnold, 6, 98, 182, 185,
    188–190, 253, 256
  Adorno on, 58
  attitudes toward Richard Strauss,
    180, 248, 251, 252
  Der biblische Weg, 208, 209
  Erwartung, 128, 181, 182, 189, 205, 251
  "Five Pieces for Orchestra," 189, 251
  Die glückliche Hand, 111, 176, 189
  Moses und Aron, 45, 69, 110,
    177, 208–9, 216, 265; its
    anti-theatricality, 7, 196,
    205–9, 215, 216, 218
  Pelléas et Mélisande, 164
  piano pieces, Op. 11, 189
  Pierrot Lunaire, 176, 177
  Variations for Orchestra, 127
  Von Heute auf Morgen, 187
Schön, Daniele, 130
Schopenhauer, Arthur, *The World as
    Will and Representation*, 150,
    155–56, 170, 171
Schröder-Devrient, Wilhelmine, 261
Schubert, Franz, 146
Schwarzkopf, Elisabeth, 90
Scott, Sir Walter, 8, 160
  Ivanhoe, 166
  Rob Roy, 172
Scribe, Eugène, 197
Scrutiny, 70, 272
Scudo, Paul, 244
Seattle Opera, 1
Second Viennese School, 253, 255, 270

Sellars, Peter, 78, 113, 191, 217, 218
Serra, Richard, 111
Shakespeare, William, 3, 21, 159, 161
    Hamlet, 166
    King Lear, 172
    Othello, 166, 241
    sonnets, 153
Shaw, George Bernard, 20, 41
Shelley, Percy Bysshe, *Defence of*
    Poetry, 148, 159
Sheppard, W. Anthony, 82
Shostakovich, Dmitri
    Lady Macbeth of Mtsensk, 183
    The Nose, 114
Shreffler, Anne C., 189
Sibelius, Jean, *Pelléas et Mélisande*, 164
Singspiel, 46–47, 50, 78, 137, 168
Sitwell, Edith, *Façade*, 177
Smetana, Bedřich, 267
    Libuše, 77
Smithson, Robert, *Spiral Jetty*, 172
Solger, K. W. F., 147, 150, 151, 153, 159
Sondheim, Stephen, *Sweeney Todd*, 79
Soyinka, Wole, *Death and the King's*
    Horseman, 82
Spenser, Edmund, 159
    The Faerie Queene, 137
Spitzer, Leo, 165
Sprechstimme, 98, 177, 206–7, 215
Sridharan, Devarajan, 122–23
Stadlen, Peter, 207
Steele, Richard, 230
Stein, Gertrude, 189
    Four Saints in Three Acts, 111,
      180, 217
    Dr. Faustus Lights the Lights, 94
    The Making of Americans, 189
    The Mother of Us All, 23, 111, 180
Steinberg, Michael P., 26
Steinheuer, Joachim, 223

Stendhal (Henri Beyle), 65
    Life of Rossini, 238–240
Stephanie, Gottlob, 48, 50
Stewart-Steinberg, Susan, 26
Stoker, Bram, *Dracula*, 73
Stramm, August, 188
Strauss, Franz, 252
Strauss, Frau Johann, 249
Strauss, Johann, *Blue Danube Waltz*, 126
    Die Fledermaus, p. 79
Strauss, Richard, 21, 99, 131, 185, 186,
    254, 257
    and modernism, 183
    and tradition of music-drama, 112
    Ariadne auf Naxos, 176, 178, 183,
      184, 209, 216
    Capriccio, 129, 216
    Don Juan, 164
    Don Quixote, 164
    Die Frau ohne Schatten, 184
    Elektra, 98, 128, 179, 181, 183, 193, 250, 253
    Macbeth, 164
    Der Rosenkavalier, 67, 77, 179, 183,
      184, 193, 261
    Salome, 98, 128, 136, 180–82, 183,
      193, 265; as example of
      "hard modernism," 179; as
      "shocker," 73; Graz premiere of,
      248–53; popularity with audiences,
      193; relation to *Tristan und Isolde*,
      179; relation to Wilde's play, 95
    theatricality of his operas, 216
Stravinsky, Igor, 134, 185, 248
    La Baiser de la fée, 210
    Le Sacre du printemps, 181
    L'Histoire du soldat, 177
    Oedipus Rex, 177, 180, 190, 193, 195
    Perséphone, 177
    Pulcinella, 210
    The Firebird, 55

The Nightingale, 187
The Rake's Progress, 67, 175, 176, 178,
   182, 187, 194, 199, 209–12, 210–11,
   215, 218; its anti-theatricality, 196;
   parodying of earlier styles, 7
Strickland, William, 255
Striggio, Alessandro, 222
Sullivan, Sir Arthur, 209
Sulzer, J. G., *General Theory of the
   Fine Arts*, 170
Surrealism, 95, 184, 191
Sutherland, Joan, 28, 260
Synaesthesia, 167, 247

Tamberlick, Enrico, 10
Tan Dun, *The First Emperor*, 82, 195
Tang Xianzu, *Peony Pavilion*, 80, 81, 82
Tarabotti, Arcangela, 227
Tasso, Torquato
   Aminta, 220, 223, 233
   Gerusalemme liberata, 114, 166, 230, 232
Tchaikovsky, Peter Ilyich, 174, 210
   Evgeny Onegin, 71–72
   Francesca da Rimini, 164
   Hamlet, 164
   Manfred Symphony, 164
   Pique Dame, 178
   Romeo and Juliet, 164
Tebaldini, Giovanni, 30
Thackeray, William Makepeace,
   Vanity Fair, 67
The Who, *Tommy*, 97, 195
Theater an der Wien, Vienna, 253
Théâtre de la Monnaie, Brussels, 88,
   114, 265
Théâtre Italien, Paris, 265
Théâtre-Lyrique, Paris, 115, 243
Thomas, Downing A., 236
Thomson, Virgil
   Four Saints in Three Acts, 111, 180, 217

The Mother of Us All, 23, 111, 180
Tieck, Ludwig, "Die schöne
   Magelone," 163
Till, Nicholas, 49
Titian (Tiziano Vecello), 158, 159, 250
Tolstoy, Leo, *War and Peace*, 62
Tomlinson, Gary, 52, 53, 163
Tommasini, Anthony, 256, 259
Toscanini, Arturo, 260
Toye, Francis, 20–21
Tragédie-lyrique, 115, 136
Tragedy, Greek, 81, 138, 144, 159,
   169, 219
Trakl, Georg, 188–89, 253
Trimpi, Wesley, 142
Trotha, General Johann von, 90
Turkish music (in early-modern
   Europe), 48–49, 51, 61
Turner, J. M. W., 146, 165–66

ut pictura poesis, 142, 160, 164

Vaget, Hans-Rudolf, 252
Valéry, Paul, *Mon Faust*, 103
Van, Gilles de, see De Van, Gilles
Velázquez, Diego, 255
Velluti, Giambattista, 238
Venetian opera
   (during seventeenth century), 57,
   59, 77, 99, 114, 135, 176, 186, 197,
   223–28, 229
Venice Biennale, 2009, 112
Verdi, Giuseppe, 18, 29, 135, 175, 185,
   193, 273, 278
   Aida, 39, 42
   composing for Paris Opéra,
      246, 266
   disparagement of, 21, 270
   Don Carlos, 21, 22, 109
   Ernani, 18, 30

Verdi, Giuseppe (cont.)
   Falstaff, 15, 21, 31, 198–99, 209
   Il trovatore, 4, 6–7, 8–43, 52, 60, 67, 69,
      127, 198, 218; cabalettas in, 10;
      high *c*'s in, 7; in film, 23–26;
      Miserere, 9–10; plot of, 8–9;
      voice ranges in, 36
   La forza del Destino, 22
   late style of, 198
   La traviata, 18, 30, 34–35, 39, 55,
      125, 135, 211
   Le Trouvère, 14–15
   ornamentation in, 29
   Otello, 21, 260
   Requiem, 61
   revival in Weimar Germany, 22
   Rigoletto, 14, 18, 21, 30, 34–35,
      39–40, 137, 194, 237
   rivalry with Wagner, 235, 238
   Simon Boccanegra, 21, 22, 137
   structure of aria in, 8, 122, 123
   supposed "naïveté," 34, 239
   Un ballo in maschera, 18
Verismo opera, 34, 67, 137, 175
Vickers, Jon, 259–60
Vienna Philharmonic, 254
Vienna State Opera, 41, 105, 107,
   180, 248, 250, 253–57
Vienna Volksoper, 250
Villégier, Jean-Marie, 85
Villon, François, 187
Vinci, Leonardo da, *Paragone*, 149
Vines, Bradley W., 133–34
Virgil, 159
   Georgics, 222
   The Aeneid, 155
Visconti, Luchino, *Senso*, 23–24, 25–26, 40
Voigt, Deborah, 257, 258–59, 260
Voltaire (François-Marie Arouet), 143
   Tancrède, 240

Wackenroder, Wilhelm,
   Herzensergießungen, 155, 161–62, 165
Wagner, Richard, 104, 114, 135, 175,
   185–86, 193, 254, 261, 272
   "Bericht über die Aufführung des
      'Tannhäuser'," 243
   Das Rheingold, 16, 101, 218
   Das Judentum in der Musik, 246
   Debussy's attitude toward, 204
   Der fliegende Holländer, 13
   Der Ring des Nibelungen, 1, 16, 107, 125,
      131–32, 133, 137, 172
   Die Meistersinger, 152, 200, 218, 238
   Die Walküre, 123, 137
   early works of, 146, 174
   Faust Overture, 164
   Götterdämmerung, 55, 73
   his relation to audiences, 21, 57,
      59, 113
   late style of, 198
   leitmotifs in, 124, 128, 131–32
   Lohengrin, 68, 94, 108, 114, 247
   Mein Leben, 16, 243
   musical structure in, 123
   narration in, 26
   Oper und Drama, 15
   Parsifal, 61, 179, 198, 199–200, 206
   rivalry with Verdi, 235, 238
   Siegfried, 213
   synaethesia in, 167
   Tannhäuser, 152, 242–47
   The Artwork of the Future, 151, 154–55
   theatricality of, 7
   theories of, 4, 15–16, 19, 45, 61, 70, 129,
      141, 142, 151, 152, 156, 171
   and tradition of music-drama, 112,
      172, 179, 185, 190, 193, 205, 210,
      216, 270
   Tristan und Isolde, 67, 123, 125, 198,
      199–200, 203, 212, 244, 256,

257–60, 278; its presence in
later composers, 179
"Über die Anwendung der Musik
auf das Drama," 156
Wagnerism, 22, 247
Waits, Tom, 93
Walpole, Horace, 84
Walton, Benjamin, 240
Walton, William, *Façade*, 177
Watson, James, 101
Watt, Ian, *The Rise of the Novel*,
64–65, 70, 71, 76
Webb, Daniel, 155
Weber, Carl Maria, 145, 167, 174,
193, 267
Der Freischütz, 69, 77, 92–93, 94
Weber, William, 145
Webern, Anton von, 190, 248, 250, 253
Trakl songs, 189, 253
Weill, Kurt, 6, 93
"Die neue Opera," 177
Aufstieg und Fall der Stadt Mahagonny,
176, 181, 194, 195, 254
Three-Penny Opera, 254
Welitsch, Ljuba, 182
Wellbery, David, 160
Wellek, René, 145
Werfel, Franz, 22
Wesendonck, Mathilde, 278

West, Thomas, *Guide to the Lakes*, 148
Wiener Festwochen, 255
Wiener Werkstätte, 254
Wiesmann, Sigrid, 22
Wilde, Oscar, *Salome*, 95, 180
Wilhelm II, emperor of Germany, 90
Williams, Bernard, 34
Williams, Raymond, 54
Wilson, Robert, 92–94, 113
Death Destruction and Detroit, 94
Einstein on the Beach, 94, 191, 192,
195, 218
The Black Rider, 93–94, 113
Winckelmann, Johann Joachim, 157, 158
Wölfflin, Heinrich, 269
Woolf, Virginia, 69, 70
To the Lighthouse, 66
Wordsworth, William, 109, 143, 278
The Prelude, 5, 6, 168
Wordsworth, William, and Coleridge,
Samuel Taylor, *Lyrical Ballads*, 145

Zajick, Dolora, 37, 42
Zandonai, Riccardo, *Francesca da
Rimini*, 194
Zatorre, Robert J., 119
Zeffirelli, Franco, 41, 106
Zemlinsky, Alexander, 248, 250
Eine florentinische Tragödie, 128, 250